'An extraordinary collection of comparative perspectives is presented in this engaging book. It is arguably more important than at any time in the past, given increasing globalisation, to consider what current themes and approaches exist across jurisdictions that can enable us all to deal with disputes effectively. It is a delight to read and engage with the perspectives of these outstanding thinkers.'

Prof. Tania Sourdin, *Dean and Head of School, Newcastle Law School*

'Anyone engaged in the serious study of legal dispute resolution should not only read this book, but also keep it at hand. Dispute resolution students, scholars, practitioners, and policymakers – especially but not only those working across borders – will find striking insights and actionable wisdom about how to research, design, and reform effective dispute resolution systems.'

Dr. Joshua Karton, *Associate Professor, Queen's University Faculty of Law*

'This pathbreaking book brings new perspectives to the study of comparative and transnational alternative dispute resolution. It promises to change the way with we understand the laws, systems, and institutions undergirding the global practice of mediation, arbitration, and other extra-judicial methods.'

Zachary Calo, *Professor of Law, Hamad bin Khalifa University College of Law and Public Policy*

COMPARATIVE AND TRANSNATIONAL DISPUTE RESOLUTION

This edited volume presents research and policy insights into the theory and practice of dispute systems reform in diverse jurisdictions. It highlights how important extra-judicial mechanisms are for resolving cross-border disputes, as evidenced both by the breadth of scholarship dedicated to the issue and the proliferation of parties resorting to non-litigious dispute resolution mechanisms in recent years.

Drawing on selected case studies, the book examines the impact of comparative research and policy analysis in advancing reform of dispute resolution institutions at both the regional and global levels. It explores the challenges and opportunities of understanding and assessing developments in systems of dispute resolution in diverse social and political contexts through comparative research.

With a growing number of disputes which have come to involve cross-border issues, anyone interested in transnational and comparative dispute resolution will find this book a useful reference.

Shahla Ali is Professor and Associate Dean (International) and Director of the LLM in Arbitration and Dispute Resolution in the Faculty of Law at the University of Hong Kong. Her research and practice centre on questions of governance, development and the resolution of cross-border disputes in the Asia Pacific region.

Routledge Research in International Law

Indigenous-Industry Agreements, Natural Resources and the Law
Edited by Ibironke T. Odumosu-Ayanu and Dwight Newman

Secession and Statehood
Lessons from Spain and Catalonia
Edited by Ana G Lopez and Jose Perea Unceta

The International Court of Justice and Municipal Courts
An Inter-Judicial Dialogue
Oktawian Kuc

Global Governance, Human Rights and International Law (2nd Edition)
Combating the Tragic Flaw
Errol P. Mendes

Small Island States and International Law
The Challenge of Rising Seas
Carolin König

Private International Law and Arbitral Jurisdiction
Faidon Varesis

Comparative and Transnational Dispute Resolution
Edited by Shahla Ali

For more information about this series, please visit www.routledge.com/Routledge-Research-in-International-Law/book-series/INTNLLAW

COMPARATIVE AND TRANSNATIONAL DISPUTE RESOLUTION

Edited by Shahla Ali

Routledge
Taylor & Francis Group
LONDON AND NEW YORK

Designed cover image: Hiroshi Watanabe

First published 2023
by Routledge
4 Park Square, Milton Park, Abingdon, Oxon OX14 4RN

and by Routledge
605 Third Avenue, New York, NY 10158

Routledge is an imprint of the Taylor & Francis Group, an informa business

British Library Cataloguing-in-Publication Data
A catalogue record for this book is available from the British Library

Library of Congress Cataloging-in-Publication Data
Title: Comparative and transnational dispute resolution / edited by Shahla Ali.
Description: Abingdon, Oxon ; New York, NY : Routledge, 2022. | Series: Routledge research in international law
Identifiers: LCCN 2022035707 | ISBN 9780367374624 (hardback) | ISBN 9781032420318 (paperback) | ISBN 9780429354625 (ebook)
Subjects: LCSH: Dispute resolution (Law)—Congresses. | International commercial arbitration—Congresses. | International business enterprises—Law and legislation—Congresses. | Conference papers and proceedings. lcgft
Classification: LCC K2390.A6 A28 2019 | DDC 347.09—dc23/eng/20221101
LC record available at https://lccn.loc.gov/2022035707

ISBN: 978-0-367-37462-4 (hbk)
ISBN: 978-1-032-42031-8 (pbk)
ISBN: 978-0-429-35462-5 (ebk)

DOI: 10.4324/9780429354625

Typeset in Bembo
by Apex CoVantage, LLC

CONTENTS

CONTRIBUTORS

Michal Alberstein, Professor, Faculty of Law, Bar-Ilan University, Israel

Nadja Alexander, Ph.D., Professor of Law and Director of the Singapore International Dispute Resolution Academy, Yong Pung How School of Law, Singapore Management University

Shahla Ali, Professor and Associate Dean (International) and Director, Program in Arbitration and Dispute Resolution, Faculty of Law, University of Hong Kong

Eleonora Ciscato, Ph.D. candidate in International and Public Law, Ethics and Economics for Sustainable Development, University of Milan

Luigi Cominelli, Associate Professor, Faculty of Law, University of Milan

Matthew S. Erie, J.D., Ph.D., Associate Professor of Modern Chinese Studies and Associate of the Centre for Socio-Legal Studies, University of Oxford

Susan Finder, Distinguished Scholar in Residence, Peking University School of Transnational Law; Supreme People's Court International Expert Committee Member, Supreme People's Court, People's Republic of China

Xin He, Professor, Faculty of Law, University of Hong Kong

Stefania Lattuille, mediator in commercial, family and environmental disputes, facilitator in participatory processes, Ascolto Attivo srl

Kwai Hang Ng, Professor, Department of Sociology, University of California, San Diego

Lola Akin Ojelabi, Professor and Head of Department of Law, Graduate School of Business and Law, RMIT University, Australia

Michael Palmer, Professor Emeritus, SOAS and IALS, University of London; Cheng Yu Tung Visiting Professor of Law, University of Hong Kong; Senior Research Fellow, HKIAPS, Chinese University of Hong Kong

Yang Su, Professor, Department of Sociology, University of California, Irvine

Xiantao Wen, Department of Treaty and Law, Ministry of Commerce, People's Republic of China

Ling Zhou, Assistant Professor, School of Foreign Languages, Shenzhen Technology University; Associate Research Fellow, Institute of Advanced Legal Studies, University of London

ACKNOWLEDGMENT

> "At each stage in human history, more complex levels of integration become not only possible, but necessary. . . . The demands of the present moment are pushing existing structures for facilitating . . . systems of conflict resolution beyond their capacity."
>
> —A Governance Befitting: Humanity and the Path Toward a Just Global Order, *Baha'I International Community (BIC) 2020*

This book was made possible thanks to the contributions of participants at the "Advances in Comparative and Transnational ADR: Research into Practice" forum at the University of Hong Kong in 2019 and thanks to the support of the Hong Kong Research Grants Council, General Research Fund 17610921. Thanks also to Ernest Kenneth Southworth for his Research Assistance.

Introduction

1

INTRODUCTION

Comparative and Transnational Dispute Resolution: Research into Practice

Shahla Ali

Introduction – Overview of the Book

Comparative and Transnational Dispute Resolution: Research into Practice presents research and policy insights into the theory and practice of dispute systems reform. Drawing on selected case studies, the book examines the impact of comparative research and policy analysis on advancing reform of dispute resolution institutions at both the regional and global levels.

Contributors to the book address current methodological understandings of transnational dispute resolution through seeking common ground to map future methodological directions. Viewing transnational dispute resolution through a "third eye,"[1] reviving the oft-neglected perspective of social phenomenon in dispute resolution and bringing to the fore "inclusive devolved reflection"[2] are all centred on the premise of refocusing dispute resolution research methodology to reflect inclusiveness grounded in dispute resolution's founding aims.

A core feature of the book is the emphasis on comparative approaches to understanding current issues in transnational dispute resolution and how those issues can be resolved through a better understanding of both common and divergent themes across nations. The book is an apt addition to existing publications on comparative dispute resolution, such as Palmer et al.'s *Comparative Dispute Resolution* (Research Handbooks in Comparative Law Series).[3] These projects advance the socio-legal analysis of dispute resolution systems beyond pure procedural examinations. Drawing insights from a cross section of jurisdictions,

1 M. S. Erie, "The New Legal Hubs: The Emergent Landscape of International Commercial Dispute Resolution," *Virginia Journal of International Law* 60, no. 2 (2020): Chapter 2.

2 S. Ali, *Court Mediation Reform: Efficiency, Confidence and Perceptions of Justice* (Chapter 3) (Edward Elgar Publishing, 2018).

3 M. Palmer, et al., *Comparative Dispute Resolution* (Edward Elgar, 2020).

DOI: 10.4324/9780429354625-2

this book offers perspectives on both questions of comparative dispute resolution methodology and policy application through analysis of procedural and ethical standards in dispute resolution practice, regulatory patterns across both mediation and arbitration and comparative approaches to advancing consumer and environmental protection that broadens our perspective of dispute resolution practices.

Theoretical Foundations

In exploring the theoretical backdrop for this book, key insights and developments in the field of comparative legal institutions underscore flourishing development through significant contributions by scholars in both the public and private law spheres.[4] As there is no one single method exclusive to comparative law, one cannot talk of a "comparative law methodology" or even of a "methodology of comparative law" but instead must speak of methods employed in comparative law research. Comparative law research is moving towards the exploration of backgrounds, contexts and interrelationships by employing a "system dynamics" approach.[5]

Synthesis of comparative commercial cross-border dispute resolution research methodology builds on existing work in comparative law generally. Comparative law refers not to a body of law resulting in the production of legal norms but to the "systematic application of the comparative technique to the field of law."[6] Such comparative undertakings generally take as their subject matter "two or more legal systems; or parts, branches or aspects of two or more legal systems" depending on whether a macro- or micro-comparison is pursued.[7]

In reflecting on the study of comparative law, scholars have conceived of the chief function of comparative legal studies as to "facilitate legislation and the practical improvement of law."[8] In light of the constant coming into existence of "new conceptions of rights and duties, owing to far-reaching changes in the political and economic structure of society," comparison of laws may pro-

4 M. Adams, J. Husa and M. Oderkerk, eds., *Comparative Law Methodology: Volumes I and II*. The International Library of Comparative Law (Edward Elgar Publishing, 2017); P. Zumbansen, "Transnational Comparisons: Theory and Practice of Comparative Law as a Critique of Global Governance," in *Practice and Theory in Comaparative Law*, ed. M. Adams and J. Bomboff, 186–211 (Cambridge: Cambridge University Press, 2012); J. Bell, "Legal Research and the Distinctiveness of Comparative Law," in *Methodologies of Legal Research: What Kind of Method for What Kind of Discipline?*, ed. M. Van Hoecke, 155–176 (Hart Publishing, 2011); R. Dixon and T. Ginsburg, *Comparative Constitutional Law* (Edward Elgar Publishing, 2011); R. Hirschl, "The Question of Case Selection in Comparative Constitutional Law," *American Journal of Comparative Law* 53, no. 1 (2005): 125–155.

5 V. Palmer, "Arbitrator Integrity," in *The Backlash against Investment Arbitration*, ed. M. Waibel, A. Kaushal, L. Chung and C. Balchin, 189–251 (Kluwer Law International, 2004).

6 W. J. Kamba, "Comparative Law: A Theoretical Framework," *International and Comparative Law Quarterly* 23, no. 3 (1974): 485–519, 486.

7 Ibid.

8 H. S. Maine, *Village-communities in the East and West* (H. Holt, 1876).

vide guidance.[9] In this vein, comparative legal studies assist us in overcoming a "deficiency in basic knowledge of other legal systems caused by the unavailability or narrow focus of comparative legal studies."[10] From such analysis, we are assisted in (i) developing better understanding of external systems; (ii) increasing understanding of one's domestic system; (iii) identifying "best" practices; and (iv) responding to doctrinal or textual questions.[11]

The methodological approach to comparative legal studies has likewise been widely theorized and discussed. Avoiding the prescription of specific comparative procedures, three "phases" of comparative law research (i.e., the descriptive, identificatory and explanatory) are influenced by a comparatist's jurisprudential outlook and social and legal contexts.[12] In recent times, a "conceptual comparisons" approach has been put forward[13] alongside empirically informed standards for comparison[14] to assist in identifying relevant normative values[15] for comparative assessment.

Within the broad field of comparative legal studies, comparative legal institutions research has likewise employed a range of approaches including "emergent" legal analytics, "complementing functionalism with participation-centered concepts . . . moving beyond the law/politics divide, theorizing doctrine as semi-autonomous and mediated by institutions, and recognizing that the pursuit of all goals and values is transformed by institutions with their own reflexive processes."[16] While comparative legal institutions literature has provided important methodological insights, much of the discussion has been confined to traditional legal institutions. Emerging comparative research in systems of dispute resolution requires distinct approaches given the legal and extra-legal dimensions of practice.

Comparative dispute resolution studies seek to consider a range of models and experiences in an effort to explore reform options in the context of sociocultural and legal cultural affinity in order to derive a better understanding of one's own system of dispute resolution and advancement of reforms within a given system.

9 H. C. Gutteridge, *Comparative Law: An Introduction to the Comparative Method of Legal Study and Research* (CUP Archive, 1974).

10 R. J. Cummins, "International Practice and Comparative Legal Studies," *Journal of Legal Education* 35 (1985).

11 V. C. Jackson, "Methodological Challenges in Comparative Constitutional Law," *Penn State International Law Review* 28 (2009).

12 Kamba, "Comparative Law."

13 O. Brand, "Conceptual Comparisons: Towards a Coherent Methodology of Comparative Legal Studies," *Brooklyn Journal of International Law* 32 (2006).

14 J. De Coninck, "The Functional Method of Comparative Law: 'Quo Vadis'?" *Rabels Zeitschrift Für Ausländisches Und Internationales Privatrecht/The Rabel Journal of Comparative and International Private Law* 74, no. 2 (2010): 318–350.

15 Jackson, "Methodological Challenges in Comparative Constitutional Law."

16 V. Nourse and G. Shaffer, "Varieties of New Legal Realism: Can a New World Order Prompt a New Legal Theory?" *Cornell Law Review* 95 (2009): 61–132.

Focusing more specifically on the subcategory of comparative dispute resolution scholarship, we can see that recent scholarship has germinated into a burgeoning array of work examining the practice, function and approach to dispute resolution in diverse settings,[17] drawing on legal analytic and quantitative frameworks, functionalist approaches and systems dynamics to study practices in the field.

Comparative dispute resolution research has taken a number of forms. Mirroring advances in the field of comparative law, no one single method has been adopted by comparative scholars. The plurality of methods and multiplicity of approaches mirrors research possibilities in this field.[18]

Dispute resolution is perhaps one of the oldest fields of law. Recently, the systems and relevant stakeholders have become increasingly more sophisticated and "regulated." Modern dispute resolution institutions have developed often in response to unique external stimuli.[19] The sheer variety of possible rules and laws that may be applied and potential jurisdictions and institutions has grown, alongside international knowledge transfer.

In the sub-field of comparative dispute resolution reform-oriented research, the proliferation of studies, surveys, statistics, academic research and other

17 See, e.g. V. Lazić and S. Stuij, *International Dispute Resolution: Selected Issues in International Litigation and Arbitration (Short Studies in Private International Law)* (The Hague: T.M.C. Asser Press, 2018); D. Hensler, C. Hodges and I. Tzankova, eds., *Class Actions In Context: How Culture, Economics and Politics Shape Collective Litigation* (Edward Elgar Publishing, 2016); A. Bjorklund, *2013–14 Yearbook of International Investment Law and Policy* (Oxford: Oxford University Press, 2015); C. J. Menkel-Meadow, "Why and How to Study 'Transnational' Law," *UC Irvine Law Review* 1, no. 1 (2011): 97–129; M. Palmer and S. Roberts, *Dispute Processes: ADR and the Primary Forms of Decision Making* (Cambridge: Cambridge University Press, 2005); Ali, *Court Mediation Reform*; T. Stipanowich, J. Yang, J. Welsh, Q. Chen, P. Robinson, J. Tan, . . . J. Zhang, "East Meets West: An International Dialogue on Mediation and Med-Arb in the United States and China," *Pepperdine Dispute Resolution Law Journal* 9, no. 2 (2009): 379–414; S. Strong, "Class Arbitration Outside the United States: Reading the Tea Leaves," *ICC Institute of World Business Law, Dossier VII – Multiparty Arbitration*, 2009, 36. https://ssrn.com/abstract=1517272; N. Alexander, "Mediation and the Myth of Universality," *Erwägen Wissen Ethik* 20 (2009): 512–513; L. Nottage, "The Vicissitudes of Transnational Commercial Arbitration and the Lex Mercatoria: A View from the Periphery," *Arbitration International* 16 (2000): 53–78; M. Woo, *East Asian Law: Universal Norms and Local Cultures* (with L. Cheng and A. Rosette) (Routledge, 2003); L. A. Mistelis, L. B. Stavros and J. D. M. Lew, ed., *The Evolution and Future of International Arbitration* (Alphen aan den Rijn: Kluwer Law International, 2016); Erie, "The New Legal Hubs," 225–298; L. Boulle, "International Enforceability of Mediated Settlement Agreements: Developing the Conceptual Framework," *Contemporary Asia Arbitration Journal* 7, no. 1 (2014): 35–68; J. J. Coe, "Transparency in the Resolution of Investor-State Disputes – Adoption, Adaption, and NAFTA Leadership," *Kansas Law Review* 54 (2008); V. Bath and L. Nottage, "Foreign Investment and Dispute Resolution Law and Practice in Asia: An Overview," in *Foreign Investment and Dispute Resolution Law and Practice in Asia* (Routledge, 2011); E. A. Feldman, "Compensating the Victims of Japan's 3–11 Fukushima Disaster," *AsianPacific Law & Policy* 16 (2015): 127; J. Lee and D. Quek Anderson, "The Global Pound Conference: A Conversation on the Future of Dispute Resolution," *Asian Journal on Mediation* 70 (2016).

18 E. Örücü, "Methodology of Comparative Law," in *Elgar Encyclopedia of Comparative Law*, ed. J. Smits, 2nd ed. (Edward Elgar Publishing, 2012).

19 A. Stone Sweet and F. Grisel, *The Evolution of International Arbitration: Judicialization, Governance, Legitimacy* (Oxford: Oxford University Press, 2017).

publications has enhanced the availability of data in this area.[20] Although the data provide a rich base of comparison, they face unique challenges including, at times, a lack of transparency, insufficient data sets and partiality, given that data informants are often beneficiaries of the same systems under review. The number of cases that can be compared in studies remain relatively low.[21] At the same time, this body of insight provides a growing base of information from which to identify strengths and areas for reform.[22] For example, the International Council for Commercial Arbitration (ICCA) and the Queen Mary University of London published their "Report on Third-Party Funding in International Arbitration" in April 2018 not for a specific reform project but as part of the ICCA Reports series "in the hopes that these occasional papers, prepared by ICCA interest groups and project groups, will stimulate discussion and debate."[23] Similarly, the International Arbitration Survey, published annually by the Queen Mary University of London, attempts to collect views of stakeholders and reflect the most recent developments in practice.[24] The 2018 instalment, "The Evolution of International Arbitration," identifies "principal drivers and stakeholders" in the continuing development of cross-border arbitration.[25] A variety of stakeholders with diverse interests, aims and ideas contribute to shaping the system,[26] including input from "associations and councils . . . departments of law firms, commercial organizations and chambers" and relevant scholarship.[27] Efforts at reform have employed a variety of approaches, including both intrinsic and extrinsic models initiated from either top-down (government or regulating

20 C. Drahozal, "The State of Empirical Research on International Commercial Arbitration: 10 Years Later," in *The Evolution and Future of International Arbitration*, ed. S. Brekoulakis, J. Lew and L. Mistelis, 453–458 (Alphen aan den Rjin: Kluwer Law International, 2016).

21 G. Harten, "Contributions and Limitations of Empirical Research on Independence and Impartiality in International Investment Arbitration," *Oñati Socio-Legal Series* 1, no. 4 (2011): 4–29.

22 T. Stipanowich and M. Vasconcellos, "The Interplay Between Empirical Studies and Commercial Arbitration Practice," in *The Evolution and Future of International Arbitration*, ed. S. Brekoulakis, J. Lew, and L. Mistelis, 471–486 (Alphen aan den Rjin: Kluwer Law International, 2016); Strong, "Class Arbitration Outside the United States."

23 International Council for Commercial Arbitration, *Report of the ICCA-Queen Mary Task Force on Third-Party Funding in International Arbitration* (The Hague, International Council for Commercial Arbitration, 2018). https://cdn.arbitration-icca.org/s3fs-public/document/media_document/Third-Party-Funding-Report%20.pdf.

24 Queen Mary University of London & White & Case LLP, *International Arbitration Survey: The Evolution of International Arbitration* (White & Case and School of International Arbitration, Queen Mary University of London, 2018). https://arbitration.qmul.ac.uk/media/arbitration/docs/2018-International-Arbitration-Survey-report.pdf.

25 Ibid.

26 E. Gaillard, "Sociology of International Arbitration," in *Practising Virtue: Inside International Arbitration*, ed. D. Caron, S. Schill, A. Smutny and E. Triantafilou, 187–203 (Oxford: Oxford University Press, 2015).

27 S. Brekoulakis, "The Evolution and Future of International Arbitration," in *The Evolution and Future of International Arbitration*, ed. S. Brekoulakis, J. Lew and L. Mistelis, 8–10 (Alphen aan den Rijn: Kluwer Law International, 2016).

body), with input from experts, or from bottom-up (initiated by stakeholders) vantage points – or through a combination of both.[28]

While this existing body of work has provided important insights into particular dispute resolution policy domains, it is now timely to analyze such approaches with the aim of contributing to a systematic understanding of the relationship between cross-border dispute resolution research methodologies and policy application.

In exploring the relationship between comparative dispute resolution research and policy reform, it is useful to look to the aims of such research, which draws on a paradigm of empowerment whereby the knowledge sought "increases awareness . . . [and] directs attention to the possibilities for social transformation inherent in the present configuration of social processes."[29] Mirroring the aims of comparative dispute resolution through the identification of the conditions in which dialogue can be developed, "people are stimulated to develop critical awareness and commit themselves to . . . transformation"[30] and positive social change.[31]

As explored in Chapter 3, the role of stakeholders in developing empirical research in arbitration and dispute resolution presents unique challenges.[32] Such system-intrinsic reflections are necessary to inform practice yet often consist of subjective observations. As noted by Stipanowich and Vasconcellos, "It must be remembered that empirical surveys on [alternative dispute resolution, ADR] practices and perspectives are not a matter of objective and observable facts, but instead rely on subjective observations, recollections, opinions and general estimates."[33] Such input provides insights into otherwise private processes and can be used to analyze emerging practices, diagnose existing problems and review existing reforms. In recent years, systematic efforts have likewise been made to introduce public input alongside insider perspectives. For example, when the United Nations Commission on International Trade Law (UNCITRAL) tackled the question of transparency in the Mauritius Convention, the question had already been the subject of vigorous public debate, oftentimes in the context of perceived arbitrator bias.[34] Similarly, the

28 Ali, *Court Mediation Reform.*

29 P. Lather, "Research as Praxis," *Harvard Education Review* 56 (1986).

30 H. C. Hsia, "Empowering 'Foreign Brides' and Community Growth Through Praxis-oriented Research. *Societies Without Borders* 1 (2006).

31 N. Andrews and S. Bawa, "'People Come and Go But We Don't See Anything': How Might Social Research Contribute to Social Change?" *The Qualitative Report* 24 (2019).

32 Stipanowich and Vasconcellos, "The Interplay Between Empirical Studies and Commercial Arbitration Practice."

33 Ibid., 479–480.

34 Cf. inter alia L. Wells, "Backlash to Investment Arbitration: Three Causes," in *The Backlash against Investment Arbitration*, ed. M. Waibel, A. Kaushal, L. Chung and C. Balchin, 341–352 (Alphen aan den Rijn: Kluwer Law International, 2010); W. Park, "Arbitrator integrity," in *The Backlash against Investment Arbitration*, ed. M. Waibel, A. Kaushal, L. Chung and C. Balchin, 189–251 (Alphen aan den Rijn: Kluwer Law International, 2010); G. Harten, "Perceived Bias in Investment Treaty Arbitration," in *The Backlash against Investment Arbitration*, ed. M. Waibel, A. Kaushal, L. Chung and C. Balchin, 433–453 (Alphen aan den Rijn: Kluwer Law International, 2010).

Singapore Convention was published after two decades of public consultation on relevant issues.[35]

It is hoped that the diverse insights into methodology and application in this book will advance understanding of the interrelation between comparative dispute resolution research and policy reform.

Structure of the Book

The chapters contained in this book form a tapestry of perspectives that contribute to the overall discussion of dispute resolution research methodology, policy reform and practice development. The chapters discuss methodological considerations and ethical and jurisprudential concerns of institutional development from a comparative and transnational perspective. In addition to a core commitment to considering transnational dispute resolution from a comparative perspective, the book also considers how hybrid forms of dispute resolution in mainland China widen our theoretical understanding of dispute resolution developments.

Following this chapter, this book proceeds to explore four themes including Methodological Considerations in Comparative and Transnational ADR; Comparative ADR Ethics, Standards and Jurisprudential Ideals; Comparative Approaches in Mediation and Arbitration; and ADR Developments and Reform in Mainland China.

Section 1: Methodological Considerations in Comparative and Transnational ADR

The first section on Methodological Considerations begins with a foundational chapter by **Matthew S. Erie** on "The Problem of Method in the Study of Transnational Dispute Resolution." This insightful chapter examines how, more so than other areas of law, transnational dispute resolution has generated a bifurcated scholarship since the late 1990s. On the one hand, the social scientific approach describes sociologists of law who have located dispute resolution practices such as international arbitration as an exclusive field of elite practitioners who generate transnational norms through their own ideologies and practices of dispute resolution. On the other hand, the legal-formalistic approach describes practitioners who, to a significant extent, dismiss such "crit" or social scientific approaches as overly vague or politicized and lacking technical rigour.

This chapter considers a third approach to transnational dispute resolution methodology by considering what Chinese anthropologist Mingming Wang (2002)

35 United Nations, General Assembly, Report of the Secretary General, Settlement of Commercial Disputes – Possible uniform rules on certain issues concerning settlement of commercial disputes: conciliation, interim measures of protection, written form for arbitration agreement, A/CN.9/WG.II/WP.108, para. 16; United Nations, General Assembly, Proposal by the Government of the United States of America: future work for Working Group II, A/CN.9/822.

has called the "third eye."[36] The third eye neither reproduces practitioners' views nor falls back on critique but rather engages in para-ethnography, which takes experts' own theories and explanations for their work seriously while also identifying divergences between academic knowledge production and business models. The chapter presents collected data from approximately two years of fieldwork in Dubai, Singapore, Astana, Hong Kong, Shenzhen and Shanghai to provide ethnographic evidence that significantly contributes to the understanding of transnational dispute resolution methodology. This chapter uses the ethnographic research on "legal hubs," one-stop shops for dispute resolution based in nonliberal regimes, as a window to consider the "third eye" approach. The conclusion drawn is that a para-ethnographic approach to transnational dispute resolution offers a bridge between the two current dominant approaches and that legal hubs offer opportunities to advance substantive knowledge about transnational dispute resolution and the methods by which we come to understand it. Thus, the chapter greatly contributes to the existing literature by endowing a comparative and interconnecting methodological approach to understanding transnational dispute resolution.

This is followed by **Michael Palmer**'s important chapter on "Modes of Dispute Response: Exploring Issues in the Range." This chapter examines how societies around the world offer disputants a range of processes that can be called into operation when "trouble" arises. At one end of the spectrum of responses lies avoidance and the "lumping" of problems, where a party with a grievance for a variety of reasons does not pursue her or his grievance and/or unilaterally readjusts a relationship in which a dispute has arisen so that tensions are mitigated or even dissolved. At one end of the spectrum another important response is the use of violence, sometimes with a degree of social acceptance, and other forms of self-help, in response to disagreement or more serious forms of tension. This chapter examines the nature and characteristics of, on the one hand, avoidance and lumping, and on the other, the threat and use of force for resolving "civil" disputes. In so doing, the chapter considers social phenomena to which texts on "alternative dispute resolution," "civil procedure" and so on tend not give a great deal of attention. The mainstream focus is, of course, primarily on the more morally appropriate and legally acceptable processes of negotiation, mediation and umpiring.

The intent of this chapter is to explore the two more neglected forms of response in order to provide a fuller understanding of the range of decision-making responses to "trouble." In this respect, the chapter contributes to the existing literature by reflecting various forms of avoidance, such as the role of an apology, in contrast to other forms of self-help, including violence, and provides a reflection on how they operate on the borders of formal ADR procedures. A

36 Mingming Wang, "The Third Eye: Towards a Critique of 'Nativist Anthropology'," *Critique of Anthropology* 22, no. 2 (2002): 149–174.

unique insight into Chinese historical and cultural understanding of these two forms of dispute resolution is provided throughout the chapter.

The last chapter of the Methods section is by **Shahla Ali** on "Advancing Research and Practice in the Governance of Dispute Resolution Institutions through Inclusive Devolved Reflection." This chapter explores how efforts to develop and reform systems of dispute resolution have been undertaken through a variety of methodologies, including commissioned research studies, citizen input, use of model laws and rules, regional accompaniment and indicator assessment. Among such efforts, this chapter focuses on the role of "devolved reflection" as a tool to support institutional dispute resolution reform. Devolved reflection can be understood as a process by which relevant stakeholders engage in earnest deliberation to arrive at a greater understanding of existing circumstances, review accomplishments, analyze challenges, learn from experience and plan next steps to improve service delivery. The United Nations Sustainable Development Goals (SDGs) include the target of building "inclusive institutions at all levels" through "citizen participation in decision making."[37] However, the dynamics of how such participation may be enhanced through reflective processes in advancing systems of dispute resolution remains understudied. The capacity to reflect as individuals and communities has increasingly been tapped to varying degrees within institutions of governance. This chapter explores what may be described as an emerging approach to devolved reflection as a mode of organizational practice, as an emerging legal principle and norm of customary international law, as an analytic and normative framework for new governance policy,[38] as an applied reflective research methodology[39] and as a component of a larger framework of learning through reflective action.[40]

The chapter draws on insights from research highlighting the role of engaged reflection and shared knowledge generation in facilitating conditions conducive to dynamic advancement within transnational dispute resolution systems – whether it be in the form of community engagement with consumer financial institutions,[41] cross-border arbitration,[42] court mediation reform[43] and development or post-disaster governance initiatives.[44]

37 See: Fariello Frank Anthony, Laurence Boisson de Chazournes, Kevin E. Davis and Samuel V. P. Lucas, eds. *Financing and Implementing the Post-2015 Development Agenda: The Role of Law and Justice Systems (English)*. The World Bank Legal Review, Vol. 7 (Washington, DC: World Bank Group, 2016). http://documents.worldbank.org/curated/en/824011473329198139/Financing-and-implementing-the-post-2015-development-agenda-the-role-of-law-and-justice-systems.

38 Ibid., 6.

39 Ibid., 8.

40 Ibid., 18.

41 Ibid., 12.

42 Ibid., 10.

43 Ibid., 11.

44 Ibid., 6.

Section 2: Comparative ADR Ethics, Standards and Jurisprudential Ideals

The second section on Comparative ADR Ethics, Standards and Jurisprudential Ideals begins with a thoughtful chapter by **Michal Alberstein**, "Comparative Judicial Conflict Resolution (JCR): Between Summary Trials and ADR." Building on the methodological framing of Section 1, this chapter examines the intersection between ADR and contemporary court systems by referring to the changing roles of judges in an age of vanishing trials[45] and the emergence of new hybrids of judicial activities.

The chapter presents research data collected from both civil and criminal fields in Israel, Italy and England and Wales. The findings suggest that judges are significantly involved only in a small number of cases that enter the courts and that most cases are settled or reach plea bargains without a substantial intervention of judges. However, when judges do intervene in legal disputes, their involvement is characterized by encouraging consent between parties regarding either process or substance. Interventions that refer to process include convincing the parties to accept a form of summary trial (Israel civil, Italy criminal), enforcing mediation through judicial orders (Italy civil) and encouraging parties to go to mediation (Israel and England and Wales) whereas interventions that refer to substance include providing predictions of the legal outcome (Israel, Italy and England and Wales), using procedural and administrative incentives (England and Wales and Israel) and addressing the negative aspects of pursuing the legal process for the parties (Israel).

The chapter reviews the variety of these forms of intervention and examines the possible connection between ADR and these new models of judicial work. In particular, the chapter questions whether the ideals of ADR resonate in judicial practices of concluding cases efficiently. The chapter identifies two trends that characterize contemporary judicial work: the diminishing of the trial and the shift to an inquisitorial process or summary trial and the development of new judicial roles related to mediation and conflict resolution. These two trajectories offer different ideals for the development of legal systems, and the chapter discusses them in reference to jurisprudential ideals on the judicial role. The chapter makes two important findings. In cases that do reach court, judicial intervention is narrow with an encouragement for the parties to settle but focuses on the specific legal issues in the case rather than the wider benefits of ADR. Further, an emphasis on judicial intervention akin to a summary trial basis is more aligned to the effective management of cases rather than jurisprudential goals of ADR.[46] The chapter concludes that a paradigmatic shift is required in designing the court

45 Marc Galanter, "The Vanishing Trial: An Examination of Trials and Related Matters in Federal and State Courts," *Journal of Empirical Legal Studies* 1, no. 3 (2004): 459.

46 Ibid., 18.

system based on preventing and resolving conflicts.[47] Thus, a substantial contribution is made to assessing the jurisprudential goals of ADR in light of emerging judicial practices.

Next is **Lola Akin Ojelabi**'s significant chapter on "The Challenges of Developing Global Ethical Standards for Mediation Practice." Alternative or Appropriate Dispute Resolution has grown exponentially in many jurisdictions. As Ojelabi explores in her chapter, in many parts of the world, the impetus for this growth has been the need to improve access to justice. ADR processes viewed as less costly, less complicated and less time consuming were promoted as better alternatives to judicial determination, and although traditional forms of dispute resolution have existed in many jurisdictions and cultures, ADR processes promoted on the back of the access to justice movement were those developed in the West. These processes have become institutionalized in many nations and form an integral part of the civil justice systems. The common source of ADR terminology and training across jurisdictions has meant that similarities exist. However, a closer look would reveal significant differences in definitions of ADR terms, standards of ADR practice and conceptions of ADR practitioner responsibilities, shaped by social and professional culture. The implication is that developing a set of global standards for ADR would require careful consideration. The chapter explores the significance of harmonizing global ADR standards in the face of localized and cultural ethical practices by looking at ADR policies and practices in various jurisdictions. Specifically, five standards/codes are examined, including the Australian National Mediator Accreditation System (Practice Standards) 2015 (NMAS Standards), The European Code of Conduct for Mediators (EU Code), the Model Standards of Conduct for Mediators, August 2005 (Model Standards), the Singapore Mediation Centre, Mediation Service Code of Conduct (SMC Code) and the IMI Code of Professional Conduct for Mediators (IMI Code). The chapter offers an analysis of both similar and diverging understandings of ADR from a multi-jurisdictional standpoint.[48] It concludes that global harmonization of ADR standards is desirable, though it is not without challenges; cultural understandings of ADR are diverse. A combination of comparative approaches and a "law-in-context" methodology is required to achieve common ground on global ADR standards.[49] The chapter, therefore, significantly contributes to the debate on harmonizing international standards through a better understanding of comparative localized standards.

Section 3: Comparative Approaches in Mediation and Arbitration

The third section on Comparative Approaches in Mediation and Arbitration begins with an insightful chapter by **Nadja Alexander** on "International

47 Ibid., 19.
48 Ibid., 7.
49 Ibid., 16.

Comparative Mediation Law: Hong Kong and Singapore in Perspective." This chapter explores how ASEAN (Association of Southeast Asian Nations) is emerging as a significant region for the development of mediation systems. In recent years, both Singapore and Hong Kong have introduced new mediation laws, institutions and credentialing for professional mediators that will impact the practice of commercial and civil dispute resolution in both domestic and cross-border matters. Further, the UN adopted a Convention on International Settlement Agreements Arising from Mediation in December 2018 – the first instrument of its kind on mediation at the international level. The chapter offers an international comparative approach, emphasizing ASEAN, to discussing the development of mediation regulatory systems and infrastructure.

Next is **Luigi Cominelli, Eleonora Ciscato and Stefania Lattuille**'s important contribution on "Environmental Mediation and Facilitation in Italy: Theoretical Insights and Practical Experience on Non-Adjudicative Mechanisms and 'Total Conflicts.'" This chapter provides insight and analysis of mediation in Italy from the unique perspective of environmental disputes. So-called environmental conflicts have existed in Italy between individuals and governmental bodies or private organizations tasked with construction waste management and disposal infrastructure throughout the country.

Finally, **Xiantao Wen**, with an introduction by **Susan Finder**, explores "Comparative Analysis of the Singapore Convention in Light of the New York and Hague Choice of Court Conventions." This significant chapter contributes to the understanding of comparative perspectives of the operation of the United Nations Convention on International Settlement Agreements Resulting from Mediation (the Singapore Convention) on cross-border relief for commercial settlement agreements. The chapter includes a focused analysis of the Singapore Convention's core provisions, including the scope of application, general principles, grounds for refusing to grant relief and reservations together with a comprehensive interpretation of key concepts such as "settlement" and "mediation." The chapter highlights the comparative thematic nature of the book by providing a comparative study of the relevant provisions from the Singapore Convention against those from the New York Convention and the Hague Choice of Court Convention in light of Chinese laws and regulations. The chapter concludes that China should actively seek to accede to the Singapore Convention and improve relevant domestic laws and regulations in an effort to accelerate the diversification of civil and commercial dispute resolution regimes, which will help establish a community of shared future for mankind.

Section 4: ADR Developments and Reform in Mainland China

The last section explores ADR Developments and Reform in Mainland China. This chapter begins with an important chapter by **Xin He and Yang Su** on "Flexibility and Authority: Keys for Informal Justice to Succeed." This chapter extends existing literature regarding flexibility and authority as key characteristics of informal injustice through considering reform and development of ADR in China from a labour dispute perspective. It investigates the dispute resolution process by following the life cycles of a sample of 810 labour disputes handled by a Chinese labour agency. The research findings show that an informal justice forum, such as the China labour agency, was both efficient and effective. This was made possible by the combination of flexibility and authority. Flexibility in this context means that the agency attracts certain types of cases that are usually screened out of the formal legal system and that agency officials use "informal," hence flexible, techniques. Authority means that the administrative agency possesses additional powers over the disputants; hence, the disputants are pressured to follow its suggestions and decisions.[50]

The chapter makes two important findings. First, it concludes that both flexibility and authority are crucial for informal justice to be effective. Further, it demonstrates that flexibility without authority is insufficient and that some informal justice forums are effective because they enjoy both.[51] The chapter contextualizes the research and considers the wider implications of its conclusions for all government-sponsored agencies offering dispute resolution forums.

Next, **Kwai Hang Ng** explores the timely question of integrating adjudication and mediation in his chapter, "Wearing Two Hats: Problems of 'In-Trial' Mediation in China." This chapter presents China as an outlier case of extreme integration between adjudication and mediation and assesses the issues associated with a fully integrated model of mediation. The chapter uses collected data from contested divorce cases as a focus of the investigation. By drawing on both fieldwork observation and court data analysis, this chapter explores and examines the feedback effects of mediation *on* adjudication under the integrated model of judicial mediation in China. The chapter offers a case study[52] that, by comparison with other models of judicial mediation, has important theoretical implications for understanding the essential "alternative" elements required of an ADR institution to make it an apt option for parties seeking dispute resolution.

As a procedural context, the chapter argues that the adversarial trial setting is poorly equipped to facilitate mediation because it places a too high burden on the judiciary to fulfil different roles. There is also evidence implicating that this integrated and yet open-ended process of court-directed mediation discourages litigants from returning to the court to seek resolution.[53] The chapter concludes by expressing caution regarding the notion that the more integration of ADR into the adversarial court structure, the merrier. It provides sentiment to the careful consideration of what "alternative" requires in a dispute resolution model.

The last chapter by **Ling Zhou**, "Thinking about Consumer Mediation in China: Some Examples from Shenzhen," explores the question of mixed

50 Ibid., 11.
51 Ibid., 15.
52 Ibid., 6.
53 Ibid., 11.

processes through the lens of consumer disputes. She explores how an emphasis on the internal integrity of the dispute process has gradually been supplanted by voices for allowing process pluralism and the inventions of hybrid forms of dispute process around the world. In mainland China, the mixing of various dispute processes is a natural dimension of a legal culture that privileges mediation and harmony and where enforcement of court judgments can be problematic. The chapter focuses on one of China's fast-growing cities, Shenzhen, and provides a unique insight into the approach to how consumer grievances are resolved both within formal and societal ADR processes and how Shenzhen, and China more generally, has responded to a new special type of user, the professional litigant. The professional litigant is typically a repeat player who, without formal training in law, skilfully uses the legal framework of consumer protection through litigation and threats of litigation to negotiate a good settlement. Among the tactics is the purchase of substandard products purposefully so as to claim punitive damages. Thus, the chapter greatly adds to existing literature by assessing the emergence of the professional litigant in consumer law in accordance with developing ADR structures within an urbanizing context.

Conclusion

This book builds upon prior volumes by offering a fresh socio-legal perspective of the interface between comparative global dispute resolution and policy reform in diverse jurisdictions. It is anticipated that this book will be of great interest to students, practitioners and scholars of transnational dispute resolution and comparative legal institutions as well as those working in global dispute systems design as it provides a comprehensive review of the contributions of comparative policy studies to the development and refinement of dispute resolution institutions, examines cutting-edge developments at the intersection of legal ethics and dispute resolution and identifies best practices in policy reform.

Acknowledgement

The author thanks Ernest Kenneth Southworth for his research support. The author also thanks the Government of Hong Kong's Research Grants Council for its support through its grant HK-17610921.

SECTION I

Methodological Considerations in Comparative and Transnational ADR

2

THE PROBLEM OF METHOD IN THE STUDY OF TRANSNATIONAL DISPUTE RESOLUTION

Matthew S. Erie

Introduction: Defining the Problem

The field of transnational dispute resolution (TDR), defined as, primarily, international arbitration, transnational litigation, and business mediation, is, by all accounts, booming. A number of indicators evince the field's health, including: number and size of arbitral awards, growth of international commercial courts, increase in legal services in the form of international law firms, and curricular reforms in law schools that focus on TDR coursework and training. Despite currents of anti-globalisation in the U.S., U.K., and western Europe, and the ongoing deleterious impact of the COVID-19 pandemic, multinational companies (MNCs) continue to produce a high volume of cross-border commercial transactions and concomitant disputes. In part, because of anti-globalisation currents, some of these deals are relocating to Asia. Regulatory responses to COVID-19 in Asia in particular have also caused a number of disputes. This chapter sets out to address the question: how are we to study TDR during a period that may be witnessing a shift from globalisation to regionalisation? More specifically as a matter of methodology, how can Asian TDR be made an object of study?

The study of TDR has attracted, generally, two main approaches. One, which I call the "legal-formalistic" approach, emphasises doctrine. The second adopts the methodologies of the social sciences, and which I thus call the "social scientific" approach. These views each have their own epistemologies and analytical languages, and each sets out to answer different types of questions. The legal-formalistic approach is, by far, the dominant approach, as it is endorsed by the practitioners of TDR. The social scientific approach, often favoured by legal sociologists and legal anthropologists as well as adherents to "law and society" and empirical legal studies, is, for the most part, marginalised, particularly by the proponents of the legal-formalistic view. While it could be said that the

DOI: 10.4324/9780429354625-4

insider-outsider dichotomy characterises legal studies more generally, the divide is particularly pronounced in the study of TDR.

This chapter proposes a different perspective by borrowing from the anthropology of experts to suggest that "para-ethnography" is one way to build synergies between the legal-formalistic approach and the social scientific one. In particular, the chapter suggests that ethnographic strategies focused on expert knowledge can elucidate the thought processes that shape TDR practices. This chapter draws on data collected for a larger project on new legal hubs (NLHs), one-stop shops for cross-border commercial dispute resolution, in financial centres, promoted as an official policy by nondemocratic or hybrid (i.e., democratic and authoritarian) states, located primarily in Asia.[1] This chapter's perspective is aimed at opening up broader conceptual grounds for methodological approaches to TDR. In the remainder of this chapter, I first identify the current methodologies for studying dispute resolution; second, provide an overview of NLHs; third, propose a new method for their study, para-ethnography; fourth, explain my use of that method; fifth, provide a succinct case study applying that method; and, last, end with a brief conclusion.

Disciplinary Blinkers

There are, traditionally, two veins of thought on how to study TDR. The first, the legal-formalistic approach, is the doctrinal perspective taught in law schools in the U.S., Europe, Asia, and elsewhere and which, similar to other areas of law covered by a legal curriculum, explains the operation of TDR with reference to the relevant substantive and procedural rules. The specific methodology used in this mode is one that traces the analysis of third-party decision-makers (whether arbitrators, judges, or mediators) in precedent cases, awards, or settlements for purposes of understanding instant or future disputes. Inherently, the legal-formalistic approach is focused on rules, so, for example, in international commercial arbitration, the interplay between international covenants (e.g., the Convention on the Recognition and Enforcement of Foreign Arbitral Awards, or "New York Convention of 1958"), domestic legislation (e.g., the Singapore International Arbitration Act of 2010, as amended in 2016), and, perhaps, the rules of institutional arbitration (e.g., Singapore International Arbitration Centre 2016 Rules).

Continuing the example of international commercial arbitration, the legal-formalistic approach focuses in on the relevant substantive and procedural rules as they affect such doctrinal questions as separability, competence-competence, enforcement of agreements, applicable law and arbitral seat, and the arbitral award. There is a preoccupation (rightly so) on choice of law concerns as they determine the substantive law governing the merits of the parties' contract, the

1 See Matthew S. Erie, "The New Legal Hubs: The Emerging Landscape of International Commercial Dispute Resolution," *Virginia Journal of International Law* 60, no. 2 (2020): 225–298, p. 229.

substantive law governing the parties' arbitration agreement, and the law applicable to the arbitral proceedings. To understand outcomes of arbitral tribunals, scholars operating in this mode parse through judicial cases that review the various legal issues pertaining to arbitration agreements and awards, given that most awards themselves are confidential.

Whereas the legal-formalistic approach is the majority or default mode, there is a second or minority one. This view occurs at the overlap of a number of different literatures, including legal sociology, legal anthropology, "law and society," and empirical legal studies. Broadly speaking, this view adopts specific social scientific approaches to data collection to examine less rules and doctrine and more the structures of power and hierarchy, or space, networks, and ritual, through which such rules operate. Rather than analysing naked rules, the social scientific approach frames rules (and rule-makers) in their multidimensional social, economic, and political contexts. Many of these studies are written by non-practitioners or outsiders to TDR, and a portion of them derive from "crit" vantages, written with the goal not to reproduce elite knowledge practices but to critique them. Empirical methodologies include both quantitative and qualitative strategies and, further, may use such material to either verify existing theories of dispute resolution or generate new models.[2] While a generalisation, empirical legal studies often uses statistical measures, legal anthropology prefers ethnographic ones, and legal sociology and sister approaches in "law and society" demonstrate a mixture.

The legal-formalistic approach and the social scientific one, while not intrinsically antagonistic, have more often than not regarded the other in such a way. Practitioners may believe that, for example, the sociology of arbitration goes too far in its rubrics of "tournament rituals," "social capital," and "fields." From the view of the practitioner, such analogies are inaccessible and impractical at best and alienating at worst. The critical edge of some observations naturally further antagonises practitioners. Line-drawing occurs on both sides. Practitioners marginalise the social scientific approach, and as practitioners are those who not only occupy arbitration tribunals and benches but also law school lecterns and other professional membership organisations, such marginalisation matters.

One case in point is Yves Dezalay and Bryant Garth's foundational study of international commercial arbitration, *Dealing in Virtue: International Commercial Arbitration and the Construction of a Transnational Legal Order* (1996), in which they contend that the relationship between academics and practitioners is one of "polarization."[3] In his review of the book, former secretary general of the Inter-

2 See, e.g., *International Arbitration and Global Governance: Contending Theories and Evidence*, eds. Walter Mattli and Thomas Dietz, 1st ed. (Oxford: Oxford University Press, 2014); Joshua D. H. Karton, *The Culture of International Arbitration and the Evolution of Contract Law*, 1st ed. (Oxford: Oxford University Press, 2013); Alec Stone Sweet, *The Evolution of International Arbitration: Judicialization, Governance, Legitimacy*. Ed. Florian Grisel. 1st ed. (Oxford and New York: Oxford University Press, 2017).

3 Yves Dézalay and Bryant G. Garth, *Dealing in Virtue: International Commercial Arbitration and the Construction of a Transnational Legal Order.* (London and Chicago: University of Chicago Press, 1996), 41.

national Chamber of Commerce (ICC) International Court of Arbitration Eric Schwartz points out that this dichotomy is overstated; rather, many academics are practitioners.[4] (At the same time, Schwartz characterises the study as, at times, "difficult to fathom" and "tedious," and he goes on to conclude: "this book paints a misleading portrait of the world of international commercial arbitration and its development."[5]) On the initial point, indeed, the distinction in contemporary TDR is between practitioner-academics who are, for the most part, formal-legalists and social scientists who are, with few exceptions, mainly non-practitioners. Nonetheless, the dichotomous way of thinking persists, itself rooted in the historical reception of social scientific approaches to law in the legal academy.[6] This way of thinking begs the question whether the two approaches are really irreconcilable or if an accommodation is possible. Before proposing a method that bridges the two disciplines, I turn to one particular formation of TDR: NLHs.

The New Legal Hubs

NLHs are "one-stop shops" for cross-border commercial dispute resolution, often located in financial centres, promoted as an official policy by nondemocratic or hybrid states. The idea of the one-stop shop derives from legal scholar Frank Sander's idea of the "multi-door courthouse."[7] Sander thought that the courts of the future would provide parties with a menu of dispute resolution mechanisms, offering not just litigation but also mediation, arbitration, and ombudsmen. An intake office, which triages disputes, was the key to the system.[8] NLHs are modern-day versions of the multi-door courthouse for sophisticated parties whose lawyers choose which mechanism to use. A second defining feature of NLHs is that they overlap with other sectoral hubs: financial, infrastructural, telecom, and insurance, to name a few. As centres of finance, hubs require clear rules for creating capital markets.[9] Third, NLHs are located mainly in nondemocratic

4 Eric A. Schwartz, "Dealing in Virtue: International Commercial Arbitration and the Construction of a Transnational Legal Order. By Yves Dézalay and Bryant Garth," *ICSID Review* 12, no. 1 (1997): 229–235, 232.

5 Ibid., 229–230.

6 Richard L. Abel, "A Comparative Theory of Dispute Institutions in Society," *Law & Society Review* 8, no. 2 (1974): 217–347, 225–226; Richard L. Abel, "Law and Society: Project and Practice," *Annual Review of Law and Social Science* 6, no. 1 (2010): 1–23, 3; Marc Galanter, "Presidential Address: The Legal Malaise; or, Justice Observed," *Law & Society Review* 19, no. 4 (1985): 537–556, 537.

7 Frank E. A. Sander, "Varieties of Dispute Processing," in *The Pound Conference: Perspectives on Justice in the Future*, eds. Leo A. Levin and Russell R. Wheeler (Eagan, MN: West Publishing Company, 1979).

8 Ibid.

9 Rumu Sarkar, *International Development Law: Rule of Law, Human Rights, and Global Finance*, 2nd ed. (Cham, Switzerland: Springer International Publishing, 2009), 432 (discussing the creation of a successful regulatory framework for capital markets); Robert B. Ahdieh, "Making Markets: Network Effects and the Role of Law in the Creation of Strong Securities," *Southern California Law Review* 76, no. 2 (2003): 277. (examining why law matters in the creation of securities markets in transitional states); Andrew T. Guzman, "Capital Market Regulation in Developing Countries: A Proposal," *Virginia Journal of International Law* 39, no. 3 (1999): 607, 609 (stating, "A country that successfully

or hybrid states, by which I mean non-Western states wherein power is concentrated in the hands of a few (or one) with the result that the system lacks true political pluralism, representation, and an electoral process.[10] Examples of forms of government include autocracies, kleptocracies, authoritarian systems, single-party states, and hybrid regimes.[11] Nondemocratic and hybrid states have different and overlapping goals, including political legitimacy (in the eyes of international business parties as well as for domestic audiences) and economic development. Legitimacy as a legal service provider can be a precondition for economic growth.[12] Depending on the relative socio-economic development of the host state, NLHs can either attract foreign direct investment (FDI) or export legal services, thus serving as a multipurpose growth strategy.

NLHs are particularly prominent in Asia. The two dominant NLHs are Hong Kong and Singapore, while a second tier of NLHs is make up of Dubai and Nur-Sultan (formerly Astana), with more nascent examples located in China – specifically, Shanghai and Shenzhen. The NLHs spanning from the Middle East and Western Asia to the Asia-Pacific Rim are part and parcel of the emergence of the macro-region in the latter half of the twentieth century – and, more recently, after the 2008 worldwide financial crisis – that has been called "Inter-Asia."[13] Following the rise of post–World War II Japan and the so-called Asian tigers of Hong Kong, Taiwan, Singapore, and South Korea in the 1980s, China, India, and the Gulf states each experienced rapid growth and integration into international trade and investment regimes. Legal services have followed suit, including TDR. Hong Kong and Singapore, for instance, are more convenient and culturally and linguistically familiar to Asia-based MNCs than, say, Paris

establishes a regulatory regime that meets the needs of investors and issuers will encourage investment in that country").

10 See, e.g., Samuel P. Huntington, *Authoritarian Politics in Modern Society: The Dynamics of Established One-Party Systems*. Ed. Samuel P. Huntington and Clement Henry Moore (New York: Basic Books, 1970).

11 See, e.g., Daron Acemoglu, Thierry Verdier and James A. Robinson, "Kleptocracy and Divide-and-Rule: A Model of Personal Rule," *Journal of the European Economic Association* 2, no. 2–3 (2004): 162–192 (arguing that kleptocracies practice a divide-and-rule strategy, enabled by weak institutions); Steven Levitsky, *Competitive Authoritarianism: Hybrid Regimes after the Cold War*. Ed. Lucan Way (Cambridge and New York: Cambridge University Press, 2010) (analysing how formal democratic institutions can serve as the means of obtaining authoritarianism); Milan W. Svolik, *The Politics of Authoritarian Rule*. Ed. Cambridge University Press (New York and Cambridge: Cambridge University Press, 2012) (providing an explanation for why politics assume different forms in different types of dictatorships).

12 See Richard L. Abel and Philip S. C. Lewis, *Lawyers in Society: An Overview* (Berkeley: University of California Press, 1995) (providing a study of the role of lawyers in emergent markets). See also David B. Wilkins, Vikramaditya S. Khanna and David M. Trubek, *The Indian Legal Profession in the Age of Globalization: The Rise of the Corporate Legal Sector and Its Impact on Lawyers and Society* (Cambridge: Cambridge University Press, 2017); Luciana Gross Cunha, *The Brazilian Legal Profession in the Age of Globalization: The Rise of the Corporate Legal Sector and its Impact on Lawyers and Society* (Cambridge: Cambridge University Press, 2018).

13 Engseng Ho, "Inter-Asian Concepts for Mobile Societies," *The Journal of Asian Studies* 76, no. 4 (2017): 907.

or Stockholm. While traditional legal hubs such as New York City and London may still attract a large number of cross-border commercial disputes, by many indicators, at least some Inter-Asian NLHs are growing in popularity.[14]

Just as with TDR elsewhere, NLHs can be examined through the lenses of either the legal-formalistic approach or the social scientific one. Accordingly, a number of studies have, pursuant to the former paradigm, demonstrated how NLHs trade on the quality of their legal frameworks.[15] Further, they may promote legal harmonisation through their adoption of international covenants and model laws. Examples include Asian states' accession to the New York Convention of 1958 and the ICSID Convention of 1965, as well as their adoption of the 1985 UNCITRAL Model Law on International Commercial Arbitration, as amended in 2006.[16] Likewise, much has been made of Singapore as the eponymous inspiration for the Convention on International Settlement Agreements Resulting from Mediation, or the Singapore Convention.[17] In the same vein, China's initiative in launching its own one-stop shops for TDR in the form of the so-called China International Commercial Court, based in Shenzhen and Xi'an, has fired the imagination of many international lawyers, resulting in not a few law firm memos and "client alerts" on the topic. A common feature of these studies is a methodology which examines the adoption of and innovation upon multiple sources of legal rules, whether international treaties, national legislation, or institutional rules, the last of which may only have legal force once parties adopt those rules into their contracts.

NLHs have been the subject of fewer social scientific approaches. Yves Dezalay and Bryant Garth's *Asian Legal Revivals: Lawyers in the Shadow of Empire* (2010) extends the qualitative method of their earlier study on international commercial arbitration – namely, elite interviews – to explain postcolonial lawyering in such countries as Singapore, Hong Kong, South Korea, and the Philippines, among other jurisdictions. So, on the one hand, some of the old tensions between the legal-formalistic view and the social scientific counterpart persist, even if on new jurisdictional terrain. On the other hand, in Asian states, there seems to be a

14 Queen Mary University of London and White & Case, *2018 International Arbitration Survey: The Evolution of International Arbitration*. Report, 2018. p. 2. www.whitecase.com/sites/whitecase/files/files/download/publications/qmul-international-arbitration-survey-2018-18.pdf (rating Shenzhen and Hong Kong as two of the world's top venues for international arbitration).

15 See, e.g., Olga Boltenko, Howard Chan and Wong Zi Wei, "Setting Aside Jurisdictional Findings by Tribunals and the Ad Hoc Admission of Counsel in Singapore and Hong Kong," *Asian Dispute Review* 22, no. 2 (2020): 70–74.

16 See Simon Greenberg, Christopher Kee and J. Romesh Weeramantry, *International Commercial Arbitration: An Asia-Pacific Perspective* (Melbourne: Cambridge University Press, 2010); Gary F. Bell, *The UNCITRAL Model Law and Asian Arbitration Laws: Implementation and Comparisons* (Cambridge: Cambridge University Press, 2018), and Anselmo Reyes and Weixia Gu, *The Developing World of Arbitration: A Comparative Study of Arbitration Reform in the Asia Pacific*, 1st ed. (London: Hart Publishing, 2018).

17 Eunice Chua, "The Singapore Convention on Mediation – A Brighter Future for Asian Dispute Resolution," *Asian Journal of International Law* 9, no. 2 (2019): 195–205.

growing number of individuals who cross over the lines between legal-formalistic "practitioner" and social scientific academic, and indeed, such individuals are carving out novel spaces for studying TDR in Asian contexts.[18]

Building on these contributions, starting in 2016 to the onset of the COVID-19 pandemic in 2019, I conducted fieldwork in and on the major NLHs, including Singapore, Hong Kong, Dubai, Nur-Sultan, Shanghai, and Shenzhen. I also conducted fieldwork in London as London's institutions for TDR are a model, in some ways, for NLHs in Inter-Asia, some of which are former British colonial territories. Early on in my fieldwork, I was struck by two features of data-gathering: first, NLHs were a result of a specific nexus of legal specialists or "entrepreneurs," including U.K. legal consultants (e.g., barristers, solicitors, arbitrators, and former judges), government officials representing the jurisdiction in which the NLH is based, and a third group I call "transnational legal elites," made up of non-U.K. nationals who nonetheless may have received legal training in the U.K. and who are arbitrators and judges. This nexus of expertise was concentrated in NLHs, but I also watched how it moved between and among different NLHs, suggesting a kind of network of knowledge practices. This "travelling knowledge" was thus one challenge to conducting fieldwork.[19]

The second observation was that the kinds of innovations NLHs exhibited were not just structural or institutional in nature but also derived from doctrine and rules. In other words, I soon realised that to study NLHs as TDR holistically, I had to make their legal entrepreneurs' legal reasoning an object of analysis, just as much as the courts and other venues that they were building. This second observation was even more of a challenge and required me to gain a fuller understanding of the substantive areas of international commercial law in question – namely, international commercial arbitration and transnational litigation. In the next section, I explain para-ethnography as a method for grappling with the particular challenges of studying TDR in NLHs.

Para-Ethnography

Anthropologists are known to study systems of behaviour and thought that differ from that of their own societies. During the formative years of anthropology at the start of the twentieth century, the objects of anthropological study were mostly pre-capitalist societies in Africa, Asia, and Latin America.[20] A leading debate was whether the thinking of members of such societies differed in nature from that of

18 See, e.g., Shahla F. Ali and Tom Ginsburg, *International Commercial Arbitration in Asia*, 3rd ed. (Huntington, NY: Juris, 2013).

19 Alyssa S. King and Pamela K. Bookman, "Traveling Judges," *American Journal of International Law* (forthcoming) (studying retired English judges serving on benches in Hong Kong, Dubai, and elsewhere).

20 Bronislaw Malinowski, *Crime and Custom in Savage Society*. Ed. Human Relations Area Files (London: Trubner, 1926).

capitalist Western societies.[21] Fast-forward a century, and the discipline has diversified significantly such that anthropologists study a wide array of modern forms of knowledge, including the bureaucratic, technical, financial, medical, legal, and artificial.[22] These studies share a commitment to ethnography, one that is grounded in explicating specific disciplinary modes of thinking. In this regard, the programming skills of a blockchain developer can be made the object of study in the same way as the rituals of a Bororo chief.[23] In both cases, the "exotic" is rendered "familiar" and vice versa through the work of ethnographic translation.

Following these inroads into contemporary professions, and dovetailing with both science and technology studies and legal studies, a literature has coalesced around an "anthropology of experts."[24] These ethnographic case studies suggest that immersion in the modes of hypothesis formation, experimentation, data collection, analysis, and argumentation in laboratories and courtrooms, for example, can shed light on how expert knowledge is generated and deployed by diverse actors, including funders, governments, academics, lay publics, and the experts themselves. The anthropology of experts has also exposed an epistemological problem that calls into question some of the analogical logic of the blockchain developer::Bororo chief. If the expert knowledge under study is rooted in the same theories as the knowledge of the ethnographer, then that shared or overlapped knowledge may be problematic for the reason that sufficient critical distance cannot be created between the researcher and the object knowledge under examination to adequately assess its contours, texture, and heft. In other words, similar to the "native anthropologist" who shares a body of assumptions

21 Lucien Lévy-Bruhl, *How Natives Think*. Ed. Lilian Ada Long Claire (London: G. Allen & Unwin Ltd, 1926) (suggesting that "primitive" man uses non-logical "mystical" modes of thought). But see Émile Durkheim, *The Elementary Forms of the Religious Life* (Joseph Ward Swain trans., 1912) (inducting the elementary forms of all religions from the totemic beliefs of Australian aborigines).

22 Laura Nader, "Up the Anthropologist: Perspectives Gained from Studying Up," in *Reinventing Anthropology*, 1st ed., ed. Dell Hymes (New York: Pantheon Books, 1972); Timothy Mitchell, *Rule of Experts: Egypt, Techno-Politics, Modernity* (Berkeley: University of California Press, 2002); Hubert Dreyfus, *What Computers Still Can't Do: A Critique of Artificial* Reason. Ed. Hubert L. Dreyfus (Cambridge, MA: MIT Press, 1992); David Graeber, *The Utopia of Rules: On Technology, Stupidity, and the Secret Joys of Bureaucracy* (Brooklyn: Melville House, 2015); Karen Zouwen Ho, *Liquidated: An Ethnography of Wall Street* (London and Durham: Duke University Press, 2009); Vilma Santiago-Irizarry, *Medicalizing Ethnicity: The Construction of Latino Identity in a Psychiatric Setting* (Ithaca, NY: Cornell University Press, 2001); Bruno Latour, *The Making of Law – An Ethnography of the Conseil D'Etat* (Cambridge: Polity Press, 2010).

23 See, e.g., Claude Lévi-Strauss, *Tristes Tropiques* (John and Doreen Weightman trans., London: Penguin: 1955[1973]).

24 Dominic Boyer, "Thinking through the Anthropology of Experts," *Anthropology in Action* 15, no. 2 (2008): 38; Harry Collins and Evans Robert, *Rethinking Expertise* (Chicago: University of Chicago Press, 2007). Penny Harvey and Hannah Knox, *Roads: An Anthropology of Infrastructure and Expertise*, 1st ed. (Ithaca: Cornell University Press, 2015); Candis Callison, *How Climate Change Comes to Matter: The Communal Life of Facts* (Durham: Duke University Press, 2014); Peter Miller, *Governing the Present: Administering Economic, Social and Personal Life*. Ed. Nikolas S. Rose (Cambridge: Polity, 2008).

with interlocutors, the anthropologist may already be normalised into a way of thinking that is thus "invisible" to him or her.

One way that anthropologists have dealt with this problem is through devising comparative strategies of reasoning between the overlapping expert knowledges, the anthropologist's and the interlocutor's. One stream of thought on this question can be traced to British anthropologist Marilyn Strathern's body of work, which has been described as a "reflexive" approach to anthropology's knowledge production vis-à-vis experts. In her own words, Strathern writes, "The reflexivity that has become routine in both anthropological and ethnographic enquiry in some senses mirrors the self-conscious auditing of present-day health policies for Aboriginal people in Australia."[25] Strathern uses the bureaucratic processes of health professionals as a mirror for anthropologists' own ceaseless re-examination of its foundations.

Strathern's approach has been influential in American anthropology as well and has spurred further methodologies of studying expert knowledge. Notable among these examples is Bill Maurer's idea of "lateral reasoning" as a basis for ethnography, as illustrated in his study of Islamic finance.[26] For Maurer, anthropological knowledge production and that of experts reside side by side, informing each other, and the job of ethnography is less to explicate expert knowledge than it is to frame this oscillation.[27] This perspective – that ethnography is not external to but immanent within expert knowledge and that experts combine their forms of knowledge with ethnographic description – is taken up by Annelise Riles in her study of collateral. Riles understands collateral not only in its traditional sense as a security given by the debtor to the creditor to guarantee payment for an obligation but also as that which is "on the sidelines somewhat of an afterthought" as in the position of legal knowledge vis-à-vis markets.[28] Further, the concept becomes, like Strathern's health bureaucracies, a conceit for expert knowledge itself (here, legal expertise), which "claims to be unique, set apart, collateral."[29] Last, Dominic Boyer has cogently articulated the problem of the anthropology of experts in his example of studying German intellectuals. He proposes:

> A dialectician studying other dialecticians did not seem quite capable of evoking the impression of critical theoretical distance of the kind that is often valued as an index of objectivity or sophistication . . . [and that this posed] the threat of an epistemological end point for anthropology in the potential doubling, collapse and/or cancellation of analytical knowledge forms.[30]

25 Marilyn Strathern, "Anthropological Reasoning: Some Threads of Thought," *HAU Journal of Ethnographic Theory* 4, no. 3 (2014): 23–37.

26 Bill Maurer, *Mutual Life, Limited: Islamic Banking, Alternative Currencies, Lateral Reason*. (Princeton, NJ: Princeton University Press, 2005).

27 Ibid., 7.

28 Annelise Riles, *Collateral Knowledge: Legal Reasoning in the Global Financial Markets* (London: University of Chicago Press, 2011), 2.

29 Ibid., 25.

30 See Boyer, "Thinking Through the Anthropology of Experts," 41.

Boyer's response to this problem is, in a move that echoes the earlier debates over primitive man as "mystical" and civilised man as "rational," to call for de-emphasising the pure rationality of expert knowledge by bringing back desire and affect in the study of expertise.[31]

The anthropology of experts, particularly the vein of thought that stresses reflexivity, may seem, to non-anthropologists (and even some anthropologists), as overly focused on questions that are internal to anthropology and of limited importance beyond the discipline. Formal-legalists, in particular, may question the relevance or utility of such approaches. I submit that there may be excesses to such meditations, but they also provide a foundation that is helpful not necessarily to circumvent an impasse between social scientific methodologies and formal-legalistic ones but to pull on both of these analytical currents to advance the study of TDR and even the hard case of NLHs.

In particular, some reflexive anthropologists propose "para-ethnography" as a specific methodology to confront and even operationalise the doubling of knowledge between anthropologist-as-analyst and expert-as-object.[32] The prefix "para-" is understood in this context as "side by side" in the sense of two experts working collaboratively (e.g., "paramedic"). Para-ethnography thus goes beyond the heuristic exercise of taking a particular cause or effect of expert knowledge (e.g., health bureaucracy or collateral) as a basis for reflexively thinking about anthropological knowledge to posit à la Boyer that there is indeed a causal relationship between the analyst's and the object's forms of knowledge. Hence, para-ethnography is a mode of academic knowledge production that is joint or fused and does not take for granted the intimate co-imbrication of multiple ethnographers. Para-ethnography shares affinities with "devolved reflection" as a method for studying dispute resolutions (Ali, this volume), although it often operates in a specific stratum of knowledge production – that of elite experts.

Seeing through the Third Eye

In response to a paper I have given or at the beginning of a question in a question-and-answer portion of an academic event, I have consistently heard this start to a sentence, "As a practitioner, I . . ." The qualifying clause fulfils two functions: one, it self-identifies the speaker as a lawyer, arbitrator, judge, or other type of legal expert. Two, it distinguishes the speaker from the listener – in this case, me. I may be a practitioner, too, but not the speaker's type of practitioner. For

31 See ibid.

32 Douglas R. Holmes and George E. Marcus, "Para-Ethnography," in *The Sage Encyclopedia of Qualitative Research Methods*, ed. Lisa M. Given (Newbury Park, CA: Sage Publications Inc, 2008), A-L 595; Douglas R. Holmes and George E. Marcus, "Fast Capitalism: Para-Ethnography and the Rise of the Symbolic Analyst," in *Frontiers of Capitalism: Ethnographic Reflections on the New Economy*, eds. Melissa S. Fisher and Greg Downey (Durham: Duke University Press, 2006), 33; George E. Marcus, "The Uses of Complicity in the Changing Mise-En-Scène of Anthropological Fieldwork," in *Ethnography Through Thick and Thin* (Princeton, NJ: Princeton University Press, 1998), 105.

example, in speaking about a research project with an arbitrator who used this phrase, it made no difference to the arbitrator that I had practiced law; rather, I was not an arbitrator and so belonged in the out-group. Starting with the works of Pierre Bourdieu, a line of scholarship has noted the monopolistic effect of legal language, remarking on the social division between lay and legal professionals.[33] These divisions seem particularly acute in the field of TDR, where the credentials of international arbitrators, judges, lawyers, and mediators may be quite high, distancing them from nonexperts. Inversely, among international arbitrators (and secondarily, international mediators), because the field is not regulated by either a self-governing professional organisation or state agency, the bar to entry may be lower, and thus there is a strong incentive to police professional boundaries.[34]

Whereas only so much can be done to shift thinking among one's expert interlocutors regarding the potential benefits of a social scientific approach to studying TDR, the researcher can change his or her own perspective. So while para-ethnography may provide a specific methodological tool that may be helpful in addressing disconnects between legal-formalistic and social scientific approaches, conducting such a methodology required me to close the gap by acquiring some of the relevant knowledge and skills possessed by TDR experts. In other words, I had to see with the "third eye," to use Chinese anthropologist Wang Mingming's concept.[35] For Wang, anthropology in China is divided between those internal and external to it. "Native anthropologists" – that is, Chinese anthropologists who study Chinese culture, in reaction to Western anthropology which they perceive to be "colonial" – tend to reproduce narratives about civilisation and progress, in line with the views of the regime, whereas Western anthropologists of China may be more limited in their linguistic skills and access to data but may be capable of a more nuanced analysis. Wang highlights a younger generation of Chinese anthropologists (himself included), trained in the U.S. and U.K., who engage with Euro-American anthropology, rather than reject it. Similarly, whereas social scientists of law may react to formal-legalistic views as hegemonic,

33 Pierre Bourdieu, "The Force of Law: Toward a Sociology of the Juridical Field," *Hastings Law Journal* 38, no. 5 (1987): 814. See also John M. Conley, *Rules Versus Relationships: The Ethnography of Legal Discourse*. Ed. William M. O'Barr (Chicago: University of Chicago Press, 1990); Michael W. McCann, *Rights at Work: Pay Equity Reform and the Politics of Legal Mobilization* (Chicago: University of Chicago Press, 1994); John M. Conley, *Law, Language and Power*. Ed. William M. O'Barr, 2nd ed. (Chicago: University of Chicago Press, 2005). Elizabeth Mertz, *The Language of Law School: Learning to Think Like a Lawyer* (New York and Oxford: Oxford University Press, 2007).

34 Catherine A. Rogers, "The Vocation of International Arbitrators," *American University International Law Review* 20 (2005): 957, Sergio Puig, "Social Capital in the Arbitration Market," *European Journal of International Law* 25, no. 2 (2014): 387–424, Florian Grisel, "Competition and Cooperation in International Commercial Arbitration: The Birth of a Transnational Legal Profession," *Law & Society Review* 51, no. 4 (2017): 790–824.

35 Mingming Wang, "The Third Eye: Towards a Critique of 'Nativist Anthropology'," *Critique of Anthropology* 22, no. 2 (2002): 149–174.

and thereby, paradoxically, reinforce divisions, following Wang, it is time for a closer engagement of social scientists of TDR with formal-legalism.

To that end, for the purposes of studying NLHs, I adopted a multipronged strategy that included learning about the field of TDR as an "insider" while also engaging with para-ethnographers. For the former, this meant studying international commercial arbitration and transnational litigation casebooks, undergoing training in international commercial arbitration at the Chartered Institute for Arbitrators in London, and even teaching international commercial arbitration in Asia, on an interdisciplinary team of instructors, to law students at Oxford, as well as to international practitioners through the American Bar Association's Section on International Law. For the latter, I conducted fieldwork for approximately two years at or on the major NLHs, visiting international commercial courts and arbitration centres, spending time with U.K. legal consultants, transnational legal elite, and government officials in formal and informal settings. I travelled to each hub, including Singapore, Hong Kong, and Shenzhen and Shanghai. Although I did not physically visit Dubai, on behalf of my academic institution, I established a memorandum of understanding (MOU) with the Dubai International Financial Centre Courts (DIFC Courts) and have participated with representatives of the DIFC Courts[36] through a number of events (either at my home institution or via conference calls and virtual meetings). Similarly, I engaged experts in Nur-Sultan through telephonic and digital communication. In visiting the legal hubs or in travelling between them, I sought out para-ethnographers, those legal experts who were systematically thinking about the construction and promotion of legal hubs. In the section that follows, I detail some of my findings, which demonstrate the benefits of working with para-ethnographic partners.

Between Doctrine and (Its) Image

One mainstay of ethnographic fieldwork is the anthropologist's contrasting of interlocutors' actions with their speech.[37] Through such juxtapositions, ethnographers can identify the slippages between individual and social action. In studying NLHs, I was struck by two domains of activity which did not easily correspond to "action" and "speech." The first comprised the sum total of innovations embarked upon by the NLHs, including procedural, doctrinal, and technological. These innovations derive from reform mainly at the level of TDR institutions and the interaction between these rules and national legislation. As such, they are the bailiwick of the legal-formalists. The constant reform of procedural institutional rules aimed to (i) increase the likelihood of enforcement of

36 See Memorandum of Understanding between the University of Oxford and the DIFC Dispute Resolution Authority, signed May 11, 2018.

37 Tom Boellstorff, et al., *Ethnography and Virtual Worlds: A Handbook of Method* (Princeton, NJ: Princeton University Press, 2012), 92.

those institutions' decisions and awards abroad, (ii) decrease transaction costs of users, and (iii) fulfil (i) and (ii) while competing with rival regional NLHs.

The second domain of activity consisted of the promotion of the foregoing. That is, it is not enough to continuously improve a TDR institution's rules; instead, these improvements must be communicated to would-be parties. Fundamentally, TDR institutions based in NLHs must convince parties to select their institution as the venue for dispute resolution in the dispute resolution clauses of their contracts. To do so, the three main legal actors in NLHs – U.K. legal consultants, local government officials, and transnational elite – engage in "image-work," narratives that are self-legitimating, to advertise their legal services to MNCs.[38] These narratives speak to the hyper-modern dispute resolution facilities, including the most up-to-date procedural rules and "lawtech," a nebulous category which seems to include artificial intelligence and machine learning, to persuade MNCs that their institutions efficiently deliver justice.

One of the main functions of image-work, then, is to counterbalance the public relations deficit of many of the jurisdictions within which NLHs are based. As most NLHs are built in nondemocratic or hybrid regimes, they do not enjoy the reputation of the legacy hubs (e.g., London, Paris, and New York City), which are all based in democracies. NLHs thus raise the wider question as to whether the provision of TDR services is dependent on good governance, understood as transparent and accountable political institutions and rules. They beget the question: can jurisdictional carve-outs sever TDR from bad politics? The recent example of two English judges resigning from the Hong Kong Court of Final Appeals due to the deterioration of democracy in Hong Kong is one such example and suggests, in the case of Hong Kong, at least, that NLHs are not severable from the politics of their larger jurisdiction.[39] As such, the promotional work of NLHs' exponents, which goes beyond the naked rules of doctrine or their narrow interpretation to consider the mutual effects of law and politics, invites a broader socio-legal approach.

These two domains of activity, which I shorthand as doctrinal innovation and image-work, were apparent in my interaction with representatives of the DIFC Courts. By way of background, the DIFC Courts, established in 2006, are designed as a jurisdictional carve-out from a legal system that is otherwise unfamiliar to MNCs given that UAE law includes Islamic law and is written in the Arabic language.[40] The DIFC Courts consist of a Court of First Instance

38 Christian De Cock, Max Baker and Christian Vokmann, "Financial Phantasmagoria: Corporate Image-Work in Times of Crisis," *Organization* 18, no. 2 (2011): 153–172.

39 UK Government, *Foreign Secretary Supports the Withdrawal of Serving UK Judges from the Hong Kong Court of Final Appeal*, March 30, 2022. www.gov.uk/government/news/foreign-secretary-supports-the-withdrawal-of-serving-uk-judges-from-the-hong-kong-court-of-final-appeal.

40 See Jayanth K. Krishnan, *The Story of the Dubai International Financial Centre Courts: A Retrospective* (Dubai: Motivate Publishing, 2018) (providing a history of the founding of the DIFC Courts) and Jayanth K. Krishnan and Priya Purohit, "A Common-Law Court in an Uncommon Environment:

and a Court of Appeal, which is the court of final appeal.[41] Modelled after the Commercial Court in London, the bench of the DIFC Courts features mainly retired U.K. judges trained in English common law. The DIFC Courts adapt English common law procedural rules to cases and substantive law chosen by parties, including a "local law" called "DIFC law," the result of legislation and common law decisions. This local law is the default law for commercial and civil disputes within the DIFC, which, in terms of its physical presence, is a 110-hectare area.[42] The DIFC Courts are part of a dispute resolution complex that includes international commercial arbitration institutions, some of which are "joint ventures" with London-based houses (i.e., the Dubai International Financial Centre–London Court of International Arbitration Centre or DIFC-LCIA Arbitration Centre). The DIFC Courts are thus purported to be "islands of transnational governance."[43]

Given their experimental nature, the DIFC Courts have initiated a set of doctrinal reforms that are unique in the field of TDR. As the central dispute resolution mechanism of the DIFC Courts is the courts themselves, the reforms have focused on enhancing the enforcement of DIFC Courts' decisions outside the DIFC, within the UAE, and beyond in other states. As a baseline, DIFC Court decisions are fully enforceable within the DIFC.[44] Beyond the DIFC, to enforce a DIFC Court decision within Dubai, the prevailing party must apply for an "execution letter" from the DIFC Courts,[45] which is then submitted to the relevant onshore Dubai court for approval. Despite a series of cases that have expanded the jurisdiction of the DIFC Courts,[46] their judgments have encountered difficulty in being recognised and enforced by courts outside of the DIFC. According to one study, as of 2014, no Emirati court outside Dubai had enforced a DIFC judgment due to "lack of faith."[47]

In addition to case law, to shore up the efficacy of DIFC Courts' judgments outside of the DIFC, the judges and administrators of the DIFC Courts

---

The DIFC Judiciary and Global Commercial Dispute Resolution," *The American Review of International Arbitration* 25, no. 3–4 (2014): 497, 506.

41 See Law No. 16 of 2011, Amending Certain Provisions of Law No. 12 of 2004 Concerning Dubai International Financial Centre Courts (hereinafter "Dubai Law No. 16"), art. 5(A), (B), www.difccourts.ae/2011/10/31/law-no-16-of-2011-amending-certain-provisions-of-law-no-12-of-2004-concerning-dubai-international-financial-centre-courts/.

42 See Dubai Law No. 12 of 2004, as amended, www.difc.ae/files/7014/5510/4276/Dubai_Law_No._12_of_2004_as_amended_English.pdf.

43 Alec Stone Sweet, "Islands of Transnational Governance," in *On Law, Politics, and Judicialization*, ed. Martin Shapiro and Alec Stone (New York and Oxford: Oxford University Press, 2002), 323.

44 See DIFC Courts, *DIFC Courts Enforcement Guide 2018*. Report (Dubai, 2018), 13, http://issuu.com/difccourts/docs/enforcement_guide_combined_single__?e=29076707/61750336.

45 Krishnan and Purohit, "A Common-Law Court," 506.

46 See, e.g., Corinth Pipeworks SA v Barclays Bank PLC [2011] DIFC CA 002 (Court of Appeal), www.difccourts.ae/2011/01/22/ca-0022011-corinth-pipeworks-sa-v-barclays-bank-plc/, accessed October 22, 2018 (expanding the DIFC Court's jurisdiction over overseas parent companies that have a subsidiary in the DIFC).

47 See Krishnan and Purohit, "A Common-Law Court," 509.

introduced a number of reforms. First, the DIFC Courts have created a latticework of MOGs and MOUs with partner institutions throughout the world. These memoranda are not enforceable, but they do show intent of courts and arbitration houses to enforce each other's decisions. The first MOG was signed with the London Commercial Court in 2013.[48] Subsequently, the DIFC Courts have signed nine MOGs with courts throughout the world.[49] Additionally, over the last decade, the DIFC Courts have signed eleven "collaboration MOUs" with courts within the UAE and the greater Gulf Cooperation Council.[50] Despite these efforts, the efficacy of the soft law instruments is in doubt. Still, there is at least one precedent for its use: in 2014, an Australian court affirmed and enforced a decision by the Court of First Instance consistent with the MOG between it and the DIFC Courts for the reason that the respondent's assets were based in Australia.[51] In addition to Australia, by 2017, DIFC Court judgments had been enforced by the U.K.[52]

Second, the DIFC Courts have introduced cross-institutional mechanisms to strengthen enforcement. One example is a mechanism by which parties opting into the jurisdiction of the DIFC Courts could also refer their final judgments for enforcement through the DIFC-LCIA Arbitration Centre.[53] The mechanism allowed the DIFC-LCIA to convert judgments into arbitral awards that could

48 See Memorandum of Understanding on Strengthening Judicial Exchange and Cooperation between Commercial Court, Queen's Bench Division, England and Wales and Dubai International Financial Centre Courts (signed January 23, 2013).

49 These include the Supreme Court of New South Wales (signed Sept. 9, 2013), the Federal Court of Australia (signed March 28, 2014), the Commercial & Admiralty Division of the High Court of Kenya (signed November 27, 2014), the Supreme Court of Singapore (signed January 19, 2015), the District Court for the Southern District of New York (signed March 22, 2015), the Supreme Court of the Republic of Kazakhstan (signed August 28, 2015), and the National Court Administration of the Supreme Court of Korea (signed November 4, 2015). In addition, the DIFC Courts have established an "MOU on References of Questions of Law" with the Supreme Court of Singapore (signed January 19, 2015).

50 These include a "collaboration MOU" with the Dubai courts (July 16, 2009); a "protocol of jurisdiction" with the Dubai Courts (May 1, 2009) for "due enforcement of the judgments rendered by the other Party"; a second such "protocol of jurisdiction" with the Dubai Courts (December 7, 2009) for "follow[ing] the concerning laws and regulations as for the jurisdiction issue between DIFC Courts and Dubai Courts"; and "collaboration MOUs" with: Notary Public Department of the Dubai Courts, Ministry of Justice of Jordan, UAE Ministry of Justice, Dubai Judicial Institute, and Ra Al Khaimah Courts; and a "service MOU" with the international Cooperation Department of the UAE Ministry of Justice.

51 See Graciela Ltd. v. Giacobbe [2014] DIFC CFI 027 (finding for the claimant in a wrongful interference in property suit).

52 DIFC Courts, *DIFC Courts Enforcement Guide 2017*. Report (Dubai, 2017), 25, http://issuu.com/difccourts/docs/enforcement_guide_e5__2017?e=29076707/48883438.

53 The DIFC – LCIA was established in 2008 as a joint venture between the DIFC and the LCIA. Following challenges to its jurisdictional reach, Dubai Law No. 7 of 2014, www.difc.ae/files/6914/5510/4274/Dubai_Law_No._7_of_2014_English.pdf was passed to establish the Dispute Resolution Authority which in turn governs the DIFC Arbitration Institute (DAI). The DAI entered into an agreement with the LCIA to relaunch the DIFC – LCIA in 2015. *See* DIFC – LCIA, *Overview*, www.difc-lcia.org/overview.aspx, accessed October 22, 2018.

then be enforceable abroad through the New York Convention of 1958.[54] While the effects of incorporating more inclusive policies into the court's operations remains to be seen, the mechanism to convert a judgment into an arbitral award, much like the MOGs and MOUs, is mainly untested. As of 2017, no party had opted to use the mechanism, likely out of concern that other jurisdictions, at the enforcement stage, may not consider the conversion of the judgment into an arbitral award to be valid because non-payment of a judgment may not be a genuine dispute capable of being referred to arbitration.[55] Adding further uncertainty and exemplary of the kinds of tensions NLHs can generate with domestic courts and tribunals, in late 2021, the Emirate of Dubai abolished the DIFC-LCIA to consolidate arbitration in the homegrown Dubai International Arbitration Centre (DIAC).[56]

The DIFC Courts thus raise important doctrinal and practical questions, particularly for conflict of laws (i.e., jurisdiction, choice of law, and enforcement concerns). These questions can be analysed pursuant to relevant case law, statutes, and international conventions. At the same time, to limit the analysis to a purely doctrinal examination would fail to reveal much of what makes the study of NLHs so compelling, particularly for the larger subject of TDR. This became apparent to me when spending time with some of the personnel behind the DIFC Courts – namely, the CEO of its dispute resolution authority, a U.K. finance lawyer and court reformer, as well as its judges, including a leading U.K.-trained arbitrator and judge from Singapore. These experts had developed their own theories for NLHs and their obstacles and potential. More specifically, they were also gathering data, often travelling between and among NLHs to do so, analysing that data, and generating explanatory frames for how NLHs could not only fit into the existing landscape of TDR but also improve upon it. This knowledge production was part and parcel of their promotional work for their own specific hub. In short, the experts were para-ethnographers.

The proponents of NLHs often had a particular conception of what NLHs are and what they do. For instance, the CEO of the DIFC Courts' dispute resolution

54 DIFC, DIFC Courts Practice Direction No. 2 of 2015 on Referral of Judgment Payment Disputes to Arbitration (16 February 2015), www.difccourts.ae/2015/02/16/difc-courts-practice-direction-no-2-2015-referral-judgment-payment-disputes-arbitration/ (stating that the parties may "further agree that any dispute arising out of or in connection with the non-payment of any money judgment given by the DIFC Courts may, at the option of the judgment creditor, be referred to arbitration under the Arbitration Rules of the DIFC-LCIA Arbitration Centre").

55 Christopher Mainwaring-Taylor and Yacine Francis, "DIFC Courts Introduce Unique Mechanism to Convert DIFC Money Judgments into Arbitral Awards," Publication. (*Allen & Overy*, 18 October 2018), www.allenovery.com/publications/en-gb/lrrfs/middleeastandafrica/Pages/DIFC-Courts-introduce-unique-mechanism-to-convert-DIFC-money-judgments-into-arbitral-awards-n.aspx. *See also* Dalma R. Demeter and Kayleigh M. Smith, "The Implications of International Commercial Courts on Arbitration," *Journal of International Arbitration* 33, no. 5 (2016): 441–469.

56 Mohammed bin Rashid Al Maktoum, Decree No. (34) of 2021 Concerning the Dubai International Financial Centre, 14 September 2021, https://dlp.dubai.gov.ae/Legislation%20Reference/2021/Decree%20No.%20(34)%20of%202021.html.

authority envisioned them as "nodules of connectivity"[57] that were interlinked by soft law and technology as much as by his and his colleagues' sharing of knowledge and problem solving, aided by their frequent travelling between the hubs. For the CEO, Dubai, Nur-Sultan, Singapore, and Hong Kong were all international nodes, and while they were established independent of China's "going out" policy of the late 1990s, they were also well positioned to facilitate Chinese cross-border transactions and their disputes. As such, they were "bridgeheads"[58] for Chinese investment: Hong Kong and Singapore for Southeast Asia, Nur-Sultan for Central Asia, and Dubai for the Middle East.

Within this network of NLHs, each individual NLH is to be a bubble of legal modernisation, influenced, to varying degree, by London's experience. As remarked by the judge:

> [We] try to give them the whole experience. So DIFC was meant to be a home away from home. So they hired retired civil servants, retired bankers from the Bank of England, the former general manager from Sydney stock exchange for their fledgling exchange. . . . [It's] like you're in your own backyard. The legal system is like that. Because Dubai is a financial centre, too, the view is that there is no messing about. The financial world is dominated by Anglo-Saxon common law, so [Dubai] needed common law.[59]

Hence, through U.K. staffing and partially transplanting English common law procedural rules, the DIFC Courts are a kind of derivative hub. Although the other NLHs have different relationships to London than Dubai (some more post-colonial than others), most have adapted some form of English common law into their procedural rules for transnational litigation – and have done so through the work of U.K. legal advisors. This interhub lex mercatoria is not complete, however, particularly in regards to enforcement of foreign judgments and orders. In the absence of an international convention on the recognition and enforcement of foreign judgments,[60] London is still trying to supply soft law to fill in the gaps in the form of the Standing International Forum for Commercial Courts' *Draft Multilateral Memorandum on Enforcement of Commercial Judgments for Money*.[61]

57 Interview, London, November 6, 2017.

58 Ibid.

59 Interview, Oxford, May 11, 2018.

60 The Hague Convention on the Recognition and Enforcement of Foreign Judgments is still being deliberated. See Special Commission on the Recognition and Enforcement of Foreign Judgments of the Hague Conference on Private International Law, 2018 Draft Convention, May 24–29, 2018 (on file with the author).

61 The *Draft Multilateral Memorandum on Enforcement of Commercial Judgments for Money* was discussed on September 27, 2018, during the second meeting of the Standing International Forum for Commercial Courts (SIFoCC) in New York City. Currently, individual members of SIFoCC, including judges from the main NLHs discussed herein (i.e., Dubai, Singapore, Hong Kong, Kazakhstan, and the People's Republic of China [PRC]), are in the process of finalising the document.

Meanwhile, the Chinese are starting to supply mega-regional soft law through their own *Joint Statement of the World Enforcement Conference.*[62]

NLHs, in fact, show how Chinese legal entrepreneurs are building on and supplementing legal infrastructure created by the British Empire for China Inc. The missionary work of NLH proponents is part of this process. Hence, image-work operates not only to attract parties to use a NLH for their dispute resolution services but also to proselytise the concept of NLHs for the purpose of producing other NLHs. The relationship between NLHs is one of both competition (e.g., between international arbitration houses) and cooperation (e.g., mutual enforcement of other hubs' judicial decisions), and thus the multiplication of hubs can potentially lead to a race to the top.

This process was evident in my conversations not only with legal experts from the DIFC Courts, who were creating links with counterparts in China, but also with PRC judges, arbitrators, and officials who were interested in building their own hubs, based, in part, on the experience of the DIFC Courts and other hubs, like Singapore. Image-work was made up of a number of self-representations, including publications with case statistics for international commercial courts or awards given from arbitration tribunals, Internet versions of the foregoing, and "road shows" whereby representatives from the hubs venture out into other jurisdictions to advertise their procedural and technological advancements. China has learned from other NLHs through these exchanges and is building its own NLHs in Shenzhen and Shanghai. Concurrently, hubs like the DIFC Courts are also studying Chinese legal reform – namely, the introduction of AI into "smart courts" for its own improvement. Some of these reforms and improvements will have traction; others, like the use of a robot to deliver sandwiches to arbitrators at Maxwell Chambers in Singapore, are merely window dressing. Nonetheless, this is the work that images do – to produce and reproduce the idea of legal and technological modernisation. It is important to note that these observations on image-work move the analysis beyond mere doctrinal questions and thus would not be as readily apparent without a social scientific approach.

Conclusion

It is something of a truism that doctrinal approaches to legal questions and "law and society" ones demonstrate more divergence than convergence. The study of TDR seems to exhibit particularly acute forms of this divergence. This chapter has essayed to challenge this assumption and the kinds of line-drawing it encourages. Rather, a methodology that incorporates para-ethnography may be one means, among others, that helps bridge these divides. The value added of para-ethnography is that it invites the analyst to grapple with the intellectual work of his or her

62 See, e.g., Supreme People's Court, *Joint Statement of the World Enforcement Conference* (drafted by the Supreme People's Court following a high-level conference in Shanghai on January 20–23, 2019, featuring presidents and chief justices of supreme courts).

interlocutors – in this case, legal entrepreneurs who champion doctrinal innovation to improve the standing of their NLH. This engagement then is principally a "legal analysis" and operates through logic, case law, and statutory reasoning. At the same time, para-ethnography, as an ethnographic method, highlights the "contextual, dynamic, and reflexive"[63] factors that motivate legal reasoning and logic. These factors become particularly salient in studying law in nondemocratic or hybrid contexts where the category of the political has particular relevance. For the foregoing reasons, para-ethnography, one that balances doctrinal analysis with empirical insights, may generate new synergies in the study of TDR.

Acknowledgement

The author thanks Shahla Ali and other participants in the "Advances in Comparative and Transnational ADR: Research into Practice" conference at the Hong Kong University Law Faculty (March 8–9, 2019) for their comments on an earlier draft. This work is part of the China, Law and Development (CLD) project, which has received funding from the European Research Council (ERC) under the European Union's Horizon 2020 research and innovation program (Grant No. 803763). All mistakes are the author's.

63 John Flood, "Socio-Legal Ethnography," in *Theory and Method in Socio-Legal Research* (Oxford: Hart Publishing, 2005), 33, 34.

3

MODES OF DISPUTE RESPONSE

Exploring Issues in the Range

Michael Palmer

Introduction

This chapter concerns the various processes used by people around the world to manage their disputes. In any society, people may be faced with difficulties in their lives. Such trouble situations may arise in one or more of several settings: financial, personal injury, family, consumer, commercial transaction, employment, and neighbours, among others. Sensing injustice or opportunity, they assert their grievance and look for remedial processes that would secure for them satisfaction and redress. The range of these remedial processes has been characterised in Figure 3.1.

Although the details differ, this sort of characterisation of remedy processes was at the heart of Frank Sander's seminal model of the multi-door courthouse, which conjectured that courts of the future would likely be dispute resolution centres that promoted processual pluralism by offering disputants choices between, and advice on, a range of processes.[1] Developments in alternative dispute resolution discourse and changes in society over the past 40 years suggest that several aspects of the continuum of response merit greater attention. Among these are prevention and avoidance, apology and violence. The intended contribution of this chapter is to examine some critical dimensions of these three processes.[2]

A dispute between two or more parties is a social relationship. The parties may use a range of possible responses to change the dynamics of their relationship when 'trouble' arises. Avoidance and prevention are at one end of the range. Avoidance may, for example, include the 'lumping' of problems – a party with a grievance

1 Frank E. A. Sander, "Varieties of Dispute Processing," in *The Pound Conference: Perspectives on Justice in the Future*, eds. A. Leo Levin and Russell R. Wheeler (West Publishing: St. Paul MN, 1979).

2 See also: Michael Palmer and Simon Roberts, "Development of Disputes, Avoidance, and Violence," Chapter 5, *Dispute Processes: ADR and the Primary Forms of Decision-Making*, 3rd ed., Law in Context (Cambridge: Cambridge University Press, 2020), 101–122.

DOI: 10.4324/9780429354625-5

>Third-party intervention<

Avoidance *Negotiation ||*Mediation *Umpiring *Self-help

*(sometimes with partisans)

FIGURE 3.1 Varieties of Response

for a variety of reasons does not pursue that grievance, allowing tensions to dissipate. Or the parties may put in place arrangements of dispute prevention – the parties anticipate problems. They therefore enter into arrangements they hope will manage potential difficulties, avoiding trouble arising in the first place. At the other end of the spectrum lies another important response to disagreement or more serious forms of tension: self-help, particularly violence. Various forms of self-help may be utilised, but a decision to use violence will likely significantly impact the parties' relationship. Situated between the two ends of the spectrum, an apology is sometimes demanded and sometimes given and may be found in all three primary processes: negotiation, mediation and umpiring.

In legal studies, and much alternative dispute resolution discourse and practice, the main concern is with the primary processes of negotiation, mediation and umpiring. Doctrinal analysis in the common law world has, in particular, focused on the application of the law by judges in deciding cases rather than other processes.[3] However, the intent of this chapter is to explore three relatively neglected forms of response – prevention and avoidance, apology and violence – seeking a fuller understanding of the range and nature of decision-making responses to 'trouble'. In the early days of ADR, these were arguably afforded more attention than they are today. Hence, the chapter is more a revival of a concern than a new start.

Dispute Responses

Early thinking on the spectrum of dispute responses is to be found in the studies by, for example, Llewellyn and Hoebel (1941),[4] Gluckman (1955),[5] Bohannan (1957),[6] Turner (1968 [1957]),[7] Gulliver (1963),[8] Nader (1965),[9] and Nader and

3 Fiona Cownie and Anthony Bradney, "Dispute Avoidance," in *Comparative Dispute Resolution*, ed. M. F. Moscati, M. Palmer and M. Roberts (Cheltenham and Northampton, MA: Edward Elgar, 2020).

4 K. N. Llewellyn and E. A. Hoebel, *The Cheyenne Way: Conflict and Case Law in Primitive Jurisprudence* (Norman, OK: University of Oklahoma Press, 1941).

5 Max Gluckman, *The Judicial Process among the Barotse of Northern Rhodesia (Zambia)* (Manchester: Manchester University Press, 1955).

6 Paul Bohannan, *Justice and Judgement among the Tiv* (London: Oxford University Press, 1957).

7 V. W. Turner, *Schism and Continuity in an African Society* (Manchester: Manchester University Press [published on behalf of the Institute for Social Research, University of Zambia], 1968 [1957]).

8 P. H. Gulliver, *Social Control in an African Society: A Study of the Arusha: Agricultural Masai of Northern Tanganyika* (London: Routledge, 1963).

9 Laura Nader, "The Ethnography of Law," *American Anthropologist* (New series, Special publication) 67, no. 6 (December 1965): pt. 2.

Todd (1978).[10] These efforts tended to be focused on binary distinctions in decision-making: force or negotiation, imposed authoritative decisions or negotiation and settlement, 'partisan' or 'neutral' third-party intervenors, advice or authoritative decision and so on. More elaborate typologies of dispute processes or 'responses to trouble' emerged, usually with, at one end, 'avoidance' and, at the other, 'force', including 'violence'. However, legal scholars and others have focused attention on the middle ground of negotiation, mediation and umpiring for a good reason: such processes potentially offer a resolution of the parties' quarrel. The polar extremes of avoidance and force offer much less certainty. Moreover, parties do not always want to settle but instead conduct themselves with a view to future opportunities to revive and pursue their grievance. Both avoidance (though not necessarily prevention) and coercion also share a common characteristic: they are both primarily unilateral modes of decision-making, unlike many aspects of the more central dispute response processes, and this too may reduce the possibility of an agreed outcome.

Value of Looking at 'Avoidance' and 'Violence' More Carefully

These early studies of the two ends of the spectrum revealed, however, that these modes of response in dispute processes are sometimes widespread and carry serious messages for both a better understanding of dispute processes and law reform agendas. In 'Naming, Blaming, Claiming', Felstiner, Abel and Sarat pointed to the need to analyse the initial stages of a dispute. First, that is when an aggrieved person is most likely to conclude that it is best not to pursue her or his grievance. Second, in the early phases of a dispute, there is a greater choice of response, for in the later stages, formal frameworks may limit options.

Moreover, limited rights' consciousness and a sense of futility have created a fundamental problem of 'grievance apathy'; it may be futile to implement civil procedural reforms which offer more equal access at the later stages of disputing, as the later stages are where inequality may have a greater impact and the disputant is in an unfamiliar institutional context. Innovations such as legal aid, waiver of court costs, small claims courts and so on may have a more limited impact than hoped for. As Felstiner, Abel and Sarat conclude, 'Such reforms would be like constructing a theory of politics entirely on the basis of voting patterns when we know that most people do not vote in most elections'.[11]

Moreover, such limitations may lead to possible violent outcomes. In the People's Republic of China (PRC) today, people's mediators may well justify very early intervention in an emerging dispute with the hope this will 'nip the

10 Laura Nader and Harry F. Todd, eds., *The Disputing Process: Law in Ten Societies* (New York: Columbia University Press, 1978).

11 William L. F. Felstiner, Richard L. Abel and Austin Sarat, "The Emergence and Transformation of Disputes: Naming, Blaming, Claiming . . .," *Law and Society Review* 15, no. 3 &4 (1980–1981): 631–654. See also, William L. F. Felstiner, "Influences of Social Organization on Dispute Processing," *Law and Society Review* 9, no. 1 (1974): 63–94.

contradiction in the bud' (扼杀了矛盾的萌芽: *eshale maodun de mengya*), thereby preventing 'degeneration' of the dispute into violence. This concern also reflects a long-standing worry in Chinese legal culture that oppressive conduct in a social relationship may well lead to suicide and that in some senses pressing the other party is the functional equivalent of homicide. Thus, in traditional China from the Ming dynasty onwards, it was a specific offence in the law of homicide for a person to act in such a manner as to drive another into committing suicide.[12]

Avoidance: Its Forms and Close Relatives

Introduction: Dispute Avoidance and Dispute Preemption

Avoidance is non-confrontational. But beyond this, it is not easy to offer a precise definition of this kind of social conduct. Philip Gulliver, in searching for a useful definition, draws an important distinction between dispute avoidance and what he describes as 'conflict management'. However, the term 'conflict management' is something of a misnomer, as Gulliver describes it in a manner that points to conduct that is 'dispute preemption' or 'prevention'.[13] Gulliver draws inspiration from Felstiner's earlier distinction between avoidance as a type of dispute processing and avoidance conduct intended to prevent disputes arising in the first place.[14] Thus, dispute avoidance is evasive conduct that occurs in an emerging dispute between individuals or groups. This evasive conduct is resorted to after disagreement has emerged or is likely to surface. Examples include 'lumping' – tolerating the injustice; ostracising the other party; 'turning the other cheek' – refusing to respond to an injustice; 'sidestepping' – diverting attention by refocusing the relationship on some other issue that is less or non-confrontational; and in some circumstances accepting a claim or offer that is unjustified but once accepted avoids further interaction. Perhaps also we should include the use of diversion to avoid further deliberating on the substantive issues giving rise to the dispute, pointing to some other area of common concern which is not so contentious.

The line between avoidance and prevention is sometimes difficult to draw, and both may become fused in an overall strategy. Thus, Gulliver in his work on rural Ireland notes that individuals often chose not to frequent places or to engage in activities where troublesome situations and difficult people would be encountered, instead, for example, crossing the road or taking another route so as not meet certain individuals. When a meeting was unavoidable, interaction

12 Geoffrey MacCormack, "Coercion and Suicide in Traditional Chinese Law: Evolution of the Statutory Rules," *Journal of Comparative Law* 13, no. 2 (2018): 217–260.

13 Philip Gulliver, "On Avoidance," in *The Politics of Cultural Performance*, eds. D. J. Parkin, L. Caplan and H. J. Fisher (Providence, ME: Berghahn Books, 1996), 125–143, 126–127.

14 William L. F. Felstiner, "Avoidance as Dispute Processing: An Elaboration," *Law & Society Review* 9, no. 4 (Summer 1975): 695–706, 695.

was carefully diverted to a conversation on superficial topics, such as the weather or non-local gossip.[15]

Here we see conduct that lies on the penumbra nestling between avoidance and preventative conduct, and Gulliver suggests that the two forms of deflective action may be used serially: both before a dispute occurs and after a grievance has been created and a dispute begins to emerge.

Preventing

For dispute preemption or prevention, the intention is, more or less knowingly – how much less is a matter of some debate, as we shall see in the following – to prevent disputes occurring or to limit involvement in circumstances in which it is anticipated that a dispute might well occur. As we have indicated, Gulliver sees this form of conduct as 'conflict management', but this does not seem to be an appropriate characterisation, not only because the distinction between 'conflict' and 'dispute' in this context is not made clear but also because avoidance is itself a way of managing an emerging disagreement. Dispute prevention is explicitly forward looking, an established part of the practice of law, and may well involve the use of legally binding contracts and other devices in a wide range of situations.[16]

Changing Legal Practice

Accordingly, it should recognise that in various ways, commercial and civil legal practice (in the common law world at least) have been drifting in the direction of dispute avoidance for some time now, making adjustments specifically intended to avoid the development of disputes. As is well known, prenuptial agreements are just one form of contract preliminary intended to avert future disputing or at least clarify the rights of the parties should disagreement arise. This is not to say that the goal of preemption is the sole influence in such developments but rather that it may well be an important consideration. Thus, in addition to preemptive contract arrangements, we may think of evolving processual innovations such as collaborative lawyering, partnering or simply better project design and

15 Gulliver, "On Avoidance," 125–143, 127.

16 See also, for example, Brockman's work on traditional Chinese contracts for long-distance trade and the use of specific contractual provisions intended to locate liability in the sometimes difficult situations that could arise in such trade in a pre-urban, pre-industrial society: Rosser H. Brockman, "Commercial Contract Law in Late Nineteenth-Century Taiwan," in *Essays on China's Legal Tradition*, ed. Jerome Alan Cohen, R. Randle Edwards and Fu-Mei Chang Chen (Princeton: Princeton University Press, 1980). On the growing need for couples contemplating marriage to foresee future divergences in their married life and try to prevent them through premarital agreements, see Olga Denti and Michela Giordano, "Till Money (and Divorce) Do Us Part: Premarital Agreements in the American and Spanish Legal Discourse," in *The Discourses of Dispute Resolution*, ed. Vijay K. Bhatia, Christopher N. Candlin and Maurizio Gotti (Berne: Peter Lang, 2010).

management. As one leading London firm advises, conflict avoidance requires clear, concise, careful and proper planning of the strategy for the execution of a project. It is also about adopting a proactive conflict avoidance approach such as risk analysis, clarity in the contract documentation or partnering.[17] More generally, such initiatives are part of a range of attempts at creating a professional culture of problem-solving, as Rosenberry points out in an understated and underestimated essay:

> Those in the legal profession who respond to a rapid change by broadening their repertoire of approaches for preventing and solving problems are more likely to be successful in their practices and feel more personally fulfilled. In a rapidly changing world, the nature of problems change; in order to respond, one needs a box full of tools. Therefore, it is important to recognize ways to facilitate creativity and creative problem-solving.[18]

Some Temporal Dimensions of Avoidance

Avoidance as a process – unlike dispute prevention – involves doing little or nothing to resolve the issues in dispute between the parties. Sometimes the approach is intended to be only *temporary*, giving a party breathing space to rethink the dispute or attract partisan support (popular or expert or both) or gather material resources. Avoidance may also in effect be a form of indirect pressure, intended to discomfort the other party who seeks a rapid resolution of the parties' disagreement. To this might be added that delaying a response may have the additional virtue of avoiding the dispute, perhaps by allowing tempers to cool and the parties to retreat. However, avoidance may become *protracted*, or even permanent, perhaps even being handed down to the disputants' heirs – a counterpart in a sense to feuding across generations. Then again, the disagreement itself may be slowly overlooked and a new, albeit circumscribed, relationship may emerge between the parties or the relationship may return to an approximation of its former state because of the common benefits it offers.[19]

Grievance Apathy and Lumping: Are They Avoidance?

Another important dimension to the conceptualisation of avoidance is the extent to which intention should be included in the characterisation. It is argued by Gulliver that avoidance is ordinarily a deliberate choice of strategy and action by which to deal with the dispute: 'It is not merely resignation because of perceived

17 See Nicholas Gould, "Conflict Avoidance and Dispute Resolution" (2019), www.fenwickelliott.com/sites/default/files/nick_gould_-_conflict_avoidance_and_dispute_resolution.indd_.pdf.

18 Katharine Rosenberry, "Organizational Barriers to Creativity in Law Schools and the Legal Profession," *California Western Law Review* 41, no. 2 (2005): 424.

19 Gulliver, "On Avoidance," 125–143, 128.

inability to do anything in the situation as the opponent appears to be overwhelmingly stronger, or out of reach, geographically or socially, or where the costs of any conceivable action are too high'.[20] From this perspective what is often referred to as 'grievance apathy' and (possibly) 'lumping' would be excluded from the characterisation as: '[avoidance] is not merely resignation because of perceived inability to do anything in the situation as the opponent appears to be overwhelmingly stronger, or out of reach, geographically or socially, or where the costs of any conceivable action are too high'.[21]

But identification by an analyst of this lack of intention is, in my view, not so easy to accomplish, and resignation in the face of overwhelming odds may well also be seen as casting doubt on the need for intention. Structural pressures may be so overwhelming that the aggrieved person feels she or he has no choice of action. That is not quite the same as saying that there is no decision-making involved.

Cultural Variation?

Avoidance and prevention happen everywhere, and while there are some analytical dangers lurking in the use of cultural embeddedness as an explanation for avoidance conduct, it seems likely that some societies encourage dispute avoidance more than others: some legal cultures and the institutions which are one part of such cultures may well contain policies that encourage avoidance ideologically and in practice. This may be as a preference for other forms of dispute resolution, but it might also be as one possibility within a range of other actions when a dispute occurs, including some form of third-party intervention such as umpiring or mediation or bilateral negotiation.[22]

Action and Ideology: The Avoidance Ethic and Harmony Ideology

Sometimes, it is claimed, a crucial moral value is supportive of and enforced by recurrent avoidance conduct. Carol Greenhouse, for example, looks at the influence of certain forms of Christian thought in the United States and identifies the idea of an 'avoidance ethic', which she characterises as 'an ethical preference to self-restraint'[23] and which represents a 'culturally appropriate means of resolving contradictions between the self-interests and the collective good'.[24] In ADR discourse, the debates surrounding civil justice have sometimes characterised the legal culture of the United States as being 'litigious', but Greenhouse among

20 Ibid.
21 Ibid.
22 Ibid., 125–143, 128–129.
23 Carol Greenhouse, "Signs of Quality: Individualism and Hierarchy in American Culture," *American Ethnologist* 19, no. 2 (1992): 233–254, 249.
24 Ibid., 233–254, 242.

others suggests it can more accurately be characterised as possessing an avoidance culture. Most people attempt to avoid confrontation, and such avoidance conduct is also linked to values of individualism and self-reliance. Avoidance does not necessarily manifest itself in real conduct, but it is, however, a foundational value that shapes understandings and explanations, shaping how ordinary people think about confrontation and indeed their own cultural identity.[25]

If we turn to China, we see a very similar ethic or 'ideology' of avoidance, albeit based on apparently different ideas about the relationship between the individual and society. The Confucian concept of 'harmony' (和: *he*) is central to traditional Chinese disputing culture and is a continuing influence in the mainland PRC today. Many popular sayings emphasise the value of 'harmony', including 'harmony is precious' (和为贵: *he wei gui*), 'harmony creates wealth' (和气生财: *he qi sheng cai*), peaceful families flourish (家和万事兴: *jia he wan shixing*) and so on.

The emphasis on harmony is entrenched in the Confucian Analects and robustly expressed in Confucius's oft-quoted revelation that 'in hearing lawsuits, I am like any other person. What is necessary, however, is to cause the people to have no litigation'. The educated gentleman would not allow himself to be drawn into a dispute against his fellows; such involvement was itself indicative of moral failing, and if a dispute did arise, he would nevertheless rise above it by practicing yielding (让: *rang*). The ideal Confucian society, for Confucius, is one without litigation, and in rural China today there are local anti-litigation societies that are still given local official and popular support. People maintain harmonious interpersonal relationships based on mutual love and respect, thereby serving the greater good and benefiting society. The Confucian ideal of harmony is also linked to Daoism, and the latter philosophy's ideas about the relationship between the human world and the cosmic order. A disturbance in society is a disruption of harmony in the cosmos. Therefore, harmony in society should be promoted by public lectures given throughout China, and today it is an ideal that is central to the Hu Jintao ideal of creating a 'socialist harmonious society' (社会主义和谐社会: *shehui zhuyi hexieshehui*).

Choice – Rational Decision-Making and the Costs of Choice: Evolutionary and 'Econocentric' Approaches

In examining the pursuit of particular strategies of dispute resolution, it seems to me that the analytical perspective and the participant's perspective are sometimes far apart. In the literature on avoidance, the tendency is to see decisions about opting for this strategy in terms of individual rational choice, a kind of careful cost-benefit analysis made on the basis of an explicit evaluation of the economic and psychological costs entailed in pursuing this strategy in relation to the

25 Ibid., 233–254, 248.

hoped-for outcome. On the other hand, the causes of the dispute may fade away and the parties' social relationship may be revived in whole or in part, especially where the parties calculate this as being in their self-interest.

Social Complexity and Avoidance

Moreover, in a manner reminiscent of some of the deep contrasts offered in classical sociology and Auerbach's history of law and non-law,[26] it is suggested that the greater anonymity and 'moral minimalism' of modern urban cultures (especially 'suburban cultures') make the costs of avoidance less of a burden.[27] Thus, avoidance is likely to increase in importance as a dispute resolution strategy where there is:

- an absence of hierarchical authority
- easy and frequent entering and leaving relationships
- a dominance of single-stranded relationships
- loose-knit social networks
- a high degree of functional autonomy and capacity to decide and act alone.

On the other hand, in more traditional rural societies where social relationships are multiplex and enduring and disputes are often polycentric in Fuller's sense, avoidance can entail heavy costs.

But deliberative decision-making may not play quite such a pronounced role as this approach suggests, especially in the early stages of disagreement, where 'maximal claims' are being made, or when there is growing frustration and hostility – this may be a juncture in the emerging dispute when emotions overcome more rational thinking or such thinking is not relevant because not enough is known about the situation. Moreover, rational decision-making may be hindered by a felt need to respond in a manner consistent with wider, entrenched, normative ideas (for example, 'harmony ideology') or a disputant's own engrained experience or by the encouragement of another person. And it is possible to point to empirical situations in which the model is plainly inapplicable. Take, for example, the case of two African tribal groupings that Gulliver studies, the Arusha and the Ndendeuli:

> In both cases . . . the conditions under which dispute avoidance was rare were the converse of the conditions in U.S. suburbia where such avoidance was common: close-knit social networks, multi-stranded relationships and little functional autonomy – in contrast to loose-knit networks and a high degree of autonomy.[28]

26 J. S. Auerbach, *Justice without Law?* (Oxford: Oxford University Press, 1983).
27 M. P. Baumgartner, "Social Control in Suburbia," in *Towards a General Theory of Social Control*, vol. 2, ed. D. Black (Orlando, FL: Academic Press, 1984), 129.
28 Gulliver, "On Avoidance," 125–143, 140.

So, we may conclude that there is a danger of over-rationalising the bases of decision-making and seeing the use of avoidance in social developmental terms.

We might also conclude that dispute prevention and dispute avoidance are important features of a wide range of societies and that ADR discourse, by focusing on negotiation, mediation and umpiring, runs the danger of continuing to underestimate the importance of prevention and avoidance, both of which are not only important ways of handling situations of potential and emerging conflict but also are important for continuity and order in social life.

Apology

In the context of a dispute, where one party is blamed by the other – the aggrieved party – for misconduct and its negative impact, a quick acceptance of responsibility by means of an apology may dissolve the emerging dispute. An effective apology is likely to contain one or more elements: a recognition that there has been a wrongdoing done to the other party, acceptance of responsibility by acknowledging fault, a statement of genuine remorse for harm done and some sort of undertaking that the blameworthy conduct will not happen again. This prompt action may produce an outcome of forgiveness. But in other situations, an apology may not be offered. Perhaps this is because there is no concern on the part of the offending party to remedy the situation or because responsibility has been effectively disguised.[29]

Across the spectrum of dispute processes, the act of apologising may become incorporated with one or more of the various primary responses to a grievance. It may be a timely way of avoiding escalation of the disagreement emerging between the two parties. It can facilitate negotiation, mediation and arbitration even when it does not become a formal part of an agreed outcome. It may be ordered by the court, typically but not exclusively as a civil law remedy.[30] It is often a very important aspect of victim-offender mediation. In domestic violence, the offering of an apology by an abuser to a victim is not only commonplace but is often accompanied by unacceptable excuses. These justifications are intended to minimise the importance of the abusive conduct that has taken place by means of

29 For a helpful sociological analysis of the apology, see N. Tavuchis, *Mea Culpa: A Sociology of Apology and Reconciliation* (Stanford, CA: Stanford University Press, 1991). Also useful are: Lee Taft, "Apology Subverted: The Commodification of Apology," *Yale Law Journal* 109, no. 5 (2000): 1135–1160; Brent T. White, "Say You're Sorry: Court-Ordered Apologies as a Civil Rights Remedy," *Cornell Law Review* 91 (2006): 1261–1331.

30 For example, in mainland China under the new Civil Code and before, apology has been one of the remedies specified for by statute: Article 179 on the 2020 Civil Code of the People's Republic of China thus provides at paragraph 11 that one remedy which may be imposed on the defending party is the requirement of an apology (赔礼道歉: *peili daoqian*). Article 995 also specifically provides for apology as a remedy in cases of infringement of personality rights. More generally, see: Andrea Zwart-Hink, Arno Akkermans and Kiliaan Van Wees, "Compelled Apologies as a Legal Remedy: Some Thoughts from a Civil Law Jurisdiction," *University of Western Australia Law Review* 38, no. 1 (2014): 100–122.

suggestions, for example, that the victim's conduct was contributory, forcing the abuser into the violent misconduct.

Like avoidance and violence, an apology is an aspect of the social interactions between the parties, and it is likely that its place in the social relationship may reflect a number of structural configurations.[31] First, there is an interpersonal apology from one individual to another; second, there is the apology from an individual to a collectivity; third, there is one from a collectivity to an individual; and finally, there is an apology from one collectivity to another. It is likely that the willingness to give an apology and the style and dynamics of the apology will vary between these four differing configurations. For example, the delegation of responsibility for providing an apology probably would not be acceptable in the case of an individual apologising to another party, whether individual or collective. Here, direct and genuine statements of contrition from the blameworthy party are expected. The relationship may also be complicated by the intervention of a third party. Differences will also likely be found depending on whether an apology is public or private: a public act of contrition is likely to be more disconcerting for the blamed party than a simple private acknowledgement of fault and a need for forgiveness. This may be especially the case when the person apologising is a state official. Analytical perspectives also differ, as the practicing lawyer is perhaps more likely to see apology as a bargaining chip in 'litigotiation'[32] and more sociologically inclined analysts are more likely to see it as a social fact with moral dimensions, especially restoration of a troubling social relationship. It is this difference in approach that may result, for example, in a financial settlement that is generous – but if this is not accompanied by an apology, then the outcome may leave the aggrieved party unhappy.

In addition, the role apology plays is complicated by several issues. One of the most important involves perceptions of the sincerity of an apology. A true and acceptable apology is likely to avoid suggestions that the injured party is exaggerating the intention to offend or the seriousness of the harm done. A genuine apology may well contain instead the elements of recognition of wrongdoing, acceptance of fault, remorse and commitment not to repeat the blameworthy conduct. An apology that fails to provide these elements may make the aggrieved party feel even more displeased because the 'false' or 'insincere' apology disguises a lack of intention to take responsibility for the misconduct that has given rise to the grievance. It is a refusal to accept that the misconduct was a mistake – and one with negative consequences for the other party.

Another difficulty, in a situation where a mistake has been made by one party with negative consequences for the other, is how best to draw the line between an apology as a social act of contrition and an apology with (potentially negative) legal consequences. With increasing recognition of the value of apology, a number of jurisdictions have decided that apologies are such an important and appropriate response to grievances and civil wrongs that they have removed legal deterrents

31 Tavuchis provides an extended analysis of these configurations – see Tavuchis, *Mea Culpa*.

32 Marc Galanter, "Worlds of Deals: Using Negotiation to Teach about Legal Process," *Journal of Legal Education* 34, no. 2 (1984): 268–276.

for apologising by enacting legislation that helps encourage the use of apology in the dispute resolution process by protecting the apology. After some deliberation, Hong Kong enacted in 2017, as one part of a broad programme of civil justice reform, an Apology Ordinance (Cap 631).[33] This provides – in the interests of preventing the escalation of disputes, facilitating amicable settlement and reducing the hostility and negative feeling of the injured party – that ordinarily an apology may not be relied on as evidence in civil proceedings and other fora for establishing liability. Only in exceptional cases may a judge (or mediator or arbitrator) admit a statement of fact contained in an apology as evidence in the proceedings – for example, where no other evidence is available for determining an issue.

In looking at dispute resolution processes from the perspective of the disputing parties, it might be surmised that apology is probably desired by disputants rather more than conventional ADR textbooks allow. For some aggrieved parties, the apology may be more important than any financial settlement or award, and a public apology may be especially sought after in disputes in which an administrative body or large business is being challenged. Such apologies might assist aggrieved parties to recover their sense of self-esteem and value, especially where power imbalances have resulted in the aggrieved person being ignored, brushed off or otherwise treated with disdain.

Violence and Its Forms

At the other end of the spectrum from avoidance are various forms of self-help, including the use of coercion and, in particular, recourse to violence, in response to disagreement or more serious forms of trouble. Sometimes self-help attracts a degree of social and even legal acceptance. A common but potentially costly and less tolerated way of dealing with conflict is to make a direct physical attack on the other party in a disagreement in an attempt to create a favourable outcome.[34] Interpersonal violence can be a significant form of response to disagreement. Like the other forms of response, the resort to violent conduct in resolving civil disagreements occurs in a social context. Where violence is carried out, it is one dimension of a social relationship. In this respect, it is like other modes of response to civil disagreements, including avoidance.

Conventionalised Violence

Violence too – even if we focus on small-scale disputes involving a small group of mutually agreed form of decision-making in advance of the actual violent confrontation. One of the best examples is the European duel, in which the parties agree to allow an outcome that is created by a violent act.

33 See: Prue Vines and Robyn Carroll, "The Apology Ordinance: Bold Steps into Some Uncharted Areas of Apology Protecting Legislation," *Hong Kong Law Journal* 48, no. 3 (2018): 925–952.

34 Costs include broken relationships, the risk of retaliation and harm to people which might be later regretted.

Violence as Non-Negotiation

In addition, the threat or use of violence may be seen as conduct that closes off other resolution possibilities. It is a declaration that coercion alone will determine the outcome. It becomes part of a process of closure. Its use is a social definition of the situation – that the outcome has to be on the terms dictated by or very favourable to the violent party. In this sense, too, there are some parallels to avoidance.[35] The use of violence in what is otherwise a civil dispute may also be a rejection of principles of procedural fairness and the need for and value of compromise – both very significant dimensions of resolving disagreements by negotiation and mediation.[36]

As I have suggested, coercion, especially violence, is found in various forms, some institutionalised, others less so. A dispute emerges between two or more parties when naming and blaming are followed by a rejected claim. One or more of the parties decides that force is the best or at least one feasible way of dealing with the trouble that has arisen. Or violence is resorted to more spontaneously in a fit of anger and discontent. Sometimes the more peaceable processes are attempted first, and when they are perceived by at least one party to fail, then violence ensues. But in other cases, the recourse to violence is more direct: there is quickly developing antagonism, rage and loss of temper. Sometimes, too, violence may be mixed in with other processes as a show of force intended to create favourable positions in negotiations. At the other end of the spectrum, violence may be more instrumentally used, as is sometimes the case in prolonged relations of domestic violence. In some societies, more than in others, the circumstances may be such that resort to violence is socially approved, perhaps even seen as noble, even where legally forbidden.[37] On the other hand, it may – as noted – be institutionalised in concrete forms of conduct, and I also identify dueling, feuding, honour killings and even vigilantism as taking on something of an institutionalised form even when not lawful.

Characterising Violence, the Nature of Violence in Disputes

In looking at recourse to violence in disputes, we see the threat or actual use of violence is a form of domination or coercion which is often physical and which

35 As Simmel noted, 'force', as usually understood, is used by one party to rob the other of every spontaneity and thereby every true 'action' that would be one side of an interaction: Georg Simmel, *Sociology: Inquiries into the Construction of Social Forms. Translated from German* (Soziologie. Untersuchungen über die Formen der Vergesellschaftung), translated and edited by A. J. Blasi, A. K. Jacobs and M. Kanjirathinkal, with an introduction by H. J. Helle (Leiden: Brill NV, 2008), 130.

36 On the value of 'compromise', see Stuart Hampshire, *Innocence and Experience* (Cambridge, MA: Harvard University Press, 1991), 74.

37 Fernanda Pirie, *Peace and Conflict in Ladakh: The Construction of a Fragile Web of Order* (Leiden: Brill, 2007), 5.

seeks to subordinate the other party into accepting an outcome that the dominant party seeks. This violence, as has been suggested, may arise from spontaneous emotion and loss of self-control, expressing anger and discontent, rather than seeking advantage. Or it may take a more prolonged and intentional character, being used strategically to seek advantage and dominate the other party.

Self-Help

Not all forms of self-help involve physical violence against the person, but nevertheless, some forms may contain an element of coercion that comes close to violence. The use of self-help is allowed in some legal systems, in the sense of permitting the aggressive assertion of one party's claims, intended to secure rights and interests without necessarily relying on formal legal processes to secure an outcome. Broadly speaking, self-help is allowed if laws are not broken and there is no breach of the peace committed – repossession of property in failed bank mortgage loans or where the property has been taken unlawfully are fairly common examples. However, if repossession in some ways creates damage, if force has to be used or if property rights such as those arising from protected tenancies are infringed, then self-help may become unlawful.

Structural Violence

Johan Galtung's work is important in the analysis of violence. For Galtung, the most pernicious and important form of violence is structural violence. This he sees as probably the most basic form of violence and as expressing social inequalities and institutional arrangements of power. These impact disproportionately on the socially marginalised in society, resulting in systemic harm of many such victims:

> Structural violence may also be about individuals acting abusively or violently in their private lives, or about individuals acting abusively or violently within the context of their institutionalized roles or public lives. More fundamentally, structural violence reinforces adversarial social organisation that incorporates both personal and impersonal ideologies of difference, privilege, and inequality.[38]

38 G. Barak, *Violence and Nonviolence: Pathways to Understanding*, Chapter 4 'Structural Violence' (Sage, 2003), https://sk.sagepub.com/books/violence-and-nonviolence. More generally, some scholars argue that law itself creates a violence in legitimating an 'intolerable' economic status quo that is unfair and exploitative, with justifications based on economic doctrines of comparative advantage. See, for example, R. Cover, "Violence and the Word," *Yale Law Journal* 95, no. 8 (1986): 1601–1629; Johan Galtung, "Cultural Violence," *Journal of Peace Research* 27, no. 3 (1990): 291–305, 300–301.

Ideologies of Violence

Systems of 'cultural violence' are also important: 'aspects of culture – exemplified by religion and ideology, language and art, empirical science and formal science (logic and mathematics) . . . can be used to justify or legitimize direct or structural violence'.[39] This is the functional reverse of Greenhouse's 'ethic of avoidance' or Laura Nader's 'harmony ideology'.[40] Just as there may be, in a society, an ideology that promotes the idea that conflict is dysfunctional and that minimising conflict and confrontation is necessary so as to achieve a peaceful and harmonious society, so there are 'ideologies of violence' in which the use of force is characterised as the correct way to resolve disputes and other disagreements. A clear example is provided by China. When the Cultural Revolution was at its height (1966–1968), disputes were to be seen in 'revolutionary' terms by a system which contrasted 'the people', to whom the communist revolution belonged (and still belongs), and 'the enemy' – that is, members of the former exploiting classes and counterrevolutionaries. From this dichotomy emerged a distinctive approach to the resolution of disputes and other forms of social conflict. Problems arising 'within the people' – primarily routine civil disputes such as matrimonial relations, landlord-tenant relations and so on – were characterised as 'non-antagonistic' – contradictions best resolved by methods of 'democracy' (that is, 'persuasion', 'self-criticism' and 'education', delivered through a highly evaluative 'mediation' process). However, similarly routine problems arising between parties who were of 'the people' on the one hand and of 'the enemy' on the other were recharacterised as 'antagonistic contradictions'. These disagreements were to be dealt with by the methods of dictatorship, including 'punishment' and thought reform. Often these processes of dictatorship took place in a public arena in which stress was placed on the importance of class conflict, political analysis of correct class position and the language of class injustice.

More generally, recent work has pointed to emerging problems of 'ideological masculinity'. Men who subscribe to this ideology believe that women's empowerment has left them victimised and discriminated against. This refurbishment of old ideas of male supremacy seeks to promote a return to a perceived period of male supremacy, now 'lost' to women's rights and self-effacing men (referred to by some members of the alt-right movement as 'beta cucks').[41]

Domestic Violence: China

In the case of mainland China, such ideas of male supremacy have never gone away. It has been very difficult to change thinking so that male-on-female

39 Johan Galtung, "Cultural Violence," *Journal of Peace Research* 27, no. 3 (1990): 291–305, 291.

40 Laura Nader, *Harmony Ideology, Justice and Control in a Zapotec Mountain Village* (Stanford, CA: Stanford University Press, 1990).

41 http://theconversation.com/ideological-masculinity-that-drives-violence-against-women-is-a-form-of-violent-extremism-99603.

partner violence in domestic disputes is seen as deviant conduct, requiring a much more robust response than the traditional management techniques of mediatory intervention aimed at reconciliation.[42] China's 2015 Anti-Domestic Violence Law was only introduced after much delay and opposition from 'patriarchal socialist' elements and has only functioned imperfectly since taking effect in March 2016. Judicial practice, however, still works hard to prevent divorce in situations of domestic violence and also demands a superior standard of proof for domestic violence when considering applications for protection orders from abused wives. Thus, the incidence of domestic violence is likely to remain a significant 'structural violence' issue for the foreseeable future, despite belated legislative reforms.

Violence and Time

While fully acknowledging that some forms of violence, such as domestic violence, are notable in no small part because of their persistence over time, it seems likely that we can agree with Randall Collins that actual resort to violence tends – unlike avoidance – in many cultures to be episodic. In his view, stereotyping images (we might add, as with Hollywood courtroom dramas and their characterisation of the practice of law as litigation theatrics) encourage us to think of violence as endemic. But, he adds, 'most of the time there is very little violence'.[43]

'Time' is important in an important dimension of the interactions between the parties involved in a dispute. The pressure on the parties to take immediate and coercive action may grow to feel keen as the antagonism between the parties develops. In general, we are socialised into interacting with others in a positive manner, and coercion is not the norm in social interaction. It is, on the contrary, an exception to ordinary social interaction. The possibility of its use creates confrontational strain and intensity, and the chances of its actual use are thereby increased. The situation of aggressive encounters only rarely allows parties to escape the confrontational tension that is generated by an imposed, coercive outcome.

42 Michael Palmer, "On China's Slow Boat to Women's Rights: Revisions to the Women's Protection Law, 2005," *The International Journal of Human Rights* 11, no. 1–2 (2007): 151–177; Michael Palmer, "Men Are Superior to Women' (*nan zun nü* bei)? Slowly Healing the Harm of Domestic Violence in Contemporary Chinese Law," In *Liber Amicorum in Honour of Professor William Butler*, eds. Natalia Iu. Erpyleva and Maryann E. Gashi-Butler (London: Wildy, Simmonds and Hill, 2014); Michael Palmer, "Domestic Violence and Mediation in Contemporary China," in *Mediation in Contemporary China: Continuity and Change*, ed. Fu Hualing and Michael Palmer (London: Wildy Simmonds and Hill, 2017).

43 Randall Collins, *Violence: A Micro-Sociological Theory* (Princeton: Princeton University Press, 2008), 14. See also, Randall Collins, "Theorizing the Time-dynamics of Violence," *Violence* 1, no. 1 (2020): 166–184; Carmelo Danisi and Nuno Ferreira, "Legal Violence and (In)Visible Families: How Law Shapes and Erases Family Life in SOGI Asylum in Europe," *Human Rights Law Review* (2021): 1–31.

Linking the Macro and the Micro

At the same time, while acknowledging that recourse to the use of violence in disputes reflects one or more of a number of facilitating structural and cultural environing factors – masculine honour, the opportunity for material benefits and a social imperative to dominate a person from another ethnic group – it is also the case that violence may also be more or less spontaneous. This is perhaps especially true of the use of interpersonal violence in the course of a dispute between two (or more) parties. Here, broadly speaking and as noted prior, a distinction may be drawn between instrumental violence and expressive violence. In looking at violence and other forms of compulsion in a dispute context, there appears to be a large divide between planned, instrumental violence, including the ritualised forms of violence noted earlier, and the more ad hoc, random and spontaneous conduct often associated with a violent loss of temper. Some acts of instrumental violence may be expressions of a wider context of structural violence, while structural violence may provide environing circumstances that are conducive to spontaneous violence. There is a need to go beyond this observation and consider in interpersonal disputes how the macro and the micro relate to each other, especially in generating specific acts of spontaneous violence. The distinguished sociologist Randall Collins's study of violence offers one explanation, as outlined in the following.

Violence Is Unusual

Disputing parties ordinarily do not use physical violence to fight with each other, a point stressed by Collins, as noted prior. Instead, they may argue, insult, gossip and so on rather than try to make their point by physically aggressive compulsion, or they may use forms of pressure against the other party that are abusive rather than physical violence. In Collins's view, when the parties do resort to physical violence, especially expressive violence, the determining conditions are to be found in the processes of the parties' short-term interaction. Negotiations between the parties in concrete encounters move away from normal interaction patterns and degenerate into alternative pathways which lead to a 'tunnel of violence'.[44] At the entrance of this tunnel is a situation of 'confrontational tension'. There is a spiralling of the tension and fears in the exchanges between the parties. These emotions may drain away, however, and the confrontational tension subside, leaving an impasse in the parties' relationship.

Other avenues to this tunnel, however, may generate increased tension and open up the tunnel entrance. One such path is 'forward panic', where the confrontational tension builds up, abruptly degenerating into violence. Unlike the positive, peaceable and cooperative social interaction in everyday life, the parties

44 See, for example, Randall Collins, *Violence: A Micro-Sociological Theory* (Princeton: Princeton University Press, 2008), 140.

may find themselves inept and unskilled in handling the tensions, intensifying the antagonisms. Other avenues that lead into the tunnel include an impulse to attack the weaker party precisely because the violent party sees that other party as weak and therefore vulnerable (as, for example, often in domestic violence). Also, the emotional state of an audience may have the significant impact of stirring up greater tensions. Clearly, these avenues are not exclusive paths to violence, and they often overlap and intertwine: the extent to which they are applicable cross-culturally has yet to be determined, as Collins draws primarily on North American data and gives little attention to anthropological accounts of disputing violence.

Social Complexity and Avoidance

I have noted that in the dispute resolution discourses on avoidance, attention has been given to issues of social and economic complexity and the use of avoidance as a dispute resolution strategy. The literature on resort to violence in the context of interpersonal dispute resolution (as opposed to violence more generally) does not seem to have shared such an 'evolutionary' concern. One notable exception is a set of observations by one of the early seminal thinkers on disputes and their resolution, namely Philip Gulliver. He takes the view that – to generalise his comments from observations on 'noncentralized, acephalous' societies – violent self-help, in the form of (for example) feuding, may emerge where there are strong, self-organised, compartmentalised groups within society. Such groups are able to manage, for a period of time, without peaceful cooperation. Where groups are more interdependent, resort to violence may be more strategic in nature and hostilities cannot long be tolerated. There are, here, echoes of Durkheim's distinction between mechanical and organic solidarity. In the case latter, we can point to, 'for example, the raid on the opponent's home, the seizure or spoliation of property, and the industrial strike. . . . [But] it leads to efforts for peacemaking'.[45]

There are some similarities also to the avoidance explanations noted earlier: put together, we see in both approaches the idea that in more 'advanced' or socially complex societies (in the words of one commentator, outer suburban communities in the United States), avoidance is a relatively feasible and attractive course of action. But in such communities too, resorting to violence may still be a feasible course of action, but it is likely to be used more strategically and instrumentally.

45 Philip Gulliver, *Disputes and Negotiations: A Cross-Cultural Perspective* (London and New York: Academic Press, 1979), 1–2.

Reflections

This chapter has given particular consideration to aspects of dispute resolution that are not given the attention they perhaps deserve mainstream in dispute resolution discourse. To some extent, this is a result of the domination of ADR discourse by lawyers, especially legal practitioners. As stressed at the beginning of the chapter, there are understandable *practical* reasons for this, as legal practitioners are necessarily focused on litigation and trial, and increasingly also negotiation and mediation, although it must be added that dispute prevention is more and more part of legal practice in many jurisdictions and that the use of apology is also increasingly formalised. But this domination does mean that there are important aspects of the continuum of response that tend to be overlooked, and it is to be hoped, by consideration of the sorts of issues taken up in this contribution, that a broader vision of the nature of alternative dispute resolution discourse will prevail.

References

Auerbach, J. S. *Justice without Law?* Oxford: Oxford University Press, 1983.

Barak, G. *Violence and Nonviolence: Pathways to Understanding*. Thousand Oaks, CA: Sage Publications, Chapter 4 "Structural Violence." 2003.

Baumgartner, M. P. "Social Control in Suburbia." In *Towards a General Theory of Social Control*, vol. 2, edited by Donald Black. Orlando, FA: Academic Press, 1984.

Bohannan, Paul. *Justice and Judgement among the Tiv*. London: Oxford University Press, 1957.

Brockman, R. H. "Commercial Contract Law in late Nineteenth Century Taiwan." In *Essays on China's Legal Tradition*, edited by J. Cohen, R. Edwards and Fu-mei Chang-Chen. Princeton, NJ: Princeton University Press, 1980.

Collins, Randall. "Theorizing the Time-dynamics of Violence." *Violence* 1, no. 1 (2020): 166–184.

Cover, Robert. "Violence and the Word." *Yale Law Journal* 95 no. 8 (1986): 1601–1629.

Cownie, Fiona and Anthony Bradney. "Dispute Avoidance. " In *Comparative Dispute Resolution*, edited by Maria Federica Moscati, Michael Palmer and Marian Roberts. Cheltenham and Northampton, MA: Edward Elgar Publishing, 2020.

Danisi, Carmelo and Nuno Ferreira. "Legal Violence and (In)Visible *Families: How Law Shapes and Erases Family Life in SOGI Asylum in Europe*." *Human Rights Law Review* (2021): 1–31.

Denti, Olga and Michela Giordano. "Till Money (and Divorce) Do Us Part: Premarital Agreements in the American and Spanish Legal Discourse." In *The Discourses of Dispute Resolution*, edited by Vijay K. Bhatia, Christopher N. Candlin and Maurizio Gotti. Peter Lang: Berne, 2010.

Felstiner, William L. F. "Avoidance as Dispute Processing: An Elaboration." *Law & Society Review* 9, no. 4 (Summer, 1975): 695–706 at 695.

Felstiner, William L. F. "Influences of Social Organization on Dispute Processing." *Law and Society Review* 9, no. 1 (1974): 63–94.

Felstiner, William L. F., R. L. Abel and A. Sarat. "The Emergence and Transformation of Disputes: Naming, Blaming, Claiming . . . " *Law & Society Review* 15, no. 3/4, Special Issue on Dispute Processing and Civil Litigation (1980–1981): 631–654.

Galtung, Johan. "Cultural Violence." *Journal of Peace Research* 27, no. 3 (1990): 291–305.

Gluckman, Max. *The Judicial Process among the Barotse of Northern Rhodesia (Zambia)*. Manchester: Manchester University Press, 1955.

Gould, Nicholas. "Conflict Avoidance and Dispute Resolution." (2019). www.fenwickelliott.com/sites/default/files/nick_gould_-_conflict_avoidance_and_dispute_resolution.indd_.pdf

Greenhouse, Carol. "Signs of Quality: Individualism and Hierarchy in American Culture." *American Ethnologist* 19, no. 2 (1992): 233–254.

Gulliver, P. H. "On Avoidance." In *The Politics of Cultural Performance*, edited by D. J. Parkin, L. Caplan and H. J. Fisher. Providence: Berghahn Books, 1996.

Gulliver, P. H. *Social Control in an African Society: A Study of the Arusha, Agricultural Masai of Northern Tanganyika*. London: Routledge, 1963.

Hampshire, Stuart. *Innocence and Experience*. Cambridge, MA: Harvard University Press, 1991.

Johnsen, D. Bruce. "A Modern Potlatch?" (24, 2) *PERC* (Property and Environment Research Center) Summer 2006. June 1, 2006. www.perc.org/2006/06/01/a-modern-potlatch/

Llewellyn, K. N. and E. A. Hoebel. *The Cheyenne Way: Conflict and Case Law in Primitive Jurisprudence*. Norman, OK: University of Oklahoma Press, 1941.

MacCormack, Geoffrey "Coercion and Suicide in Traditional Chinese Law: Evolution of the Statutory Rules." *Journal of Comparative Law* 13, no. 2 (2018): 217–260.

Moscati, Maria Federica, Michael Palmer and Marian Roberts, eds. *Comparative Dispute Resolution*. Cheltenham, UK and Northampton, MA: Edward Elgar Publishing, 2020.

Nader, L. "The Ethnography of Law." *American Anthropologist*, New Series, Special Publication 67, no. 6 (1965): pt. 2.

Nader, L. *Harmony Ideology, Justice and Control in a Zapotec Mountain Village*. Stanford, CA: Stanford University Press, 1990.

Nader, L. and H. F. Todd, eds. *The Disputing Process: Law in Ten Societies*. New York: Columbia University Press, 1978.

Palmer, Michael. "Domestic Violence and Mediation in Contemporary China." In *Mediation in Contemporary China: Continuity and Change*, edited by F. U. Hualing and Michael Palmer. London: Wildy Simmonds and Hill, 2017.

Palmer, Michael. "'Men Are Superior to Women' (*nan zun nü bei*)? Slowly Healing the Harm of Domestic Violence in Contemporary Chinese Law." In *Liber Amicorum in Honour of Professor William Butler*, edited by Natalia Iu Erpyleva, Maryann E. Gashi-Butler and Jane Hendersen. London: Wildy, Simmonds and Hill, 2014.

Palmer, Michael. "On China's Slow Boat to Women's Rights: Revisions to the Women's Protection Law, 2005." *The International Journal of Human Rights* 11, nos. 1–2 (2007): 151–177.

Palmer, Michael. "Violence." In *Comparative Dispute Resolution*, edited by Maria Federica Moscati, Michael Palmer and Marian Roberts. Cheltenham and Northampton, MA: Edward Elgar Publishing, 2020.

Palmer, Michael and Simon Roberts. "Development of Disputes, Avoidance, and Violence." In Chapter 5 *Dispute Processes: ADR and the Primary Forms of Decision-Making*, 3rd ed., 101–122. Law in Context. Cambridge: Cambridge University Press, 2020.

Pirie, Fernanda. *Peace and Conflict in Ladakh: The Construction of a Fragile Web of Order*. Leiden: Brill, 2007.

Rosenberry, Katharine, "Organizational Barriers to Creativity in Law Schools and the Legal Profession." *California Western Law Review* 41, no. 2 (2005): 423–457.

Simmel, Georg. *Sociology: Inquiries into the Construction of Social Forms*. Translated from German (*Soziologie. Untersuchungen über die Formen der Vergesellschaftung*) and edited by

A. J. Blasi, A. K. Jacobs and M. Kanjirathinkal, with an introduction by H. J. Helle. Leiden: Brill NV, 2008.

Taft, Lee. "Apology Subverted: The Commodification of Apology." *Yale Law Journal* 109, no. 5 (2000): 1135–1160.

Tavuchis, Nicholas. *Mea Culpa: A Sociology of Apology and Reconciliation*. Stanford, CA: Stanford University Press, 1991.

Turner, V. W. *Schism and Continuity in an African Society*. Manchester: Manchester University Press (published on behalf of the Institute for Social Research, University of Zambia), 1968 (1957).

Vines, Prue and Robyn Carroll. "The Apology Ordinance: Bold Steps into Some Uncharted Areas of Apology Protecting Legislation." *Hong Kong Law Journal* 48, no. 3 (2018): 925–952.

White, Brent T. "Say You're Sorry: Court-Ordered Apologies as a Civil Rights Remedy." *Cornell Law Review* 91 (2006): 1261–1331.

Zwart-Hink, Andrea, Arno Akkermans and Kiliaan Van Wees. "Compelled Apologies as a Legal Remedy: Some Thoughts from a Civil Law Jurisdiction." *University of Western Australia Law Review* 38, no. 1 (2014): 100–122.

4

ADVANCING RESEARCH AND PRACTICE IN THE GOVERNANCE OF DISPUTE RESOLUTION INSTITUTIONS THROUGH INCLUSIVE DEVOLVED REFLECTION

Shahla Ali

Efforts to develop and reform systems of dispute resolution have been undertaken through a variety of approaches. This chapter focuses on the role of "devolved reflection" as a tool to support institutional dispute resolution reform. Devolved reflection can be understood as a process by which relevant stakeholders engage in earnest deliberation to arrive at a greater understanding of existing circumstances, review accomplishments, analyse challenges, learn from experience and plan next steps in an effort to improve service delivery. The capacity to reflect as individuals and communities has increasingly been tapped to varying degrees within institutions of governance. An emerging approach to devolved reflection functions as an applied reflective research methodology and as a component of a larger framework of systematic learning. The chapter draws on insights from research highlighting the role of engaged reflection and shared knowledge generation in facilitating conditions conducive to dynamic advancement within transnational dispute resolution systems.

Introduction: Devolved Reflection and Organisational Progress

Echoing Goal 16 of the UN's Sustainable Development Goals of promoting "just, peaceful and inclusive societies" by building "effective, accountable and inclusive institutions at all levels" through "citizens' participation in decision making,"[1] recent scholarship has described an important shift in organisational structure

1 Mahmoud Mohieldin, "Foreword," in *The World Bank Legal Review, Volume 7. Financing and Implementing the Post-2015 Development Agenda: The Role of Law and Justice Systems*, ed. Frank Fariello, Laurence Boisson de Chazournes, and Kevin Davis (Washington, DC: World Bank, 2016). https://openknowledge.worldbank.org/bitstream/handle/10986/24997/9781464805455.pdf?sequence=2&isAllowed=y.

DOI: 10.4324/9780429354625-6

aspiring toward equipping such entities to "draw out more human potential"[2] through reflective dialogue so as to enable them to address increasingly complex and critical social and environmental challenges.[3] Among the defining features of such organisations is a shift in orientation toward structures in which "purpose . . . [is] the guiding principle."[4] Such organisational systems operate on the basis of "peer relationships"[5] and are assisted to advance through joint reflection by asking "the . . . questions that help teams to find their own solutions"[6] while "trust[ing] in the collective intelligence of the system."[7] Such an approach resonates with emerging work in "Global Experimentalist Governance," which traces how participatory and multilevel problem solving advances when particular problems are framed in an open way and are subject "to periodic revision by various forms of peer review in light of locally generated knowledge."[8]

Reflecting "a shift from [a] deficit to [a] strength-based paradigm"[9] through a process of devolved "collective . . . self-reflection,"[10] recent research has found that "among the great number of innovative . . . [management] practices . . . joint reflection" is credited with contributing to significant advances in organisational culture and functioning.[11] In such settings, "collective insights emerge, as well as decisions and initiatives [to be] carried out,"[12] assisting "the whole organization [to] gro[w] its way through one topic after another."[13] At the same time, reflective spaces permit organisations to regularly acknowledge and affirm practices that are working well in order that they may be strengthened.[14]

The significance of devolved reflective process in organisational advancement can be linked to a rich body of scholarship highlighting the role of social capital in supporting cooperative, cohesive and creative social behaviour, enhancing productivity[15] and facilitating collective action for mutual benefit,[16] including improved social welfare and reduced corruption.[17] Social capital, understood as

2 Frederic Laloux, *Reinventing Organizations: A Guide to Creating Organizations Inspired by the Next Stage of Human Consciousness*, 1st ed. (Brussels, Belgium: Nelson Parker, 2014), 4.
3 Ibid., 5.
4 Ibid., 50.
5 Ibid.
6 Ibid., 69.
7 Ibid., 85.
8 Gráinne De Búrca, Robert O. Keohane and Charles Sabel, "Global Experimentalist Governance," *British Journal of Political Science* 44, no. 3 (2014): 477–486. https://doi:10.1017/S0007123414000076.
9 Ibid.
10 Ibid., 154.
11 Ibid.
12 Ibid.
13 Ibid., 156.
14 Ibid., 160.
15 Robert D. Putnam, "Bowling Alone: America's Declining Social Capital," *Journal of Democracy* 6, no. 1 (1995): 65–78.
16 Michael Woolcock, "Social Capital and Economic Development: Toward a Theoretical Synthesis and Policy Framework," *Theory and Society* 27, no. 2 (1998): 151–208.
17 Putnam, "Bowling Alone," 1.

a set of norms, values, attitudes, beliefs and relationships,[18] is largely formed through the creation of spaces within a community that foster changes in thinking, attitudes and behaviour and the formation of trust[19] – built through collective exchange, learning and action.[20] It is strengthened by consultative processes through which stakeholders continually elaborate a common understanding of collective objectives,[21] articulate their interests and mediate their differences[22] in order to promote development for the collective whole.[23] Inclusivity is an important component of social capital and has been enriched by recent scholarship showing that cluster rather than individualised group membership selection can significantly enhance group diversity in multiple contexts.[24]

Drawing on insights from devolved reflection processes, this chapter examines how such an approach is increasingly echoed in emerging legal principles and norms (Part II), in analytic and normative frameworks for new governance policy (Part III), in applied reflective research (Part IV) and as aspiring toward systematic learning (Part V).

Devolved Reflection as an Emerging Legal Principle and Norm of Customary International Law

In addition to the growing use of devolved reflective principles in organisational governance, such principles, including the principle of community-based decision-making has increasingly been referenced in emerging customary norms[25] in the realm of humanitarian assistance and resource use planning.

In the field of humanitarian assistance, states are increasingly being required to facilitate the establishment of mechanisms enabling participation[26] and reflective planning.[27] The Good Humanitarian Donorship consortium of states emphasises the need to involve communities in "the design, implementation, monitoring and

18 *See* Vladislav Valentinov, "Toward a Social Capital Theory of Cooperative Organization," *Journal of Cooperative Studies* 3 (2004): 37.

19 *See* Putnam, "Bowling Alone," 1.

20 UN Development Program, *Strategy Note on Governance for Human Development*, 2004. See also World Bank Group, http://siteresources.worldbank.org/INTSOCIALCAPITAL/Resources/Social-Capital-Initiative-Working-Paper-Series/SCI-WPS-24.pdf.

21 World Bank Group, http://siteresources.worldbank.org/INTSOCIALCAPITAL/Resources/Social-Capital-Initiative-Working-Paper-Series/SCI-WPS-24.pdf.

22 UNDP, 2004 Strategy Note.

23 *See* "Social Capital Research & Training," www.socialcapitalresearch.com/.

24 *See* Richard R. W. Brooks and Valerie Puride-Vaughns, "Supermodular Architecture of Inclusion," *Harvard Journal of Law & Gender* 30 (2007): 379.

25 For complete discussion *see*: Shahla F. Ali and Tom Kabau, "A Human Rights-Based Approach to the Global Regulation of Humanitarian Relief: The Emerging Obligation to Incorporate Local Participation," *Brooklyn Journal of International Law* 40, no. 3 (2015): 791–826.

26 For complete discussion *see*: Shahla F. Ali, *Governing Disasters: Engaging Local Populations in Humanitarian Relief* (New York, NY: Cambridge University Press, 2016), vii–xix, 1–321.

27 Brigitte I. Hamm, "A Human Rights Approach to Development," *Human Rights Quarterly* 23, no. 4 (2001): 1005–1031, 1011.

evaluation" of relief activities.[28] Article 2(c)(ii) of the 2012 Food Assistance Convention stipulates that one of the key governing principles in the provision of food assistance is the involvement of communities "in the assessment of their needs and in the design, implementation, monitoring and evaluation" of relief activities.[29]

A range of qualitative guidelines and standards are emerging from treaties, resolutions of states and self-regulatory instruments, including the Sphere Charter, requiring that local participants be involved, at minimum, "in the design, implementation, monitoring and evaluation" of humanitarian relief activities.[30] This includes access to appropriate and safe venues for meetings,[31] balanced representation,[32] understandable language,[33] transparent and effective feedback mechanisms,[34] use of local resources and skills[35] and engagement with progressive local norms[36] given that resource use questions are "inherently infused with value judgments"[37] and that the reduction of such questions to a single metric implies "significant loss to those values."[38] Such guidelines are emerging to ensure uniform and objective qualitative standards of participation in various stages of relief.

Devolved Reflection as an Emerging Framework for New Governance Policy and Evaluation

Elements of devolved reflection may be traced within the emerging field of new governance scholarship.[39] This area of inquiry has provided a framework for both

28 Good Humanitarian Donorship, "Principles and Good Practice of Humanitarian Donorship," (endorsed in Stockholm, 17 June 2003) paragraph 7, www.goodhumanitariandonorship.org/gns/principles-good-practice-ghd/overview.aspx, accessed May 19, 2014.

29 *Food Assistance Convention*, London, 25 April 2012, *United Nations Treaty Series*, vol. 2884, no. 50320, 3, https://treaties.un.org/Pages/ViewDetails.aspx?src=TREATY&mtdsg_no=XIX48&chapter=19&clang=_en, accessed May 11, 2013.

30 *Food Assistance Convention*, Article 2(c)(ii). *See also*: Good Humanitarian Donorship, "Principles and Good Practice of Humanitarian Donorship"; United Nations and the Inter-Agency Standing Committee, "Civil-Military Guidelines and Reference for Complex Emergencies" (2008), 19, https://docs.unocha.org/sites/dms/Documents/ENGLISH%20VERSION%20Guidelines%20for%20Complex%20Emergencies.pdf, accessed May 5, 7, 2014; Emergency Capacity Building Project, "Impact Measurement and Accountability in Emergencies: The Good Enough Guide" (2007), 34–35, www.ecbproject.org/inside-the-guide/view-the-good-enough-guide, accessed May 19, 2014.

31 Sphere Project, *Sphere Handbook: Humanitarian Charter and Minimum Standards in Humanitarian Response, 2011*, 3rd ed. (Rugby, UK: Sphere Project, 2011), 55.

32 Ibid.

33 Ibid.

34 Ibid.

35 Ibid.

36 Ibid.

37 Jim Rossi, "Participation Run Amok: The Costs of Mass Participation for Deliberative Agency Decisionmaking," *Northwesten University Law Review* 92, no. 172 (1997): 198.

38 Sheila Foster, "Environmental Justice in an Era of Devolved Collaboration," *Harvard Environmental Law Review* 26, no. 2 (2002): 459.

39 For further discussion, *see*: Shahla F. Ali, "Towards Peer Presence in Post-Disaster Governance: An Empirical Study," *Hastings International and Comparative Law Review* 38, no. 2 (2015): 243–274.

policy making and evaluation of policy outcomes through recognition of the value of expanded participation and partnership on the part of governments and non-state actors in solving public problems;[40] a learning-focused orientation;[41] the use of public-private partnership in regulatory reform;[42] the role of the state as a convener, catalyst and coordinator;[43] and development of problem-solving capabilities.[44] Recent scholarship has likewise examined the challenges facing new governance, including ensuring that participants have the necessary skills for participation,[45] developing managerial and procedural safeguards,[46] achieving stakeholder participation under conditions of social conflict[47] and overcoming representational and distributional inequalities.[48]

New governance places opportunities for stakeholder participation and reflection as central to decision-making processes.[49] Stakeholders, including organisations (institutions, public agencies, private firms and NGOs), interact, share responsibility and together generate policy.[50] States and localities are expected to be better situated to facilitate participatory processes, and once solutions are found, they are best suited to monitor implementation.[51]

Among the normative values identified with new governance[52] are ownership, responsibility and follow-through by stakeholders given that solutions are derived from community input.[53] Deliberation and reflection on the part of diverse participants, it is suggested, yields wiser results,[54] and collaboration may give rise to higher levels of transparency and accountability.[55]

40 Orly Lobel, "The Renew Deal: The Fall of Regulation and the Rise of Governance in Contemporary Legal Thought," *Minnesota Law Review* 89, no. 2 (2004): 342, 381–382; Jason M. Solomon, "Law and Governance in the 21st Century Regulatory State," *Texas Law Review* 86, no. 4 (2008): 819–856.

41 Solomon, "Law and Governance" loc. cit.; Amy J. Cohen, "Negotiation, Meet New Governance: Interests, Skills, and Selves," *Law & Social Inquiry* 33, no. 2 (2008): 501–562, 503.

42 Lisa T. Alexander, "Stakeholder Participation in New Governance: Lessons From Chicago's Public Housing Reform Experiment," *Georgetown Journal on Poverty Law & Policy* 16, no. 1 (2009): 117.

43 Michael C. Dorf and E. Charles, "A Constitution of Democratic Experimentalism," *Columbia Law Review* 98, no. 2 (1998): 267–473, 267; Solomon, "Law and Governance," loc. cit.; Cohen, "Negotiation, Meet New Governance," loc. cit.

44 Cohen, "Negotiation, Meet New Governance," loc. cit.

45 Ibid.

46 Lester M. Salamon, "The New Governance and the Tools of Public Action: An Introduction," *The Fordham Urban Law Journal* 28, no. 5 (2001): 1611.

47 Alexander, "Stakeholder Participation," loc. cit.

48 Ibid.

49 Ibid., 333.

50 Ibid.

51 Orly, "The Renew Deal," 381–382.

52 E.g. *see* Charles F. Sabel and Jonathan Zeitlin, *Experimental Governance in the European Union: Towards a New Architecture*, ed. Charles F. Sabel and Jonathan Zeitlin (Oxford: Oxford University Press, 2010).

53 Ibid.

54 Beth Simone Noveck, "The Single Point of Failure," in *Innovating Government*, eds. Simone Van der Hof and Marga M. Groothuis (The Hague: Asserr Press, 2011), 77–99, 85.

55 *See* Jerome van der Heijden, "Experimentation in policy-design: Insights from the building sector," *Policy Sciences* 47, no. 3 (2014): 249–266.

When effectively facilitated, devolved governance efforts respond to the aspiration for broad-based contribution to decision-making.[56] However, when implemented without regard to issues of universal representation and disparate access to resources, the process has the potential of replicating and possibly exacerbating existing representation problems[57] and simply offering a means of providing input to existing plans rather than originating plans at the community level. Similar to the challenges facing responsive law,[58] such as the existence of subjectivity in rule-making and the danger of getting the moral question wrong through caving into power politics (as advanced through special interests, for example), new governance approaches likewise face the potential danger of rendering community resource problems "less visible or subject to scrutiny, because the farther the process is removed from a centralized decision-maker, the less accountability there will be."[59] Research has suggested that in order to benefit from devolution and decentralisation,[60] the necessary conditions for its success should include (1) the broadest possible degree of stakeholder participation compatible with effective decision-making, (2) effective and informed monitoring,[61] (3) ensuring participants have the necessary skills for participation,[62] (4) the development of procedural safeguards[63] and (5) ensuring stakeholder participation under conditions of social conflict[64] and distributional inequalities.[65] The challenge at present is to examine ways

56 *See* Philip Nonet, *Law and Society in Transition: Toward Responsive Law*. Ed. Philip Selznick, 1st ed. (New Brunswick: Transaction Publishers, 1978). "Responsive Law" is described in relation to both "Repressive Law" (law as servant of repressive power) and "Autonomous Law" (law as differentiated institution capable of taming repression and protecting its own integrity). Repressive law generally takes little note of affected interests. A "common source of repression is the poverty of resources available to governing elites" in circumstances where "urgent tasks must be met under conditions of adequate power but scarce resources." Autonomous law can be characterised by the "rule of law" born when legal institutions acquire enough independent authority to impose standards of restraint on the exercise of governmental power. Specialised legal institutions claim qualified supremacy within defined spheres of competence. Autonomous law reflects a transition from blanket certification of the source of power to a sustained justification of its use. "Legal institutions purchase procedural autonomy at the price of substantive subordination." The downside is that the application of rules ceases to be informed by a regard for purposes, needs and consequences (64).

57 Foster, "Environmental Justice," 485.

58 Among the challenges noted by Nonet and Selznick include the fact that "responsive law is a precarious ideal whose achievement and desirability are historically contingent and depend especially on the urgencies to be met and the resources that can be tapped." Specifically, there is the danger of subjectivity in rule-making and "getting the moral question wrong." The achievement of responsive ideals depends a great deal on the development of "cognitive competence" (within the judiciary) to consider social conditions and gather relevant information from outside sources in order to search for a solution, rather than arbitrarily lay down a rule: Sheila Foster, Environmental Justice, 485.

59 Ibid.

60 Lisa T. Alexander, "Reflections on Success and Failure in New Governance and the Role of the Lawyer," *Wisconsin Law Review* 2010, no. 2 (2010): 737, 738.

61 Ibid., 740–741; see also: Shahla F. Ali, "Measuring Success in Devolved Collaboration," *Journal of Land Use and Environmental Law* 26, no. 1 (2010): 93–112.

62 Ibid.

63 Salamon, "The New Governance," 1611.

64 Alexander, "Reflections on Success," loc. cit.

65 Ibid.

in which reflective devolved decision-making processes might be strengthened to address potential disparities, the focus of the following sections of this chapter.[66]

Devolved Reflection as a Research Methodology and Approach to Policy Refinement

In an effort to advance participatory reflective approaches in comparative dispute resolution, numerous research approaches have been developed. These include citizen input, use of model laws and rules and indicator assessment. This section reports on the author's efforts to apply elements of a devolved reflective research process in a series of comparative dispute resolution research projects to draw out lessons learned as to how local engagement responds to and shapes global norms in an effort to enhance access to justice. This approach echoes elements of the para-ethnographic approach discussed by Matthew S. Erie in this volume. Insights from four projects highlighting the role of engaged participation and shared knowledge generation in consumer financial dispute resolution, cross-border arbitration and post-disaster governance initiatives are examined. The work traces the role of capacity building, cohesion and collective contribution to knowledge generation.

In examining the dynamics by which selected dispute resolution organisations change and develop, rather than through fundamental or top-down shifts in structure, they appear to advance through "iterative revolutions" in thinking and organisation. The idea of iterative revolutions, building on the concept of scientific paradigmatic shifts as described by Kuhn,[67] implies that over time, organisations develop through experiencing new challenges, asking new questions and addressing these questions through a collective body of shared knowledge and practice. This is similar to Kuhn's notion that the evolution within scientific theory does not emerge from the mere accumulation of facts but rather from a set of changing intellectual circumstances and possibilities.[68] A core element of this process requires exploring alternatives to "long-held, obvious-seeming assumptions" through asking questions and reflecting on experience. In contrast to the traditional scientific model in which a lone scientists engages in paradigm-challenging experiments, this process implies the collective work of groups, organisations and communities engaged in a joint exploration of knowledge.

Engaging in Reflective Process as Scholars, Users and Practitioners: Case Studies

At present, existing literature provides useful insights into efforts at establishing reflective spaces within existing ADR organisations. For example, in Nancy Welsh's article on "Magistrate Judges, Settlement and Procedural Justice," she

66 *See:* Ali, "Measuring Success," 93–112.
67 Thomas S. Kuhn, *The Structure of Scientific Revolutions* (Chicago: University of Chicago Press, 1962).
68 Ibid.

examines emerging opportunities for feedback and self-reflection among mediation administrators in an effort to improve overall quality and procedural fairness in mediation.[69]

In addition to policy reflection within court settings, reflective research approaches have been used to advance understanding of how comparative systems of ADR function and advance in diverse contexts. The following highlights three dispute resolution research projects that have employed a process of devolved reflective engagement with practitioners working in institutions involved in the arbitration of cross-border disputes, consumer financial grievance mechanisms, post-disaster humanitarian aid and court mediation reform and development.

What unites each of these projects is a concern with the development of comparative reflective spaces to address what has been working well, challenges and suggestions for improvement in the context of diverse cultural and social environments. The core impetus for this approach is the notion that "the realization of justice is dependent upon universal participation and action among all members and agencies of society."[70]

Within this reflective approach, the aim is to create spaces where a growing number of individuals and practitioners can share insights that contribute to the ongoing improvement, refinement and progress of dispute resolution institutions. By examining what has been working in advanced organisations, it is possible to synthesise "more than a collection of case studies" but rather explore "patterns and commonalities that point to a coherent new model."[71]

In general, this research approach builds upon a mixed methodology that involves a combination of survey work and comparative case studies. Each of the three studies examines: (1) the key approaches to reflective engagement employed, (2) relevant insights and (3) limitations.

Arbitration of Cross-Border Disputes

Building on the observation that "for none is self-sufficiency any longer possible, inasmuch as political ties unite all peoples and nations, and the bonds of trade and industry, of agriculture and education, are being strengthened every day,"[72] the first project, *Resolving Disputes in the Asia Pacific Region: International Arbitration and Mediation in East Asia and the West*,[73] sought to examine how diverse cultures

69 *See:* Nancy Welsh, "Magistrate Judges, Settlement, and Procedural Justice," *Nevada Law Journal* 16 (2015–2016): 983.

70 Bahá'í International Community, "Prosperity of Humankind". Statement. United Nations World Summit on Social Development, Copenhagen, Denmark, 3 March 1995.

71 Laloux, "*Reinventing Organizations*," 4.

72 Abdu'l-Bahá, *Paris Talks*, 11th ed. (Oakham, UK: Bahá'í Publishing Trust, 1972).

73 *For* full discussion, *see:* Shahla F. Ali, *Resolving Disputes in the Asia Pacific: International Arbitration and Mediation in East Asia and the West* (New York and London: Routledge, 2010; 2012 reprint), v–xiv, 1–146.

approach the resolution of conflict in the context of the integration of global markets.[74]

Approach to Reflective Engagement

This project sought to apply a framework of reflective engagement by (1) widening the base of survey participants to reflect the diversity of the international arbitration community and (2) engaging diverse practitioners in conversations regarding survey design and interpretation. Insights from reflection were synthesised into concrete observations regarding areas of advancement, challenge and suggestions for improving the system of cross-border arbitration.

First, in extending much of the existing western-focused research on international arbitration as practiced in Europe and North America, this project sought to provide empirical understanding of the attitudes and perceptions of over 115 arbitrators, judges, lawyers and members of the rapidly expanding arbitration community in China, Hong Kong, Korea, Japan, Singapore and Malaysia alongside counterparts in North America and Europe.[75] The project covered both international commercial arbitration and mediation, providing an empirical analysis of how both types of dispute resolution are conducted in the East Asian context.[76]

Second, a principal orientation of the research project focused on participation from those immediately and substantially affected by the potential outcome of the research. Participants were given a voice in framing and reframing the interview question under study, a voice in selecting the means of answering the question defined by the research and a voice in determining the criteria to decide whether the question has been validly answered.[77] Likewise, the research drew on the model of "social science as public philosophy" described by Robert Bellah which "accepts the cannons of critical disciplined research" but at the same time "does not imagine that such research exits in a vacuum or can be 'value free.'"[78] In this light, the research placed special attention on examining the underlying values that inform contemporary processes of dispute resolution in diverse regions.[79] This approach drew on recent insights in the field of socio-legal studies regarding the growing need for legal study to be underpinned by theorising that treats generalisations across legal families, traditions, cultures and orders as problematic,[80] as

74 Ibid.

75 Ibid.

76 Ibid.

77 Rhett Diessner, "Action Research," in *Converging Realities* 1, no. 1 (Switzerland: Landegg Academy, 2000).

78 Robert N. Bellah, et al., *Habits of the Heart: Individualism and Collectivism in American Life* (New York: Harper and Row, 1985).

79 For full discussion, *see:* Ali, *Resolving Disputes*, v–xiv, 1–146.

80 *See:* William Twining, *Globalization and Legal Theory* (London: Butterworths, 2000) and William Twining, "Have Concepts, Will Travel: Analytical Jurisprudence in a Global Context," *International Journal of Law in Context* 1, no. 1 (March 2005).

well as the need to examine those underlying universal norms that guide dispute resolution processes.[81]

Insights from Devolved Reflection

The results of the 115-person survey and 64 follow-up interviews highlight the importance of two major factors at work in the field of international arbitration: global convergence and informed diversity.[82] The major finding of the research was that due to the relatively flexible nature of the United Nations model law structure of international arbitration which allows countries to gradually and selectively adopt particular provisions of the model law, a relatively high degree of substantive legal uniformity in arbitration rules (convergence) can coexist and be enriched by procedural variation in settlement processes and techniques (diversity) across regions.[83] At the same time, based on the norm of "global deliberative equality" and the basic moral precept that "our species is one, and each of the individuals who compose it is entitled to equal moral consideration,"[84] the enriching influence of regional diversity enhances the range of arbitral technique and enables the global examination of best practices from a wide range of experiences. Regional distinctions are reflected in varying arbitrator perceptions regarding the arbitrators' role in settlement, whether settlement is regarded as a goal in arbitration and the types of efforts made during the course of arbitration to settle disputes. For example, the survey found a greater openness to exploring settlement options and a greater degree of support for arbitrator-initiated settlement discussions among practitioners working in East Asia.[85] Such diverse experiences are understood as not static but fluid, as a set of learned institutional and ideological expressions based on shared norms and beliefs about the world.[86]

Drawing on 64 open-ended interviews and follow-up field work, practitioner insights focused on what international arbitration practitioners could do to assist in improving the practice of international arbitration in a cross-cultural context. Such insights included the need for greater cross-cultural training of arbitrators, disciplinary and multicultural panels, bilingual arbitrators, widening the pool of arbitrators from diverse backgrounds, greater transparency, strengthening of local arbitration tribunals and finally greater training of counsel and arbitrators as to the uses and timing of mediation. In addition, nearly all arbitrators interviewed

81 See: Philip Selznick, *Law and Society in Transition: Toward Responsive Law*, 1st ed. (New Brunswick: Transaction Publishers, 1978); and Philip Selznick, *The Moral Commonwealth: Social Theory and the Promise of Community* (Berkeley: University of California Press, 1992).

82 *See* also: Anne Marie Slaughter, *A New World Order* (Princeton, NJ: Princeton University Press, 2004).

83 For full discussion, *see* Ali, *Resolving Disputes*, v–xiv, 1–146.

84 Ibid., 245.

85 For full discussion, *see* Ali, *Resolving Disputes*, v–xiv, 1–146.

86 Michael R. Karlberg, *Beyond the Culture of Contest: From Adversarialism to Mutualism in an Age of Interdependence* (Oxford: George Ronald Publishers Ltd., 2004).

felt that extensive adversarial practices in arbitration were not advantageous or beneficial to the parties or practice in general.

Limitations

While the study sought to extend existing understanding of international arbitration practice in diverse regions by extending the survey pool to international arbitrators working in East Asia, a key limitation of the study was its bifurcated presentation of perspectives of practitioners working in two distinct regional groupings. While an effort was made to address this limitation by focusing on an arbitrator's primary region of practice rather than nationality, future studies may examine how to draw on such regional insights in the context of an inherently interconnected global community.

Consumer Financial Dispute Resolution

With the objective of enhancing capacities that enable institutions to "respond creatively to challenges . . . [through] . . . the ability to . . . uphold standards of fairness and equity,"[87] the project *Consumer Financial Dispute Resolution in a Comparative Context* examined how governments and self-regulatory organisations design and administer financial dispute resolution mechanisms in the context of increasingly turbulent financial markets.[88]

Approach to Reflective Engagement

Drawing on comparative research about the development and design of grievance mechanisms in East Asia, North America and Europe, this project sought to apply a framework of reflective engagement by: (1) identifying relevant globally accepted principles and standards pertinent to addressing consumer financial disputes; (2) drawing on selected principles to serve as a lens by which to analyse processes giving rise to the development of accessible, efficient and equitable financial ombuds and arbitration systems in seven jurisdictions; and (3) engaging practitioners in conversations about achievements, challenges and lessons learned in the resolution of consumer financial disputes. Drawing on insights from a multi-jurisdictional survey, the project examined the emergence of global principles that influence the design of financial dispute resolution models, considered structural variations between the ombuds and arbitration systems and synthesised practitioner insights.

First, drawing on an exploration of the development of global principles that influence to varying degrees the design of consumer financial dispute resolution systems in diverse societies, emerging standards were synthesised from the

87 Bahá'í International Community, "Overcoming Corruption".

88 For full discussion, *see:* Shahla F. Ali, *Consumer Financial Dispute Resolution in a Comparative Context: Principles, Systems and Practice* (Cambridge: Cambridge University Press, 2013), vii–xiv, 1–267.

Equator Principles, the Basel Accords and the UN Millennium Development Goals, including the need for accessible grievance mechanisms, transparent risk disclosure and risk mitigation, impartiality, equity, accountability and fairness.[89]

Second, the project drew on these selected global principles to serve as a lens by which to analyse processes and structures that give rise to the development of accessible, efficient and equitable financial ombuds and arbitration systems in seven jurisdictions. It examined comparative institutional dispute resolution structures and results in selected financial centres in East Asia, North America and Europe in order to glean best practices. Through comparison among corresponding financial dispute resolution centres in seven jurisdictions, the aim of the research was to understand how these jurisdictions addressed consumer complaints through distinct structures of financial dispute resolution including ombuds, arbitration and multi-tier processes.[90]

Third, drawing on relevant global principles to assess how arbitrators and ombuds viewed the benefits of particular methods of consumer financial dispute resolution alongside challenges and suggestions for improvement, a survey was conducted between the fall of 2011 and the summer of 2012. Nearly 100 survey questionnaires were distributed to practitioners throughout the world. A total of 48 arbitrators and ombudspersons from East Asia, North America, Europe, the Middle East and Africa responded. The participants represented experienced practitioners, members of government regulatory ombuds services and private arbitration commissions.[91]

Insights from Reflection

The question of how systems of consumer financial dispute resolution can be designed in diverse contexts to effectively and fairly administer the resolution of financial disputes; how such centres can draw on emerging global principles of accessibility, efficiency, impartiality and fairness; and how such centres might consequently contribute to the health of the broader economic environment engages with insights from socio-legal dispute processing literature regarding how mechanisms can be developed to limit the effect of the power/knowledge gap of "repeat players" in institutional dispute resolution settings through appropriate regulations and policies. Previous studies in respect of litigation process tend to suggest that "haves" (i.e. large businesses, financially well-endowed organisations) tend to fare better in courts than "have nots."[92] Therefore, attention to procedural safeguards aimed at addressing structural inequities in the design and development of such systems is required to effectively address such disputes.[93]

The results of the comparative cross-jurisdictional analysis of consumer financial dispute resolution centres suggest that such centres in general offer a flexible

89 Ibid.

90 Ibid.

91 Ibid.

92 *See:* Marc Galanter, "Why the Haves Come Out Ahead: Speculations on The Limits of Legal Change," *Law and Society Review* 9, no. 1 (1974): 95–160.

93 For full discussion, *see:* Ali, "Consumer Financial Dispute Resolution," vii–xiv, 1–267.

and relatively fast way to resolve financial disputes but are not without their challenges. Such challenges include the potential for mismatch between regulatory consistency and individualised case handling.[94] Determining how best to overcome such challenges while addressing a growing number of finance-related disputes are pressing questions facing governments, legislatures and aggrieved citizens.[95]

Ombuds processes were viewed as particularly useful in providing an independent and accessible review mechanism for financial customers. At the same time, the service also helped to identify areas of systematic risk that could inform regulatory reform of banking institutions.[96] Such benefits likely explain the growing use of ombuds processes in recent years. Practitioners also acknowledged areas for continued improvement including the need for greater public education,[97] oversight and quality assurance of ombuds processes.[98]

Arbitration practitioners likewise viewed the benefits of arbitration in consumer financial disputes as providing disputants with technical expertise "where the parties are not arguing over the law, but application of financial/accounting principles."[99] Among the challenges include "proof issues, imbalance of power and information, lack of full discovery options/rights."[100] In addressing resource disparities due to "repeat-user" advantage,[101] practitioners noted the need for "good program design [including] exit evaluations [and] grievance processes to allow parties to file complaints against neutrals who do not perform well" and provision of information regarding relevant standards and rules in order to ensure fairness and confidence in the process.[102]

Limitations

The project's global, principle-based perspective was helpful in identifying relevant achievements and gaps in existing practice. At the same time, the small sample size of the survey pool (n = 48) limited the generalisability of the findings.

Court Mediation Reform

With the aspiration toward justice as a means for the expression of "dignity and equality,"[103] the project *Court Mediation Reform: Efficiency, Confidence and Perceptions of Justice* was premised on the idea that as judicial systems advance, evolving conceptions of justice are reflected in varying emphasis on the role, place and

94 See Douglas W. Arner, Berry F. C. Hsu and Antonio M. Da Roza, "Financial Regulation in Hong Kong: Time for a Change," *Asian Journal of Comparative Law* 5 (2010): 71–114.
95 For full discussion, *see:* Ali, "Consumer Financial Dispute Resolution," vii–xiv, 1–267.
96 Survey No. 1 (July 2011 – March 2012).
97 Ibid.
98 Survey No. 4 (July 2011 – March 2012).
99 Survey No. 8 (July 2011 – March 2012).
100 Survey No. 10 (July 2011 – March 2012).
101 Survey No. 14 (July 2011 – March 2012).
102 Survey No. 10 (July 2011 – March 2012).
103 Abdu'l-Bahá, *Paris Talks*, 154.

practice of mediation in civil courts.[104] How such programs, whether voluntary or mandatory, provide opportunities for party-directed reconciliation on the one hand while ensuring access to formal legal channels remains an area for continued exploration.[105]

Approach to Reflective Engagement

This project sought to apply a framework of devolved reflective engagement by: (1) engaging 83 court mediation practitioners in conversations about the dynamics, challenges and lessons learned in the context of mandatory and voluntary court mediation programs and the impact of program type, if any, on perceptions of confidence, fairness and efficiency; and (2) examining institutional developments, cultural context and outcomes of mediation programs within 10 jurisdictions using governance indicators to trace developments in judicial quality, efficiency and access to courts over a five-year time period.[106]

Insights from Reflection

Significant variation in the implementation of court mediation reforms currently exists. Such variation reflects tensions between self-determination and party choice[107] alongside differing notions of who bears responsibility for the costs of conflict within society as a whole. Given that "public means available for financing dispute resolution are not unlimited,"[108] a balancing of individual process choices and social efficiency requires careful investigation.[109]

The principal finding of the 10 country case studies, survey research and analysis of civil justice indicators indicate that overall, while both voluntary and mandatory mediation programs demonstrate unique programmatic strengths and are associated with positive gains in the advancement of civil justice quality over a five-year period since implementation, sampled voluntary mediation program regions are associated with a slightly higher proportion of longitudinal advancement in levels of efficiency and perceptions of justice with a nearly equal proportion of advancement in levels of confidence and impartial and effective ADR.[110]

104 For complete discussion, *see:* Shahla F. Ali, *Court Mediation Reform: Efficiency, Confidence and Perceptions of Justice* (Cheltenham and Northampton, MA: Edward Elgar Publishing, 2018), viii–x, 1–291.

105 For complete discussion, *see:* Ali, "Governing Disasters," vii–xix, 1–321.

106 Ibid.

107 Felix Steffek, Hannes Unberath, Hazel Genn, Reinhard Greger and Carrie Menkel-Meadow, *Regulating Dispute Resolution – ADR and Access to Justice at the Crossroads* (Oxford: Hart, 2013).

108 Ibid.

109 For complete discussion, *see:* Ali, "Governing Disasters," vii–xix, 1–321.

110 For purposes of the study, efficiency is measured through an aggregation of the following indicators:

- *Efficiency of Legal Framework in Settling Disputes:* This indicator appears in the Global Competitiveness Report. It measures the efficiency of the legal framework in settling

With respect to advancing program quality, the survey findings provide insights into the dynamics, challenges and lessons learned from the perspective of those directly engaged in the work of administering, representing and mediating civil claims. In particular, the findings indicate that practitioners working in mandatory court mediation programs identify several key benefits, including normalising party-driven resolution and enhanced efficiency through effective case screening, while practitioners working in voluntary programs identified the key strengths of such programs as the encouragement of self-determined engagement. Practitioner suggestions for improving the overall court mediation process ranged from enhanced training in cultural sensitivity and implicit bias to greater flexibility in settlement arrangements and public education. Practitioners also highlighted that key to improving court mediation programs was the need for greater party understanding of the mediation process, overcoming conflicts of interest, enhancing mediator quality, developing greater capacity to manage power imbalances and resource support through ongoing monitoring and evaluation.

---

disputes. Data was collected from the Executive Opinion Survey where participants rate the efficiency of the legal framework in their countries on a scale of 1 to 7. Data from the World Economic Forum was also used in generating the results

- *Accessibility and Affordability:* This indicator appears in the World Justice Project Rule of Law Index. It indicates people's awareness of available remedies and the accessibility and affordability of courts, legal advice and representation. It also examines the extent to which court procedures and costs affect the accessibility and affordability of civil justice.
- *No Unreasonable Delay:* This indicator appears in the World Justice Project Rule of Law Index. It indicates the level of delay in adjudicating disputes and general perception of delay.

Likewise, confidence is measured through an aggregation of:

- *Overall Civil Justice Ranking:* This ranking is included in the World Justice Project's Rule of Law Index and measures the overall ranking of civil justice systems.
- *Impartial and Effective ADR:* This indicator appears in the World Justice Project Rule of Law Index. It measures the accessibility, impartiality, efficiency and effectiveness in enforcing decisions reached through mediation. It also examines whether mediation is free of improper influence.
- *Effective Enforcement:* This indicator appears in the World Justice Project Rule of Law Index. It indicates levels of effectiveness in enforcing judgments and the delays in enforcing decisions.

Finally, perceptions of justice are examined through the following indicators:

- *Level of Discrimination:* This indicator appears in the World Justice Project Rule of Law Index. It indicates the extent to which a person's economic and social status, e.g. sex, race, religion, place of origin or sexual orientation, affect one's access to civil justice.
- *Rule of Law:* The Worldwide Governance Indicators defines rule of law as the "perceptions of the extent to which agents have confidence in and abide by the rules of society, and in particular the quality of contract enforcement, property rights, the police, and the courts, as well as the likelihood of crime and violence" (World Bank, Worldwide Governance Indicators: FAQ, https://info.worldbank.org/governance/wgi/Home/FAQ).

Limitations

The question of voluntary or mandatory program design is highly context dependent. As noted in an earlier study of mandatory and voluntary programs, "the differences in the structure and court environments of . . . programs mean that each program . . . is unique: they cannot simply be lumped together and viewed generically."[111] While the study reports on the program's correlation with the same measures including efficiency, confidence and perceptions of justice, the results must be seen as reflecting the unique conditions of each particular program and "any cross-program comparisons must therefore take into account the impact of programmatic and environmental differences on these results."[112] Indicator analyses, while providing useful insights, as noted by Davis, Kingsbury and Merry, are influenced by governance structures and also exert a corresponding influence on such structures in their conceptualisation of problems.[113] Moreover, given the existence of intervening and exogenous variables, court judicial quality data is supplemented by contextual case investigation of civil justice dynamics and survey data. In addition, given the small sample size of the country case studies (n = 10) and survey research (n = 83), and the fact that in some regions, elements of voluntary and mandatory systems may co-exist, the results cannot be considered generalisable but rather aim at offering initial insights into the dynamics of diverse civil mediation policy approaches in the selected regions. The aim is that future studies will continue to refine and develop increasingly more accurate approaches to the analysis of such relationships. Further studies will also benefit from in-depth analysis of program features, procedural safeguards and training systems leading to high-quality mediation outcomes.

Summary

The aforementioned projects sought to apply a framework of devolved reflective engagement by first engaging practitioners in conversations about study design and reflection about the dynamics, challenges and lessons learned in the development of dispute resolution programs; second, identifying relevant standards and principles to serve as benchmarks to measure advancement; and third, examining the institutional and cultural contexts surrounding program advancement in order to reflect on broader patterns contributing to efficacy in program design. Elements of both doctrine and law in context methodologies were employed.

Efforts to apply devolved reflective practice in dispute resolution research alongside developments in new governance scholarship echo a common concern

111 Heather Anderson and Ron Pi, *Evaluation of the Early Mediation Pilot Programs*. Report, Judicial Council of CA Administrative Office of the Courts, 27 February 2004.

112 Ibid.

113 Kevin E. Davis, Benedict Kingsbury and Sally Engle Merry, "Indicators as a Technology of Global Governance," *Law & Society Review* 46, no. 1 (2012): 71–104.

with the importance of community engagement and deliberation. Such efforts represent an initial step in applying principles of reflection in research and practice settings. However, reflection isolated from a broader framework of collective study, consultation and action inhibits comprehensive advancement that results from reflective practice woven into a wider tapestry of study, consultation and action, which is discussed in the final section.

Devolved Reflection and Systematic Learning

In advancing devolved reflective processes within organisations and governance institutions, it is useful to consider some experiences pertaining to the use of reflective practices in the context of community development. Such experiences shed light on the interplay among consultation, action and study in contributing to social progress.

As noted previously, several challenges have been identified in the context of devolved governance, including the potential of replicating and possibly exacerbating existing representation problems,[114] simply offering a means of providing "input" to existing plans rather than originating plans at the community level, the existence of subjectivity in rule-making, the danger of getting questions wrong through caving into power politics (as advanced through special interests) rendering community resource problems "less visible or subject to scrutiny, because the farther the process is removed from a centralised decision-maker, the less accountability there will be . . ."[115] Research has suggested that in order to benefit from devolution and decentralisation,[116] the necessary conditions for its success should include (1) the broadest possible degree of stakeholder participation compatible with effective decision-making,[117] (2) ensuring participants have the necessary skills for participation,[118] (3) the development of managerial and procedural safeguards[119] and (4) ensuring stakeholder participation in conditions of adversity and wider social conflict.[120]

Reflection forms one component of a broader framework consisting of (1) studying/reading society; (2) consultation; (3) action and (4) reflection on action that together contribute to the achievement of social justice and organisational advancement.[121]

The first stage of "reading society and formulating a vision" involves "understanding . . . the nature and state of society, its challenges, the institutions operating

114 Foster, "Environmental Justice," 485.

115 Ibid.

116 Alexander, "Reflections on Success," 738.

117 Ibid., 740–741; *see also*: Ali, "Measuring Success."

118 Ibid.

119 Salamon, "The New Governance," 1611.

120 Alexander, loc. cit.

121 Office of Social and Economic Development at the Baha'i World Centre, *Statement on Social Action*, Statement, 26 November 2012.

in it, the forces influencing it, and the capacities of its peoples."[122] At this stage "conditions need to be understood progressively, both from the perspective of a particular endeavour's purpose and in the context of a vision of collective existence."[123]

In contrast to the notion of "participation" as offering a means for providing "input" rather than originating plans within the community, the process of "reading society and formulating a vision . . seeks to involve the people themselves in the generation and application of knowledge."[124] Individuals, regardless of location of origin, can "be a source of strength, contributing innovative ideas and local knowledge which, when mobilised and used appropriately, can lead to solutions that can make a fundamental contribution" to community life.[125]

In reading society, community members jointly formulate a vision which "express[es] a general idea of how goals are to be achieved: the nature of the strategies to be devised, the approaches to be taken, the attitudes to be assumed, and . . . some of the methods to be employed."[126] Such a vision, over time, becomes "more and more precise . . . to accommodate constantly evolving and ever more complex action"[127]

The second stage, involving consultation among members of a community, may be applied in "analysing a specific problem, attaining higher degrees of understanding on a given issue, or exploring possible courses of action."[128] In each case, "consultation may be seen as collective search for truth."[129] It is understood that "participants in a consultative process see reality from different points of view, and as these views are examined and understood, clarity is achieved."[130] From this perspective, "truth is not a compromise between opposing interest groups. Nor does the desire to exercise power over one another animate participants in the consultative process. What they seek, rather, is the power of unified thought and action."[131] This has direct implications for achieving community participation and overcoming conditions of social conflict.

With regard to the nature of reflection and participation in the consultative process, it aims to be "substantive and creative; it must allow the people themselves access to knowledge and encourage them to apply it."[132] At times,

122 Ibid.
123 Ibid.
124 Ibid.
125 Phong Tran, Rajib Shaw, Guillaume Chantry and John Norton, "GIS and Local Knowledge in Disaster Management: A Case Study of Flood Risk Mapping in Viet Nam," *Disasters* 33, no. 1 (2009): 152–169, 152.
126 Office of Social and Economic Development, *Statement on Social Action*.
127 Ibid.
128 Ibid.
129 Ibid.
130 Ibid.
131 Ibid.
132 Institute for Studies in Global Prosperity, "Science, Religion and Development: Some Initial Considerations" (New York: Institute for Studies in Global Prosperity, 1997).

consultation might be exploratory, advisory or decisional in nature.[133] The process is not an "end in itself" but rather a means for "heightening collective consciousness, and fostering unified action."[134] The Institute for Studies in Global Prosperity has identified a number of capabilities needed for effective participation. Among these include:

- to think systematically in understanding problems and searching for solutions;
- to use methods of decision-making that are non-adversarial and inclusive;
- to contribute to the effective design and management of community projects.[135]

Describing the interrelationship between consultation and reflection, this interrelationship ensures that decision-making

> benefit[s] from a diversity of perspectives through a consultative process which, understood as the collective investigation of reality, promotes detachment from personal views, gives due importance to valid empirical information, does not raise mere opinion to the status of fact or define truth as the compromise between opposing interest groups.[136]

A key concern is learning

> how to maintain such a mode of learning in action, how to ensure that growing numbers participate in the generation and application of relevant knowledge and how to devise structures for the systemization of an expanding worldwide experience and for the equitable distribution of the lessons learned.[137]

In particular,

> As effort is made to welcome increasing numbers into thoughtful discussion on the direction of their collective development, decision-making processes become more consultative and participatory . . . attain deeper understanding of complex issues, and evaluate courses of action with clarity and impartiality.[138]

133 Michael Karlberg, "Media and Public Discourse: Normative Foundations," in *Religion and Public Discourse in an Age of Transition: Reflections on Baha'i Practice and Thought*, ed. Geoffrey Cameron and Benjamin Schewel (Waterloo: Wilfrid Laurier University Press, 2018).

134 Shahriar Razavi, "Baha'i Participation in Public Discourse: Some Considerations Related to History, Concepts, and Approaches," in *Religion and Public Discourse in an Age of Transition: Reflections on Baha'i Practice and Thought*, ed. Geoffrey Cameron and Benjamin Schewel (Waterloo: Wilfrid Laurier University Press, 2018).

135 Ibid.

136 Universal House of Justice, Letter to Baha'i Community in Iran, March 2, 2013.

137 Ibid.

138 Bahá'í International Community, "Rising Together: Building the Capacity to Recover from Within," Statement. United Nations World Summit on Social Development, Istanbul, Turkey, 17 May 2016. www.bic.org/statements/rising-together-building-capacity-recover-within#DfamHkoftFVFGomQ.97.

At the level of global reflection and discourse, new approaches to socio-economic development by stakeholders in the development process have increasingly come to draw on consultative principles to raise questions "about the salient assumptions . . . of the development process and to identify avenues of research and action in relation to those questions."[139] Such a process recognises that ethical and social values lie at the heart of individual and collective ordering[140] and views stakeholders not as "beneficiaries" but rather as active "protagonists of development."[141]

Consultative processes have been increasingly attempted in the virtual online-offline space, including an initiative to promote meaningful deliberation among large numbers of participants on matters of social concern. One such process, "vTaiwan," has been used to facilitate conversations on the regulation of a range of social concerns including offensive online images, ride-sharing services and Fin-Tech. The "focused conversation" method consists in defining objectives, crowd-sourcing agendas, and reflection and interpretation followed by decision-making.[142] Stakeholders contribute to the interpretation of data and potential lines of inquiry through its website, meetings and hackathons. As of February 2018, 26 cases were discussed through the platform, and 80% resulted in concrete policy action.[143]

The entire learning process, defying traditional new governance categorisation of "either 'top-down' or 'bottom-up'" governance approaches, is characterised rather by "reciprocity and interconnectedness."[144] For example, as "a group of people working at the grassroots begins to gain experience in social action, the first lessons learned may consist of little more than occasional stories, anecdotes, and personal accounts."[145] However, "over time, patterns tend to emerge which can be documented and carefully analysed" by local institutions that extend beyond "opinion or the mere collection of various experiences."[146] At the same time, such learning processes, to be effective, are connected "to a global process . . . with structures "at all levels, from the local to the international, to facilitate learning about development."[147] At the international level, "such learning calls for a degree of conceptualization that takes into account the broader processes of global transformation

139 Matthew Weinberg, "Contributions to International Development Discourse: Exploring the Roles of Science and Religion," in *Religion and Public Discourse in an Age of Transition: Reflections on Baha'i Practice and Thought*, eds. Geoffrey Cameron and Benjamin Schewel (Waterloo: Wilfrid Laurier University Press, 2018).

140 Ibid, *see also*: Wendy M. Heller, "The Religious Foundations of Civil Society (Part 1 and 2)," *Journal of Baha'i Studies* 10, no. 1–2 (2000): 27–70.

141 Farzam Arbab, "Promoting a Discourse on Science, Religion and Development," in *The Lab, The Temple and the Market: Reflections at the Intersection of Science, Religion and Development*, ed. Sharon M. P. Harper (Ottawa: International Development Research Centre, 2000).

142 *See:* vTaiwan, https://info.vtaiwan.tw.

143 Ibid.

144 Office of Social and Economic Development, *Statement on Social Action*.

145 Ibid.

146 Ibid.

147 Ibid.

under way and which serves to adjust the overall direction of development activities accordingly."[148]

Conclusion

This chapter explored what may be described as "devolved reflection" as a mode of reflective organisational practice, as an emerging norm of humanitarian assistance, as an analytic and normative framework for new governance policy and as an applied reflective research methodology. In examining the application of this framework, it examined lessons learned from research into how local engagement both responds to and shapes global norms in an effort to enhance access to justice. The reflections drew on insights from work highlighting the role of engaged participation and shared knowledge generation in facilitating conditions conducive to dynamic advancement within governance systems – whether in the form of community engagement with consumer financial institutions, cross-border arbitration or post-disaster governance initiatives. The work traces the relevance of reflective engagement as well as its potential to contribute to institutional advancement when carried out within a broader systematic context of study, consultation and action oriented toward the collective contribution to knowledge generation.

Acknowledgement

The author thanks participants at the "Advances in Comparative and Transnational ADR: Research into Practice" conference at the University of Hong Kong in March 2019 for their valuable feedback. The author also thanks Professors Kevin Davis and Richard Brooks for their kind invitation to share these findings at the NYU School ofLaw. Thanks also to Victor Ali and Matthew Weinberg for their helpful comments and input. Thanks also to GRF RGC research grant (HK 17604318) for support.

148 Ibid.

SECTION II

Comparative ADR Ethics, Standards and Jurisprudential Ideals

5

COMPARATIVE JUDICIAL CONFLICT RESOLUTION (JCR)

Between Summary Trials and ADR

Michal Alberstein

Introduction

The original presentation of the declining rate of verdicts, and the depiction of this phenomenon as "the vanishing trial," was made by Marc Galanter in reference to the U.S. legal system, both on the federal and state levels.[1] Contemporary discussions on this matter in the U.S. include reference to "the diminished trial" and the "extinct trial" and various frames of what exactly has vanished have been developed.[2] The Judicial Conflict Resolution (JCR) Research Project, sponsored by the European Research Council (ERC),[3] aims to provide a clear and nuanced definition of settlements and vanishing trials, a comparative perspective on vanishing trials in other legal systems and continents and a new model to capture the relationships between judges' involvement and case dispositions.

Focusing on Italy, Israel and England and Wales, we first ask to what extent trials are vanishing and further examine the role of mediation and ADR. We conducted quantitative mapping in each country and analysed the relationships among the stages of the case processing, judicial activities and case disposition. We developed a model to capture these relationships.

The inspiration for the JCR research project was the ADR (alternative dispute resolution) revolution in the previous century and the aspiration expressed by some

1 Marc Galanter, "The Vanishing Trial: An Examination of Trials and Related Matters in Federal and State Courts," *Journal of Empirical Legal Studies* 1, no. 3 (2004): 459.

2 Nora Freeman Engstrom, "The Diminished Trial," *Fordham Law Review* 86, no. 5 (2018): 2131; Marc Galanter, "The Decline of Trials in a Legalizing Society," *Valparaiso University Law Review* 51, no. 3 (2017): 559; Béatrice Coscas-Williams and Michal Alberstein, "A Patchwork of Doors: Accelerated Proceedings in Continental Criminal Justice Systems," *New Criminal Law Review* 22, no. 4 (2019): 585.

3 Michal Alberstein, "Judicial Conflict Resolution (JCR): A New Jurisprudence for an Emerging Judicial Practice," *Cardozo Law Journal of Conflict Resolution* 16 (2015): 879.

DOI: 10.4324/9780429354625-8

proponents of the field both in the U.S. and Europe to transform the adversarial legal culture and insert alternative modes of conflict resolution and soft methods into the legal system. Support of mediation as an alternative paradigm to adjudication was promoted as part of the 2008 European Mediation Directive. In Israel, Italy and England and Wales, reforms supported by court administrations were accompanied by mandatory or institutionalised mediation programs and training for professional mediators. This revolution has nevertheless not transformed legal culture but rather joined the prevalent push for efficiency in these countries. The JCR research hypothesises that unique hybrids of non-adversarial practices, coupled with managerial incentives embedded in the local legal culture, have developed in each country. It aims to examine whether contemporary adjudication includes elements of conflict resolution and mediation, whether mediation inside the court has been co-opted by adjudication and if co-optation should be supported or resisted.

How do judges perceive their role between adjudication and conflict resolution? How are the boundaries between mediation inside and outside the courtroom demarcated in each legal system?

In order to understand the background for the empirical inquiry, an overview of the regulative framework in each research country is needed. Each legal system allows judges to use different forms of conflict resolution, and settlement practices of judges are influenced by various regulative schemes. Legal rules and precedents, ethical conduct rules, ombudsperson decisions and administrative court reforms aim to incentivise judges' behaviour and increase settlement rates in each research country. The JCR research asks what forms and modes of conflict resolution are available for judges by various regulative systems. We examine the gap between JCR in books and JCR in action by conducting court observations and interviews with judges. Following our findings and accumulated data during the research, we ask what should be the preferred court Dispute System Design (DSD).

This chapter therefore first briefly outlines the regulative framework of the three research countries as the background for understanding the empirical findings, which are summarised in the second section for the three countries, while focusing on broader findings from Israel. The third section outlines main new judicial procedures, delineating process and substance interventions and reflecting on their nature. The last section portrays the co-optation authority journey of mediation and conflict resolution in and out of the court system and presents the challenges and concerns it raises for comparative ADR studies.

Comparative Study of the Regulative Framework for JCR

A comparison of the regulative mapping of the three legal systems revealed some equivalent tendencies.[4] In recent decades, the three countries have promoted

4 Michal Alberstein and Nourit Zimerman, "Judicial Conflict Resolution (JCR) in Italy, Israel and England and Wales: A Comparative Look on the Regulation of Judges' Settlement Activities," in *Comparative Dispute Resolution: Research Handbooks in Comparative Law*, ed. M. Moscati, M. Roberts, and M. Palmer, 298 (Cheltenham, UK: Edward Elgar Publishing, 2020).

mediation programs that are connected to the courts and some legislation to promote settlement activities by judges. In England and Wales, we witness a series of reforms, among them the comprehensive reforms that were implemented following the Woolf and Jackson reports. These reports reframed the overriding objective of the legal system as reaching settlement and defined adjudication as the last resort. The reports suggest a new managerial scheme to allocate cases and manage them effectively in order to promote efficiency and access to justice. Although some explicit directives refer to the role of judges in promoting settlement, in reality, active involvement of judges, such as issuing a settlement proposal, persuasion or other JCR activities, are rarely conducted in English courts. Cost-management sessions and structured allocation and management of legal cases seem currently to be the main effect of the new reforms on judges' work in the civil sphere.

In Israel, a series of legislative and administrative changes aim to promote settlement without framing an explicit, overarching goal. The introduction of a set of inquisitorial and problem-solving tools into the pretrial stage through civil regulations during the 1990s has significantly increased the ability of judges to promote settlement in court. Management departments in courts and internal guidelines in various tribunals have a central role in promoting settlement. In addition, the computerisation of the Israeli system in 2008 created close surveillance and monitoring of judges' case management activities. We found that judges expressed this change to be a significant factor of influence on their work. These incentives are balanced by an ombudsperson for judges who regulates judges' activities, including judges' active involvement in settlement.

In Italy, new mediation legislation was introduced in the last decade, mostly following the 2008 European Mediation Directive. Mediation was made mandatory in certain types of cases, yet this requirement was overruled by the Court of Cassazione and finally reintroduced in a revised formula. Two new instruments for judges to help promote settlement were introduced during that time in specific legislation: the judicial mediation order and the judicial conciliation proposal. We found that these tools are implemented by judges to a different extent, mainly according to the preference and style of the judge. We found no central monitoring system to control judges' work and settlement rate, except for some experimental and anecdotal activities conducted by individual judges and in specific courts.

The regulative mapping activity in the three research countries revealed diverse legal regimes and cultures in reference to settlement activities of judges. A comparison of the regulation of JCR activity in the three countries revealed differences among the types of guidance available in this field. In England, the broad objective of promoting compromise is presented and procedural incentives are offered, while preserving the traditional roles of the judge. In Italy, special formal JCR tools are created. In Israel, pretrial inquisitorial powers are granted, allowing informal space for JCR actions by judges, and incentives are provided through a computerised file-tracking system.

Empirical Findings on Judicial Conflict Resolution (JCR)

Following our research questions as discussed in the introduction, the JCR research included the collection of data on the phenomenon of court-connected settlements. It included court docket data analysis; pilot interviews with lawyers, judges and court administrators; and qualitative observations in trial courts. The goals of these activities were to provide context and framework for studying the phenomenon of JCR in each research country and to outline the scope of the comparative aspect of the research. The first empirical task was the quantitative measuring of the scope of vanishing trials, tracing the track of legal cases along the different stages of legal proceedings and capturing the relationship between judicial activities and case dispositions. The quantitative mapping of case dispositions in the three research countries revealed the following:

In England and Wales, out of 29,614,374 civil claims commenced in county courts between 2000 and 2015, 16% of the claims were defended, 9% were allocated to track (small claims, fast-track or multi-track) by a judge and only 3% of the claims were considered at a hearing or trial.

In Italy, we found that 42% of the cases in the Florence court reached a verdict, 24% reached settlement and an additional 20% were probably settled – i.e., following a hearing, parties did not show up for two subsequent legal hearings (thus ending the case according to Italian law and indicating that they settled).

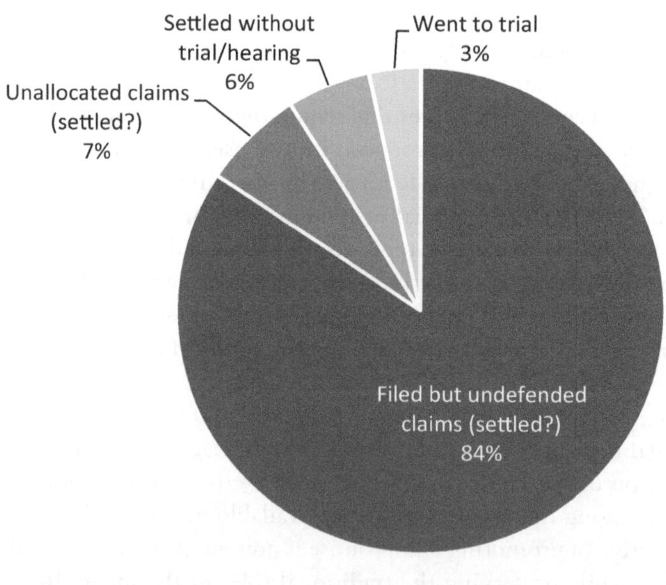

FIGURE 5.1 England – Data on Claims in Country Courts (Based on Averages between 2000 and 2015).

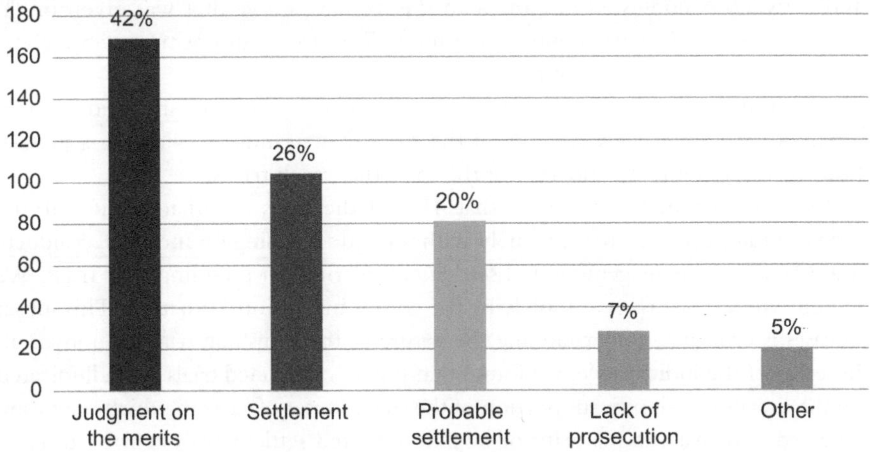

FIGURE 5.2 Italy – Modes of Dispositions during Trial, Florence, 2016 (n = 402, 100% of Cases)

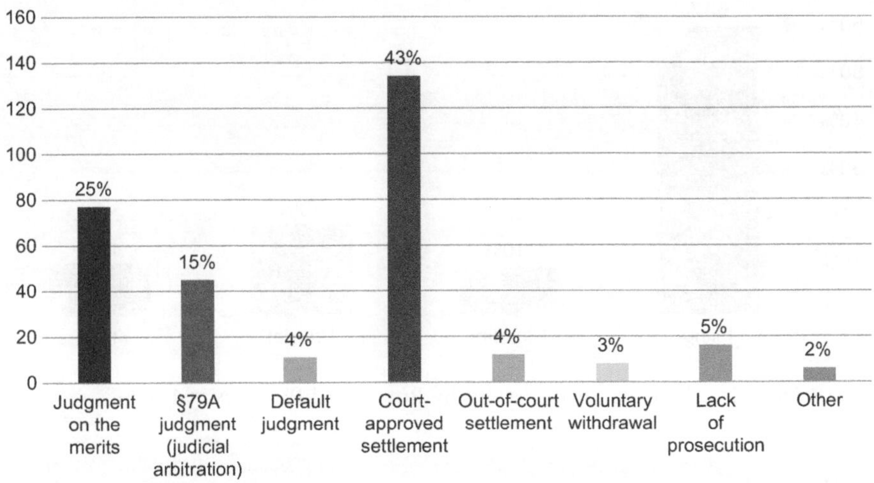

FIGURE 5.3 Israel – Case Dispositions during Pretrial and Trial, 2010–2011 (n = 309, 30% of Cases)

An analysis of a representative sample of 1,036 Israeli civil trial court cases revealed a relationship between judges' procedural involvement (JPI) in litigation and the lawsuits' mode of disposition (MoD). We found that litigants and lawyers interact with the judge in the courtroom in only 30% of the cases: 19% terminate during or after a pretrial hearing, and 11% terminate during or after the trial. It follows that the majority of cases (70%) terminate during the filing and pleading phases, without any in-person encounter among the judge, litigants and lawyers. A contested judgment in the format of a verdict was given in 8% of the cases, while settlements constituted 47% of case dispositions (35% court approved and 12% out of court).

According to the study, the subset of cases in which judges are involved includes intensive settlement activity: 60% of the cases that terminate following a pretrial hearing are settlements, and 16% of the cases that reach trial settle.

Our findings in Israel suggest that 41% of the cases terminated without any type of judicial involvement, namely without a judge ruling on motions, conducting pretrial case management and settlement hearings or presiding over trials. We identify these cases as served solely by the court's institutional function. This subset of cases is crucial to understanding the nature of the vanishing trial phenomenon. In terms of the judicial role, we found that judges conducted trials and adjudicated on the merits in a significant portion of the small subset of cases in which they were involved and that the majority of litigation-related settlements occurred in cases that included some form of judicial activity.

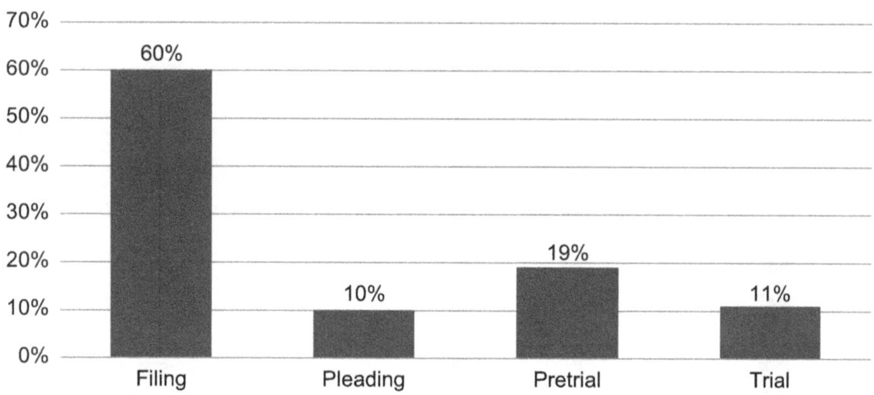

FIGURE 5.4 Israel – Case Terminations by Procedural Phase (N = 1,036)

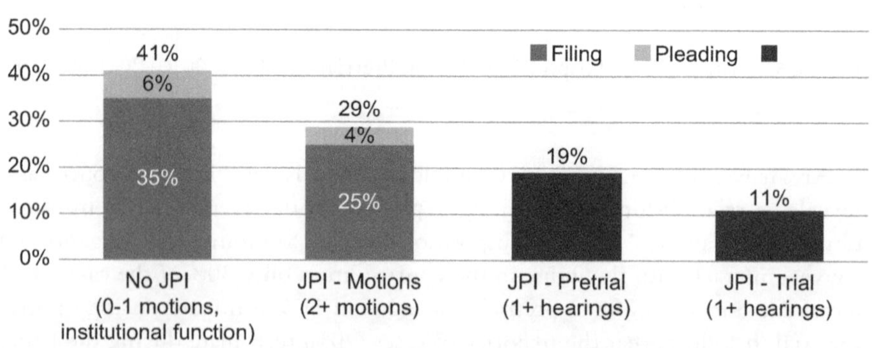

FIGURE 5.5 Israel – Case Terminations by Judicial Procedural Involvement (N = 1,036)

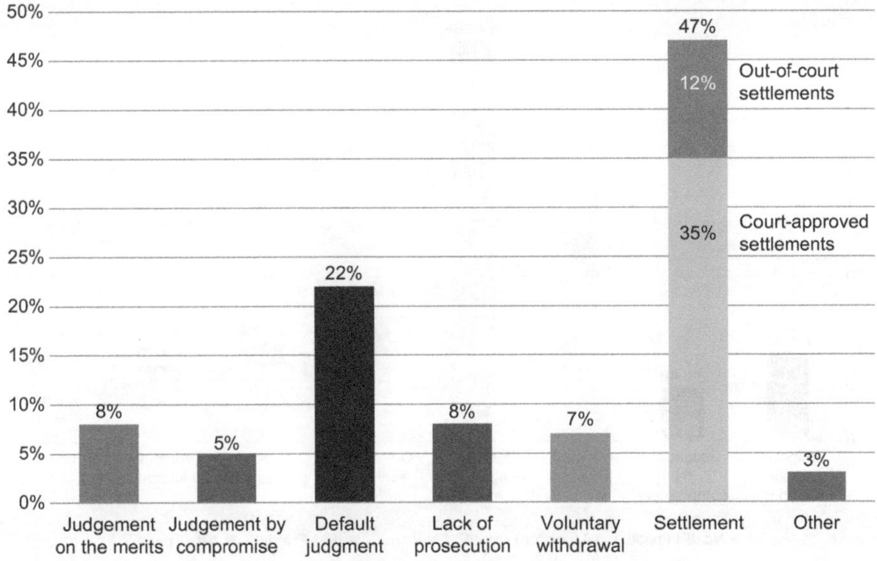

FIGURE 5.6 Israel – Case Terminations by Mode of Disposition (N = 1,036)

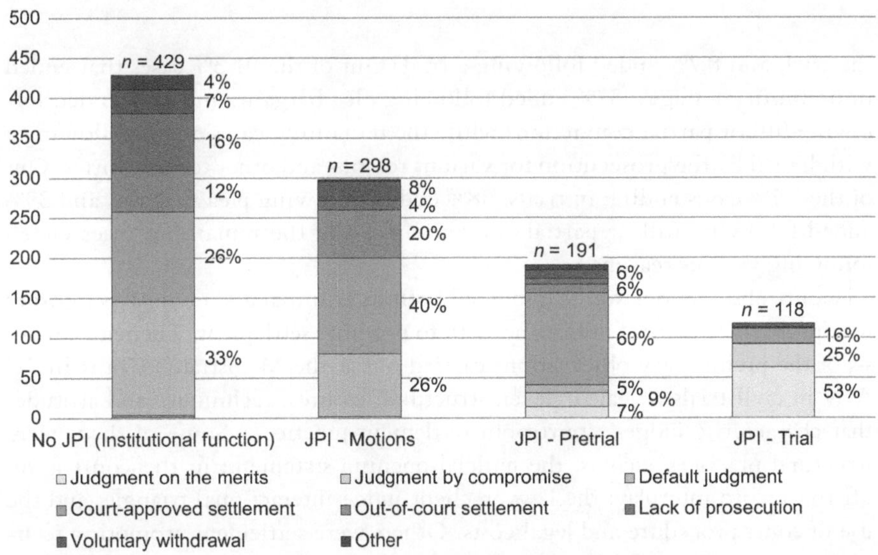

FIGURE 5.7 Israel – Judicial Procedural Involvement by Mode of Disposition (N= 1,036)

In the criminal sphere, an analysis of a representative sample of 1,606 criminal cases tried in magistrate courts in Israel during 2010 revealed that the majority of cases end during the preliminary stage of the legal process: 91.3% of the cases ended in pretrial procedures before judges who will not preside on

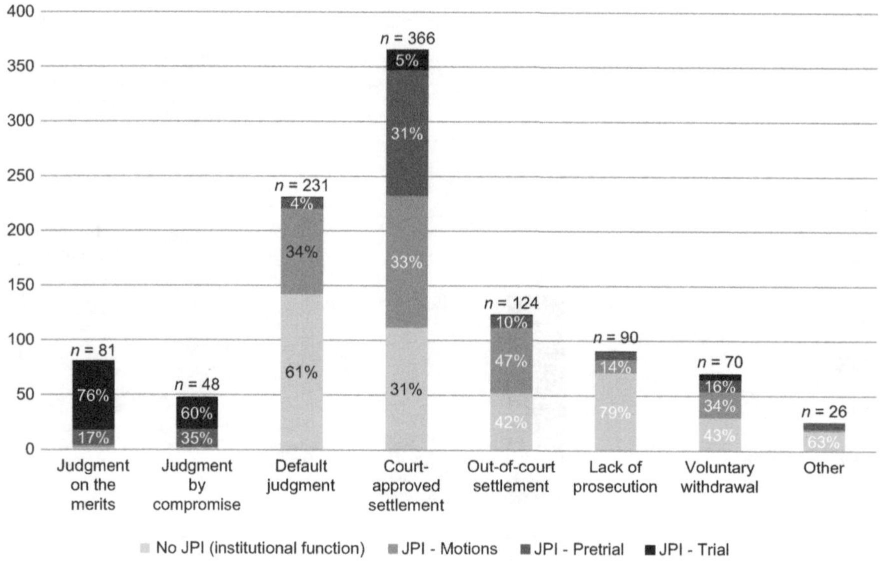

FIGURE 5.8 Israel – Modes of Disposition by Judicial Procedural Involvement ($N = 1{,}036$)

the trial, and 8.7% ended following a trial. Out of the 91.3% cases that ended in preliminary stages, 57% ended following plea bargains and 14% ended following full or partial convictions while the remaining cases ended following a withdrawal by the prosecution for various reasons and other technicalities. Out of the 8.7% cases ending in trials, 38% ended following plea bargains and 39% ended following full or partial convictions while the remaining cases ended following various reasons.

Court observations were conducted both in criminal and civil cases in order to capture the nature of judicial activity to promote settlement. Thematic analysis of the preliminary observations carried out at the Magistrate's Court in Tel Aviv in civil trials revealed eleven structural features, techniques and attitudes that characterise judges' courtroom settlement practices.[5] Some of them were structural practices such as: the judicial opening statement; in-the-courtroom, off-the-record interplay; the lawyer-client-judge interactional triangle; and the use of court procedure and legal costs. Others were settlement promotion techniques such as: direct facilitation of litigotiation, prediction of the legal outcome, procedural contracts and quasi-arbitration, portraying negative aspects of the legal process or outcome, and ADR techniques. Additionally, we found that

5 Ayelet Sela, Nourit Zimerman and Michal Alberstein, "Judges as Gatekeepers and the Dismaying Shadow of the Law: Courtroom Observation of Judicial Settlement Practice," *Harvard Negotiation Law Review* 24 (2018): 83.

there is a carryover effect in proximate hearings and a unique significance to the style and tone of judicial interventions. Contrary to our expectations, we observed only a few instances of judges who engaged in broad conflict resolution practices that are akin to ADR methods.

Observations of criminal trials in Israel were conducted in pretrial stages as well. These are preliminary hearings conducted by a judge who will not preside on the trial. In the preliminary hearings, appearance of defendants is verified, indictments are read, appointment of public defence lawyers is made and plea bargains are proposed and approved. The main purpose of the preliminary hearing is to minimise the number of cases that reach trial, and all legal cases must go through this stage. Possibilities of narrowing disagreements on facts or legal issues are considered during these hearings, sentencing is conducted and facilitation of plea bargains between the prosecution and defendants is encouraged. Senior representatives of the prosecution are present in the courthouse during these days, usually sitting in an adjacent room, and they authorise bargains when necessary. We found that during these days, cases are disposed mostly after negotiation between the prosecution and the defence without the need of the judge to intervene apart from enabling this litigotiation and encouraging it. We found that although only in a small portion of cases in each hearing day, active JCR interventions are conducted by the judges, the overall tendency is to prolong the preliminary phase and enable more hearings until an agreement between the parties can be reached. Our findings suggest that judges have limited involvement in plea facilitation and that their involvement within the main door of the criminal court is mostly managerial and technical. We compare these findings to parallel observation studies conducted by our research team in pretrial hearings of civil cases in the Tel Aviv Magistrate's Court as described previously and find that the involvement of judges in reaching settlements is more active and complex in those civil cases. Civil judges are more involved in encouraging settlements during the pretrial hearings, though 70% percent of the cases end without a hearing before a judge. In criminal cases, overall, the judges are less involved during the hearings, but in a similar way to the civil cases, approximately 70% of the cases require only administrative involvement of judges.

A comparative inquiry into continental criminal justice systems reveals that although proceedings equivalent to plea bargains have been introduced into jurisdictions such as Italy and France, it appears that plea bargains have had less of an impact in continental jurisdictions. Findings indicate that less than 15% of criminal cases in these jurisdictions are concluded through processes similar to the plea bargain, the *patteggiamento* and *comparution sur reconnaissance préalable de culpabilité*. Nevertheless, these findings do not mean that the phenomenon of the vanishing trial has not manifested in these jurisdictions.[6] Rather, it takes a different form constantly evolving in line with European Union policy

6 Coscas-Williams and Alberstein, "A Patchwork of Doors."

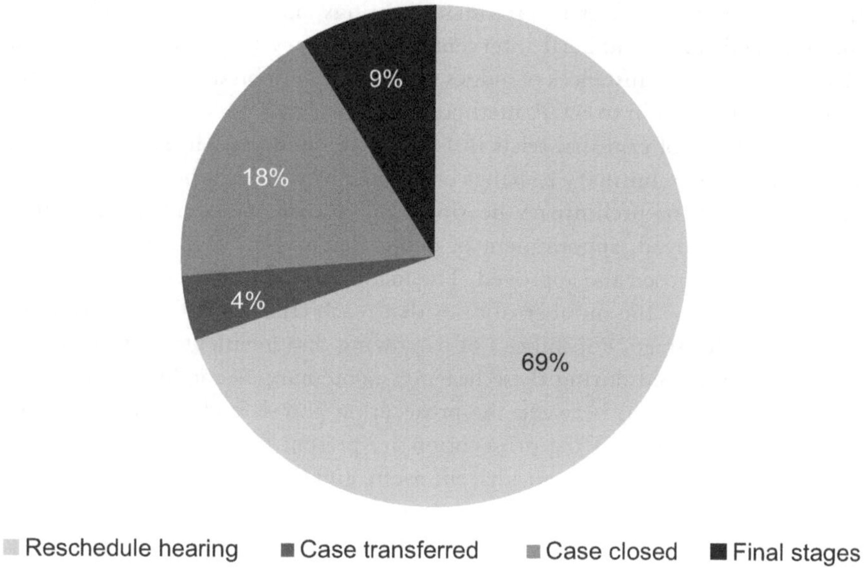

FIGURE 5.9 Israel – Modes of Disposition Pretrial Criminal Hearing ($N = 717$)

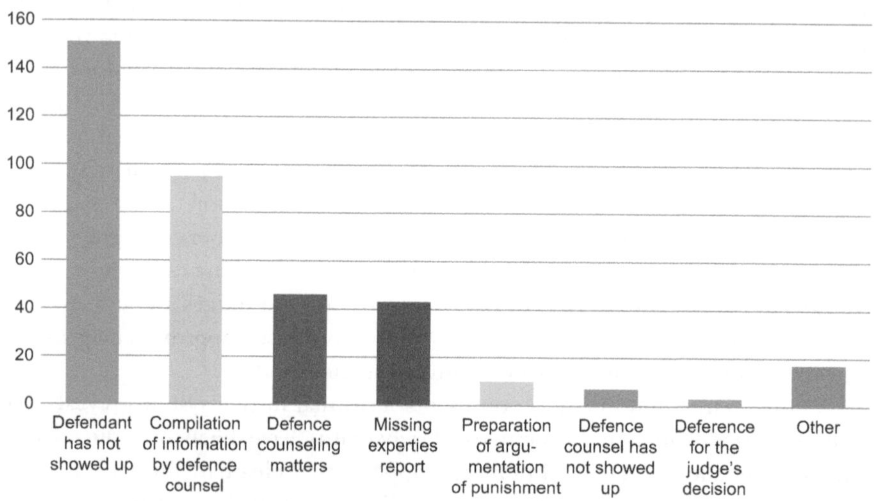

FIGURE 5.10 Israel – Hearing Rescheduling Causes ($N = 498$)

and local needs: while in the United States, the "multi-door" courthouse has evolved around the realisation of the plea bargain, in France and Italy, the "multi-door" phenomenon is different, and it is the investigation that tends to be waived. Indeed, less than 4% of all criminal cases in France in 2014 were addressed by an investigation judge.

Judicial Interventions: Between Process and Substance

Our findings both in the civil and criminal fields suggest that judges are significantly involved only in a small proportion of cases that enter the courts and that most cases are settled or reach a plea bargain without substantial intervention by judges. When judges do intervene in legal disputes, their involvement encourages consent between parties regarding process or substance. Interventions that refer to process include convincing the parties to accept a form of summary trial (Israel civil, Italy criminal), enforcing mediation through judicial orders (Italy civil) and encouraging parties to go to mediation (Israel, Italy and England and Wales). Interventions that refer to substance include providing predictions of the legal outcome (Israel, Italy and England and Wales), using procedural and administrative incentives (England and Wales and Israel) to affect the substance of negotiations between the parties and addressing the negative aspects of pursuing the legal process for the parties (Israel).

Process Interventions

Adjudication by Compromise (Judicial Arbitration) (Israel)

In Israel, §79A of the Israeli Courts Law enables litigants to authorise the judge to rule on a matter partly or fully "by way of compromise." The law provides no definition for this form of ruling, and it does not specify the role of the judge in ruling as such. However, the "law in action" appears to be that the article is used to provide a bottom-line final outcome without a reasoned decision, to render a judgment that does not necessarily result from direct application of the law or to create a fair settlement between the parties. Thus, it may be considered a unique form of judicial arbitration through which judges can create private procedural arrangements.[7] In one observation, the judge referred to a ruling according to §79A in contractual terms as "a tri-party agreement between the defendant, the plaintiff and the court." Nearly all judges emphasise that a judgment by way of compromise is final, does not pronounce the reasoning behind the decision and can rarely be appealed. In our sample prior, 15% of civil cases which reached a court encounter terminated through this method.

Criminal Abbreviated Trial (Italy)

In 1988, the Italian legislature decided to abandon the old Italian criminal justice system, which was based on an inquisitorial approach to proceedings, and introduce in its place an adversarial criminal justice system inspired by the U.S. criminal justice model. However, the transplantation of an adversarial model onto

7 Yuval Sinai and Michal Alberstein, "Court Arbitration by Compromise: Rethinking Delaware State Sponsored Arbitration Case," *Cardozo Public Law, Policy & Ethics Journal* 13 (2014–2015): 739.

a historically inquisitorial legal system was not a success. Over time, inquisitorial features were reintegrated into the criminal justice system. This newly created criminal system thus evolved into a blend of two normative methods, in which the structure is adversarial but the heart remains inquisitorial. Alongside the Italian version of plea bargaining – the *patteggiamento* – a new form of abbreviated trial (*giudizio abbreviato*) has developed as part of the search for efficiency. Inspired by the English procedure of summary trial, the abbreviated trial was conceived as a form of negotiated justice, in which the defendant may ask for the case to be assessed on the basis of the investigative file record, renouncing his right to a trial.

In return for sparing the state the expense of a full trial, the defendant is given a one-third reduction of the sentence and is not required to plead guilty. Under these proceedings, the defendant may submit two possible requests:

- A simple request, in which the defendant can ask for the case to be assessed on the basis of the investigative file record.
- A complex request, in which the defendant includes a request that the judge carry out further investigation. This request is predicated by the defendant's assertion that more evidence will be acquired during the proceeding.

The judge – *giudice dell'udienza preliminare* (GUP) – will then review the evidence, including the written record of the case, and hear oral arguments from the defence and prosecution. The verdict is delivered on the basis of the investigation dossier as presented at the preliminary hearing and ends the proceedings.

As opposed to the *patteggiamento*, there are almost no limitations regarding the cases that can be determined under this procedure.

Mediation Order (Italy)

According to the Italian Civil Code, at any stage of the trial and also during appeal, a judge may issue a mediation order: an official court order that requires the parties to attempt to mediate the case out of court. A mediation order is a detailed and reasoned document in which the judge must explain and justify the referral to mediation (i.e., clarify why the case is suitable for mediation). Judges in the Firenze Tribunal where we conducted our research were intensively encouraged to use this instrument, and specific guidance was given to them by interns and legal academics on screening cases and diagnosing their "mediability."

Mediation Encouragement and Incentivising (Italy, Israel, England and Wales)

Judges' active encouragement of parties to voluntarily peruse mediation was observed and acknowledged in the three research countries. In various stages during the course of the legal case, parties are called to consider mediation, and they sometimes must indicate what efforts have been made to promote settlement (England and Wales) or attend a free, mandatory pre-mediation meeting (Israel).

Substance Interventions

Prediction of the Legal Outcome (Italy, Israel, England and Wales)

Article 185*bis* of the Italian Civil Code states that starting from the first hearing and until the end of the preliminary hearing, a judge can make a conciliation proposal to the parties. This article is the first to introduce direct judicial settlement activity into the Italian legal system. Until the article was introduced, a settlement proposal made by a judge was generally considered an appropriate reason for the judge's recusal from the case. While initially ignored by the judiciary, we found that judges have begun to use conciliation proposals to reduce the caseload.

In Israeli civil cases, typically the same judge presides over both pretrial and trial hearings. Therefore, a glimpse into the judge's preliminary take on the lawsuit provides valuable information to the parties: a highly relevant prediction of the outcome of adjudication (albeit based on the limited information that is available in the early stages of the proceedings). Accordingly, this category refers to a judge's indication regarding the expected legal outcome of the case. In some cases, judges provide an explicit prediction of the outcome; in others, they assert their view about the strengths and weaknesses of the parties' claims. Sometimes the judicial prediction is accompanied by due reservation given the early stage of the proceedings.

In England and Wales, we found that judges barely use prediction, even in preliminary hearings, when they do not preside on a case. The Woolf report on access to justice from 1996 recommended the introduction of wide case management powers to the courts, as well as pre-action protocols, in order, among other things, "to promote more, better and earlier settlements."[8] Woolf's recommendations were swiftly integrated into the system through the 1998 Civil Procedure Rules (CPR). For the first time, the court was given a duty to actively manage cases, and this is the state of affairs to this day. This means that judges must "encourage the parties to co-operate with each other in the conduct of the proceedings," as well as actively "[help] the parties to settle the whole or part of the case." During court observations in England, we found that judges' involvement through prediction exists, though it is very limited compared to Israel.

Use of Court Procedure and Legal Costs (England and Wales, Israel)

Judicial interventions to substantially affect the conditions for negotiation through procedural arrangements and authority to rule on legal costs are common in Israeli civil pretrial hearings. Examples include affirmatively setting

8 Lord Woolf, Access to Justice: Final Report, Lord Chancellor's Department (1996).

another pretrial hearing or refusing to advance the case to trial in order to allow the parties another opportunity to settle. Relatedly, some judges reference the busy court schedule and set a distant trial date and then invoke again the opportunity for a timely settlement. Another frequently observed JCR practice in this category is judges' reference to their expected ruling on costs should a settlement not be reached. Under Israeli law, judges have full discretion to assign legal costs at the end of civil proceedings, including the amount and allocation between litigants. According to the rules of civil procedure, the judge may take into account the behaviour of the parties during litigation. Thus, judicial disapproval of parties' refusal to settle and references to the expected ruling on costs can be seen as ways to persuade the parties to settle.

In England and Wales, there is a cost-shifting principle, which entails that the loser is also liable for paying the winner's litigation costs, in addition to his or her own litigation costs (though there are exceptions to this rule). The loser does not just pay the value of the claim itself but also the added costs of litigation, which often exceed the value of the claim. Judges are not exposed to parties 'settlement proposals and therefore cannot use them in court to encourage settlement, but they conduct cost hearings in preliminary stages, providing a realistic evaluation of the expected cost in reference to the claim amount. Since the cost of litigation is very high in England and Wales, only a very small percentage of cases (less than 3%) proceed to trial after pre-commencement procedures and cost hearings.

Emphasising Negative Aspects of the Legal Procedure and Outcome (Israel)

This category includes references to uncertainty with respect to the final outcome, negative "externalities" of the litigation process (such as emotional distress associated with testimonies), reputational damage due to information recorded in a publicly available formal case record, the extended wait for a final determination (compared to an early settlement) and other associated costs. The Israeli judges we observed commonly underscored the potential negative implications stemming from factual or legal uncertainties identified in the case. In some instances, judges criticised parties' decision to refuse settlement and proceed to trial, proclaiming it irrational, unjust or even immoral.

Using the Courtroom Setting to Encourage Agreements (Israel)

Judges in Israel use the courtroom setting in pretrial to promote substantive agreements between the parties.

Lawyer-client-judge triangle: Parties are required to appear in person at the pretrial, and during the hearing, judges may speak directly with the parties if they are present in the courtroom. Judges may also ask the parties about their wishes, expectations, needs and interests in litigation and point to additional considerations that impact the parties' preferences and position regarding settlement. Thus, judges may help increase litigants' sense of participation and involvement in the settlement process. In some instances, we observed judges implicitly referring to the attorneys' interest in settlement. For example, we observed judges noting the advantages of an attorney's expected compensation as part of a proposed settlement. In other instances, we observed judges praising the lawyer while addressing the client in what appeared to be an attempt to increase the client's trust in the attorney or lend support to a certain settlement proposal that the lawyer seemed to support. Such interventions are aimed to harness the lawyer-client relationship to encourage settlement. More rarely, judges may insinuate that an attorney is objecting to settlement against the best interests of the client.

Carry-over effects: Pretrial hearings are typically held consecutively, such that each judge holds several hearings in a single courtroom sitting, usually in the morning. However, there are considerable variations in the number and frequency of hearings. We have seen judges schedule between one and ten pretrial hearings in a single, one-hour timeslot. Accordingly, the duration of hearings in our sample ranges from a few minutes to a full hour. Litigants and their lawyers usually wait for their hearing inside the courtroom, seated on the public benches at the back of the courtroom, and they advance to the plaintiff and defendant seats when called upon by the judge. In such a setting, the judge's behaviour and pronounced attitude regarding settlement in one case, or in a series of cases, can impact those who wait in the courtroom for their case to be heard. As a result, judicial practices in one hearing, or a series of hearings, may frame and set the tone for settlement discussions in subsequent hearings.

In the courtroom, off the record: The general requirement to keep full transcripts of court hearings is relaxed in pretrial hearings. According to the Israeli Courts Law, in pretrial hearings judges are allowed, with the parties' consent, to record only the main points discussed in the hearing. Under this regime, using courtroom observations, we were able to capture the importance of judges' off-the-record activities in achieving settlement. We found that JCR activities occur almost invariably off the record. For some judges, the default in pretrial hearings is that discussions are off the record unless otherwise instructed (for example, by directing the court recorder to type or by formally announcing that the discussion will now be recorded).

When overviewing the various modes of JCR interventions found in our research while adding a comparative perspective, it becomes clear that the search for fast and effective justice has a global effect on judicial practices and case processing. Courts today have gone through a paradigm shift in which the emphasis on management and effectiveness has transformed the notion of law and adjudication as we study it theoretically. While much attention has been given to judicial activities that focus on substantive consent between the parties, we found that much happens in terms of process emphasis and the emergence of new procedural contracts and abbreviated modes of trials. In adversarial systems, much focus has transferred to the preliminary stages of the case both in civil and criminal cases, and enabling legal prediction in these stages makes judicial intervention inquisitorial in a sense. In inquisitorial systems, adversarial elements have penetrated the criminal process, and abbreviated forms of trial have developed in order to promote efficiency. More procedural and less substantive interventions of judges occur in both inquisitorial and adversarial systems, and in civil cases the emphasis in inquisitorial systems is on referral to external mediation. In these countries, trials do not vanish, yet their rate decreases substantially.

The Future of the Judicial Role and the Promise of ADR

Although the past fifty years have seen the development of ADR and restorative justice and their promotion as the solution for resolving civil and criminal disputes, in practice this promise has not been achieved, and ADR processes such as mediation have not become the main framework to address legal conflicts. ADR was viewed by many as the optimal means to lessen the burden on the courts while broadening the courts' focus to address the needs of the parties. This promise formed the basis of the "multi-door courthouse," as suggested by Frank Sander, the founder of the ADR movement.[9] The vision was that parties and their disputes would be triaged in a client-centred and holistic approach. Disputes would be directed to the most appropriate method for resolution, taking into account the needs of the parties.[10] Despite this promise and the interest that it has invoked, courts have not become conflict resolution centres and have remained focused on legal issues. In our JCR study as discussed prior, we assumed that many legal cases were disposed following consensual processes and that judges play a role in many of these processes. We assumed that judges used various methods of conflict resolution to convince the parties not to pursue adjudication. Our findings suggest that when cases reach pretrial or other forms of preliminary hearing, judges encourage parties to settle yet focus, at most, on the narrow legal issues. Only rarely do judges apply a conflict resolution approach that includes the emotional and relational aspects of the dispute as postulated in the promise of ADR. Therefore, our findings suggest that most legal cases reaching court are neither resolved through full adjudication nor a systematic ADR approach.

Legal systems in which mediation has been institutionalised many times are not transformed, and there is tendency to co-opt court-annexed mediation to become much more authoritative in nature. In fact, we find that a new emerging model – authority-based mediation[11] – has come out of the journey of mediation from outside the court into the vanishing trial scene. This model could have been

9 Frank E. A. Sander, "Varieties of Dispute Processing," *Federal Rules Decisions* 70 (1976): 111.

10 Frank E. A. Sander and Lukasz Rozdeiczert, "Matching Cases and Dispute Resolution Procedures: Detailed Analysis Leading to a Mediation Centered Approach," *Harvard Negotiation Law Review* 11 (2006): 1.

11 Amos Gabrieli, Nourit Zimerman and Michal Alberstein, "Authority-Based Mediation," *Cardozo Journal of Conflict Resolution* 20 (2018): 1.

considered the nightmare of ADR pioneers, yet it is an integral part of an adversarial system in which the pursuit of settlement is the only guiding principle. Authority-based mediation is conducted in an evaluative manner, combining in-depth legal discussion with a soft dialogue that relates to emotions and interests and results in a settlement, usually following one extended mediation meeting. The incorporation of mediation and ADR into the court system has resulted, in most cases, in a failure to insert the deep values of mediation, together with the decline of adjudication as the main form of pursuing justice. The following diagram can portray the gradual shift of the originally conceived alternative process (without authority) as it has become incorporated into courtroom processes.

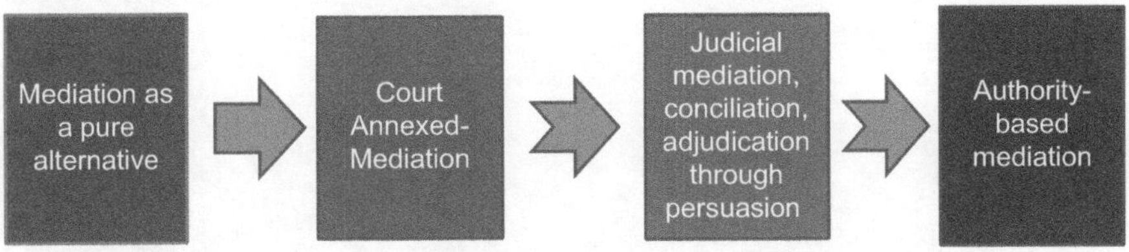

Following the relative failure of mediation to transform the adversarial model and inspire the courts with a model of conflict resolution, the other emerging model which seems to prevail is the heuristic abbreviated mode ofjudicial decision-making, which compromises some of the requirements of an ideal functioning adjudication with all its various stages and procedural and evidentiary constrains. The implementation of such a model in many cases is conditioned by prior consent of the parties, which agree to waive some of their procedural rights in return for a shorter process. This is the case with the Israeli model of 79a in civil cases and some criminal abbreviated trial forms in Italy. In some places agreement to participate in such abbreviated trials is not even needed and they become a standard form of judicial involvement.

It can be argued that the search for efficiency and the vanishing trial phenomenon suggest two possible trajectories for the judicial role: One is the more conflict resolution-oriented judge – responsive, therapeutic, relational, exercising mediation skills, a problem solver. The second is the summary trial judge – providing a short, heuristic and fast decision or prediction, in an effort to promote a reluctant compromise. The relative failure of the first model makes the parallel move to abbreviated and summary trial only natural. The problem with such a shift is the lack of any coherent justice perspective behind it. If more effective management is the overarching goal, what are the values which underlie new judicial roles? Such values could have been inspired by an ADR-conflict resolution perspective, yet currently no strong institutional support is given for this track of development. Our conclusion following three years of comparative research on the role of judges in the age of vanishing trials is therefore that unless a strong paradigmatic shift will design the court system based on the goals of preventing and resolving conflicts and provide an alternative image for a declining system of adjudication, substantive globalisation and incorporation of ADR into the court system and into the role of judges will not be achieved.

Acknowledgement

This research was supported by the European Research Commission (ERC) Consolidator Grant 647943/14 "Judicial Conflict Resolution (JCR): Examining Hybrids of Non-Adversarial Justice" (2016–2020). I thank Nofit Amir for editing work and the JCR research team for data collection and intellectual elaboration. http://jcrlab.com/

6

THE CHALLENGES OF DEVELOPING GLOBAL ETHICAL STANDARDS FOR MEDIATION PRACTICE

Lola Akin Ojelabi

Introduction

Mediation has grown exponentially in many jurisdictions and has become a globally recognised and acceptable process for the resolution of disputes, particularly those that affect communities, families and commerce, and it has become an integral part of the civil justice system in most jurisdictions. In addition, the history of the development of mediation shows that the process, perhaps due to its simplicity and resemblance with traditional processes of dispute resolution, can 'move beyond borders' and has a 'global, cross-cultural appeal'.[1] Modern mediation[2] has developed within nations. On both levels – that is, the local and global – there have been inconsistencies in relation to practice, practitioner roles and expected outcomes. For instance, there are various models of mediation with different practitioner roles and expected outcomes.[3] In some, the expectation is a settlement, while in others, providing the opportunity for parties to engage in a facilitated conversation aimed at better clarity around disputed issues is sufficient.

Although mediation has gained momentum and has settled in many jurisdictions as a dispute resolution process, questions continue to arise in relation to process and practice quality and the protection offered to mediation users.[4]

1 Nadja Alexander, "Four Mediation Stories from Across the Globe," *Rabel Journal of Comparative and International Private Law* 74 no. 4 (2010): 732–758, 753.

2 Alexander defines 'modern mediation' as 'a movement that gathered momentum in the 1970s in the United States, in the 1980s in Australia and the UK, and in the 1990s in much of civil law Europe and South Africa'. See Nadja Alexander, "Global Trends in Mediation: Riding the Third Wave," in *Global Trends in Mediation*, ed. N. Alexander (Alphen aan den Rijn: Kluwer Law International, 2006), 1.

3 Models include evaluative, transformative, facilitative and settlement focused. See Laurence Boulle, *Mediation: Principles, Process, Practice*, 3rd ed. (Chatswood: Lexis Nexis, 2005), 43–48.

4 This phenomenon is not peculiar to mediation.

DOI: 10.4324/9780429354625-9

While ethical standards have been developed in many jurisdictions, the ascendancy of mediation as a universally recognised dispute resolution process being exported to developing nations and utilised in cross-border disputes necessitates discussion of ethical standards beyond national boundaries. Ethical issues that arise in relation to exportation,[5] expansion and practice can be addressed at the global level. This chapter explores these issues. Overall, it argues that while a set of global standards is desirable for several reasons, including improving quality, raising public confidence, achieving consistency in theory and practice and protecting users of mediation, there are significant challenges in relation to jurisdictional constraints and complexity of the field of mediation as well as different categories of users and contexts of mediation. The chapter examines the preliminary question of whether there is a need for global standards before considering uses and practices of mediation and the role of ethical standards in the global practice of mediation followed by a discussion on diversity and similarities between five mediation standards. The cultural challenges of creating ethical standards are discussed, and the chapter concludes by addressing the usefulness of comparative research in developing global ethical standards.

Is There a Need for Global Ethical Standards?

Globalisation – that is, 'the expansion and intensification of social relations and consciousness across world-space and world-time'[6] – is particularly evident in economic, political and cultural interactions. It involves the way in which 'transnational actors and international institutions' influence domestic policy.[7] In relation to mediation, an almost universal access to justice movement has led to the acceptance and embedding of mediation within the civil justice systems of most nations as a means of improving access to justice for citizens due to related costs of adjudication and delay.[8] The globalisation of mediation has occurred through transportation of the process and skills training by transnational actors with significant influence on domestic dispute resolution policy

5 Alexander raises this issue in relation to the 'International Story' of mediation, which 'deals with the explosion in international mediation services and cross-border regulatory instruments on mediation. It also addresses the issue of ethics in relation to the export of mediation from the so-called first world to the third world'. See Alexander, "Four Mediation Stories," 753.

6 Paul James and Manfred B. Steger, "A Genealogy of 'Globalization': The Career of a Concept," *Globalizations* 11, no. 4 (2014): 417–434, 425.

7 Linda Weiss, "Globalisation," in *Oxford Companion to Australian Politics*, ed. Brian Galligan and Winsome Roberts (Oxford: Oxford University Press, Online 2008).

8 Ellen Waldman and Lola Akin Ojelabi, "Mediators and Substantive Justice: A View from Rawls' Original Position," *Ohio State Journal on Dispute Resolution* 30, no. 3 (2016): 391–430, 393. The authors assert that

> mediation continues to be a growth industry, both in developing nations and developed economies. As an alternative to traditional adversary forms, mediation has established a beachhead in virtually every region around the globe. Movement into previously uncharted subject matter areas parallels this geographic expansion.

and practice. Multiple actors, ideologies and processes have shaped mediation law and practice.[9]

In addition, transportation of process and training has occurred mostly without transportation of quality assurance and accountability procedures. Arguably, the opportunity to train should also come with the responsibility to offer a system for maintaining quality and accountability. An explanation for failure to transport quality and accountability mechanisms could, however, be linked to the origins and nature of modern mediation practice coupled with the enthusiasm of mediation protagonists and the assumed benefits of mediation: efficiency in cost and time for dispute resolution. Furthermore, the mediation movement was led by community organisations, and at the time it gained momentum, it was not recognised as a profession. Practitioners from different professional backgrounds relied on knowledge and skills acquired in their professions, and even in transporting jurisdictions (mostly the US), formal regulation was a later development; in some instances, it did not commence until after institutionalisation.[10] Where standardisation has occurred, it has been voluntary self-regulation where practitioners have mobilised to have a set of standards with the goal of professionalising.[11] Given the history of the growth of mediation, it is apparent that there is a need for a conversation about and development of global ethical standards which can be adopted and adapted by jurisdictions. Additionally, a significant increase in cross-border disputes as well as the universal character of mediation has meant that mediators are increasingly working across jurisdictions, including those without an effective regulatory system. A set of global standards will promote certainty and consistency in practice, improve the quality of mediation and reduce the risk of harm to users. Global ethical standards will also ensure that mediators to which the standards apply continue to act professionally in jurisdictions where domestic accountability systems are weak and where there is less scrutiny on the conduct of professionals.

Finally, there is a desire to have global ethical standards within the mediation field itself. Developments in many jurisdictions and within mediation organisations point to this. In some jurisdictions, the effort has been national or regional,[12] and in others, various organisations have developed codes of conduct for panel

9 Nadja Alexander, "Harmonisation and Diversity in the Private International Law of Mediation: The Rhythms of Regulatory Reform," in *Mediation: Principles and Regulation in Comparative Perspective*, ed. Klaus J. Hopt and Felix Steffek (Oxford: Oxford University Press, 2013), 131–193.

10 Australia is an example. See National Alternative Dispute Resolution Advisory Council, *Who Says You Are A Mediator? Towards a National System for Accrediting Mediators*, 2004. The US Model Standards of Conduct for Mediators was prepared only in 1994 by the American Arbitration Association, the American Bar Association's Section of Dispute Resolution and the Association for Conflict Resolution.

11 An example is Australia. See Mediator Standards Board, "National Mediator Accreditation System (NMAS) – A History of the Development of the Standards," https://msb.org.au/themes/msb/assets/documents/a-history-of-the-development-of-the-standards.pdf, accessed April 2019.

12 Australia, "The Mediator Standards Board Oversees Existing Accreditation System and the EU Code of Conduct," https://rm.coe.int/cepej-2018-24-en-mediation-development-toolkit-european-code-of-conduc/1680901dc6.

mediators.[13] Also, the 2016/2017 Global Pound Conference Series involving 29 conferences held in 24 countries indicates an attitude in favour of international collaboration and internationalisation of ADR generally.[14] A group of practitioners are also collaborating on a Universal Disclosure Protocol for Mediation (UDPM) described as a 'Code of Disclosure' in the absence of universal standards for mediators.[15] The next section addresses the extent to which the use and practice of mediation are consistent and the ethical standards that apply.

Uses of Mediation and Ethical Standards

Mediation is practised and utilised in many ways across the globe. It is part of the civil justice system in some jurisdictions, and in others, it is a private system of justice. It is used in a variety of contexts across many fields, including health, education, utility, consumer and government. Mediation contexts differ in relation to model, subject matter, process steps and practices. The many contexts in which mediation is used also highlights differences in user demographics. Some users may be sophisticated and better resourced while others may be significantly disadvantaged and less resourced. A recognition of differences in user demographics is important for mediation standards particularly in relation to process type, role of mediator and flexibility in relation to types of third-party interventions. A goal of mediation standards is the protection of users against unscrupulous practices, but there is a gap between the theory and practice of mediation.

Ethical standards, where they exist, have not fully addressed identified gaps between mediation theory and practice.[16] As a result, practical and ethical dilemmas arise for mediators, and ethical requirements often compete or conflict.[17] For example, there may be a challenge to the principle of self-determination where there is significant power imbalance between parties which arguably warrants a reconceptualisation of the role of the mediator in facilitative mediation.[18] The diversity in models, practice and use of mediation, as well as in users of mediation, makes global ethical standards more challenging.

In any profession, ethical standards support the quality of practice with the aim of improving public confidence. Ethical standards or codes increase 'the probability that people will behave in some ways' – that is, how they ought to behave as agreed by the profession. Thus a 'code of ethics can give people a reason – perhaps

13 For example, the US.

14 International Mediation Institute, "Global Pound Conference Series 2016–17," www.globalpound.org/, accessed April 2019.

15 Universal Disclosure Protocol for Mediation (UDPM). See https://universaldisclosureprotocolmediation.com/.

16 Arghavan Gerami, "Bridging the Theory-and-Practice Gap: Mediator Power in Practice," *Conflict Resolution Quarterly* 26, no. 4 (2016): 433–451. See also Boulle, *Mediation*, 13.

17 Mary Anne Noone, Lola Akin Ojelabi and Lynn Buchanan, *Ethics and Justice in Mediation* (Pyrmont, NSW: Lawbook Co. Thomson Reuters, 2018).

18 Waldman and Akin Ojelabi, "Mediators and Substantive Justice," 391–430.

a decisive reason – to act in one way rather than another' regardless of whether or not sanctions are attached.[19] The benefit of ethical standards is stated as follows:

> Codes of ethics, then, by encouraging or even requiring standards of behaviour among a group of people sharing views and interests, can affect both their motivation to act and the nature of their acts. When the encouragement provided by codes is reinforced by sanctions for non-compliance, their effect on these principles is even greater.[20]

A report on developing standards for mediation practice in Australia noted the 'overwhelming support for the development of standards in ADR in order to improve and maintain the quality and status of ADR, educate and protect consumers and develop Australia's international ADR profile'.[21] Having a set of ethical standards leads to positive perception of a profession by the public and increases the profile of that profession beyond geographical boundaries. In relation to global ADR, the agenda of promoting greater confidence in ADR, leading to greater confidence in ADR processes and ultimately to organisations, governments and small businesses embracing ADR as the primary means of resolving disputes, could be a driving force in the development of ethical standards.[22] Having a set of standards will also facilitate transportation of mediation in a manner that takes into account the need for quality and accountability in mediation practice in 'transportee' jurisdictions. Mediation 'transporters' may be able to recommend the global standards for adoption and adaptation by a transportee nation.

While the importance of ethical standards cannot be overemphasised, developing standards that will be acceptable to all is challenging. Addressing the tension between diversity and consistency is a key issue in developing standards in a field of practice as broad as mediation.[23] As noted by Alexander, on the one hand, there is 'a desire to experiment and develop mediation as a process able to accommodate the relationship needs of all stakeholders in a world in which geo-political borders have decreasing importance' and, on the other hand, 'a push to provide users of mediation with consistency, predictability and quality in procedures and outcomes'.[24]

19 Judith Lichtenberg, "What are Codes of Ethics For?" in *Codes of Ethics and the Professions*, ed. Margaret Coady and Sidney Bloch (Melbourne: Melbourne University Press, 1996), 15.

20 Lichtenberg, "What are Codes of Ethics For?," 23.

21 National Alternative Dispute Resolution Advisory Council, *A Framework for ADR Standards*, Report to the Commonwealth Attorney General (April, 2001). Similarly, the Preamble to the US Model Standards of Conduct for Mediators, August 2005 sets three goals: to guide the conduct of mediators, inform the mediating parties and promote public confidence in the process of mediation.

22 For example, the International Mediator Institute's code of conduct can be found here: IMI, "Code of Professional Conduct," www.imimediation.org/practitioners/code-professional-conduct/.

23 National Alternative Dispute Resolution Advisory Council, *A Framework for ADR Standards*, 4–5.

24 Nadja M. Alexander, *International and Comparative Mediation: Legal Perspectives* (Alphen aan den Rijn: Kluwer Law International, 2009), 74–76.

While the global regulation of mediation quality through an agreement on standards is challenging and yet to be achieved, significant steps are being taken in many jurisdictions to standardise mediation.[25] For example, in Europe, the EU Directive on Mediation[26] saw 18 member states introduce binding quality control mechanisms for mediation by 2017. The report, however, indicated that 19 member states require the development of and adherence to codes of conduct.[27] The EU Directive specifically refers to the European Code of Conduct for Mediators in counselling that the principles of flexibility, effectiveness, impartiality, competency and confidentiality are to be embraced by member states.[28] It is also important to note that the EU Directive applies only to cross-border civil and commercial disputes, but member states may choose to transpose it to domestic mediation processes.[29]

The recent adoption by the UN General Assembly of the United Nations Convention on International Settlement Agreements Resulting from Mediation (the Singapore Convention, 2018) will further strengthen cross-border mediation by enabling signatories to enforce mediated settlement agreements in accordance with each state's applicable procedural rules and additional conditions stipulated by the convention.[30] While the convention is silent on quality issues, it does raise the issue of mediator/mediation standards by providing that the competent authority of a state party may refuse to grant relief sought on grounds, among other things, that a serious breach of standards applicable to the mediator or the mediation has occurred. In addition, a refusal to grant relief may occur on account of a mediator's failure to disclose relevant information (conflict of interests) where that failure has raised justifiable doubts as to the mediator's impartiality or independence and has had a material impact or unduly influenced a party.[31] Thus, the convention indirectly applies mediation standards recognised in domestic jurisdictions. The implication is that there may be inconsistencies, then, in the application of and the outcomes of application of the convention. For example, where no applicable standards exist in a jurisdiction in which enforcement is sought, it will be up to the domestic courts to fill the lacuna. In addition,

25 In Europe, Directive 2008/52/EC of the European Parliament and of the Council on Certain Aspects of Mediation in Civil and Commercial Matters, 21 May 2008 has been an impetus for this.

26 Directive 2008/52/EC of the European Parliament and of the Council on Certain Aspects of Mediation in Civil and Commercial Matters, 21 May 2008.

27 European Parliament (2014–2019), Report on the Implementation of Directive 2008/52/EC of the European Parliament and of the Council on Certain Aspects of Mediation in Civil and Commercial Matters (the 'Mediation Directive'), June 2017.

28 Paragraphs 16 and 17, Directive 2008/52/EC of the European Parliament and of the Council on Certain Aspects of Mediation in Civil and Commercial Matters, 21 May 2008.

29 Paragraphs 8 and 9, Directive 2008/52/EC of the European Parliament and of the Council on Certain Aspects of Mediation in Civil and Commercial Matters, 21 May 2008.

30 Article 4, *United Nations Convention on International Settlement Agreements Resulting from Mediation* 2018.

31 Article 5, *United Nations Convention on International Settlement Agreements Resulting from Mediation* 2018.

inconsistencies in mediation standards may also mean that circumstances warranting non-enforcement in some jurisdictions may be immaterial in others.

The two instruments referred to prior are testament to a global recognition of the need to have ethical standards for mediators. Both instruments rely on states to regulate mediation practice and quality within their jurisdictions. To the extent that the EU Directive refers to the European Code of Conduct for Mediators (EU Code) applicable to civil and commercial matters, it is important to note that the EU Code is not binding on mediators within the EU and no regulatory body oversees its application. However, organisations may prescribe the Code for Mediators registered with them.

At an organisational level, the not-for-profit organisation International Mediation Institute (IMI)[32] has been involved in developing global standards applicable internationally. The goal of the organisation is to promote consensus and access to justice, and one of its missions is to 'set and achieve high mediation standards'.[33] The competency standards developed by IMI are to support users in selecting mediators, and the organisation assesses and accredits mediators based on competency standards. In addition, IMI's Professional Code of Conduct for Mediators, revised in 2017, presents ethical standards that users can expect from IMI certified mediators.[34] In revising the code, IMI notes the committee took into consideration the fact that:

> mediation takes place in a wide variety of contexts and that many practitioners must comply with a complex array of legal requirements and restrictions. The Ethics Committee members tried to be sensitive to these constraints, while moving the ethical goalposts forward toward more reflective, thoughtful practice.[35]

The IMI Code recognises that challenges may arise in developing ethical standards for mediators operating in different jurisdictions. The IMI recently reinstated its Ethics Committee for purposes of reviewing the body's ethical standards in view of the Singapore Convention.[36]

32 www.imimediation.org/. IMI is the only organisation in the world to adopt an *international* vision and mission for mediation. IMI is a not-for-profit charity registered in The Hague and supported practically and financially by corporate users and a group made up of the main international ADR service providers.

33 IMI, "International Migration Institute," www.imimediation.org/about-imi/vision-and-mission/, accessed February 2019.

34 Available at IMI, "Code of Professional Conduct," www.imimediation.org/practitioners/code-professional-conduct/, accessed February 2019.

35 IMI, "Launch of the revised IMI Code of Professional Code of Conduct for Mediators," www.imimediation.org/2017/03/10/launch-revised-imi-code-professional-code-conduct-mediators/, accessed February 2019.

36 See the terms of reference at IMI, "Ethics Committee," https://imimediation.org/about/who-are-imi/ethics-committee/, accessed February 2019.

From the foregoing, what is visible at the international level is self-regulation,[37] for instance, through the IMI and formal regulatory framework limited to the EU. Globally, the current landscape of mediation regulation also focuses on big business and high-value transactions, but mediation is not only utilised by big business and in high-value transactions.[38] There is an opportunity, then, for standardising mediation to promote better access to justice for those less advantaged and to support less-resourced nations in their quest to focus resources on non-adversarial dispute resolution. Furthermore, having a set of global ethical standards will boost efforts in achieving the sustainable development goal (SDG 16.3) of ensuring equal access to justice for all.[39]

What is currently visible is a fragmented approach to global mediation standards regardless of the global practice of mediation.[40] This theme is explored further by looking at areas of tension in regard to the ethical practice of mediation. The chapter does this by comparing mediation ethical standards across different jurisdictions, highlighting differences in relation to fundamental principles of mediation.

Mediation Standards across the Globe: Diversity and Similarities

Considerable work has been undertaken in relation to comparative mediation by authors including Alexander,[41] Hopt and Steffek[42] and Steffek and Unberath.[43] These academic works offer comprehensive discussion of various aspects

37 Alexander, identifying four forms of regulation – market-contract regulation which is 'based on free market and contract law concepts and derives from values such as freedom of the individual, choice and competition and commitment to contractual undertakings'; self-regulation which refers to 'collective, community and industry-led regulatory initiatives'; a formal regulatory framework which may take 'the form of legislative or executive instruments such as international conventions, directives, legislation and model laws'; and formal legislative regulation which 'relies primarily on legislation supported by formal institutions, such as the executive and judiciary' – concluded that most jurisdictions would have at least two of the identified regulatory forms depending on how embedded mediation is within the jurisdiction. See Alexander, *International and Comparative Mediation*, 77–92.

38 The recent Global Pound Conference focused on commercial disputes, with parties interviewed being in-house counsels and executives. See Global Pound Conference Series, *Global Data Trends and Regional Differences*, 5–6. Also, the Singapore Convention focuses on cross-border commercial disputes.

39 There is a push to have access to civil justice recognised as an important aspect of achieving SDG Goal 16. See article published by the SDG Knowledge Hub: Peter Chapman and Sumaiya Islam, "Equal Access to Civil Justice for All: How Will We Know When We Get There?" http://sdg.iisd.org/commentary/guest-articles/equal-access-to-civil-justice-for-all-how-will-we-know-when-we-get-there/. See also *United Nations, Peace, Justice, and Strong Institutions: Why They Matter*, www.un.org/sustainabledevelopment/wp-content/uploads/2017/01/16-00055p_Why_it_Matters_Goal16_Peace_new_text_Oct26.pdf, accessed March 2019.

40 *United Nations Convention on International Settlement Agreements Resulting from Mediation* 2018.

41 Alexander, *International and Comparative Mediation*.

42 Klaus J. Hopt and Felix Steffek, eds., *Mediation: Principles and Regulation in Comparative Perspective* (Oxford: Oxford University Press, 2013).

43 Felix Steffek and Hannes Unberath (in cooperation with Hazel Genn, Reinhard Greger and Carrie Menkel-Meadow), eds., *Regulating Dispute Resolution: ADR and Access to Justice at the Crossroads* (Oxford: Hart Publishing, 2013).

of mediation laws and regulation. As such, the focus of this chapter is on ethical standards for mediators. These standards are discussed comparatively to identify similarities and differences between them with suggestions, where easily deciphered, of what might account for those.

A comparative analysis of five mediation standards or codes of ethics is undertaken. The comparison is in relation to the definition of mediation embedding the role of mediators and other principles of mediation, including confidentiality and impartiality, with an emphasis on how these provisions may make harmonisation of ethical standards on a global scale challenging. A comparison of codes of conduct in relation to justice has been undertaken elsewhere.[44] Five standards/codes are examined, including the Australian National Mediator Accreditation System (Practice Standards) 2015 (NMAS Standards); the European Code of Conduct for Mediators (EU Code); the Model Standards of Conduct for Mediators, August 2005 (Model Standards); the Singapore Mediation Centre, Mediation Service Code of Conduct (SMC Code); and the IMI Code of Professional Conduct for Mediators (IMI Code).

These codes have been chosen based on the long history and sophistication of mediation in selected jurisdictions and the jurisdictional scope of the standards, particularly the EU Code of Conduct and the IMI Code. The EU Code sets basic standards which other EU countries may adopt, and the IMI Code applies to mediators who subscribe to it. The IMI Code is subscribed to by mediators from all over the world who are certified IMI mediators and in the private practice of mediation. The Model Standards is a model code prepared by a group of ADR organisations[45] and applies as guidelines in all areas of mediation practice, and the NMAS Standards applies nationally to all mediators who subscribe to it, though subscription to the standards is commonplace in Australia.[46] The Singapore Code applies to mediators appointed by the Singapore Mediation Centre.

The culture of dispute resolution differ across jurisdictions, and differences may be in relation to party and outcome expectations as well as the perceived cultural role of dispute practitioners. Arguably, these expectations, as discussed later, may be reflected in standards and principles of mediation adopted in different cultures.[47] Ethical standards may emphasise cultural understandings of the dispute resolution process. Standards may also be reflective of the extent to which the mediation field is inclusive of practitioners from different professional backgrounds and the influence of lawyers in setting mediation standards. An interesting comparison, which is not undertaken in this paper, is the extent to

44 Waldman and Akin Ojelabi, "Mediators and Substantive Justice," 391–430.

45 The American Arbitration Association, The American Bar Association's Section of Dispute Resolution and the Association for Conflict Resolution.

46 Noone, Akin Ojelabi and Buchanan, *Ethics and Justice in Mediation.*

47 Lola Akin Ojelabi and Mary Anne Noone, "Jurisdictional Perspectives on Alternative Dispute Resolution and Access to Justice: introduction," *International Journal of Law in Context* 16, no. 2 (2020): 103–107.

which ethical standards differ between civil and common law jurisdictions and what may account for identified differences.

Ethical Aspects of the Definition of Mediation

As noted prior, ethical codes set standards of behaviour for members of a profession. It is therefore not unusual for codes to define who the practitioners are as a starting point for prescribing or encouraging certain behaviour.[48] Definitions also indicate the role of parties and that of mediators. Hopt and Steffek analysed the definitions of mediation in many jurisdictions[49] and concluded that there is 'broad consensus in terms of (1) dispute, (2) voluntary nature, (3) systematic promotion of communication between the parties and (4) resolution for which the parties bear responsibility and where there is no decision-making power on the part of the intermediary'.[50] A closer look at definitions reveals significant differences between codes.

The NMAS Standards' definition of mediation focuses on process, participants and self-determination. The role of the mediator is to support the parties in their communication in order to identify interests, needs and issues; consider alternatives; generate options; and make their own decision.[51] Process and party self-determination are important for facilitative mediators who are expected to do no more than provide support to parties to self-determine. Emphasising the supportive role of mediators, the NMAS Standards also specifically state that the facilitative mediator is not to 'evaluate or advise on the merits of, or determine the outcome of, disputes'.[52] While not specifying behaviour that will qualify as support, encouraging or assisting parties in their communication, being prescriptive about steps to be taken, views to be formed or agreement to be reached is directly prohibited. In comparison, the SMC Mediation Procedure to which the Code of Conduct is annexed gives the mediator greater control. It provides that the mediator will 'facilitate negotiations between the parties and steer the direction of the discussion with the aim of finding a mutually acceptable solution'.[53] This defined role of the mediator arguably gives greater scope for intervention in the process beyond that of supporting parties in their communication. The SMC Code appears to emphasise the need for the mediator to guide or direct the parties in their discussion *aimed at finding a solution*. The mediation process is

48 See Boulle, *Mediation*, 23.

49 France, Germany, Italy, Spain, Austria, Switzerland, Norway, US, England, Ireland, Australia, New Zealand, Russia, Bulgaria, Hungary, Japan and China.

50 Klaus J. Hopt and Felix Steffek, "Mediation: Comparison of Laws, Regulatory Models, Fundamental Issues," in *Mediation: Principles and Regulation in Comparative Perspective*, eds. Klaus J. Hopt and Felix Steffek (Oxford: Oxford University Press, 2013), 13.

51 Clause 2.1 specifically provides that the mediator is to assist participants in making their own decisions. See National Mediator Accreditation System (NMAS), Practice Standards, 2015.

52 National Mediator Accreditation System (NMAS), Practice Standards, Clause 2.

53 Singapore Mediation Centre, Mediation Service, 'The Mediation Procedure', Clause 4.4. (d). The Code of Conduct specifically refers to SMC's Mediation Procedure. It provides that the mediator will act in accordance with the Mediation Procedure. See Clause 2.2. Singapore Mediation Centre, Mediation Service, Code of Conduct.

solution focused. This can be viewed both from the defined role of the mediator as steering parties toward a mutually acceptable solution and the leeway given to mediators to, in the absence of a settlement, make recommendations upon parties' requests as to how the matter might be resolved.[54] Similarly, the EU Code focuses on the process of mediation with the third-party mediator assisting parties to reach an agreement. There appears to be a greater emphasis, in comparison with other codes, on an agreement to settle the dispute.[55]

Mediators practising under the NMAS Standards may only provide advice, when using a blended process such as advisory or evaluative mediation, upon the consent of parties and must ensure that they have current knowledge and experience, hold professional registration and are covered by current professional indemnity insurance or have statutory immunity. While advice giving is allowed under this provision, the principle of self-determination is still paramount.[56]

There are similarities between the Model Standards and the NMAS Standards. The Model Standards focus on the role of the mediator within the process of mediation. The mediator, as an impartial third party, facilitates communication and negotiation and promotes voluntary decision-making.[57] The third party facilitates communication similar to the mediator under the NMAS Standards but is required to 'promote' voluntary decision-making. What the mediator can do to promote decision-making may appear wide in scope, but the enshrined principle of self-determination provides the boundary, similar to the NMAS Standards.[58] The paramountcy of the principle of self-determination is highlighted in both jurisdictions.

The IMI Code defines mediation with a focus on the process and de-emphasises settlement by defining the mediator's role as that of assisting parties in engaging in a dialogue oriented toward managing or resolving a dispute. The only difference in this regard, between the NMAS Standards and the Model Standards on the one hand and the IMI Code on the other is that those codes list other outcomes of the mediation process aside from settlement.[59]

Mediation literature shows that the expectation of reaching a settlement in mediation may lead to unscrupulous behaviour on the part of some mediators.[60] In some mediation services, a mediator's settlement rate may be a determining factor in whether that mediator is retained on the panel and, if retained, whether they are given the opportunity to mediate. It is also common knowledge that the success of a mediator or mediation program is mostly determined based on the num-

54 Singapore Mediation Centre, Mediation Service, 'The Mediation Procedure', Clause 7.5.
55 Preamble to the European code of Conduct for Mediators.
56 NMAS Practice Standards, Clause 10.2.
57 The Model Standards of Conduct for Mediators 2005, *Preamble*.
58 The Model Standards of Conduct for Mediators 2005, Standard I.A.
59 See Clause 2.2, NMAS Standards and Preamble to The Model Standards of Conduct for Mediators 2005. It is important to note that there is no mention of 'agreement' or 'settlement' in the NMAS Standards while the US Model Standards refer to 'mutually satisfactory agreement'.
60 Lola Akin Ojelabi, "Ethical Issues in Court-Connected Mediation," *Civil Justice Quarterly* 38, no. 1 (2019): 73.

ber of cases that have settled.[61] There are, however, provisions that may address these gaps. For example, the Model Standards provide that a mediator is not to 'undermine party self-determination . . . for reasons such as higher settlement rates, egos, increased fees, or outside pressures from court personnel, program administrators, provider organisations, the media or others'.[62] Of the codes analysed here, only the Model Standards specifically refer to pressure from the mediator and how that pressure may arise. The IMI Code is close, providing that the mediator must be procedurally fair in conducting the process and 'take reasonable steps to prevent any misconduct that might invalidate an agreement reached or aggravate an hostile environment'. Mediators under the IMI Code are also required to ensure that 'parties have reached agreement of their own volition and knowingly consent to any resolution', although there is no mention of self-determination.[63] The NMAS Standards refers to the mediator 'supporting participants to reach agreements freely, voluntarily, without undue influence and on the basis of informed consent',[64] but it does not specifically mention pressure from the mediator, although the provision could be read to apply to those circumstances. The SMC Code does not address the issue of party/party or mediator/party pressure. A global code may fill this gap. In addition, other provisions of codes in relation to the fundamental values of mediation may address this gap. These are discussed in the following.

Underlying Values of Mediation

The underlying values of mediation are those principles that are fundamental to the practice of mediation. The development of mediation has witnessed an erosion of some of the underlying values – in particular, voluntariness.[65] Court-ordered mediation is now prevalent, with parties having no choice as to whether they attend mediation. As discussed previously, however, voluntariness in relation to participation in the mediation and reaching an agreement or settlement remains. It is important to see how jurisdictions compare in relation to the important principles of impartiality, avoidance of conflicts of interests and confidentiality.

Impartiality

In most jurisdictions, a mediator is referred to as an impartial third party required to act fairly, equitably and free from bias or favouritism.[66] The Model Standards

61 See for example Hopt and Steffek, who write that 'the success rate of mediation, understood formally as the conclusion of a settlement or similar agreement' indicating that success is equivalent to settling the matter. See Hopt and Steffek, "Mediation: Comparison of Laws," 103.

62 The Model Standards of Conduct for Mediators 2005, Standard I.B.

63 The IMI Code of Professional Conduct for Mediators, para 4.2.2 and 4.2.3.

64 The NMAS Practice Standards, Clause 7.4.

65 Noone, Akin Ojelabi and Buchanan, *Ethics and Justice in Mediation*, 6.

66 See The NMAS Practice Standards, Clause 7.1; the IMI Code, para 3; The EU Code, para 2.2; The US Model Standards, Standard II; The SMC Code of Conduct, Clause 2.

and the IMI Code both specifically mention how bias may arise, including from mediators' perceptions of parties' personal characteristics, background, beliefs and values. In addition, the IMI Code mentions professional or financial interests or pre-existing relationships while the Model Standards mention performance at a mediation or other reasons. The list is not exhaustive. These provisions are significant because they specifically address bias based on parties' personal attributes, including, for example, race, ethnicity or religion. It also raises awareness of the mediator to unconscious bias by highlighting discriminatory tendencies on the part of the mediator.[67] These are important in relation to a global ethical code, and it is not surprising that the IMI Code, which applies multi-jurisdictionally, and the Model Standards, which applies in a jurisdiction where race issues are prevalent, both include this provision.

The EU Code simply requires mediators to act impartiality toward parties and to serve all parties equally with respect to the mediation.[68] The NMAS Standards requires the mediator to act in an impartial way,[69] and the SMC Code requires mediators to be impartial and fair to parties.[70] It must be noted that the NMAS Standards requires mediators to have knowledge of cross-cultural issues. This provision identifies that cross-cultural issues may arise in a mediation but does not go as far as identifying implicit or unconscious bias as issues which may arise. The difficult question of whether impartiality and neutrality provisions address implicit or unconscious bias is raised, and it should not be assumed that they do,[71] as Izumi has noted:

> The veneer of neutrality is stripped away by research findings that show convincingly that mediators fall far short of the ethical duty to treat parties impartially and without bias. Under current conditions, we are failing to meet our articulated goals and the expectations of the parties. Surely, it is naive to think we can completely eliminate bias in mediation. It is equally certain that nondiscrimination in mediation is attainable only with more deliberate, informed, and selfconscious practices by mediators.[72]

A global ethical standard could fill this gap.

67 This bias on the part of mediators has been identified as occurring. See for example, Richard Delgado, Chris Dunn, Pamela Brown, Helena Lee and David Hubert, "Fairness and Formality: Minimizing the Risk of prejudice in ADR," *Wisconsin Law Review* (1985): 1359–1404; Carol Izumi, "Implicit Bias and the Illusion of Mediator Neutrality," *Washington University Journal of Law and Policy* 34 (2010): 71.

68 EU Code of Conduct for Mediators, Clause 2.2.

69 NMAS Standards, Clause 7.1.

70 SMC Code of Conduct, Clause 2.1.

71 This assumption can be seen in Hopt and Steffek's work, where they state as follows: 'The success and the expectation of substantive justice of mediation are based to a significant degree on the trustworthiness of mediators, itself resting essentially upon their neutrality'. This statement indicates an acceptance of mediator neutrality, although literature shows the challenges of mediators remaining neutral. Hopt and Steffek, "Mediation: Comparison of Laws," 75.

72 Izumi, "Implicit Bias," 155.

Conflicts of Interest

All codes require the mediator to disclose situations that might give rise to a perception of, or actual conflict of interests. The SMC Code requires the mediator to disclose information that may lead to an impression that the mediator may not be impartial or fair.[73] The Model Standards has separate provisions for impartiality and conflict of interests, but there is a relationship: disclosure is required where a potential or actual conflict of interest 'could be reasonably seen as raising a question about the mediator's impartiality'.[74] The EU Code requires disclosure where there are circumstances that may, or may be seen to, affect a mediator's independence or give rise to a conflict of interests.[75] The NMAS Standards require disclosure of potential grounds for bias or conflict of interest.[76] The obligation imposed on mediators to disclose potential or actual conflict of interest continues throughout the mediation process.[77] The IMI Code provides that mediators, before accepting an appointment, will conduct reasonable enquiries to identify any perceived or real conflict of interest. Where mediators are of the opinion that such a conflict will affect their ability to remain impartial, they must decline the appointment.[78]

Determining when disclosure is required creates ethical dilemmas for mediators. Nonetheless, this dilemma should not stall the effort made in developing global ethical standards, but cultural factors may influence perceptions of when disclosure is required and otherwise. Research conducted in Australia shows differences among mediators on willingness to continue with a mediation after disclosing the fact that the mediator's children and those of one of the parties are members of the same sporting club, a fact which the mediator only came to be aware of in the room.[79] The question about whether or not facts disclosed may affect the mediator's impartiality may turn on the personal values of the mediator, which may also be influenced by his or her cultural background and what is or is not acceptable within different cultures.

Confidentiality

Confidentiality is fundamental to mediation and is considered an important advantage. Within jurisdictions, rules relating to confidentiality remain complicated

73 SMC Code, Clause 2.1; EU Code, Clause 2.

74 The Model Standards of Conduct for Mediators 2005, Standard III.

75 EU Code of Conduct for Mediators, Clause 2.1.

76 NMAS Standards, Clause 7.2.

77 See NMAS Standards, Clause 7.2; EU Code, Clause 2.1; IMI Code, Clause 3.2. See Standard III (D), which provides for disclosure where the mediator becomes aware of facts that create a potential or actual conflict of interest.

78 IMI Code, Clause 1.3.3.

79 Noone, Akin Ojelabi and Buchanan, *Ethics and Justice in Mediation*, 66.

and difficult to apply in some circumstances.[80] There are complexities in relation to the scope of confidentiality, particularly when it concerns public interest matters, minor offences and admissions made in private sessions.[81] The extent to which mediators are required to abide by confidentiality rules creates ethical dilemmas for mediators, warranting greater clarity and consistency. Hopt and Steffek report a lack of consistency among jurisdictions surveyed but opine that this inconsistency has had no adverse effect on mediation because of the application of other professional rules and the ability of parties to enter into confidentiality agreements which are binding.[82] Having a global statement on mediation confidentiality will be beneficial to new jurisdictions introducing mediation into their legal systems and will help provide a model which states may rely on for reform. It has been recommended that regulation of confidentiality should be broad enough to cover various actors and situations and prevent abuse.[83]

There are similarities in the confidentiality provisions of jurisdictions considered here – for instance, confidentiality of all information obtained by the mediator must be maintained unless agreed to by parties – but there are significant differences. The Model Standards include an obligation not to communicate information about parties' actions in the mediation to non-participants, but the mediator may complete a report providing information on parties' attendance at mediation and whether a settlement was reached. The Model Standards do not list exceptions to confidentiality.[84] The SMC Code is similar, providing that all persons in mediation keep all information obtained in the course of mediation confidential with no exceptions listed.[85] The IMI Code requires confidentiality with a number of exceptions, including where a mediator is compelled to disclose by law or by a governmental agency with authority and jurisdiction, or the information comes into the public domain or where disclosure is necessary to prevent death or imminent bodily harm.[86] Similarly, the NMAS Standards require confidentiality but list exceptions, including where an obligation exists under law, where ethical guidelines require or where it is necessary to disclose to prevent actual or potential threat to human life or safety.[87] A significant provision in the NMAS Standards is that confidentiality is based on arrangement

80 For the position in Australia, see Boulle, *Mediation*, 669–715.

81 See in relation to the NMAS Practice Standards, Noone, Akin Ojelabi and Buchanan, *Ethics and Justice in Mediation*, 61–80.

82 Klaus J. Hopt and Felix Steffek, "Mediation: Comparison of Laws, Regulatory Models, Fundamental Issues," in *Mediation: Principles and Regulation in Comparative Perspective*, ed. Klaus J. Hopt and Felix Steffek (Oxford: Oxford University Press, 2013), 5–121 at 52.

83 Felix Steffek and Hannes Unberath (coordinators), "Guide for Regulating Dispute Resolution: Principles," in *Regulating Dispute Resolution: ADR and Access to Justice at the Crossroads*, ed. Felix Steffek and Hannes Unberath (with Hazel Genn, Reinhard Greger and Carrie Menkel-Meadow) (Oxford: Hart Publishing, 2013), 3–32, 23–24.

84 Model Standards for Mediators, Standard V.

85 SMC Code, Clause 11.

86 IMI Code, Clause 5.

87 NMAS Standards, Clause 9.1.

concluded between the parties and the mediator at the start of the process. There is, however, an obligation on the part of the mediator to inform parties of the confidentiality applicable to the sessions prior to commencement.[88] The EU Code requires the mediator to keep all information arising out of or in connection with the mediation confidential unless compelled by law or public policy grounds to disclose.[89]

Another difference between codes is in relation to the confidentiality rules that apply to information disclosed in private sessions. The EU Code provides that information disclosed in confidence by one party must not be disclosed to the other party. Similar provisions appear in the Model Standards,[90] but the NMAS Standards simply require the mediator to discuss confidentiality rules applicable to private sessions with parties.[91] The IMI and SMC Codes do not include provisions on confidentiality of private sessions.

The inconsistencies between codes indicate the difficulty of defaulting to national/domestic standards and invariably raise challenges for the development of global ethical standards.

Challenges of Creating Global Ethical Standards

The aforementioned discussion points to challenges in developing global ethical standards for mediation, although this may be desirable. Staying true to the traditional underpinnings and goals of mediation will continue to be challenged by the institutionalisation, growth and internationalisation of mediation.[92]

Mediation grew exponentially on the back of the access to justice system with the imperative of improving access to dispute resolution processes for those who are disadvantaged and unable to afford the services of lawyers to defend their rights. The internationalisation of mediation appears to challenge this imperative due to the use of mediation for high-value commercial disputes involving lawyers and large corporations. While the use of mediation in this context is a good development, the regulation of mediation must consider the need for mediation to continue to improve access to justice for the disadvantaged,[93] particularly in jurisdictions with fragile justice systems. In addition, consumer dispute resolution usually involves large/multinational corporations in dispute with individuals or small to medium-sized enterprises that may not be as sophisticated and well-resourced and may require further protection to ensure fairness of process and outcome.[94] Access to justice in dispute resolution should be about access to a

88 NMAS Standards, Clause 9.2.

89 EU Code, para 4.

90 The Model Standards of Conduct for Mediators, 2015, Standard V(B).

91 NMAS Standards, Clause 9.2.

92 Akin Ojelabi, "Ethical Issues in Court-Connected Mediation," 61–77.

93 Note mention of focus of Global Pound Conference Series on ADR, 2016–2017.

94 The EU Directive on Alternative Dispute Resolution for Consumer Disputes 2013 is an example of specific regulation of consumer dispute resolution.

relevant process as well as equality, freedom and justice – in other words, procedural and substantive justice.[95]

As has been seen prior, the definitions of mediation across jurisdictions reveal the goals and purposes of mediation. Definitions and articulation of goals and purposes of mediation may be dependent on cultural knowledge and understandings of disputing and dispute resolution within jurisdictions. Dispute resolution literature shows that preference for particular types of dispute resolution processes and role of third parties are influenced by culture.[96] In some cultures, the preference may be for non-adversarial resolution of disputes based on community values and to achieve harmony, while in others, strict application of legal principles may be preferred. In addition, some cultures may prefer a role for the third party to provide advice and make determinations and recommendations to parties, while in others, strict self-determination may be preferred. These preferences are indicated in relevant literature in the distinction between low-context and high-context cultures and between individualism and collectivism.[97] In addition, because culture is not static, jurisdictions may not fit neatly into one categorisation. Another overlay of culture is professional culture, which may be driving forms of regulation and practice.

Professional culture may have an influence on how mediation is regulated and for what purpose at the global level. Traditionally, mediation is open to members of different professions who bring their own professional knowledge and values into the practice of mediation.[98] Increasingly, ADR generally is becoming dominated by the legal profession, which might result in the influence of legal culture in the mediation landscape.[99] As lawyers have embraced mediation, a model that fits well within the adversarial mode of dispute resolution is being adopted. Research shows that lawyers prefer evaluative mediation or other processes, which allow them to provide advice and use their lawyering skills in the mediation.[100] In developing a global ethical code, differences between the adversarial legal culture, which is slowly creeping into mediation practice and whether that matters, and the purely non-adversarial culture of ADR need to be considered. A possible outcome might be a proposal to regulate models of

95 Mary Anne Noone and Lola Akin Ojelabi, "Ensuring Access to Justice in Mediation within the Civil Justice System," *Monash University Law Review* 40, no. 2 (2014): 528–563.

96 See Kevin Avruch, *Context and Pretext in Conflict Resolution: Culture, Identity, Power and Practice* (New York: Routledge, 2013); Lola Akin Ojelabi, *Culture and Its Impact on Conflict, Conflict Resolution Processes and Outcomes*, PhD Thesis (La Trobe University, 2008); David Spencer, Lise Barry and Lola Akin Ojelabi, "Culture and Dispute Resolution," in *Dispute Resolution in Australia: Cases Commentary and Materials*, 4th ed. (Pyrmont, NSW: Lawbook Co., Thomson Reuters, 2018), 677–736.

97 Avruch, *Context and Pretext*, 17–20; Spencer, Barry and Akin Ojelabi, "Culture and Dispute Resolution," 677–736.

98 Boulle, *Mediation*, 14.

99 This appears to be the case within the EU and other jurisdictions.

100 Akin Ojelabi, "Ethical Issues in Court-Connected Mediation," 61–77.

mediation that allow evaluation and advice, as well as those that involve hybrid processes and practices, separate from models that do not.

There are other challenges of jurisdictional constraints in relation to regulation, including institutions and other actors. An example is the difference between common law and civil law traditions. These distinctions are, however, becoming less significant as globalisation takes hold. Nevertheless, attention must be paid to how they influence preferences in developing global standards. The challenges discussed prior further complicate an already complex field of mediation ethics. Developing ethical standards is by no means an easy task, and debates exist around what may be the best approach: whether to take a minimalist approach, which provides only basic ethical principles to be applied in context, or to be more prescriptive.[101] As noted previously, the UDPM has been developed only with a focus on matters a mediator should disclose to parties before the mediation rather than a set of standards. Whether or not a disclosure protocol is sufficient in standardising mediation and promoting accountability requires consideration. These are important discussions if, and when, developing global ethical codes becomes desirable. Further comparative research will be helpful in exploring these issues and more.

Benefits of Comparative Research

Comparative legal research is useful to understand differences among the law, legal institutions and practices of different countries, with the aim of achieving harmonisation, domestic law reform or determining the evolution of law.[102] Many methods of comparative legal research exist, including the functional method, which seeks to identify solutions to legal problems, particularly whether different jurisdictions have similar solutions to legal problems without considering structure and context.

Another method is the structural approach, which focusses on the legal 'structures hidden within the phenomenon being studied'.[103] The analytical method is used to determine similarities and differences in legal concepts, and the law-in-context method (socio-legal research) considers the context in which the law and its institutions operate. In particular, 'law in context aims at *understanding* the law, as a foreigner to that legal system and, hence, *explaining* why the law is as it is'.[104] The historical method focuses on the 'historical origins of the present-day

101 See Ellen Waldman, ed., *Mediation Ethics: cases and Commentaries* (San Francisco, CA: Jossey-Bass, A Wiley Imprint, 2011); Omer Shapira, *A Theory of Mediators' Ethics – Foundations, Rationale, and Application* (Cambridge: Cambridge University Press, 2016); Noone, Akin Ojelabi and Buchanan, *Ethics and Justice in Mediation*.

102 Mark Van Hoecke, "Methodology and Comparative Legal Research," *Law and Method*. https://doi.org/10.5553/REM/.000010, accessed March 2019.

103 Van Hoecke, "Methodology and Comparative Legal Research."

104 Ibid.

laws'.[105] Van Hoecke argues that one method may be insufficient for comparative legal research and that structural and analytical methods will generate better results and greater understanding of the phenomenon when combined with the law-in-context method. In relation to the development of global ethical standards, comparative research using a combination of methods, which includes the law-in-context method, will lead to greater understanding of ethical standards and the usefulness of those standards in practice, including the results.

Comparative research in relation to ethical standards may focus on questions of how ethical rules operate in practice, whether ethical dilemmas faced by mediators are similar across jurisdictions, whether relevant ethical rules assist in addressing them and whether existing ethical rules apply and are sufficient in all mediation contexts. Conducting empirical research will generate robust data based on which a conversation may be had of the need for, and the benefits of, developing global ethical standards.[106]

Conclusion

This chapter explored the desirability of developing global ethical standards for mediation and the challenges that might arise due to the complexity of multi-field, multi-context and multi-jurisdictional uses of mediation for the resolution of civil and commercial disputes. While developing global ethical standards is clearly challenging, comparative research which seeks to understand approaches to regulation in various jurisdictions and how such regulation applies in practice assist to resolve ethical dilemmas, promote quality and public confidence in mediation is desirable. Without such research, overcoming the challenges of developing global standards for mediation practice will be difficult. As noted prior, significant work has been completed in relation to some aspects of regulation, but more work is required.

105 Ibid.

106 An example of a similar research is reported in Noone, Akin Ojelabi and Buchanan, *Ethics and Justice in Mediation*.

SECTION III

Comparative Approaches in Mediation and Arbitration

7

INTERNATIONAL COMPARATIVE MEDIATION LAW

Hong Kong and Singapore in Perspective

Nadja Alexander

Introduction

Contemporary mediation systems are emerging throughout Asia. In 2019, 16 jurisdictions from Asia and the Pacific region signed the UN Convention on International Settlement Agreements Resulting from Mediation (the Singapore Convention),[1] including Asia's three largest economies,[2] five Association of Southeast Asian Nations (ASEAN) countries and seven members of the Regional Comprehensive Economic Partnership (RCEP).[3]

Why is this important? In a strict legal sense, the Singapore Convention is an instrument to facilitate the enforcement of international mediated settlement agreements (iMSAs). However, its broader objective is to facilitate cross-border trade and investment. This is reflected in its preamble, which reiterates the view that "the establishment of a framework for [iMSAs] that is acceptable to States with different legal, social and economic systems would contribute to the development of harmonious international economic relations."[4]

1 UN General Assembly (UNGA), Resolution 73/198, United Nations Convention on International Settlement Agreements Resulting from Mediation (December 20, 2018). These are Brunei, China, India, Kazakhstan, Lao PDR, Malaysia, Maldives, Philippines, Singapore, South Korea, Sri Lanka, Timor-Leste, Turkey, Fiji, Palau and Samoa.

2 Namely, China, India and South Korea.

3 The RCEP includes the 10 ASEAN states, plus China, Japan, South Korea, Australia and New Zealand.

4 Recital 3 of the preamble of the Singapore Convention. The UNGA has noted that the use of mediation "results in significant benefits, such as reducing the instances where a dispute leads to the termination of a commercial relationship, facilitating the administration of international transactions by commercial parties and producing savings in the administration of justice by States." UNGA, Resolution 57/18, Model Law on International Commercial Conciliation of UNCITRAL, A/Res/57/18 (January 24, 2003). See also recital 6 of Council Directive 2008/52/EC, Certain Aspects of Mediation in Civil and Commercial Matters, 2008 O.J. (L 136) 3, which acknowledges mediation's benefits.

DOI: 10.4324/9780429354625-11

The Singapore Convention promises to leave a significant impact on both international dispute resolution and trade and investment flows. According to Edna Sussman, the Convention has also inspired proposed changes to the International Centre for Settlement of Investment Disputes (ICSID) rules on conciliation such that parties to ICSID conciliation can sign settlement agreements that would benefit from the Singapore Convention's iMSA enforcement regime.[5] Matthew S. Erie observes that global capital flows post-2008 increasingly occur within Asia, which means that more cross-border disputes are being resolved in the region.[6] In this regard, naming the Convention after an Asian city-state may be serendipitous symbolism. The Convention has the capacity to enhance mediation's attractiveness within regional initiatives, such as the Belt and Road Initiative (BRI),[7] and support regional economic growth, which continues despite the global downturn following Covid-19.[8]

International commercial disputes form part of the cost of doing business. But how much conflict actually costs depends on how disputes are managed and resolved. From a user perspective, the Singapore Convention offers a risk-management mechanism accessible in terms of its commercial and cultural sensitivity, flexibility and affordability to cross-border business players – be it multinational corporations; micro, small and medium enterprises (MSMEs); indigenous communities; governments of emerging economies; or industrialised states. Further, the Convention will support the regulatory robustness of cross-border online mediation initiatives, which have surged in the wake of pandemic-related travel restrictions.[9]

During this period of growth in, and digitisation of, mediation practice, choices concerning mediation law's design and implementation will directly and significantly impact how mediation develops (or not) globally. Vitally, such choices must be informed by:

- insights from jurisdictions with experience regulating (cross-border) mediation and relevant empirical evidence;

5 Edna Sussman, "The Singapore Convention – Promoting the Enforcement and Recognition of International Mediated Settlement Agreements," *ICC Dispute Resolution Bulletin* 3 (2018): 54, citing ICSID Secretariat, "Proposals for Amendment of the ICSID Rules – Synopsis," vol. 1 (August 2, 2018), para 95, https://icsid.worldbank.org/sites/default/files/amendments/volume-1/Synopsis_English.pdf.

6 Matthew S. Erie, "The New Legal Hubs: The Emergent Landscape of International Commercial Dispute Resolution," *Virginia Journal of International Law* 60, no. 2 (2020): 227.

7 World Bank, "Belt and Road Initiative," March 29, 2018, www.worldbank.org/en/topic/regional-integration/brief/belt-and-road-initiative.

8 International Monetary Fund, "World Economic Outlook, April 2019: Growth Slowdown, Precarious Recovery," April 2019, www.imf.org/en/Publications/WEO/Issues/2019/03/28/world-economic-outlook-april-2019#Chapter%202. According to 2019 figures, Asia accounted for almost two-thirds of global growth.

9 See, for example, the proposed Asia-Pacific Economic Cooperation (APEC)-wide online dispute resolution (ODR) framework set to provide access to commercial justice for MSMEs in cross-border business-to-business (B2B) disputes. Asia-Pacific Economic Cooperation, "APEC Collaborative Framework for Online Dispute Resolution of Cross-Border Business-to-Business Disputes – Endorsed," August 2019, http://mddb.apec.org/Documents/2019/EC/EC2/19_ec2_022.pdf. On ODR, see the commentary to Art. 2(2).

- available resources that may support mediation law and its implementation, for example, existing laws, infrastructure and institutions; and
- the expertise of the professional mediation community.

To this end, I take a deep dive into the laws applicable to cross-border commercial mediation in two Asian jurisdictions considered leaders in dispute resolution: Hong Kong and Singapore. Throughout the past decade, I have been active in the professional mediation community in both jurisdictions, first Hong Kong and then Singapore, and contributed to their regulatory initiatives on mediation. It is from this dual "insider/outsider" perspective that this chapter is situated, as it draws upon empirical studies, academic literature and legal analysis throughout.

Before introducing a framework for comparison, it should be emphasised that law is essential but not sufficient to build mediation capacity. Equally essential are aspects of the mediation ecosystem such as infrastructure, including digital technology, a cadre of professional mediators, institutions offering international mediation services, regulatory and institutional connections between mediation and other dispute resolution systems like arbitration and litigation, a supportive judiciary, ongoing educational initiatives and monitoring and review mechanisms. This chapter targets one piece of the mediation puzzle – law.

Law forms the foundation of mediation systems and international mediation hubs. As Gloria Lim states, commercial dispute resolution users value "a sound, transparent and predictable trusted legal framework and environment." Where mediation clauses are drafted years before disputes arise, "commercial parties [must] be assured that with the passage of time, such clauses remain honoured . . . as the parties had envisaged."[10] In the Singapore Convention's wake and with much institutional and regulatory activity in the investor-state mediation space,[11] designing and implementing comprehensive (cross-border) mediation law will be an important initial task across jurisdictions.

Meaning of Mediation "Law" and "Regulation"

Not all mediation law is contained in legislation. In fact, statutory intervention alone captures only a thin slice of how cross-border mediation practice is regulated; further, it represents an outdated view of regulation. Contemporary theories suggest that the terms "regulation" and "law" have broad meaning that include notions of soft and hard law, embrace pluralistic thinking and view regulation as a system composed of a range of regulatory instruments and interactions with diverse mediation stakeholders.[12] In the mediation context,

10 Gloria Lim, "International Commercial Mediation: The Singapore Model," *SAcLJ* 31 (2019): 386–387.

11 Rules or guides concerning investor-state mediation have been published in recent years by the International Bar Association (2012), the Energy Charter Secretariat (2016) and ICSID (2022).

12 See Christine Parker et al., eds., *Regulating Law* (Oxford: Oxford University Press, 2004) especially: Hugh Collins, "Regulating Contract Law," 29, Colin Scott, "Regulating Constitutions," 227, and

the involvement of various regulatory actors leads to engagement with forms of so-called soft law, such as codes of conduct, institutional mediation rules and standard mediation agreements and clauses. In addition, regulation by private contract (specific mediation agreements and clauses adapted to client needs) and the market laws of supply and demand play important roles in shaping the regulatory landscape. Soft forms of regulation are generally more responsive to changing circumstances. Whereas legislation often applies generally and even mandatorily, mediation agreements only bind their parties and may be varied to suit their needs (albeit subject to overriding legislation).

With globalisation, regulatory activities can expand beyond boundaries and occur increasingly on an international scale (led, for example, by professional mediation communities and international law firms and corporations). These equally offer opportunities for harmonisation and (through their adaptive nature) diversity. As argued elsewhere, both diversity and harmonisation are important values, and their tensions are vital to achieving sustainable and responsive international mediation practice.[13] As a result, a mix of regulatory forms is desirable.[14]

Turning from the form of law to its contents, the key question is what aspects of mediation law might be regulated. A useful approach for comparing the content of mediation laws is to consider four key functions such laws may serve:[15]

1. facilitating access to mediation pathways and triggering the mediation process (triggering mechanisms);
2. regulating the conduct of the mediation (process and procedure);
3. supporting the development and recognition of the mediation profession (professional and ethical standards); and

---

John Braithwaite and Christine Parker, "Conclusion," 270 *ff*; Peter Drahos, ed., *Regulatory Theory: Foundations and Applications* (Australian National University Press, 2017), especially "Section 2: Theories and Concepts of Regulation," 115–247; Klaus J. Hopt and Felix Steffek, "Chapter 1 Mediation: Comparison of Laws, Regulatory Models, Fundamental Issues," in Klaus J. Hopt and Felix Steffek, eds., *Mediation: Principles and Regulation in Comparative Perspective* (Oxford: Oxford University Press, 2013), 114.

13 Nadja M. Alexander, "Harmonization and Diversity in the Private International Law of Mediation: The Rhythms of Regulatory Reform," in Hopt and Steffek, eds., *Mediation: Principles and Regulation*.

14 For example, see Council Directive 2008/52/EC, Certain Aspects of Mediation in Civil and Commercial Matters, 2008 O.J. (L 136) 3. The Directive identifies aspects of mediation requiring regulation by member-states. The recitals recognise different forms of regulation, including self-regulation (recital 14), referring to the European Code of Conduct for Mediators, and market-based solutions (recital 17). Recital 16 encourages member-states to ensure appropriate quality control mechanisms for mediation services. Article 4 requires member-states to encourage mediators and mediation organisations to adhere to voluntary codes of conduct and other quality control mechanisms.

15 For an application of this functional content approach to analysing mediation law, see Nadja M. Alexander, *International and Comparative Mediation: Legal Perspectives* (Alphen aan den Rijn: Kluwer Law International, 2009), and Nadja Alexander, Sabine Walsh and Martin Svatos, eds., *EU Mediation Law Handbook: Regulatory Robustness Ratings for Mediation Regimes* (Alphen aan den Rijn: Wolters Kluwer, 2017).

4. protecting participants by clarifying their respective rights and obligations (rights and obligations).

Bringing regulatory form and content together, we can now ask: what aspects of mediation are regulated *and how*? Comprehensive regimes for mediation strategically combine diverse regulatory forms (hard and soft law) to fulfil the four aforementioned functions. Further, it is important how well harmonised cross-border and domestic mediation regulations are. These issues are examined in the following.[16]

Armed with this inclusive and structured definition of mediation law, let us turn to the case study jurisdictions, Hong Kong and Singapore.

Two Asian Cities

While cross-border mediation practice remains in its infancy, there are signs of its emergence as a standalone dispute resolution process and a part of mixed mode procedures.[17] Already leading international arbitration hubs[18] with strong rule of law and business legislation rankings,[19] Hong Kong and Singapore are leading the way in creating legal environments supportive of cross-border mediation.[20]

16 See the later section entitled "Congruence of Laws."

17 Nadja Alexander, Vakhtang Giorgadze and Allison Goh, "Singapore International Dispute Resolution Academy International Dispute Resolution Survey (SIDRA Survey): 2020 Final Report," 5–6, 46–60, 71–76, https://sidra.smu.edu.sg/sites/sidra.smu.edu.sg/files/survey/index.html.

18 The SIDRA Survey identified Singapore as the most commonly used arbitration seat, with Hong Kong ranking third. The Singapore International Arbitration Centre (SIAC) was selected as the most commonly used arbitration institution, with the Hong Kong International Arbitration Centre (HKIAC) in fourth place: see 34 and 39. See also White & Case LLP and Queen Mary University of London School of International Arbitration, "2018 International Arbitration Survey: The Evolution of International Arbitration," May 9, 2018, 9 and 13 (the 2018 Queen Mary Survey), which revealed that Singapore and Hong Kong were the third and fourth most preferred international arbitration seats respectively, while the SIAC and HKIAC were the third and fourth most preferred institutions.

19 Both placed within the top three Asian countries in the World Justice Project "Rule of Law Index 2020," https://worldjusticeproject.org/sites/default/files/documents/WJP-ROLI-2020-Online_0.pdf. In the Global Competitiveness Report 2019, both countries ranked within the top three under the 'efficiency of legal framework in settling disputes' sub-factor: "Global Competitiveness Report 2019," World Economic Forum, http://www3.weforum.org/docs/WEF_TheGlobalCompetitivenessReport2019.pdf. In the International Institute for Management Development (IMD) World Competitiveness Ranking, 'business legislation' was a key attractiveness indicator for both: "Competitiveness Country Profiles," IMD World Competitiveness Centre, https://imd.cld.bz/IMD-World-Competitiveness-Booklet-2022/102/. In the Fraser Institute's "Economic Freedom of the World" 2020 annual report, both were ranked top two in Asia for 'legal system and property rights': "Economic Freedom of the World: Annual Report 2020," Fraser Institute, 4 and 11–15, www.fraserinstitute.org/sites/default/files/economic-freedom-of-the-world-2020.pdf.

20 On the emergence of Hong Kong and Singapore as dispute resolution hubs, see Nobumichi Teramura, Shahla Ali, and Anselmo Reyes, "On Expanding Asia-Pacific Frontiers for International Dispute Resolution: Conclusions and Recommendations," in Luke Nottage, et al., eds., *New Frontiers in Asia-Pacific International Arbitration and Dispute Resolution* (Alphen aan den Rijn: Wolters Kluwer, 2020), and Erie, "The New Legal Hubs".

It was not until the 1990s,[21] around the time when mediation was becoming a credible commercial dispute resolution mechanism in England, that the mediation phenomenon emerged in Hong Kong and Singapore. At government and institutional levels, both have embraced mediation as a policy congruent with Asian cultures.[22] In Hong Kong, principles of harmony feature in academic and policy presentations on mediation.[23] In multi-ethnic and multi-religious Singapore, mediation is considered central to sustaining Singapore's social fabric.[24] The term "mediAsian" was coined to symbolise the strong relationship Asian cultures have with mediation, in both historical and contemporary settings.[25]

While neither country was an early adopter of generally applicable mediation legislative frameworks, this has become an advantage for regulating cross-border commercial mediation, enabling both jurisdictions to cherry-pick from diverse mediation legal regimes around the world.[26] Next, a contextual overview of

21 Loukas A. Mistelis, "ADR in England and Wales: A Successful Case of Public Private Partnership," in Nadja Alexander, ed., *Global Trends in Mediation*, 2nd ed. (Alphen aan den Rijn: Kluwer Law International, 2006), 144.

22 See, for example, the Foreword of Department of Justice of The Government of the Hong Kong Special Administrative Region, "Report of the Working Group on Mediation," February 2010, www.doj.gov.hk/en/legal_dispute/pdf/med20100208e.pdf; Jaime Lye, "Mediating the ASEAN Way," in Joel Lee and Marcus Lim, eds., *Contemporary Issues in Mediation Volume 1* (Singapore: World Scientific, 2016); Parliament of Singapore, "White Paper on Shared Values," Paper Cmd No. 1 of 1991: para 4; Tan Dawn Wei, "Singapore, China to Set up Mediators' Panel for Belt and Road Projects," *The Straits Times*, January 25, 2019, www.straitstimes.com/asia/east-asia/singapore-china-to-set-up-mediators-panel-for-belt-and-road-projects, referring to a speech by the then-Minister of State for Law and Health, Mr Edwin Tong. On mediation and Asian values, see also "Asian Culture: A Definitional Challenge" in Joel Lee and Teh Hwee Hwee, eds., *An Asian Perspective on Mediation* (Singapore: Academy Publishing, 2009), 55–57; Joan V. Bondurant, *Conquest of Violence: The Gandhian Philosophy of Conflict* (Berkeley: University of California Press, 1965), 195; Thomas Weber, "Gandhian Philosophy, Conflict Resolution Theory and Practical Approaches to Negotiation," *Journal of Peace Research* 38, no. 4 (2001): 495. See also Eunice Chua, "The Singapore Convention on Mediation – A Brighter Future for Asian Dispute Resolution," *Asian Journal of International Law* 9 (2019): 203–205.

23 Jeffrey K. L. Lee, "Mediation in Mainland China and Hong Kong: Can They Learn from Each Other?" *City University of Hong Kong, CityU Institutional Repository* (2013). See also: The Hon Chief Justice Andrew Kwok-nang Li at the conference on "Mediation in Hong Kong: The Way Forward," November 30, 2007, www.hkcfa.hk/filemanager/speech/en/upload/68/Speech%20by%20the%20Chief%20Justice%20at%20Mediation%20Conference(30-11-2007)en.pdf and The Hon Madam Justice Lisa Wong's speech at the "Mediate First" Pledge Mediation Forum 2019, May 24, 2019, https://mediation.judiciary.hk/en/doc/The%20Hon%20Madam%20Justice%20Lisa%20Wong%27s%20speech%20at%20the%20the%20Mediate%20First%20Pledge%20Mediation%20Forum%202019.pdf.

24 Pravin Prakash, "The Leviathan and its Muscular Management of Social Cohesion in Singapore," in *Social Cohesion in Asia: Historical Origins, Contemporary Shapes and Future Dynamics*, Aurel Croissant and Peter Walkenhorst (Oxfordshire: Routledge, 2019).

25 George Lim SC, "Back to 'MediAsian'," July 2014, www.mediatewith.me/portfolio/back-to-mediasian-august-2014/.

26 Singapore's ADR Committee Report of 1997 states, "Singapore can take an eclectic approach. We should select the best features from these and other countries." *Report of the Committee on Alternative Dispute Resolution* (1997), 3, as reported in Lim, "The Singapore Model," 381.

mediation law in Hong Kong and Singapore is offered, followed by a comparative review.

Hong Kong: Background and Context

Hong Kong's development as a centre for international dispute resolution has been described as "organic."[27] Mediation as an alternative dispute resolution (ADR) form first appeared in the 1980s[28] and 1990s, primarily on an ad hoc basis.[29] In 2007 Hong Kong's then chief executive foreshadowed a transformation of the dispute resolution landscape through mediation, and its commitment to promoting the development of mediation locally, regionally and internationally has since been repeatedly reaffirmed.[30] While most initiatives focus generally on mediation in civil and commercial disputes, their reach extends to cross-border matters as policymakers envisaged.

A number of significant Department of Justice initiatives include:

- The Working Group on Mediation (2008–2010), which produced the Hong Kong Mediation Report 2010.[31] The report's 48 recommendations included creating a legislative framework, a premier accreditation body, sectoral mediation schemes, a corporate mediation pledge, promoting mediation to litigants and the legal profession, integrating mediation into school and higher education curricula and introducing apology legislation.
- The Mediation Taskforce (2010–2012), which considered and implemented the report's recommendations. Its work led to the enactment of the Mediation Ordinance (MO)[32] and a mediator accreditation and standards body, HKMAAL.[33]
- The Steering Committee on Mediation (since December 2012), which continues to monitor and promote mediation practice.[34]

27 Erie, "The New Legal Hubs": 225.

28 Family mediation was first introduced by non-governmental organisations such as the Hong Kong Family Welfare Society and the Hong Kong Catholic Marriage Advisory Council.

29 A notable example from the 1990s is the Hong Kong airport construction project, which used a mixed mode dispute resolution process composed of mediation, adjudication and arbitration: Mark Wilson, "Hong Kong's New Airport and the Resolution of Disputes," *Hong Kong Law Journal* 25 (1995): 363–382.

30 See e.g., Teresa Cheng, Speech by SJ at opening ceremony of "Mediate First" Pledge Event (May 24, 2019), www.info.gov.hk/gia/general/201905/24/P2019052400773.htm; Chun-ying Leung, "The 2014 Policy Address: Support the Needy, Let Youth Flourish, Unleash Hong Kong's Potential," Hong Kong Government, 12; Chun-ying Leung, "The 2013 Policy Address: Seek Change, Maintain Stability, Serve the People with Pragmatism," Hong Kong Government, 9.

31 Department of Justice of Hong Kong, "Report of the Working Group on Mediation."

32 Mediation Ordinance (Cap 620) (MO) (H.K.).

33 Department of Justice of Hong Kong, "Mediation Task Force Terms of Reference," (2011), 2–3, www.doj.gov.hk/en/legal_dispute/pdf/mediation20110729e.pdf. HKMAAL is the Hong Kong Mediation Accreditation Association Limited.

34 Department of Justice of Hong Kong, "Steering Committee on Mediation, Terms of Reference," www.doj.gov.hk/en/legal_dispute/mediationCommittee.html.

- The Inclusive Dispute Avoidance and Resolution Office (since 2019), established to better coordinate and implement the department's initiatives in dispute avoidance and resolution.

A number of regulatory instruments are noteworthy. The starting point for many regulatory developments was Practice Direction 31, introduced in 2010. It requires parties to mediate unless it is unreasonable to do so. The Mediation Ordinance followed in 2013, while apology legislation came into force in 2017. This made Hong Kong the first Asian jurisdiction to enact apology legislation to encourage apology-making with a view to preventing dispute escalation and facilitating amicable resolution (e.g., through mediation). The link between mediation and apologies was visible in the legislation's design, drafting and implementation.[35] Also in 2017, as part of its bid to make international mediation as attractive to international players as arbitration, Hong Kong passed third-party funding legislation for mediation (and arbitration).[36]

In relation to investment matters, a mediation mechanism has been adopted under the Mainland and Hong Kong Closer Economic Partnership Arrangement (CEPA) Investment Agreement[37] to help resolve investment disputes between investors and the mainland or Hong Kong. This has been supported by dedicated training for investor-state mediators.[38] Capitalising on its unique relationship with China, the territory has also made a major push to promote mediation in the Greater Bay Area.[39] Online dispute resolution has been spearheaded by eBRAM (Electronic Business Related Arbitration and Mediation), a technology start-up whose institutional members include legal service providers and professional associations. It offers online mediation services for cross-border commercial and investment disputes and mediation under Hong Kong's 2020 Covid-19 ODR.[40]

Finally, in 2020 Hong Kong announced its legal hub,[41] which aims to provide a premier platform for dispute resolution and business expansion in Asia.

35 Apology Ordinance (Cap 631) (H.K.).

36 Arbitration and Mediation Legislation (Third Party Funding) (Amendment) Ordinance 2017 (Ord. No. 6 of 2017) (H.K.). The sections lifting the prohibition on third-party funding were operational as of February 1, 2019, following the issuance of the Code of Practice for Third Party Funding of Arbitration (GN 9048) and a concurrent gazetted notice. At the time of writing, the provisions on mediation remain inoperative.

37 Mainland and Hong Kong Closer Economic Partnership Arrangement (CEPA), Investment Agreement (June 28, 2017), www.tid.gov.hk/english/cepa/legaltext/cepa14.html.

38 Carrie Lam, Speech by CE at International Dispute Resolution Conference 2019 (April 17, 2019), www.info.gov.hk/gia/general/201904/17/P2019041700390.htm.

39 National Development and Reform Commission, "Framework Agreement on Deepening Guangdong-Hong Kong-Macao Cooperation in the Development of the Greater Bay Area," www.bayarea.gov.hk/filemanager/en/share/pdf/Framework_Agreement.pdf.

40 eBRAM, "Covid-19 Online Dispute Resolution (ODR) Scheme," www.ebram.org/covid_19_odr.html.

41 Government of Hong Kong, "Hong Kong Legal Hub," www.legalhub.gov.hk.

Space from central government offices and the former French Mission Building is being made available to dispute resolution and law-related organisations internationally.[42]

Since Practice Direction 31 (PD 31) was introduced in 2010, Hong Kong has moved quickly to develop itself as a centre for cross-border mediation. While most initiatives have been of general (domestic and international) application, cross-border commercial and investor-state mediation have received increasing attention recently. In the words of the Secretary for Justice Teresa Cheng SC, "Moving forward, we will step up our efforts in promoting the use of mediation and enhancing public awareness of its benefits with the aim of strengthening Hong Kong's position as an international legal and dispute resolution services centre."[43]

Singapore: Background and Context

Singapore's path, while equally ambitious, is one where design features more strongly. Building on strong domestic mediation institutional and regulatory foundations dating back to the mid-1990s,[44] Singapore shifted its focus to international mediation in the early 2010s. Having already designed and implemented a domestic mediation system and an international arbitration system, it established the Working Group to Develop Singapore into a Centre for International Commercial Mediation (ICM WG) in early 2013 – its mandate reflected unmistakeably in its title.[45] The ICM WG Report set out six key recommendations: namely, (1) to design and implement a legislative framework for international commercial mediation, (2) to extend existing tax exemptions and incentives for foreign arbitrators to foreign mediators, (3) to review rules and court procedures to encourage greater use of mediation, (4) to establish international mediation services including innovative user-centric products, (5) to establish a professional standards and accreditation body for mediation professionals and (6) to undertake relevant promotional activities in target markets and industries.[46]

Following directly from the ICM WG Report, the Singapore International Mediation Centre (SIMC), an institutional service provider dedicated to international mediation, and the Singapore International Mediation Institute (SIMI),

42 Ting Kwok Iu, "Face to Face with Hong Kong's Secretary for Justice," interview with Teresa Cheng SC, *Kluwer Mediation Blog* (Aug. 2, 2020), http://mediationblog.kluwerarbitration.com/2020/08/02/interview_with_hksj/.

43 Cheng, Speech by SJ.

44 For an insightful overview of Singapore's mediation ecosystem's development, see Lim, "The Singapore Model."

45 "Report and Recommendations of the Working Group to Develop Singapore into a Centre for International Commercial Mediation" (November 2013) (ICM WG Report), as cited in Lim, "The Singapore Model."

46 ICM WG Report (2013).

a credentialing and standards body, were established in 2014. Within months, the SIMC, together with the SIAC, launched their innovative Arb-Med-Arb Protocol as the first of a number of user-centric protocols anticipated by the recommendations.[47] Tax exemptions for non-resident mediators were implemented in 2015, while certain exemptions applicable to arbitration were extended to foreign mediators and foreign-qualified counsel in 2016 through amendments to the Legal Profession Act. Legislation applicable to international commercial mediation – the Mediation Act (MA) – was enacted in 2017.[48] In 2019, Singapore introduced a review of the Civil Procedure Rules (CPR)[49] to further integrate mediation into Singapore's dispute resolution ecosystem.[50] This led to changes to the Rules of Court (ROC)[51] and the Supreme Court Practice Directions[52] in 2021.

The implementation of the ICM WG's recommendations also inspired further developments. Sustained by a long-term vision for cross-border mediation as an integrated element of international dispute resolution, the government set up a platform for thought leadership and applied research in international mediation and dispute resolution, the Singapore International Dispute Resolution Academy (SIDRA).[53] The construction of a new state-of-the-art international dispute resolution facility was completed in 2019; Maxwell Chambers Suites extends and improves Maxwell Chambers' existing facilities. Already home to numerous foreign dispute resolution institutions such as the International Chamber of Commerce (ICC),[54] Singapore's initiatives continue to attract such institutions, with the Permanent Court of Arbitration (PCA) establishing its first Asian office in Singapore. Further, as chair of the United Nations Commission on International Trade Law (UNCITRAL) Working Group II deliberations that led to the Singapore Convention's adoption, Singapore is at the forefront of its promotion: it was the first country both to sign and ratify the Convention in August 2019 (with implementing legislation, the Singapore Convention on Mediation Act 2020 (SCMA), following soon after).[55] Singapore now conducts the UNCITRAL Academy on cross-border mediation together with UNCITRAL and hosts Singapore Convention Week annually. Finally in the wake of Covid-19, online

47 Online at: https://simc.com.sg/v2/wp-content/uploads/2019/03/SIAC-SIMC-AMA-Protocol.pdf.

48 Mediation Act 2017 (Act No. 1 of 2017) (MA) (Sing.).

49 Civil Procedure Rules – Rules and Directions (UK), www.justice.gov.uk/courts/procedure-rules/civil/rules.

50 "Public Consultation on Civil Justice Reforms: The Recommendations of the Civil Justice Review Committee and Civil Justice Commission," Supreme Court of Singapore (October 26, 2018), https://www.mlaw.gov.sg/files/Annex_A_Public_consultation_paper_on_civil_justice_reforms.pdf/.

51 Cap 322, R 5, 2021 Rev Ed. (Sing.), O 5 r 1 and 3.

52 Supreme Court Practice Directions (Sing.) (updated March 27, 2019), para 53.

53 In 2020 SIDRA is a centre at the Singapore Management University and continues being funded by the Ministry of Law.

54 https://iccwbo.org/. Other foreign dispute resolution organisations with an office in Singapore include the International Centre for Dispute Resolution (ICDR) and the World Intellectual Property Organization (WIPO).

55 Official website of the Singapore Convention: https://www.singaporeconvention.org.

mediation practice has grown. The SIMC Covid-19 Protocol provides "expedited, economical and effective" online mediation, while the recently signed Japan International Mediation Centre (JIMC)-SIMC Joint Protocol is the first of its kind between two international dispute resolution centres and offers online mediation services to cross-border businesses.[56]

Through targeted policymaking and a collaborative and inclusive approach to regulatory activity, Singapore has seen significant regulatory-institutional changes in under a decade, designed to build (international) mediation into most industries' and government procurement systems' dispute resolution processes.[57] As Minister Edwin Tong states, "Should there be a dispute, [businesses investing in Singapore ultimately] want to know that it will be resolved impartially in a transparent manner, quickly, expeditiously, and cost effectively. Mediation offers all of this."[58]

Next, both jurisdictions' cross-border mediation laws will be examined from a comparative perspective. The analysis will follow the four aforementioned functional categories: triggering laws, procedural laws, standards and rights and obligations.

Triggering Laws

Triggering regulations, policies and initiatives activate a pathway to mediation processes. They encourage mediation's use in different ways and with varying influence. Generally, triggers may include court-referral mechanisms contained in practice directions and procedural rules, mediation clauses in commercial contracts and legislative provisions. A global review has shown that having diverse triggering mechanisms is the most effective approach to encouraging mediation's use across sectors.[59]

Both countries' court practice directions and rules contain triggering laws. In Hong Kong, PD 31 requires civil litigants to consider and reasonably engage in mediation before trial, on pain of costs sanctions.[60] It applies to all writ-initiated civil proceedings in the Court of First Instance and the District Court, subject to

56 Singapore International Mediation Centre, "Singapore and Japan International Mediation Centres Launch Joint Mediation Protocol to Help Cross-Border Businesses Resolve Disputes Swiftly and Inexpensively," *SIMC News* (September 13, 2020), https://simc.com.sg/blog/2020/09/13/singapore-and-japan-international-mediation-centres-launch-joint-mediation-protocol-to-help-cross-border-businesses-resolve-disputes-swiftly-and-inexpensively/.

57 Sundaresh Menon, "Building Sustainable Mediation Programs: A Singapore Perspective," *Dispute Resolution Magazine* 22 (Fall 2015): 42–45.

58 Edwin Tong, "Speech by Mr Edwin Tong, Senior Minister of State for Law and Health, at the SIMC Singapore Specialist Mediators Appointment Ceremony," (January 3, 2020), https://simc.com.sg/blog/2020/01/04/speech-by-mr-edwin-tong-senior-minister-of-state-for-law-and-health-at-the-simc-singapore-specialist-mediators-appointment-ceremony/.

59 See Alexander, "Chapter 3: Pre-Mediation I: Selection and Referral," in *International and Comparative Mediation*; Alexander, Walsh, and Svatos, eds., *EU Mediation Law Handbook*; and generally, Hopt and Steffek, eds., *Mediation: Principles and Regulation*.

60 Hong Kong Practice Directions, PD 31, paras 4 and 5. Note: a revised PD 31 came into effect on 1 November 2014. For similar PDs in other HK courts, see Nadja Alexander et al., eds., *Hong Kong Mediation* (Hong Kong: LexisNexis, 2021).

Appendix A's exceptions (specialised lists address these).[61] PD 31 effectively establishes an opt-out mechanism, provided a legitimate and reasonable ground exists.[62] Legal advisers must advise clients of non-compliance's consequences.[63] Similarly, Singapore's Supreme Court Practice Directions make it the professional duty of lawyers to advise clients on appropriate forms of ADR[64] and require ADR to "be considered before the commencement and during the course of any action or appeal in order to facilitate the just, expeditious and economical disposal of civil cases."[65] Further, lawyers must advise clients of potential adverse costs orders under Order 21 rule 4(c) ROC for unreasonable refusals to engage in ADR.[66] In the State Courts, where lower value cross-border commercial disputes may be routed, a presumption of ADR exists (though parties may opt out).[67] At the Singapore International Commercial Court (SICC), judges have broad discretion to recommend (but not compel) mediation.[68]

Empirical evidence on court-related mediation suggests that mechanisms which nudge parties towards mediation (like those in Hong Kong and Singapore) tend to favour efficient dispute settlement more than mandatory directives.[69]

Mediation clauses (and mixed mode clauses incorporating mediation) can also trigger mediation processes. Indeed, the 2020 SIDRA Survey found the existence

61 Some specialised PDs adopt mechanisms like PD 31. E.g. PD 18.2 of the Employees' Compensation List requires use of the standard forms of Mediation Certificate, Mediation Notice and Mediation Response contained in PD 31's appendices, although it allows modifications to suit PD 18.2 proceedings (including proceedings on any cause or matter begun by originating summons but ordered to be continued as if begun by writ). See O 28 r 8 of the Rules of the High Court (Cap 4A) and Rules of the District Court (Cap 336) (HK), and also PD 31, para 2.

62 PD 31, para 18.

63 PD 31, para 4.

64 Supreme Court Practice Directions (Sing.), para 53(2). Appendix D further sets out Guidelines for Advocates and Solicitors Advising Clients About ADR. See also Legal Profession (Professional Conduct) Rules 2015 (No. S 706/2015), rr 17(2)(e)(i) and (ii) (a legal practitioner must evaluate with clients whether the expense of or risk in pursuing a matter is justified and has a complementary duty to evaluate the use of ADR).

65 Supreme Court Practice Directions (Sing.), para 53(4). On ADR Offers, see para 54.

66 Rules of Court (Chapter 322, R 5, 2021 Rev Ed.) (Sing.), O 21 r 4(c). See Legal Profession (Professional Conduct) Rules 2015, rule 5 (suggesting that lawyers should furnish information concerning resort to ADR when advising clients). See Dorcas Quek Anderson, "Supreme Court Practice Directions (Amendment No. 1 of 2016): A Significant Step in Further Incorporating ADR into the Civil Justice Process," *The Singapore Law Gazette* (March 2016), http://v1.lawgazette.com.sg/2016-03/1524.htm. Singapore courts not infrequently impose costs sanctions when matters should have been resolved through mediation instead of litigation (see *HSBC Institutional Trust Services (Singapore Ltd) v. Toshin Development Singapore Pte Ltd* [2012] 4 SLR 738, paras 68–72).

67 State Courts Practice Directions (Sing.), para 34(5).

68 SICC Practice Directions (effective August 1, 2022). Paragraph 77(11) states (emphasis added),

> Where parties are not willing to attempt mediation or any other form of ADR, the Judge *may* direct that the issue of mediation or any other form of ADR be considered at the next Case Management Conference or at a specified stage in the proceedings.

69 Shahla F. Ali, "Nudging Civil Justice: Examining Voluntary and Mandatory Court Mediation User Experience in Twelve Regions," *Cardozo Journal of Conflict Resolution* 19, no. 2 (Winter 2018); Charmaine Yap Yun Ning, "What's in a Nudge? How Choice Architecture Surrounding Dispute Resolution Options Can Increase Uptake of Mediation," in Joel Lee and Marcus Lim, eds., *Contemporary Issues in Mediation Volume 4* (Singapore: World Scientific Research, 2019).

of mixed mode dispute resolution clauses to be the most common reason why users enter mixed mode procedures involving mediation and arbitration.[70] In Singapore[71] and Hong Kong,[72] these clauses are prima facie judicially recognised and enforceable.[73] Mediation clauses must be *meticulously drafted*[74] to avoid unenforceability owing to uncertainty. However, recent Hong Kong[75] and Singapore[76] legislation acknowledges mediation clauses in different ways and may potentially relax drafting requirements. Hong Kong's legislation only covers mediations conducted pursuant to "agreements to mediate" (i.e., a mediation clause or mediation agreement).[77] Singapore's legislation contains a similar provision (on "mediation agreement[s]");[78] however, it goes further by expressly permitting discretionary stay of proceedings when parties institute court proceedings over matters covered by a mediation clause/agreement.[79]

This examination shows that both countries have pro-mediation judiciaries that recognise and support mediation triggering mechanisms and provide practice directions to encourage mediation. While Singapore makes the court's discretion explicit, both jurisdictions' courts conceivably have an inherent power to stay proceedings in circumstances of non-compliance with mediation clauses.[80]

Regulation of Procedural Aspects

Mediation is a flexible dispute resolution process. Its flexibility is particularly linked to its procedure, aspects of which include:

- the nature of preliminary meetings and intake;
- the nature and contents of agreements to mediate;

70 SIDRA Survey, 71–72.

71 *International Research Corp PLC v. Lufthansa Systems Asia Pacific Pte Ltd and another* [2014] 1 SLR 130, especially para 54.

72 *Hyundai Engineering and Construction Co Ltd v. Vigour Ltd* [2005] HKEC 258, paras 17–33, 37–41.

73 For Singapore, see *Zhongguo Remittance Pte Ltd v. Samlit Moneychanger Pte Ltd and others* [2020] SGDC 73; *Ling Kong Henry v. Tanglin Club* [2018] 5 SLR 871, para 25; *Heartronics Corporation v. EPI Life Pte Ltd and others* [2017] SGHCR 17; *International Research Corp PLC* [2014] 1 SLR 130; *HSBC v. Toshin* [2012] 4 SLR 738, para 43; Sundaresh Menon, speech by CJ on "Judicial Attitudes towards Arbitration and Mediation in Singapore" at the ALA and KLRCA Talk and Dinner (October 25, 2013), para 22. For Hong Kong, see *Hui Ling Ling v. Sky Field Development Limited* (unreported, July 22, 2009; HCA 35/2007) [2009] HKCU 1216, paras 5–6; *Hyundai Engineering and Construction* [2005] HKEC 258; *Dragomar S.p.A. v. Geoworks Contractors (HK) Limited* (unreported, January 27, 1998; 1997, NO. A5399) [1998] HKCU 63.

74 In Singapore, see *International Research Corp PLC* [2014] 1 SLR 130, para 54.

75 MO (H.K.), ss 2 and 6.

76 MA (Sing.), s 8.

77 MO (H.K.), s 5.

78 MA (Sing.), s 6.

79 MA (Sing.), ss 8(1) – (2).

80 See for Singapore, Nadja Alexander, et al., *Singapore Mediation Handbook* (Singapore: LexisNexis, 2019) at 9.157–9.159; *Tomolugan Holdings Ltd v Silica Investors* [2016] 1 SLR 373 (request for court to exercise inherent powers of case management under O 92 r 4 to stay litigation in favour of litigating certain matters first).

- how mediators expect participants to prepare;
- whether there will be a single mediator or co-mediators;
- how mediators are appointed and paid;
- how discussions are structured;
- how agenda items are framed;
- the extent to which private meetings are utilised;
- the specific constellations of participants in private meetings;
- how outcomes are documented and by whom; and
- the extent of post-mediation follow-up meetings.

A global review of regulatory practice shows that most jurisdictions regulate these through softer regulatory forms (e.g., mediation agreements, institutional rules and codes).[81] These offer greater elasticity than legislation, can be varied by parties and are easily updatable by institutions. Both Hong Kong and Singapore follow this trend.

Consistent with the rationale of the Hong Kong Mediation Report's Recommendation 37, the MO does not address mediation's process aspects, apart from issues concerning mediator appointment and non-lawyer and foreign lawyers' participation.[82] Similarly, Singapore's ICM WG recommended establishing a standards-setting professional body and mediator credentialing system.[83]

Mediation clauses and agreements are also relevant here. Their provisions may regulate mediation's procedural aspects or, in many cases, incorporate relevant institutional rules. For example, two leading service providers, the SIMC[84] and the HKIAC,[85] provide sample clauses incorporating institutional mediation rules.[86] In terms of institutional rules and codes, SIMI provides its Code of Professional Conduct[87] that extends to procedural matters, and in Hong Kong, the HKMAAL Mediation Code with attached Sample Agreement to Mediate[88] is the most relevant text. Both address mediator appointment, fees, confidentiality, impartiality and other important matters. The HKMAAL Code requires mediators to inform parties and their advisers about the mediation process and the roles of all participants including the mediator. It then offers procedural guidance for facilitative mediation (e.g., the Sample Agreement to Mediate's clause

81 See Felix Steffek, "Mediation in Europa und der Welt – Rechtsvergleichende Forschung zur Umsetzung der Mediationsrichtlinie," *Zeitschrift für Konfliktmanagement* 12, no. 1 (2009): 23.

82 MO (H.K.), s 7.

83 Lim, "The Singapore Model," 386.

84 E.g. SIMC Model Clause, https://siac.org.sg/the-singapore-arb-med-arb-clause.

85 E.g. HKIAC Suggested Mediation Clause, www.hkiac.org/mediation/rules/hkiac-mediation-rules.

86 See also Hong Kong's Law Society's sample Mediation and Med-Arb clauses, www.hklawsoc.org.hk/pub_e/mas/clauses.asp, and Mediation Rules, www.hklawsoc.org.hk/pub_e/mas/rules.asp. For Singapore's Law Society's sample clauses and rules, see https://www.lawsociety.org.sg/for-lawyers/dispute-resolution-schemes/law-society-mediation-scheme/agreement-to-mediate/.

87 SIMI Code of Professional Conduct: www.simi.org.sg/What-We-Offer/Mediators/Code-of-Professional-Conduct.

88 HKMAAL Mediation Code: www.hkmaal.org.hk/en/HongKongMediationCode.php.

2 outlines some basic process steps in interest-based mediation). Clause 4 confirms mediators' non-advisory and non-determinative role, which influences how they conduct the process. Of course parties are free to vary these standard terms and do so in practice. The SIMI Code takes a different approach and requires that mediators obtain the informed consent of parties and their advisers on their mediation approach (facilitative, directive or otherwise) and explain what to expect in terms of procedural characteristics and participant and mediator roles.[89] Such disclosure typically leads to a discussion with parties and advisers about their mediation preferences, promoting party autonomy. The code adds that SIMI mediators "should draw on their expertise and experience to assist the parties in developing sustainable settlements during the mediation" with parties' consent. However, mediators are simultaneously warned to "guard against prescribing solutions or offering any statement, suggestion, or value judgement which may create an undue influence on any one party towards accepting a specific outcome."[90]

Specialised Protocols have emerged in both jurisdictions in the wake of Covid-19. One of the earliest was SIMC's Covid-19 Mediation Protocol, which features streamlined procedures, reduced fees and an online mediation option. Subsequently, the JIMC-SIMC Joint Covid-19 Protocol followed, supporting co-mediation for commercial disputes along the Singapore-Japan corridor.[91] Hong Kong's Covid-19 ODR Scheme introduced in 2020,[92] focuses especially on MSMEs that may be adversely affected by Covid-19, with claim amounts capped at HK$500,000. eBRAM's e-mixed mode procedure, which begins with e-negotiations and offers e-arbitration as the final option, also incorporates e-mediation services.

Some mixed mode dispute resolution protocols also address mediation procedure. Examples include eBRAM's ODR Protocol, the SIMC-SIAC Arb-Med-Arb Protocol and SIMC-SMC[93] Singapore Infrastructure Dispute Management Protocol (SIDP).[94]

This overview highlights a regulatory focus in both jurisdictions on the actions and initiatives of mediation users, mediators and dispute resolution institutions and on maximising party autonomy. Their active and flourishing

89 SIMI Code of Professional Conduct, para 5. While the HKMAAL Code has a similar provision (para 3), it should be read in context of the provisions outlining facilitative mediation principles.

90 SIMI Code of Professional Conduct, para 5.10.

91 JIMC Kyoto and SIMC, "JIMC-SIMC Joint Covid-19 Protocol" (September 12, 2020), http://simc.com.sg/v2/wp-content/uploads/2020/09/JIMC-SIMC-Joint-Protocol_FINAL-for-web.pdf. See also Nadja Alexander, "Japan-Singapore Joint Mediation Protocol Announced," *Kluwer Mediation Blog* (September 16, 2020), http://mediationblog.kluwerarbitration.com/2020/09/16/japan-singapore-joint-mediation-protocol-announced/.

92 eBRAM, "Covid-19 ODR Scheme."

93 Singapore Mediation Centre.

94 The SIDP, launched in 2018, promotes use of Dispute Boards for large construction and infrastructure projects. See: www.mediation.com.sg/wp-content/uploads/2019/06/Guide-to-Singapore-Infracture-Disputre-Management-Protocol-Booklet.pdf.

professional mediation communities mean that more innovation in soft law procedural regulation is foreseeable.

Setting Standards

Setting standards offers access to an internationally recognised pool of local and foreign mediators of appropriate qualification and skill. As part of the international professionalisation of mediation practice, there is a discernible trend towards mediator credentialing (or certification or accreditation).

While early civil law regulation often employed legislation, both Singapore and Hong Kong deliberately developed non-legislative uniform mediator credentialing and ethical practice standards designed by the professional mediator community. SIMI and HKMAAL were established as premier mediator credentialing institutions respectively. Institutional mediation service providers and professional associations also frequently have separate standards for mediations under their auspices; for example, both countries' law societies have standards for solicitor-mediator members.[95]

To remain adaptable to changing circumstances and needs, both jurisdictions have generally embraced responsive regulation through uniform institutional and industry-based mediator standards with the buy-in of mediation users, professional mediator communities and referrers (e.g., courts, lawyers). Significantly, the establishment of credentialing and standards institutions independent of mediation service providers and training institutions signals a commitment to quality assurance.

HKMAAL's aim when it came into existence in 2013 was to establish a uniform accreditation system with minimum standards, against a backdrop where divergent credentialing standards were being offered by over 30 organisations. Its membership presently includes the Law Society, Bar Association, HKIAC, Hong Kong Mediation Centre (HKMC) and various other organisations, which now all follow HKMAAL's credentialing system plus any additional, organisation-specific standards. Importantly, mediators can be accredited and placed on HKMAAL's panel without being part of a member organisation. This approach ensures that all member organisations, which make up the vast majority of Hong Kong's institutional mediation service providers, meet uniform minimum standards for quality while retaining the flexibility to tailor-make higher standards.

Local and foreign mediators who meet the eligibility, training and assessment requirements (e.g., minimum three years working experience) can be accredited;

95 See Law Society of Singapore, *Mediation Scheme Handbook 2017*: 24–28. From 2013, the Hong Kong Law Society's Mediator Admission Scheme has followed the HKMAAL requirements with the additional requirement of being a solicitor. It also follows the HKMAAL Mediation Code's ethical practice standards: see Law Society of Hong Kong, *Mediator Admission Scheme Information Package* (October 2017): 3–6 and 9–11, www.hklawsoc.org.hk/pub_e/mas/doc/MediatorAdmiisioinSchemeInfoPack_201710.pdf.

an experience-based path is available to mediators who are credentialed elsewhere and/or highly experienced.[96] Family mediation is a specialisation with separate credentialing.[97] While not a precondition to practising in Hong Kong, Justice Secretary Teresa Cheng has noted that HKMAAL credentialing helps attract foreign mediators to Hong Kong.[98]

Established one year later, in 2014, SIMI was established in a different mediation environment, where most credentialing had been done by a single body (SMC). Unlike HKMAAL's system of institutional membership, SIMI's members are its mediators, though it also works with partner organisations on various initiatives. Furthermore, SIMI's system has no comparable work experience or degree requirements. Its four-tier accreditation system is designed for local and foreign mediators and relevant to domestic and international practice.[99] The highest tier corresponds to the International Mediation Institute's (IMI) certification. SIMI certified mediators may apply to become IMI certified mediators without additional assessment, giving them credibility to work across borders and appeal to international parties.[100] The service provider, SIMC, requires its local and foreign mediators to be recognised and certified (to the highest level) by SIMI, offering a transparent, independent and international quality standard of services, alongside a degree of international diversity of mediators. Further, the enforcement mechanisms of the MA only apply to "designated" service providers (e.g., SIMC) and "approved" mediators (e.g., SIMI credentialed), encouraging foreign mediators to work through designated institutions and obtain SIMI recognition. Tax exemptions for foreign mediators further enhance Singapore's attractiveness.[101]

Diverse mediators bring diverse practices, which raises the question of how standards bodies manage diversity. Both HKMAAL and SIMI are grounded in facilitative mediation[102] yet accept other approaches, including more directive approaches should parties consent.

Renewal requirements are an integral part of both systems.[103] Both also set standards and approval requirements for training courses. Overall HKMAAL's system is more centralised; for example, whereas HKMAAL conducts mediator assessments itself, SIMI approves training bodies to assess and determine mediator competency.

96 HKMAAL, "How to become a Mediator – General Mediator," www.hkmaal.org.hk/en/HowToBecomeAMediator_G.php.

97 Ibid.

98 See Iu, "Face to Face with Hong Kong's Secretary for Justice."

99 SIMI, "About the SIMI Credentialing Scheme," www.simi.org.sg/What-We-Offer/Mediators/SIMI-Credentialing-Scheme.

100 Ibid.

101 Singapore Ministry of Law, "Tax Exemption for Income Derived by Non-resident Mediators for Mediation Services Rendered in Singapore" (2016), www.mlaw.gov.sg/files/IndustryCircular29042016.pdf/.

102 For Singapore see the SIMI Code of Professional Conduct, para 5.10 and the meaning of mediation in MA (Sing.), s 3. For Hong Kong see the HKMAAL Sample Agreement to Mediate, clause 2 and the meaning of mediation in MO (H.K.), s 4.

103 SIMI, "Renewal requirements," www.simi.org.sg/What-We-Offer/Mediators/Renewal-Requirements.

HKMAAL's panels are made up of general mediators, family mediators, assessors and supervisors, whereas SIMI features panels at each of its four levels.

Beyond credentialing, standards for ongoing ethical practice are increasingly important with the Singapore Convention's coming into force in 2020 – where one ground for refusing iMSA enforcement may involve a breach of mediator standards. Examples of standards (or codes of ethics, practice standards and professional codes of conduct) include the HKMAAL Code of Conduct[104] and SIMI Code of Professional Conduct.[105]

Also central are channels for user feedback and complaints. HKMAAL and SIMI have complaints and disciplinary procedures.[106] It is conceivable that legal proceedings for civil remedies could be commenced against mediators.[107]

Neither jurisdiction mandates professional indemnity insurance; however, SIMI provides its mediators with basic professional indemnity insurance.[108] Lawyers acting as mediators in either jurisdiction would typically be covered under existing professional indemnity insurance.[109]

This regulatory overview shows well-developed independent institutional credentialing schemes in both jurisdictions and codes of ethical practice supported by respective primary credentialing organisations. While Singapore's MA only applies to mediators meeting credentialing or institutional standards, Hong Kong's MO has no such condition. As breach of mediator standards is recognised as a ground for refusing iMSA enforcement, standards and feedback and complaints mechanisms will be increasingly scrutinised.

Rights and Obligations

The rules governing mediation participants' rights and obligations – including mediators, parties, lawyers, experts, translators and administrative staff – link

104 HKMAAL Code of Conduct (or "Hong Kong Mediation Code"), www.hkmaal.org.hk/en/HongKongMediationCode.php.

105 SIMI Code of Professional Conduct, www.simi.org.sg/What-We-Offer/Mediators/Code-of-Professional-Conduct.

106 HKMAAL Rules for the Handling of Complaints Against an Accredited Mediator, www.hkmaal.org.hk/en/MediationRules_RulesForTheHandling.php; SIMI Mediator Feedback Form, www.simi.org.sg/Mediator-Feedback; and SIMI Assessment of Professional Conduct for SIMI Mediators, www.simi.org.sg/Portals/0/Code%20of%20Conduct/SIMI%20Assessment%20Of%20Professional%20Conduct%20%5BJAN%202017%5D.pdf.

107 See, e.g., *Chan Gek Yong v. Violet Netto* [2018] SGHC 208, where allegations that mediators pressured the plaintiff into signing a mediated settlement agreement were dismissed. These were made in litigation where the mediators were non-parties. At the time of writing, no action against the mediator has been pursued.

108 SIMI Professional Indemnity Insurance, www.simi.org.sg/Portals/0/Events/Indemnity%20Insurance/Professional%20Indemnity%20Insurance.pdf.

109 See Law Society of Singapore, Professional Insurance Cover, www.lawsociety.org.sg/For-Public/Professional-Indemnity-Insurance; Hong Kong Law Society, Solicitors (Professional Indemnity) Rules, https://www.hklawsoc.org.hk/en/Support-Members/Professional-Support/Professional-Guide/The-hong-kong-solicitors-guide--to-professional-conduct--volume-2; Hong Kong Bar Association, Professional Indemnity Association, https://hkbarpiadmin.com/.

the mediation process and its participants directly to the legal system,[110] be it its legislation, case law, general law principles or the terms of mediation agreements (and the institutional rules they incorporate).[111] This discussion[112] focuses on legislation with some case references, issues of enforceability of mediation clauses and mediated settlement agreements and the confidentiality and admissibility of mediation communications in arbitration or court proceedings. Apology legislation and third-party funding legislation are briefly considered.

Hong Kong's MO,[113] which came into force in 2013, and Singapore's MA,[114] which came into force in 2017, form our starting point. Both have similarities; in fact, Singapore's took inspiration from several MO provisions. This promotes a harmonised approach in the region in relation to mediation confidentiality and admissibility of mediation communications in evidence. But Singapore's MA goes further in addressing enforceability and (indirectly) credentialing.

Both laws aim to encourage and facilitate dispute resolution through mediation.[115] They are remarkably similar in several ways:

1 their broad definitions of mediation that simultaneously reflect an interest-based approach;[116]
2 their scope of application, i.e., mediations occurring
   a pursuant to written mediation agreements (or agreements to mediate in Hong Kong); and
   b wholly or partly in the country, or where the mediation agreement provides that the legislation or the law of Hong Kong or Singapore, as the case may be, applies;[117]
3 their detailed and similarly worded regimes for confidentiality and admissibility of mediation communications in subsequent proceedings;[118]
4 both permit foreign lawyers to represent parties in mediations conducted in the country;[119] and
5 both bind the government.[120]

While credentialing and standards are primarily regulated by institutionally generated soft law in both jurisdictions, Singapore's MA only applies when

110 Nadja Alexander and Felix Steffek, *Making Mediation Law* (Washington, DC: World Bank Group International Finance Corporation, 2016), 36.
111 E.g. on confidentiality, see HKMAAL Mediation Code, para 4, and SIMC Mediation Rules, rule 9.
112 For deeper consideration, see Alexander et al., *Hong Kong Mediation*, and Alexander et al., *Singapore Mediation Handbook*.
113 MO (H.K.).
114 MA (Sing.).
115 MO, s 3; MA, long title.
116 MO, s 4; MA, s 3.
117 MO, ss 2 and 5; MA, ss 4 and 6.
118 MO, ss 8–10; MA, ss 9–11.
119 MO, s 7; MA, s 17.
120 MO, s 6; MA, s 5.

parties engage a designated service provider or mediator accredited under a designated scheme.[121] This regulatory approach encourages diversity in mediation practice by standards-setting to institutional bodies while promoting high ethical and competency standards by requiring MA-qualifying mediations to be conducted by mediators and service providers approved by the minister. While Hong Kong's MO is silent on standards, an earlier draft identified HKMAAL as the default mediator appointing body.[122] This was removed in subsequent drafts as HKMAAL's incorporation did not occur until after the MO's enactment. Future MO amendments may reintroduce this default, just as the Arbitration Ordinance identifies the HKIAC as the default arbitrator appointment body.[123]

Notably, only the MA addresses iMSA enforcement. During the MO's drafting from 2011 to 2013, such provisions were considered unnecessary as the general law already enforced iMSAs either as contracts, settlement deeds or consent arbitral awards.[124] Furthermore, for matters at any stage of litigation (including mediations pursuant to PD 31), parties can agree to record their iMSAs as court consent orders.[125] Indeed, the variety of enforcement options was viewed as positive and consistent with mediation's flexible nature. Another reason related to international commercial mediation's nascent state at the time; to be effective, sufficient international buy-in was required. From 2015, we have seen international buy-in through UNCITRAL's efforts, culminating in the Singapore Convention.

As indicated previously, Singapore's MA was passed in 2017, amid UNCITRAL WG II discussions leading up to the Singapore Convention, which Singapore chaired. Global interest in international commercial mediation and enforcement issues was growing. Section 12 of the MA broke new ground at the time by permitting the recording of a commercial iMSA reached *outside of any legal proceedings* as a court order.[126]

With the passing of the SCMA in 2020,[127] Singapore implemented the Convention including its enforcement provisions, offering another pathway for direct iMSA enforcement. Relief under a qualifying iMSA may be obtained from the High Court[128] by submitting the signed written settlement agreement

121 MA, s 7.

122 See, e.g., comments on cl 7 concerning default appointments in Law Society of Hong Kong, "Draft Mediation Bill – Submission of the Law Society," LC Paper No. CB(2)2415/10–11(02) (July 2011), www.legco.gov.hk/yr10-11/chinese/panels/ajls/papers/aj0721cb2-2415-2-ec.pdf.

123 Arbitration Ordinance (Cap 609) (H.K.), s 24.

124 Arbitration Ordinance (H.K.), s 66. cf International Arbitration Act (Cap 143A, 2002 Rev Ed.) (Sing.), s 18.

125 Rules of the High Court (Cap 4A) (H.K.), O 42 r 5A; Rules of the District Court (Cap 336H) (H.K.), O 42 r 5A. For other mechanisms. see Michael Wilkinson, et al., *A Guide to Civil Procedure in Hong Kong*, 6th ed. (Hong Kong: LexisNexis, 2017), paras 13–74 to 13–92.

126 MA (Sing.), s 12. Note the potential reciprocal recognition and enforcement of court orders recording iMSAs pursuant to this section; for example, via the Foreign Judgments Act 1991 (Cth) (Austl.) or the Reciprocal Enforcement of Foreign Judgments Act (Cap 177, 2000 Rev. Ed.) (Brunei).

127 Singapore Convention on Mediation Act 2020 (Act 4 of 2020) (Sing.).

128 SCMA, s 4.

with evidence that it results from mediation[129] and applying to have the iMSA recorded as a court order for the enforcement[130] or invocation.[131] Whereas MA applications must occur within eight weeks of the iMSA, the SCMA imposes no time limit. At the time of writing, Hong Kong has no equivalent legislation, as China has yet to ratify the Convention.[132]

Apart from the MA and SCMA enforcement mechanisms, iMSAs may also be recognised in Singapore contracts, settlement deeds, arbitral consent awards[133] and consent court orders.[134]

Other legislation such as apology and third-party funding legislation also have a role in the international mediation landscape. Hong Kong's Working Group on Mediation left the possibility of enhancing settlement through introducing apology legislation to fuller consideration by an appropriate body.[135]

Introduced seven years later in 2017, the Hong Kong Apology Ordinance (AO)[136] embodies this aim. Research confirms that apologies can restore and build relationships, offering insights to those involved – values mediation shares.[137]

The AO features a broad and inclusive definition of apology which includes an express or implied admission of fault. It supports mediation by protecting apologies made pre-mediation from qualifying as admissions of liability. An early apology made without such a concern may encourage settlement negotiations and use of mediation. Further, while apologies during mediations are usually protected by legislative confidentiality provisions, these face exceptions, which may create doubt in parties' minds over whether to apologise. Finally, apologies made pursuant to iMSAs may not be protected by the MO's confidentiality provisions[138] but would prima facie receive AO protection. Apology legislation is thus significant in enhancing the mediation regulatory regime by providing apologies better

129 SCMA, s 6.

130 SCMA, ss 4(1)(a)(i) and 5.

131 SCMA, ss 4(1)(a)(ii) and 5. Alternatively, invocation is possible by fulfilling section 6's requirements without applying for a court order: s 4(1)(b).

132 Hong Kong Basic Law, art 153.

133 International Arbitration Act (Cap 143A, 2002 Rev Ed.) (Sing.), s 18.

134 On the pre-MA practice of recording litigation-related iMSAs as court consent orders, see Dorcas Quek Anderson, "A Coming of Age for Mediation in Singapore? Mediation Act 2016," *SAcLJ* 29 (2017): 287; *HSBC v. Toshin* [2012] 4 SLR 738; *International Research Corp PLC* [2014] 1 SLR 130. See also SICC Practice Directions (effective August 1, 2022), para 77(12). On iMSA enforcement generally, see Eunice Chua, "The Enforcement of International Mediated Settlement Agreements without the Singapore Convention on Mediation," *SAcLJ* 31 (2019).

135 Hong Kong Department of Justice, "Report of the Working Group on Mediation": *Recommendation* 43.

136 Apology Ordinance (Cap 631) (H.K.), s 3.

137 Jennifer K. Robbennolt, "Apologies and Legal Settlement: An Empirical Examination," *Michigan Law Review* 102, no. 3 (2003); Robyn Carroll, "Beyond Compensation: Apology as a Private Law Remedy," in Jeff Berryman and Rick Bigwood, eds., *The Law of Remedies: New Directions in the Common Law* (Toronto: Irwin Law, 2010); Ian Austen and Jason Horowitz, "Pope Rejects Call for Apology to Canada's Indigenous People," *The New York Times*, March 28, 2018.

138 Even where iMSAs contain a confidentiality clause, its scope and impact will depend on its interpretation (e.g. by the courts).

protection and apologisers a broader safe harbour. Singapore has no equivalent legislation.

Legislation paving the path for third-party funding was introduced in both jurisdictions in 2017.[139] This development reflects shifting international attitudes and practices coupled with a desire to keep a close eye on third-party funding's development through regulatory measures.[140] Singapore's legislation extends to Med-Arb and Arb-Med-Arb but not standalone mediation. The SIAC's Investment Arbitration Rules, released in anticipation of the amendments, give tribunals discretionary authority to require disclosure of funding details.[141] Guided by flexibility and party autonomy, the Singapore Institute of Arbitrators[142] and Law Society[143] released non-binding guidance notes on third-party funding.

Hong Kong passed the Arbitration and Mediation Legislation (Third Party Funding) (Amendment) Ordinance in June 2017.[144] Like the SIAC, the HKIAC's new Administered Arbitration Rules (HKIAC Rules) entered into force on November 1, 2018, with amended provisions on third-party funding.

The main distinction in developments for the time being concerns legislative scope. The Ordinance permits third-party funding in both international and domestic arbitrations *and mediations*, along with related proceedings (e.g., ancillary court proceedings) and mixed mode procedures. However, the provisions concerning standalone mediation remain inoperative. In comparison, Singapore's Civil Law Act permits such funding only for international arbitrations and related proceedings (e.g., Arb-Med-Arb and similar mixed mode procedures), although the then-Senior Minister of State for Law, Indranee Rajah SC, has indicated a possibility of its extension to other dispute resolution processes.[145]

A second distinction concerns disclosure requirements. In Singapore, legal representatives of funded parties have disclosure obligations.[146] Contrarily, and consistent

139 For Singapore, see Civil Law Act (Cap 43, 2020 Rev Ed.), ss 5A-5B and Civil Law (Third Party Funding) Regulations 2017 (No. S 43/2017). For Hong Kong, see the Code of Practice for Third Party Funding of Arbitration (G.N. 9048) and Arbitration and Mediation Legislation (Third Party Funding) (Amendment) Ordinance 2017 (Ord. No. 6 of 2017). See also the 2018 Queen Mary Survey: 9.

140 Although third-party funding, particularly of litigation and arbitration, has become part and parcel of dispute resolution practice in jurisdictions like England, Australia and the US, it is only just emerging but quickly gaining traction: 2018 Queen Mary Survey: 18.

141 SIAC Investment Arbitration Rules, 1st ed. (January 1, 2017), r 24(l).

142 Singapore Institute of Arbitrators, SIArb Guidelines for Third Party Funders (May 18, 2017).

143 Law Society of Singapore, "Guidance Note 10.1.1 – Third Party Funding" (effective April 25, 2017).

144 Ord. No. 6 of 2017. The Ordinance was gazetted on June 23, 2017, but sections lifting the prohibition on third-party funding for arbitration were operational only from February 1, 2019, following the issuance of the Code of Practice for Third Party Funding of Arbitration (G.N. 9048) and a concurrent *Gazette* notice.

145 Indranee Rajah SC, "Third Party Funding – Reinforcing Singapore as a Premier International Dispute Resolution Centre," (January 24, 2017). See also Marla Decker and Nicholas Lingard, "Third Party Funding in Asia: Arrived, and Set to Thrive," *Above the Law Blog* (December 12, 2018).

146 Legal Profession (Professional Conduct) Rules 2015 (No. S 706/2015), Part 5A, added by the Legal Profession (Professional Conduct) (Amendment) Rules 2017 (No. S 69/2017).

with the Ordinance, Art 44 of the HKIAC Rules places funded parties under a continuing obligation to disclose to each party, the tribunal and HKIAC the fact that funding agreements have been made and the funder's identity.

While their immediate focus and impact is on international arbitration, these amendments have opened the door to third-party funding of international mediation in Asia's two top-ranking dispute resolution jurisdictions.

Finally, both jurisdictions feature a small but developing body of case law addressing the rights and obligations of mediators, mediation parties, lawyers and others involved in mediation.[147] Cases deal variously with enforceability and invocation of iMSAs[148] and mediation or mixed mode clauses,[149] the scope of confidentiality in mediation processes[150] and parties' and lawyers' obligations in mediation settings.[151] Cases in both jurisdictions require mediation clauses to be meticulously drafted to avoid being rendered unenforceable for uncertainty.[152] In Hong Kong, mediation agreements should precisely define the specific steps needed for the mediation process to take place when the dispute resolution

147 For Singapore cases, see Nadja Alexander and Shouyu Chong, "Mediation and Appropriate Dispute Resolution," *Singapore Academy of Law Annual Review of Singapore Cases* 21 (published on e-First on July 9, 2020), https://ink.library.smu.edu.sg/cgi/viewcontent.cgi?article=5256&context=sol_research; Alexander et al., *Singapore Mediation Handbook*: 370 ff. For Hong Kong, see Alexander, et al., *Hong Kong Mediation*; Anna K. C. Koo and Shahla Ali, "Mediation in Hong Kong SAR," in Wang Guiguo and Yang Fan, eds., *Mediation in Asia Pacific: A Practical Guide to Mediation and its Impact on Legal Systems* (Hong Kong: CCH Hong Kong, 2013).

148 For Singapore, see, e.g., *Navin Jatia and others v. Ram Niranjan and another* [2020] SGCA 31; *Inngroup Pte Ltd v. M Asset Pte Ltd* [2020] SGHC 197; *Chan Gek Yong v. Violet Netto* [2018] SGHC 208; *Lock Han Chng v. Goh Jessiline* [2008] 2 SLR(R) 455, para 34. For Hong Kong, see, e.g., *Hyundai Engineering and Construction* [2005] HKEC 258.

149 For Singapore, see, e.g., *Zhongguo Remittance v. Samlit Moneychanger* [2020] SGDC 73; *Ling Kong Henry v. Tanglin Club* [2018] 5 SLR 871, para 25; *Heartronics Corporation v. EPI Life* [2017] SGHCR 17; *International Research Corp PLC* [2014] 1 SLR 130; *HSBC v. Toshin* [2012] 4 SLR 738, para 43. For Hong Kong, see, e.g., *Hui Ling Ling v. Sky Field Development Limited* (unreported, July 22, 2009; HCA 35/2007) [2009] HKCU 1216, paras 5–6; *Hyundai Engineering and Construction* [2005] HKEC 258; *Dragomar S.p.A. v. Geoworks Contractors (HK) Limited* (Unreported, January 27, 1998; 1997, NO. A5399) [1998] HKCU 63.

150 For Singapore, see, e.g., *LVM Law Chambers LLC v. Wan Hoe Keet and another* [2020] SGCA 29; *Ernest Ferdinand Perez De La Sala v. Compañia De Navegación Palomar, SA and others* [2018] 1 SLR 894, para 98; *Chan Gek Yong v. Violet Netto* [2018] SGHC 208; *Krishna Kumaran s/o K Ramakrishnan v. Kuppusamy s/o Ramakrishnan* [2014] 4 SLR 232, para 15. For Hong Kong, see, e.g., *Chu Chung Ming & Anor v. Lam Wai Dan & Ors* [2012] 4 HKLRD 897; *S v. T* [2011] 1 HKLRD 534, paras 3–4; *Wu Wei v. Liu Yi Ping* (unreported, January 30, 2009; HCA 1452/2004) [2009] HKCU 126; *Hyundai Engineering and Construction* [2005] HKEC 258, para 40.

151 For Singapore, see, e.g., *Heartronics Corporation v. EPI Life* [2017] SGHCR 17; *HSBC v. Toshin* [2012] 4 SLR 738, para 43–45; *International Research Corp PLC* [2014] 1 SLR 130, paras 90–97; *Asia Pte Ltd v. EZ-Import. Com Pte Ltd* [2004] SGDC 64. For Hong Kong, see, e.g., *WW v. LLN* [2020] HKCA 178; *LLC v. LMWA* [2019] 2 HKLRD 529; *Chan Shun Kei v. Hong Kong Construction (Hong Kong) Ltd* (unreported, CACV192/2014, March 7, 2016); *Wing Hong Investment Co Ltd v. Fung Sok Han & Others* (unreported, HCA 2075/2009, November 19, 2015).

152 It is trite in English law that contractual clauses should be sufficiently certain: *Scandinavian Trading Tank v. Flota Petrolera Ecuatoriana (The Scaptrade)* [1983] QB 529, at 540.

clause is triggered.[153] For example, specifying a mediation service provider or formalised mediation procedures[154] would be preferable over a mere reference to a "Third Party Mediation procedure."[155] Timetables should set out when various steps must be taken.[156] Notably, these cases were decided before the MO's introduction. It remains to be seen how its express reference to, and acknowledgement of, agreements to mediate would influence subsequent judicial interpretation and enforcement.

Singapore's MA[157] applies to mediations conducted pursuant to a "mediation agreement" (the equivalent of Hong Kong's "agreement to mediate"), which includes mediation clauses.[158] Section 8 permits courts to stay proceedings pursuant to such agreements, removing any doubt as to the prima facie validity of mediation clauses and the court's power to stay proceedings to give effect to them. Like Hong Kong, the Singapore precedents on their enforceability predate the legislation and adopt a similar approach. For instance, its Court of Appeal has indicated that mediation clauses should be worded clearly and establish in a definitive and mandatory fashion (and with sufficient specificity) the personnel required to attend the dispute resolution process and each meeting's purpose.[159] It remains to be seen if the Singapore courts take a more or less stringent approach following the MA.[160]

Overall, the court decisions suggest that both jurisdictions have a pro-mediation judiciary familiar with mediation's regulatory framework, mediation practice's nuances and associated legal issues.

Congruence of Laws

Legal and client users benefit from congruent domestic and international legal frameworks. Where domestic and cross-border elements are present in the same or related disputes, mediation would be potentially difficult if different laws applied to the domestic and cross-border aspects. Mediation promises the flexibility to address related disputes together and to address issues not technically part of the legal statement of claim. Harmonised legal frameworks would make this aspect of mediation significantly easier.

Hong Kong law does not differentiate between domestic and international MSAs. Lawyers must be familiar with the common law rules, the court practice directions and rules for litigation matters resolved at mediation and the Arbitration Ordinance for iMSAs recorded as consent arbitral awards. Once China

153 *Hyundai Engineering and Construction* [2005] HKEC 258, at para 29.
154 Rogers V. P. considered *Cable & Wireless Plc. v. IBM UK Ltd.* [2002] EWHC 2059.
155 *Hyundai Engineering and Construction* [2005] HKEC 258, at paras 29–30.
156 *Hyundai Engineering and Construction* [2005] HKEC 258, at para 30.
157 MA (Sing.).
158 The terms "mediation agreement" and "agreement to mediate" are largely used interchangeably in international mediation circles.
159 *International Research Corp PLC* [2014] 1 SLR 130, para 54.
160 *International Research Corp PLC* [2014] 1 SLR 130.

ratifies the Singapore Convention and Hong Kong implements its provisions, there will be an enforcement option open to iMSAs unavailable to domestic MSAs. However, given the international buy-in to the Convention and the absence of other legislation addressing commercial iMSA enforceability, this is unlikely to cause confusion. Rather, it will likely enhance Hong Kong's iMSA enforceability regime.

Singapore's legal frameworks for domestic and international mediation are comprehensive and largely integrated. Domestic and cross-border commercial mediation with a Singapore element are regulated in the same way by the same rules, like the MA.[161] The SCMA makes the iMSA enforcement regime slightly more complex, as it addresses commercial iMSAs (and not MSAs) but without the MA's prerequisites.

Practitioners will need to familiarise themselves with these options. Significantly, both the MA and SCMA apply to iMSAs involving disputes where litigation proceedings have not commenced.[162] Their broad scope enables disputants to save time and costs associated with commencing litigation while pursuing early settlement options that promise direct and perceptible enforcement relief. Granted, there are differences that will influence choices and strategies. For example, the MA only applies to mediations at least partly conducted in Singapore or where Singapore law applies; mediation service providers and mediators must meet certain standards; and parties have eight weeks to apply for a consent order reflecting the iMSA's terms. These requirements do not apply to the SCMA; moreover, under the SCMA only one party must apply to record the iMSA as a court order – i.e., the party seeking relief. Should parties record their iMSA as a court order under the MA, they will be precluded from recording it with a view to enforcement under the SCMA.

As in Hong Kong, domestic and international MSAs continue to be enforceable as contracts under the common law. Further, where litigation commences before a Singapore court, enforcement procedures for court-referred mediation may be available. Finally, when mediation forms part of mixed mode procedures, iMSAs may also be enforceable as consent arbitral awards. In short, parties have numerous enforcement options, and practitioners must familiarise themselves with the variegated iMSA enforcement regimes.

Conclusion

The law applicable to iMSAs in Hong Kong and Singapore demonstrates their leadership in regulating cross-border mediation, although their regulatory developments have varied in some ways.

Both jurisdictions feature hard and soft law approaches to regulation. Mediation clauses and court practice directions and rules form the primary trigger

161 MA, s 6(1), (wholly or partly conducted in Singapore or where the mediation agreement provides for Singapore law or the MA's application).

162 The SCMA does not apply to iMSAs that have been court approved or concluded in the course of court proceedings (SCMA, s 3(2)(a) read with Singapore Convention, art 1(3)(a)(i)).

mechanisms for mediation, whereas internal aspects of the mediation process are largely left for the parties' and mediators' determination, embodying the principle of party autonomy and mediation's procedural flexibility. Institutions in both jurisdictions play leading roles in credentialing and setting ethical and practice standards, and notably Singapore's MA only applies to mediations conducted by designated mediators or service provider institutions. In terms of legislation, both Hong Kong's MO and Singapore's MA and SCMA primarily address the rights and obligations of mediators and participants.

It is noteworthy that the general legislation applicable to both cross-border and domestic commercial mediation contains many similar provisions, suggesting a harmonised approach by Asia's two leading dispute resolution jurisdictions, especially over the confidentiality and admissibility of mediation communications. Regulatory approaches differ most noticeably in their direct enforcement provisions for pre-litigation iMSAs: only Singapore provides for this through the MA and SCMA. At the time of writing, neither jurisdiction has operative legislative provisions on third-party funding for standalone mediation, although this will likely change. Unique in Asia is Hong Kong's apology legislation, designed to encourage the use of mediation (including cross-border commercial mediation) by protecting apologies.

Mediation-related case law in both jurisdictions indicates a judiciary well versed in the nuances of mediation and supportive of its development. Further, its overall tenor is largely consistent across jurisdictions, differences being one of degree not principle.

The tale of two cities, Hong Kong and Singapore, bodes well for cross-border mediation law's future development, regionally and internationally. Jurisdictions seeking to introduce or amend such laws stand to learn from Hong Kong and Singapore's regulatory initiatives and experiences. Finally, the presence of active professional mediation communities and stakeholders in both jurisdictions, combined with supportive judiciaries and governments, suggests that we can expect ongoing leadership and regulatory innovation into the future.

Acknowledgment

I wish to thank Ong Kye Jing for his outstanding research and editorial work on this chapter. A longer and earlier version of this research appears in "The Emergence of Mediation Law in Asia: A Tale of Two Cities," *Transnational Dispute Management* 3 (2021), www.transnational-dispute-management.com.

Bibliography

Alexander, Nadja M. "Harmonization and Diversity in the Private International Law of Mediation: The Rhythms of Regulatory Reform." In Mediation: Principles and Regulation in Comparative Perspective, edited by Klaus J. Hopt and Felix Steffek, 131–204. Oxford University Press, 2013.

Alexander, Nadja M. International and Comparative Mediation: Legal Perspectives. Alphen aan den Rijn: Kluwer Law International, 2009.

Alexander, Nadja. "Japan-Singapore Joint Mediation Protocol Announced." Kluwer Mediation Blog. September 16, 2020. http://mediationblog.kluwerarbitration.com/2020/09/16/japan-singapore-joint-mediation-protocol-announced/.

Alexander, Nadja and Shouyu Chong. "Mediation and Appropriate Dispute Resolution." Singapore Academy of Law Annual Review of Singapore Cases 21 (2020). Published on e-First on July 9, 2020. https://ink.library.smu.edu.sg/cgi/viewcontent.cgi?article=5256&context=sol_research.

Alexander, Nadja, Vakhtang Giorgadze and Allison Goh. "Singapore International Dispute Resolution Academy International Dispute Resolution Survey (SIDRA Survey): 2020 Final Report." https://sidra.smu.edu.sg/sites/sidra.smu.edu.sg/files/survey/index.html.

Alexander, Nadja, Iu Ting Kwok, Rimksy Yuen and Ada Chen, eds. Hong Kong Mediation. Hong Kong: Lexis Nexis, 2021.

Alexander, Nadja, Joel Lee and Lum Kit-Wye. Singapore Mediation Handbook Singapore Mediation Handbook. Singapore: Lexis Nexis, 2019.

Alexander, Nadja and Felix Steffek. Making Mediation Law. World Bank Group International Finance Corporation, 2016. http://documents1.worldbank.org/curated/en/899611503551941578/pdf/119067-WP-REV-11-9-2017-15-33-48-MakingMedLaw.pdf.

Alexander, Nadja, Sabine Walsh and Martin Svatos, eds. EU Mediation Law Handbook: Regulatory Robustness Ratings for Mediation Regimes. Alphen aan den Rijn: Wolters Kluwer, 2017.

Ali, Shahla F. "Nudging Civil Justice: Examining Voluntary and Mandatory Court Mediation User Experience in Twelve Regions." Cardozo Journal of Conflict Resolution 19, no. 2 (Winter 2018).

APEC. "APEC Collaborative Framework for Online Dispute Resolution of Cross-Border Business-to-Business Disputes – Endorsed." August 2019. http://mddb.apec.org/Documents/2019/EC/EC2/19_ec2_022.pdf.

Austen, Ian and Jason Horowitz. "Pope Rejects Call for Apology to Canada's Indigenous People." The New York Times. March 28, 2018.

Bondurant, Joan V. Conquest of Violence: The Gandhian Philosophy of Conflict. Berkeley: University of California Press, 1965.

Carroll, Robyn. "Beyond Compensation: Apology as a Private Law Remedy." In The Law of Remedies: New Directions in the Common Law, edited by Jeff Berryman and Rick Bigwood, 323–385. Toronto: Irwin Law, 2010.

Chan, Sek Keong. "Launch of the SMU – Centre for Dispute Resolution – Speech by Chief Justice Chan Sek Keong." April 16, 2009. www.supremecourt.gov.sg/news/speeches/launch-of-the-smu–centre-for-dispute-resolution–speech-by-chief-justice-chan-sek-keong, last accessed January 12, 2022.

Cheng, Teresa. Speech by SJ at opening ceremony of "Mediate First" Pledge Event. May 24, 2019. www.info.gov.hk/gia/general/201905/24/P2019052400773.htm.

Chua, Eunice. "The Enforcement of International Mediated Settlement Agreements Without the Singapore Convention on Mediation." SAcLJ 31 (2019): 572–597.

Chua, Eunice. "The Singapore Convention on Mediation – A Brighter Future for Asian Dispute Resolution." Asian Journal of International Law 9 (2019): 195–205.

Decker, Marla and Nicholas Lingard. "Third Party Funding in Asia: Arrived, and Set to Thrive." Above the Law Blog. December 12, 2018.

Department of Justice of the Government of the Hong Kong Special Administrative Region. "Mediation Task Force Terms of Reference." 2011. www.doj.gov.hk/en/legal_dispute/pdf/mediation20110729e.pdf.

Department of Justice of the Government of the Hong Kong Special Administrative Region. "Report of the Working Group on Mediation." February 2010. www.doj.gov.hk/en/legal_dispute/pdf/med20100208e.pdf.

Department of Justice of the Government of the Hong Kong Special Administrative Region. "Steering Committee on Mediation, Terms of Reference." www.doj.gov.hk/en/legal_dispute/mediationCommittee.html.

Drahos, Peter, ed. Regulatory Theory: Foundations and Applications. Acton: Australian National University Press, 2017.

eBram. "Covid-19 Online Dispute Resolution (ODR) Scheme." www.ebram.org/covid_19_odr.html.

Erie, Matthew S. "The New Legal Hubs: The Emergent Landscape of International Commercial Dispute Resolution." Virginia Journal of International Law 60, no. 2 (2020): 225–298.

Fraser Institute. "Economic Freedom of the World: Annual Report 2020." www.fraserinstitute.org/sites/default/files/economic-freedom-of-the-world-2020.pdf.

Government of the Hong Kong Special Administrative Region. "Hong Kong Legal Hub." www.legalhub.gov.hk.

Hopt, Klaus J. and Felix Steffek. "Chapter 1 Mediation: Comparison of Laws, Regulatory Models, Fundamental Issues." In Mediation: Principles and Regulation, edited by Hopt and Steffek, 3–130. Oxford: Oxford University Press, 2013.

ICSID Secretariat. "Proposals for Amendment of the ICSID Rules – Synopsis." vol. 1. August 2, 2018. https://icsid.worldbank.org/sites/default/files/amendments/volume-1/Synopsis_English.pdf.

IMD World Competitiveness Centre. "Competitiveness Country Profiles." https://imd.cld.bz/IMD-World-Competitiveness-Booklet-2022/102/.

International Monetary Fund. "World Economic Outlook, April 2019: Growth Slowdown, Precarious Recovery." April 2019. www.imf.org/en/Publications/WEO/Issues/2019/03/28/world-economic-outlook-april-2019#Chapter%202.

Iu, Ting Kwok. "Face to Face with Hong Kong's Secretary for Justice." Interview with Teresa Cheng SC. Kluwer Mediation Blog. August 2, 2020. http://mediationblog.kluwerarbitration.com/2020/08/02/interview_with_hksj/.

Koo, Anna K. C. and Shahla Ali. "Mediation in Hong Kong SAR." In Mediation in Asia Pacific: A Practical Guide to Mediation and its Impact on Legal Systems, edited by Wang Guiguo and Yang Fan. Hong Kong: CCH Hong Kong, 2013.

Lam, Carrie. Speech by CE at International Dispute Resolution Conference 2019. April 17, 2019. www.info.gov.hk/gia/general/201904/17/P2019041700390.htm.

Lee, Jeffrey K. L. "Mediation in Mainland China and Hong Kong: Can They Learn from Each Other?" City University of Hong Kong, CityU Institutional Repository (2013).

Lee, Joel and Teh Hwee Hwee, eds. An Asian Perspective on Mediation. Singapore: Academy Publishing, 2009.

Leung, Chun-ying. "The 2013 Policy Address: Seek Change, Maintain Stability, Serve the People with Pragmatism." Hong Kong Government. 2013.

Leung, Chun-ying. "The 2014 Policy Address: Support the Needy, Let Youth Flourish, Unleash Hong Kong's Potential." Hong Kong Government. 2014.

Li, Kwok-nang Andrew. Speech at the conference on "Mediation in Hong Kong: The Way Forward." November 30, 2007. www.hkcfa.hk/filemanager/speech/en/upload/68/Speech%20by%20the%20Chief%20Justice%20at%20Mediation%20Conference(30-11-2007)en.pdf.

Lim, George S. C. "Back to 'MediAsian'." July 2014. www.mediatewith.me/portfolio/back-to-mediasian-august-2014/.

Lim, Gloria. "International Commercial Mediation: The Singapore Model." SAcLJ 31 (2019): 377–404.

Lye, Jaime. "Mediating the ASEAN Way." In Contemporary Issues in Mediation Volume 1, edited by Joel Lee and Marcus Lim. Singapore: World Scientific, 2016.

Menon, Sundaresh. "Building Sustainable Mediation Programs: A Singapore Perspective." Dispute Resolution Magazine 22 (Fall 2015): 42–45.

Menon, Sundaresh. Speech by CJ on "Judicial Attitudes towards Arbitration and Mediation in Singapore" at the Asean Law Association Malaysia (ALA) and Kuala Lumpur Regional Centre for Arbitration (KLRCA) Talk and Dinner. October 25, 2013.

Mistelis, Loukas A. "ADR in England and Wales: A Successful Case of Public Private Partnership." In Global Trends in Mediation, edited by Nadja Alexander, 2nd ed. Alphen aan den Rijn: Kluwer Law International, 2006.

National Development and Reform Commission. "Framework Agreement on Deepening Guangdong-Hong Kong-Macao Cooperation in the Development of the Greater Bay Area." www.bayarea.gov.hk/filemanager/en/share/pdf/Framework_Agreement.pdf.

Parker, Christine, Colin Scott, Nicola Lacey and John Braithwaite, eds. Regulating Law. Oxford: Oxford University Press, 2004.

Parliament of Singapore. "White Paper on Shared Values." Paper Cmd No. 1 of 1991.

Prakash, Pravin. "The Leviathan and its Muscular Management of Social Cohesion in Singapore." In Social Cohesion in Asia: Historical Origins, Contemporary Shapes and Future Dynamics, edited by Aurel Croissant and Peter Walkenhorst. Oxfordshire: Routledge, 2019.

Quek Anderson, Dorcas. "A Coming of Age for Mediation in Singapore? Mediation Act 2016." SAcLJ 29 (2017): 275–293.

Quek Anderson, Dorcas. "Supreme Court Practice Directions (Amendment No. 1 of 2016): A Significant Step in Further Incorporating ADR into the Civil Justice Process." The Singapore Law Gazette (March 2016). http://v1.lawgazette.com.sg/2016-03/1524.htm.

Robbennolt, Jennifer K. "Apologies and Legal Settlement: An Empirical Examination." Michigan Law Review 102, no. 3 (2003): 460–516.

Singapore International Mediation Centre. "Singapore and Japan International Mediation Centres Launch Joint Mediation Protocol to Help Cross-Border Businesses Resolve Disputes Swiftly and Inexpensively." SIMC News. September 13, 2020. https://simc.com.sg/blog/2020/09/13/singapore-and-japan-international-mediation-centres-launch-joint-mediation-protocol-to-help-cross-border-businesses-resolve-disputes-swiftly-and-inexpensively/.

Steffek, Felix. "Mediation in Europa und der Welt – Rechtsvergleichende Forschung zur Umsetzung der Mediationsrichtlinie." Zeitschrift für Konfliktmanagement 12, no. 1 (2009): 21–25.

Supreme Court of Singapore. "Public Consultation on Civil Justice Reforms: The Recommendations of the Civil Justice Review Committee and Civil Justice Commission." October 26, 2018. https://www.mlaw.gov.sg/files/Annex_A_Public_consultation_paper_on_civil_justice_reforms.pdf/.

Sussman, Edna. "The Singapore Convention – Promoting the Enforcement and Recognition of International Mediated Settlement Agreements." ICC Dispute Resolution Bulletin 3 (2018): 42–54.

Tan, Dawn Wei. "Singapore, China to Set up Mediators' Panel for Belt and Road Projects." The Straits Times. January 25, 2019. www.straitstimes.com/asia/east-asia/singapore-china-to-set-up-mediators-panel-for-belt-and-road-projects.

Teramura, Nobumichi, Shahla Ali and Anselmo Reyes. "On Expanding Asia-Pacific Frontiers for International Dispute Resolution: Conclusions and Recommendations." In New Frontiers in Asia-Pacific International Arbitration and Dispute Resolution, edited by Luke Nottage, Shahla Ali, Bruno Jetin and Nobumichi Teramura. Alphen aan den Rijn: Wolters Kluwer, 2020.

Tong, Edwin. "Speech by Mr Edwin Tong, Senior Minister of State for Law and Health, at the SIMC Singapore Specialist Mediators Appointment Ceremony." January 3, 2020. https://simc.com.sg/blog/2020/01/04/speech-by-mr-edwin-tong-senior-minister-of-state-for-law-and-health-at-the-simc-singapore-specialist-mediators-appointment-ceremony/.

Weber, Thomas. "Gandhian Philosophy, Conflict Resolution Theory and Practical Approaches to Negotiation." Journal of Peace Research 38, no. 4 (2001): 493–513.

White & Case LLP and Queen Mary University of London School of International Arbitration. "2018 International Arbitration Survey: The Evolution of International Arbitration." May 9, 2018. https://arbitration.qmul.ac.uk/media/arbitration/docs/2018-International-Arbitration-Survey-report.pdf.

Wilkinson, Michael, Eric Cheung and Gary Meggitt. A Guide to Civil Procedure in Hong Kong, 6th ed. Hong Kong: Lexis Nexis, 2017.

Wilson, Mark. "Hong Kong's New Airport and the Resolution of Disputes." Hong Kong Law Journal 25 (1995): 363–382.

Wong, Lisa. Speech at the "Mediate First" Pledge Mediation Forum 2019. May 24, 2019. https://mediation.judiciary.hk/en/doc/The%20Hon%20Madam%20Justice%20Lisa%20Wong%27s%20speech%20at%20the%20the%20Mediate%20First%20Pledge%20Mediation%20Forum%202019.pdf.

World Bank. "Belt and Road Initiative." March 29, 2018. www.worldbank.org/en/topic/regional-integration/brief/belt-and-road-initiative.

World Economic Forum. "Global Competitiveness Report 2019." http://www3.weforum.org/docs/WEF_TheGlobalCompetitivenessReport2019.pdf.

World Justice Project. "Rule of Law Index 2020." https://worldjusticeproject.org/sites/default/files/documents/WJP-ROLI-2020-Online_0.pdf.

Yap, Yun Ning Charmaine. "What's in a Nudge? How Choice Architecture Surrounding Dispute Resolution Options Can Increase Uptake of Mediation." In *Contemporary Issues in Mediation Volume 4*, edited by Joel Lee and Marcus Lim, 3–13. Singapore: World Scientific Research, 2019.

8

ENVIRONMENTAL MEDIATION AND FACILITATION IN ITALY

Theoretical Insights and Practical Experience on Non-Adjudicative Mechanisms and "Total Conflicts"

Luigi Cominelli, Eleonora Ciscato and Stefania Lattuille

The Environmental Conflict in Italy

The environmental conflict, in the broad sense, is one of the fields of dispute resolution that is currently attracting the most attention. The growing awareness of the environmental risks of climate change and environmental pollution has facilitated the rising of disputes that can involve public and private subjects at all levels (individual and collective actors, urban and rural areas) and that require effective and innovative management paradigms. This mega-trend concerns the whole world, both developed and developing areas, where until recently the needs to grow and build civil and industrial infrastructures seemed to overshadow any other consideration. Sometimes, the environmental conflict takes an international character and involves independent sovereign subjects, with potential consequences of even greater size.[1]

Besides, the complexity of the triggered problems leads to paradoxical situations, where local communities even oppose constructing "green" disposal plants as they impact the local environment. Italy, for example, has a structural shortage of infrastructure for processing waste, which then has to be processed abroad. This is not economically sustainable,[2] thus facilitating the onset of illegal disposal activities and, consequently, widespread environmental damage. This leads to the well-known NIMBY (Not In My Back Yard) phenomena of resistance and civil mobilisation, arising when the local community perceives that the costs of a

1 John Dryzek and Susan Hunter, "Environmental Mediation for International Problems," *International Studies Quarterly* (2017): 87–102.

2 Jacopo Giliberto, "Ecomondo, inquinamento: le emissioni di gas serra non calano da cinque anni," *Il Sole 24 ore*, November 13, 2019, www.ilsole24ore.com/art/economia-verde-che-cosa-e-accaduto-ecomondo-ACNaZjx.

DOI: 10.4324/9780429354625-12

given intervention exceed the supposed benefits and the possibility to litigate (as now universally possible) is foreseen.[3]

The "Atlante italiano dei conflitti ambientali"[4] (Italian Atlas of Environmental Conflicts), part of the Global Atlas of Environmental Justice, financed and periodically updated with the European ERC funds allocated to the EnvJustice project, mapped 157 environmental conflicts on Italian national soil (a conservative estimate). Many of these are now over, but most of them are still active and of "average" intensity, and some of them have been ongoing for years or even decades now.

This work has focused on the alternative dispute resolution of Italian environmental conflicts. We intend to give an overview of a fast-changing system by combining the academic and professional experience of the authors. Given its multifaceted nature, and the involvement of citizens and external stakeholders that are not entitled to litigate but are partially involved in the issue, the environmental conflict has always been considered one of the most suitable areas for application of non-adjudicative methods of dispute resolution, especially of mediation and facilitation. On the other hand, the environmental conflict is often complex to deal with because it falls within the competence of different administrative and judicial authorities, depending on the specific problem and the parties involved.

Starting from this analysis, the issue of common goods management has also been addressed. In a broader sense, today more than ever, individuals and collectivities are ready to litigate in courts over such "environmental common goods", getting to results that are not always rapid and satisfactory.[5] Finally, we thought it was also important to underline and deepen the point of view of practitioners in cases of domestic facilitation/mediation.

Environmental Conflicts as Total Conflicts

Power plants, extractive and productive factories, big infrastructures and waste storage facilities are increasingly at the centre of conflicts, where groups of citizens confront private or public bodies.[6] These are the so-called environmental conflicts in which human intervention, potential or already in place, becomes a source of disturbance in the physiological ability of ecosystems to regenerate, causing scarcity. It can be physical scarcity due to over-exploitation or impoverishment in the quality of public space.[7] Along with chemical and biological

3 Douglas H. Yarn, "Environmental Mediation: Great Promise, Some Problems," *Water Environment & Technology*, no. 7 (1995): 80–81.

4 "Atlante italiano dei conflitti ambientali," https://it.ejatlas.org/country, accessed November 23, 2020.

5 Giovanni Ruocco and Marianna Stori, "La democrazia alla prova dei conflitti ambientali," *Associazione A Sud – CDCA* (2016): 49.

6 Centro documentazione conflitti ambientali, *Dossier Conflitti Ambientali: Mappe, saperi, strumenti per le ecologie di domani* (Roma: CDCA, 2019).

7 Stephan Libiszewski, "What is an Environmental Conflict?" *Occasional Paper No. 1* (Zurich: Center for Security Studies and Conflict Research, 1993).

processes, however, social phenomena also arise, as the result of the conflicting interaction between stakeholders. Therefore, conflicts are not only the result of broken ecological balance but become "total conflicts" that involve sociological, economic, political and institutional aspects. Although situations can differ considerably, the perception of existing or potential environmental degradation usually triggers the creation of citizens' groups that self-organise to claim their rights to live in a healthy environment. Legal instruments are increasingly seen by communities as a useful resource to deal with injustices and report abuses, better if accompanied by media coverage.[8]

In addition to this, there are more and more instances where the right to self-determination is advanced, understood as the effective ability to participate in the decision-making process.[9] This social aspect is particularly relevant in terms of the conflict dynamics: the claims are not individual but always have a collective scope. Besides, they increasingly intercept legally debated issues such as environmental justice and the rights of future generations,[10] in a way intertwining with the claims of global social movements such as Fridays for Future or Extinction Rebellion.[11]

Increasingly, the political (though in many cases non-partisan) side emerges: groups of environmentalists and citizens criticise the economic paradigm based on individualism and consumerism that led, as anticipated by Polanyi,[12] to an indiscriminate commodification of the environment and people's lives. The environmental conflict also involves economic assessments: clashes often concern the real economic benefits of the projects under discussion (even when they should favour the collectivity)[13] as well as the benefits-costs dimension. Finally, environmental conflicts also interest institutions. Indeed, institutions are involved not only as counterparties, but their role is questioned when they are perceived as non-transparent, incapable of making participatory processes effective or, even worse, subjugated to expertise that struggles in finding its neutral dimension.[14]

In this "contentious politics"[15] of dynamics, actors, interests and implications, finding adequate responses to the growing number of environmental conflicts is

8 Michael McCann, "Law and Social Movements: Contemporary Perspective," *Annual Review of Law and Social Science*, no. 2 (2006): 29–31.

9 Luigi Bobbio and Alberico Zeppetella, *Perché proprio qui? Grandi opere e opposizioni locali* (Milano: FrancoAngeli, 1999).

10 In this sense, it is interesting to evaluate, also in the mediation context, the time frame used as a reference and how it can be legally justifiable. As Passerini (1998) pointed out, the "social time horizon" may vary from community to community, with its implications.

11 Xenia Chiaramonte, "The Struggle for Law: Legal Strategies, Environmental Struggles and Climate Actions in Italy," *Oñati Socio-Legal Series* 10, no. 4 (2020): 939.

12 Karl Polanyi, *The Great Transformation* (New York: Farrar and Rinehart, 1944).

13 Consider, for example, the conflicts arising from the construction of TAV in Val di Susa, the incinerator in Trento or the wind turbine plants in Abruzzo.

14 Luigi Pellizzoni, *Conflitti ambientali. Esperti, politica, istituzioni nelle controversie sociologiche* (Bologna: Il Mulino, 2011).

15 Charles Tilly and Sidney Tarrow, *Contentious Politics* (New York: Oxford University Press, 2006).

no easy task. As surveys pointed out,[16] the increased awareness of environmental risks or social media communication only partly justifies the growing involvement of citizen groups in environmental litigation. Rather, it seems to be crucial that clean water, air and soil are among the non-replaceable essential goods on which people's well-being, health and life depend.

The public debate is increasingly taking up the idea that the environment is a "common good,"[17] meaning that the resources are fundamental in meeting the most basic needs of individuals and should, therefore, be protected in the public interest.[18] These resources, as defined by Ostrom,[19] are non-excludable and rivalrous. To avoid their deterioration, misuse or even depletion, management should be organised in a way that is adequate, sustainable and, as has been pointed out by various studies, capable of involving local communities. Several scholars, starting from Axelrod[20] and Ostrom,[21] analysed the issue of property rights and, through systematic empirical studies, highlighted the contexts that favoured collective action to govern common goods, providing fundamental ideas and incentives in guiding policies as well as assessing forms of dispute resolution.

Analysing the dynamics of environmental conflicts in Italy[22] – but this concept can be extended worldwide – it emerges that some factors contribute specifically to conflicts, such as the irreversibility of interventions foreseen or the pre-existing vulnerability of the territory.[23] Other relevant elements to assess the likelihood of an environmental conflict are degradation observability and perceived weak governance.[24] Strong governance, far from any simple reduction, is the one capable of deep analysis and action, to be inclusive, transparent and able to recognise, involve and empower citizens. In this sense, Sen[25] and Nussbaum's[26] works can help clarify, theoretically, how justice should not be

16 Eurobarometer, *Special Eurobarometer 468: Attitudes of European Citizens Towards the Environment* (Brussels: Directorate-General for Communication, 2017).

17 The academic literature dealing with common goods is extremely broad and cannot be addressed here for space constraints, but here are some of the main references that should be considered: Hardin (1968), Ostrom (1990), Demsets (1967) and Boyle (2003). In Italy, we should mention Marella (2014), Mattei (2011), Rodotà (2013) and Sacconi and Ottone (2015), among others.

18 Maria Rosaria Marella, "The Commons as a Legal Concept," *Law Critique, Springer*, no. 28 (2017): 61–86.

19 Elinor Ostrom et al., *Rules, Games and Common-Pool Resources* (Michigan: University of Michigan Press, 1994).

20 Robert Axelrod, *The Evolution of Cooperation* (New York: Basic Books, 1984).

21 Elinor Ostrom, *Governing the Commons. The Evolution of Institutions for Collective Action* (Cambridge: Cambridge University Press, 1990).

22 Luigi Pellizzoni, *Conflitti Ambientali. Esperti, Politica, Istituzioni Nelle Controversie Sociologiche* (Bologna: Il Mulino, 2011).

23 Alessandra Oppio et al., "Exploring the Relationship Among Local Conflicts and Territorial Vulnerability: The Case Study of Lombardy Region," *Land Use Policy*, no. 43 (2015): 239–247.

24 Renard Sexton, "Unpacking the Local Resource Curse: How Externalities and Governance Shape Social Conflict," *Journal of Conflict Resolution* 64, no. 64 (2020): 640–673.

25 Amartya K. Sen, *Development as Freedom* (New York: Knopf, 1990).

26 Martha C. Nussbaum, *Creating Capabilities: The Human Development Approach* (Cambridge, MA: Harvard University Press, 2011).

conceptualised only in terms of distribution but as possibilities to living worthy lives, considering goods and opportunities in terms of capabilities and functioning of individuals.

This process, while not easy, can be developed by taking into account both expertise and lay knowledge of citizens and movements, through transparent information and, in essence, the inclusion of different perspectives.[27] Environmental disasters are often caused by human beings' direct action, and legal responses are often inadequate because of the technical difficulties in defining liabilities in scientific uncertainty and because of the complexity of the issues at stake. The non-linear relationship among expertise, representation and perception makes it even more difficult to face the threats of irreversible damages and social conflicts. The environmental mediation, involving stakeholders and public authorities, can potentially be instrumental in identifying generative and legitimate practices to preserve environmental quality and at the same time manage social conflicts.

Mediation and Facilitation of Environmental Conflicts

Mediation is considered particularly suitable for collective disputes involving two or more parties that can also formally represent a variety of subjects. In multiparty litigation, the variety of interests and individual perceptions can be grasped and summarised with even greater difficulty than in dyadic litigations. Moreover, the issues at stake affect a given collectivity for a significant period and concern issues that tend to be long lasting (such as environmental damage or the construction of an infrastructure).

It is no coincidence that in the United States environmental disputes were entrusted to the Federal Mediation and Conciliation Services (FMCS), created in 1947 to mediate in trade union negotiations and today in charge of ADR procedures involving public administration at all levels.[28] However, environmental disputes are recognised to be more complex than industrial relations, even from the perspective of the diversity of the parties involved and on the heterogeneity of the issues entailed.[29]

When an environmental dispute enters litigation, argue Danielson and Watson, the case usually focuses on side issues over substantive ones: whether alternatives have been assessed fairly, whether enough consultations have been held or whether the relevant data has been submitted correctly.[30] It is for this reason that the majority of environmental disputes involving the allocation of scarce

27 Rosalba Altopiedi, "Ambiente, Giustizia e Diritto," *Sociologia del diritto*, no. 2 (2020): 104–105.

28 Lawrence E. Susskind, "Environmental Mediation and the Accountability Problem," *Vermont Law Review*, no. 6 (1981).

29 Michael R. Greenberg, "Up-Front Environmental Mediation," *Geographical Review*, no. 67 (1977): 235.

30 Luke J. Danielson and John L. Watson, "Environmental Mediation," *Natural Resources Lawyer*, no. 15 (1983): 689.

resources, the setting of public priorities or the definition of qualitative environmental standards should be amenable to mediation.[31]

We do not explain here in detail the distinction between disputes that can or cannot be mediated, but we still believe the general criteria developed by Carrie Menkel-Meadow[32] recognising the full compatibility of non-adjudicative methods with the principles of the right of defence are fully applicable. Considering the cost-benefit analysis perspective, and despite the complication of measuring its benefits and even though it does not guarantee a decision on the dispute or set a precedent, mediation reduces transaction costs and allows for the establishment or maintenance of better relationships between parties, also facilitating satisfactory solutions.[33]

Susskind so summarises the nine elements that require particular attention in environmental mediation:[34] 1) identify all parties holding a potential interest in the dispute; 2) adequately involve all the relevant interest groups in the process; 3) address the substantial differences in values among the parties; 4) develop an adequate number of alternative solutions; 5) define the temporal and substance limits of the environmental impact assessment; 6) carry out, collectively, the balancing, the scaling and the cost-benefit assessments; 7) negotiate compensatory and impact mitigation actions; 8) carefully assess the legitimacy and financial sustainability of the agreements; and 9) make sure mechanisms are in place so that all parties are required to meet their commitments.

Several of these aspects are common to any non-adjudicative procedure, but some of the steps, given the specificity of the environmental dispute, become crucial. It has been stressed, for example, that the list of stakeholders should be formalised, as should be the addressed issues, whether or not they were included in the ongoing or potential judicial litigation. Moreover, a timeline that ensures the problem is handled timely can be helpful.[35] Likewise, the issue of compliance with the content of the agreement is particularly thorny: in several cases, the settlement reached in mediation is only opportunistically agreed upon by one of the parties to achieve appeasement, without the intention to respect it.[36] Moreover, the time factor can have particular implications for the "political side", which, having the possibility to proceed unilaterally, has an excellent alternative to reaching a consensus agreement but at the same time bears the risk of a non-re-election or the possible disinvestment by private investors.[37]

31 Susskind, "Environmental Mediation and the Accountability Problem," 13.

32 Carrie Menkel-Meadow, "Whose Dispute is it Anyway?: a Philosophical and Democratic Defense of Settlement (in Some Cases)," *Georgetown Law Journal*, no. 83 (1995): 2663–2969.

33 Lawrence E. Susskind, "Confessions of a Public Dispute Mediator," *Negotiation Journal* (2000): 131.

34 Susskind, "Environmental Mediation and the Accountability Problem," 14.

35 Ane D. Deister, "Environmental Mediation Strategies for Success: Summaries of Two Consensus-Based Cases – Florida's Growth Management Act Legislation and the Los Angeles River Watershed Task Force," *The Urban Lawyer* 32 no. 1 (2000): 87.

36 David Nicholson, *Environmental Dispute Resolution in Indonesia* (Leiden: Brill, 2000), 189.

37 John Harrison, "Environmental Mediation: The Ethical and Constitutional Dimension," *Journal of Environmental Law* 9, no. 1 (1997): 94.

Alongside mediation, and perhaps before it, environmental disputes have been dealt with through "facilitation" procedures. When it comes to facilitation, a wide and heterogeneous set of practices and "participatory processes" is now usually considered. They are increasingly regulated and defined as "public debates" which, without establishing a formal process of mediation and generally working pre-emptively, aim at preventing the dispute from ending up in a judicial dispute through consultation and with the involvement of all stakeholders. These processes help define the ongoing or potential dispute (consensus conferences, citizen juries, planning cells, scenario workshops) but can also lead to so-called *negotiated rule-making.*[38]

The facilitator (or, more often, the team of facilitators) follows all the stages of the facilitation, even once it is concluded. The organisational effort is considerable, given the large number of players involved and given that the facilitators cannot always rely on a stable organisation. Their tasks are: setting the pace of the meetings, moderating (facilitate, indeed) the debate and the following negotiation in its most controversial aspects, bringing out the differences and deepening the issues discussed and involving those whose consensus is important for reaching the final agreement.

In carrying out this task, the techniques may vary considerably, but the practice of dividing the participants into subgroups (or *caucuses*, just as the confidential sessions used in mediation) is recurrent. When diverging opinions within "coalitions" emerge (for example, between committees of citizens or residents and the public entity interested in enforcing environmental legislation against a private entity), creating a sub-group can prevent the debate from reaching an impasse or positions from becoming polarised.

Another way of using the caucus is to create sub-groups where every stakeholder has a representative and to assign each of them a controversial aspect of the dispute to discuss. Once the sub-group has reached an agreement on that specific aspect, each member, no matter which group of interest they belong to, will commit to having the compromise accepted by the other members of their group as well. It has been observed that with interaction and mutual knowledge, caucuses, even though they incorporate diverse and conflicting interests, start to work as a unitary decision-making groups, collectively and cooperatively. This mechanism helps produce proposals that are not labelled anymore as "the environmental position" or "the engineer's preference".[39] Another task of the facilitator is that of ensuring the continued and ongoing involvement of participants. Facilitating processes requires considerable commitment in terms of time and energy, and avoiding intermittent and unfocused participation of the parties is essential for success.[40]

38 Luigi Pellizzoni, "'Decidiamo insieme!' Conflitti tecnologici e deliberazione pubblica," *Quaderni di Sociologia*, no. 41 (2006): 5; Howard Bellman and Susan L. Podziba, "Public Policy Mediation: Best Practices," *GPSolo Magazine* 33, no. 3 (2016): 73.

39 Deister, "Environmental Mediation Strategies for Success," 93.

40 Ibid., 95.

There is also a significant difference from mediation processes in terms of confidentiality. While confidentiality in joint or separate mediation sessions is strictly protected, what happens in the facilitation of environmental conflicts needs to be adequately publicised, considering the collective impact and the public relevance of the dispute. In many cases, maintaining confidentiality is not practically possible, like when parties with a low level of cohesion are involved in the process, such as citizens' committees or protest groups.[41] When confidentiality needs to be protected at least during the exploratory phase, some of the sessions should be open to the public or the media or the procedure should be flanked by a public regulatory process.[42] It should be recalled that when the power of the authority of a public entity is involved, the decision-making process of mediation and facilitation should be normally followed by a formalised decision-making process.[43]

Legal Instruments for Environmental Conflict Management

When they agree to mediate, governments and institutions renounce the possibility to act unilaterally.[44] In a sense, this is the cause of the controversy over the use of ADRs when public interests are at stake. In such cases, many fear that using ADR would imply an abdication of the state jurisdiction from its functions of interpreting constitutional norms and protecting the weaker party.[45] Considering the environmental field, in particular, the main concern is that the general interest in maintaining a healthy environment or in conserving resources will be abandoned when the decision-making process results in a private transaction between actors that may lack democratic legitimacy.[46]

Some have objected by highlighting that while it is true that the interpretation of rules of public interest should be litigated in a court of law, not all environmental matters necessarily imply the interpretation of such rules.[47] More often, it is a question of balancing public interests of a comparable weight, whose

41 Harrison, "Environmental Mediation: The Ethical and Constitutional Dimension," 87.

42 Susskind, "Environmental Mediation and the Accountability Problem," 44–45.

43 Harrison, "Environmental Mediation: The Ethical and Constitutional Dimension," 95; Susan L. Podziba, *Civic Fusion. Mediating Polarized Public Disputes* (Chicago: American Bar Association, 2012).

44 Susskind, "Confessions of a Public Dispute Mediator," 130.

45 Owen M. Fiss, "Against Settlement," *Yale Law Journal* 93, no. 6 (1984): 1073–1090; David Luban, "Settlements and the Erosion of Public Realm," *The Georgetown Law Journal*, no. 83 (1995): 2619–2662; William Twining, "Alternative to What? Theories of Litigation, Procedure and Dispute Settlement in Anglo-American Jurisprudence: Some Neglected Classics," *The Modern Law Review* 56, no. 3 (1993): 380–392.

46 Harrison, "Environmental Mediation: The Ethical and Constitutional Dimension," 79.

47 Carrie Menkel-Meadow, "For and Against Settlement: Uses and Abuses of the Mandatory Settlement Conference," *UCLA Law Review*, no. 33 (1985): 485–514; Carrie Menkel-Meadow, "Whose Dispute is it Anyway?: A Philosophical and Democratic Defense of Settlement (in Some Cases)," *Georgetown Law Journal*, no. 83 (1995): 2663–2969; Eligio Resta, "Giudicare, Conciliare, Mediare," *Politica del Diritto* 30, no. 4 (1999): 541–575.

assessment could be better made by the individuals and entities concerned rather than by the court. However, in a country of "formalistic and bureaucratic legal and administrative tradition, public and private", such as Italy, it is clear that the spaces available for such negotiations can be even narrower,[48] especially if the public administration culture is conceived as an imperative definition of the closest arrangements to an abstract idea of public interest, rather than as a political negotiation of what the public interest is.[49]

Therefore, mediation has often been accused of being the Trojan horse, used by private industry or public bureaucracy to co-opt the most malleable side of environmental groups, cool down the conflict and legitimise a watered-down compromise. By focusing on negotiable aspects of the dispute and leaving out the non-negotiable ones, the final outcome would favour the strongest party, with the consequence of crystallising the imbalance between the respective interest groups.[50]

On the contrary, although the mediator is by definition neutral and impartial, this does not mean he or she is obliged to mediate a dispute where the imbalance between the parties is excessive or where the essential interests of the absent stakeholder are overlooked.[51] In this sense, there are situations where the mediator can and must take an active role and go beyond neutrality,[52] actively seeking to rebalance the dispute[53] without jeopardising her credibility.

The most critical aspects of environmental mediation under this profile are the impact of the agreement on under-represented groups or groups that cannot be represented in court, its long-term consequences and the precedent the agreement establishes.[54] The ethical responsibility for the consequences of the agreement rests on the mediator, who may raise doubts while remaining impartial, maybe even suggesting the parties rely on an external consultant or withdraw from litigation.[55]

The Italian regulatory framework also needed to be amended for the administrative power to become "negotiable". Constitutional doctrine had in the past been inflexible on this point, depriving public entities of the opportunity to participate in nonjudicial processes, such as mediation and facilitation. Today, however, there is greater flexibility in accepting that at least the practical arrangements in pursuing the public interest can be within certain limits discretionally

48 Pellizzoni, "Decidiamo insieme!," 2.

49 Robert D. Putnam, *The Comparative Study of Political Elites* (Englewood Cliffs, NJ: Prentice-Hall, 1976).

50 Amy J. Douglas, "The Politics of Environmental Mediation," *Ecology Law Quarterly* 11, no. 1 (1983): 1–19.

51 Susskind, "Environmental Mediation and the Accountability Problem," 14.

52 Nicholson, "Environmental Dispute Resolution in Indonesia," 52.

53 Susskind, "Environmental Mediation and the Accountability Problem," 130.

54 Ibid., 46.

55 Harrison, "Environmental Mediation: the Ethical and Constitutional Dimension," 102.

negotiable.[56] In this sense, domestic legislation accepted the notion of "public law contracts"[57] while constitutional doctrine created the two distinct concepts of "private-law transactions involving relations governed by public law" and "public law transactions".[58]

Full institutionalisation and recognition of ADRs in such disputes were certainly expected, especially in a complex framework, where the theoretical feasibility of mediation did not entirely convince the public officials. The traditional problem for public officials in promoting a settlement agreement on behalf of a public entity has always been the risk of being held accountable for the damage to the Treasury. Public officials sometimes sought preventive legal advice from the attorney general (*avvocatura dello stato*), but ambivalent answers were given that, for example, recognised the convenience of environmental mediation only in cases of "modest" damage and suggested it exclusively for limited aspects such as restoration, compensation for "provisional losses" and possibly some forms of non-financial damage to the public entity.[59]

Facilitation for environmental issues has finally been recognised at the national level, after limited mechanisms of participatory decision-making processes had been foreseen at the local level[60] or in sectoral legislation. The 1998 Aarhus Convention[61] represented a benchmark, as it transposed the tenth principle of the Rio Declaration on Environment and Development (1992), thus regulating and promoting access to information, public participation in decision-making processes and access to justice in the environmental field. At the state level, the most relevant precedent for public debate and participatory processes was the French Law "Barnier" (No. 95–101 of 2 February 1995) on environmental protection.

The Public Debate was first outlined by art. 22 of the Italian Code on public procurement (Legislative Decree 18 April 2016, n. 50). In 2018, a decree by the president of the Council of Ministers (DPCM No. 76 of 10 May 2018 – entered into force on 24 August 2018) established the National Public Debate Commission, in charge of supervising the public discussion, through facilitation processes, of the feasibility of infrastructures and architecture works of social importance, impacting the environment, cities and the territory and falling under the public procurement code (roads, airports, ports, railways or works

56 Jacopo Polinari, "La possibile deflazione delle controversie amministrative. Transazione e altri mezzi di prevenzione e/o risoluzione. Premesse ad uno studio sull'arbitrato nel diritto amministrativo," *Rassegna Avvocatura Dello Stato*, no. 4 (2010): 287.

57 Ibid., 288.

58 Ibid. In some countries, when public agencies are not involved, agreements are implemented in 67% of cases, while when they are, the rate of implementation is 85%: see Harrison, "Environmental Mediation: the Ethical and Constitutional Dimension," 90.

59 Luisa Giampietro, "I procedimenti di mediazione in materia ambientale: spunti di riflessione," *Ambiente & Sviluppo*, no. 3 (2011): 251.

60 "Progettare insieme la città," Allegati alle Deliberazione Giunta Comune Milano n. 1079/2016.

61 UNECE Convention on Access to Information, Public Participation in Decision-making and Access to Justice in Environmental Matters (Aarhus Convention, 1998).

related to energy, water, industrial settlements or connected to cultural, sports, scientific and touristic purposes).

The Public Debate (art. 2) is "the process of information, participation and public debate on the opportunities and design solutions for works, projects or interventions". A national commission will supervise these public debates and will be chaired by an administrative judge and will have the power to propose to the competent ministry the appointment of up to three experts in mediation and facilitation that will take part in its proceedings (without voting rights). Each public debate will be attended by national or local members of the parliament, administrative judges, representatives of authorised national environmental associations, representatives of customers and "qualified personalities", meaning any representative of the relevant stakeholders.

Each public debate will be organised and managed considering the characteristics of the social and territorial context and will consist of information and follow-up meetings, discussions and conflict management, especially in those territories that are directly affected, as well as in the collection of proposals from citizens, associations and institutions (art. 8).

A coordinator (facilitator) will be assigned to each work for which a public debate is initiated, in order to follow the process and make it open to the general public. The design and preparation phase of the debate will last one month, to allow the facilitator to adapt the process to the local context as for the modalities, timing and dissemination among the public (art. 6). The public debate will last approximately four months, after which a final report will be presented, that will also be taken into account by the public administration or the contracting authority in the impact assessment and in deciding the following stages (art. 9).

With regard to those works that do not qualify for the public debate procedure, the process can also be initiated voluntarily following the initiative of qualified subjects (which, obviously, can take into account informal requests by citizens), and other procedures of institutionalised participation provided for in the official environmental impact assessment can be applied, even though these do not prioritise the facilitation aspect.

The "Canal" Mediation

It is useful here to recount a recent environmental mediation conducted in northern Italy which did not follow the official public debate procedure but lends itself to a description of its possible functioning. Following the initiative by a public entity in Lombardy, this mediation was carried out from September 2019 to March 2020 to resolve the differences on a project for the recovery of an ancient irrigation canal, polluted by sewage waters, within a protected natural area.[62] The mediation involved the local public bodies and the companies in

62 The mediation was conducted by Stefania Lattuille, one of the co-authors of this article.

charge of the redevelopment work, the various technical consultants appointed by these bodies, the company that owned a significant portion of the area and two associations of citizens active in the protection of their territory.

The mediator in charge organised the process throughout seven meetings, coordinating the plenary sessions and those of the technical committee, attending the inspection in the territory impacted by the project and taking care of the exchanges of documentation that took place. She then led the closing meeting of the mediation and the further contacts and exchanges to promote the implementation of the amended project, until a new convention between the three public bodies was signed.

With respect to this environmental mediation, two aspects deserve to be highlighted: on the one hand, the planning and organisation of the mediation process, and on the other hand, the result achieved, which constitutes a noteworthy precedent because through creative confrontation it was possible to discuss, redesign and modify a public project that was already underway. In the pre-mediation meeting, after the initial round of presentations, the mediator illustrated the working method and the characteristics of environmental mediation, and then she invited all the participants to specify their points of view, maintaining a reserved space for speaking in order to allow mutual listening and learning of the relevant aspects of such complex affair.

In essence, the problems to be solved that emerged were: 1) the fact that the technical solution for the recovery of the canal envisaged by the project did not take into account the needs of the local community (in particular, that of maintaining unspoiled the historical landscape of the place) and 2) that the chosen solutions, in particular the hydraulic ones, had not been shared and understood, and for this reason they too were opposed and questioned.

In the light of what emerged at the first meeting, having asked if all the interlocutors were present, the need to involve the financing entity was highlighted, which in the end took an important role. The participants then outlined in a more precise way the objectives of the mediation, setting a maximum time frame for the process at three to four months, which was then extended to six months.

The participants themselves made a list of the documents that it was necessary or appropriate to share, through the mediator, and then, in the following days, they were able to view all the materials relating to the executive project, the numerous additional technical documents and the observations from the two citizens' associations. However, the group initially decided to keep the process and the exchanges of documentation and reports of the various meetings confidential, with the agreement to re-evaluate this aspect in light of the outcome of the mediation itself.

In the two subsequent meetings, all twenty participants at the table were able to first deepen their respective positions and points of view, addressing the various information and differences, even on technical solutions, sometimes in a very heated way. However, they came together to draft the agenda of the issues to be addressed during the mediation process; therefore, they were able to discuss ideas, entering into the merits of the exchanged documentation, and then examine some first proposals to change the executive project. The parties jointly requested a specific opinion to the Superintendency on Archaeology, Fine Arts and Landscape, whose answer could have required a different path for the canal.

During the third meeting, the parties discussed the opportunity to have sessions with the technical consultants and representatives of various bodies, with the task of investigating the numerous technical issues and making emerge a proposal for a variant to the project that took into account all the critical remarks and the proposed changes. The parties thus appointed a "technical committee", to which all those interested could still participate as observers.

Finally, a date was agreed to carry out an on-field inspection, which the mediator proposed in accordance with the principle that *the map is not the territory*. During the three-hour inspection, all the participants in the mediation could move around those three areas which were considered most crucial for the variants to the project – and, seeing them all together in person, they managed to discuss every controversial aspect, thus reaching a better understanding of the different points of view and possible solutions.

They also realised that a further topic to be explored was related to the water flow that would have resulted upstream of the project at the end of the works. On this occasion, however, not only did the participants create a more jovial atmosphere among themselves, but, observing together the beauty of the landscape and sharing the need to protect it, they took the story of the canal's recovery even more to heart.

The two subsequent meetings were dedicated to the so-called technical committee, during which it was possible to discuss at length and in depth the technical solutions to each issue, to evaluate together a first and then a second new plan with a variant to the project, to ask all the clarifications (also by the two citizens observers), and then to address all the remarks and objections by technicians from the entities involved, aimed at further improving the variant itself and reconciling all the interests with economic viability.

In March 2020, in consideration of the Covid-19 health emergency, all the participants met by videoconference: a first session was dedicated to the technical committee and to the final exchange on technical and economic aspects, in the light of the documents shared via email, and with an explanation of the new version of the redevelopment project. A second plenary session was held to summarise the path taken, the issues addressed and the changes to the project that resulted, with the definition of the further steps which were needed to arrive at the new agreement between the public bodies involved.

At the end of this last meeting, all the participants shared their appreciation for the dialogue and the great work done collaboratively. The parties decided to override the confidentiality agreement in order to spread knowledge of the process and its positive outcome by publishing a final summary dossier. They also adhered to the mediator's wish to disseminate the use of alternative methods of dispute resolution in order to create more contexts of dialogue between citizens and governmental bodies and to prevent and resolve environmental conflicts.

Finally, after further telephone and email exchanges and tenacious work by the public representatives at the table, a new convention regulating the relations between the various public bodies involved in the recovery of the canal was signed. This convention not only accepts the outcomes of the mediation process but, in order to continue the virtuous path started with this experience, provides for the involvement of the stakeholders during the construction works and for information meetings on its progresses – in particular, in the event of any further variation that may be necessary.

In conclusion, the dispute was resolved with the representatives of the local community, thus avoiding the litigation that would have probably arisen, and which could have blocked the project. The project is now judged by the same participants as better than the initial one, because it is the result of the collective intelligence that was able to express itself in a space of dialogue and constructive exchange, harmonising the technical aspects with the values of landscape protection.[63]

Conclusions

The acceleration of the climate crisis, combined with increased environmental pollution all around the world, is attracting more and more attention. The perceived risks for human health and the ecosystem following the construction of big infrastructures and facilities, paired with the depreciation of natural resources, is fuelling so-called environmental conflicts.

These have collective character and imply the confrontation of several stakeholders, such as institutions, private entities and civil society, effectively making them "total conflicts" with economic, social, environmental, political and institutional consequences. Often, the points of contention are those resources such as water, forests or land that are limited in quantity and essential for life. Because of the potential long-term consequences of inappropriate management, they should be treated with kid gloves, imagining innovative management paradigms as well as more inclusive dispute resolution mechanisms.

After sketching the main features and problematic aspects of environmental conflicts, the authors hold that flexible dispute resolution mechanisms focusing on interests more than on positions seem to be the better option in the field. For this reason, environmental mediation and facilitation techniques need further institutionalisation, especially in the Italian context, where they still have limited application. The case study on the recovery of an ancient and polluted

63 See also: Luisa Giampietro, Mario Dotti, Veronica Dini, Daniele Gizzi, Vittorio Giampietro and Stefania Lattuille, *Conflitti ambientali: mediazione, transazione, accordi* (Milano: Wolters Kluwer E-books, 2018); Marianella Sclavi and Lawrence E. Susskind, *Confronto creativo. Come funzionano la co-progettazione creativa e la democrazia deliberativa. Perché ne abbiamo bisogno* (Milano: Ipoc, 2016).

irrigation canal in a protected natural area in the North of Italy exemplifies how environmental mediation is conducted, but even more, it shows how the facilitation process can effectively lead to shared solutions even in presence of thorny environmental issues.

Bibliography

Altopiedi, Rosalba. "Ambiente, Giustizia e Diritto." *Sociologia del diritto*, no. 2 (2020): 95–122.

Axelrod, Robert. *The Evolution of Cooperation*. New York: Basic Books, 1984.

Bellman, Howard and Susan L. Podziba. "Public Policy Mediation: Best Practices." *GPSolo Magazine* 33, no. 3 (2016).

Bobbio, Luigi. "Conflitti territoriali: sei interpretazioni." *Trimestrale del Laboratorio Mobilità e Ambiente* 4, no. 4 (2011): 79–88.

Bobbio, Luigi and Alberico Zeppetella. *Perché proprio qui? Grandi opere e opposizioni locali.* Milano: FrancoAngeli, 1999.

Boyle, James. "Foreword: The Opposite of Property?" *Law & Contemporary Problems*, no. 66 (2003): 1–32.

Centro documentazione conflitti ambientali. *Dossier Conflitti Ambientali: Mappe, saperi, strumenti per le ecologie di domani.* Roma: CDCA, 2019.

Chiaramonte, Xenia. "The Struggle for Law: Legal Strategies, Environmental Struggles and Climate Actions in Italy." *Oñati Socio-Legal Series* 10, no. 4 (2020): 932–954.

Danielson, Luke J. and John L. Watson. "Environmental Mediation." *Natural Resources Lawyer*, no. 15 (1983): 687–723.

Deister, Ane D. "Environmental Mediation Strategies for Success: Summaries of Two Consensus-Based Cases – Florida's Growth Management Act Legislation and the Los Angeles River Watershed Task Force." *The Urban Lawyer* 32, no. 1 (2000): 73–96.

Demsetz, Harold. "Toward a Theory of Property Rights." *The American Economic Review* 57, no. 2 (1967): 347–359.

Douglas, Amy J. "The Politics of Environmental Mediation." *Ecology Law Quarterly* 11, no. 1 (1983): 1–19.

Dryzek, John and Susan Hunter. "Environmental Mediation for International Problems." *International Studies Quarterly*, no. 31 (2017): 87–102.

Fisher, Frank. *Democracy and Expertise. Reorienting Policy Inquiry.* Oxford: Oxford University Press, 2009.

Fiss, Owen M. "Against Settlement." *Yale Law Journal* 93, no. 6 (1984): 1073–1090.

Giampietro, Luisa. "I procedimenti di mediazione in materia ambientale: spunti di riflessione." *Ambiente & Sviluppo*, no. 3 (2011): 247–252.

Giampietro, Luisa, Veronica Dini, Mario Dotti, Vittorio Giampietro, Daniele Gizzi and Stefania Lattuille. *Conflitti ambientali: mediazione, transazione, accordi.* Milano: Wolters Kluwer E-books, 2018.

Greenberg, Michael R. "Up-Front Environmental Mediation." *Geographical Review*, no. 67 (1977): 235.

Hardin, Garrett. "The Tragedy of the Commons." *Science, New Series* 162, no. 3859 (1968): 1243–1248.

Harrison, John. "Environmental Mediation: The Ethical and Constitutional Dimension." *Journal of Environmental Law* 9, no. 1 (1997): 79–102.

Libiszewski, Stephan. "What is an Environmental Conflict?" *Occasional Paper No. 1.* Zurich: Center for Security Studies and Conflict Research, 1993.

Luban, David. "Settlements and the Erosion of Public Realm." *The Georgetown Law Journal*, no. 83 (1995): 2619–2662.

Marella, Maria Rosaria. "The Commons as a Legal Concept." *Law Critique, Springer*, no. 28 (2017): 61–86.

Marella, Maria Rosaria. *Oltre il pubblico e il privato. Per un diritto dei beni comuni*. Verona: Ombre Corte, 2012.

Mattei, Ugo. *Beni comuni. Un manifesto*. Roma: Laterza, 2011.

McCann, Michael. "Law and Social Movements: Contemporary Perspective." *Annual Review of Law and Social Science*, no. 2 (2006): 17–38.

Menkel-Meadow, Carrie. "For and Against Settlement: Uses and Abuses of the Mandatory Settlement Conference." *UCLA Law Review*, no. 33 (1985): 485–514.

Menkel-Meadow, Carrie. "Whose Dispute Is It Anyway?: A Philosophical and Democratic Defense of Settlement (in Some Cases)." *Georgetown Law Journal*, no. 83 (1995): 2663–2969.

Nicholson, David. *Environmental Dispute Resolution in Indonesia*. Leiden: Brill, 2000.

Nussbaum, Martha C. *Creating Capabilities: The Human Development Approach*. Cambridge, MA: Harvard University Press, 2011.

Nussbaum, Martha C. *Women and Women Development: The Capabilities Approach*. Oxford: Oxford University Press, 2000.

Oppio, Alessandra, Stefano Corsi, Sergio Mattia and Andrea Tosini. "Exploring the Relationship Among Local Conflicts and Territorial Vulnerability: The Case Study of Lombardy Region." *Land Use Policy*, no. 43 (2015): 239–247.

Ostrom, Elinor. *Governing the Commons. The Evolution of Institutions for Collective Action*. Cambridge: Cambridge University Press, 1990.

Ostrom, Elinor, Roy Gardner, James Walker and Arun Agrawal. *Rules, Games and Common-Pool Resources*. Michigan: University of Michigan Press, 1994.

Passerini, Eve. "Sustainability and Sociology." *The American Sociologist* 29, no. 3 (1998): 59–70.

Pellizzoni, Luigi. *Conflitti ambientali. Esperti, politica, istituzioni nelle controversie sociologiche*. Bologna: Il Mulino, 2011.

Pellizzoni, Luigi. "'Decidiamo insieme!' Conflitti tecnologici e deliberazione pubblica." *Quaderni di Sociologia*, no. 41 (2006): 91–114.

Podziba, Susan L. *Civic Fusion. Mediating Polarized Public Disputes*. Chicago: American Bar Association, 2012.

Polanyi, Karl. *The Great Transformation*. New York: Farrar and Rinehart, 1944.

Polinari, Jacopo. "La possibile deflazione delle controversie amministrative. Transazione e altri mezzi di prevenzione e/o risoluzione. Premesse ad uno studio sull'arbitrato nel diritto amministrativo." *Rassegna Avvocatura Dello Stato*, no. 4 (2010): 268–313.

Putnam, Robert D. *The Comparative Study of Political Elites*. Englewood Cliffs, NJ: Prentice-Hall, 1976.

Resta, Eligio. "Giudicare, conciliare, mediare." *Politica del Diritto* 30, no. 4 (1999): 541–575.

Rodotà, Stefano. *Il terribile diritto. Studi sulla proprietà privata e i beni comuni*. Bologna: Il Mulino, 2013.

Ruocco, Giovanni and Marianna Stori. "La democrazia alla prova dei conflitti ambientali." *Associazione A Sud*. CDCA, 2016.

Sacconi, Lorenzo and Stefania Ottone. *Beni comuni e cooperazione*. Bologna: Il Mulino, 2015.

Sclavi, Marianella and Lawrence E. Susskind. *Confronto creativo. Come funzionano la coprogettazione creativa e la democrazia deliberativa. Perché ne abbiamo bisogno*. Milano: Ipoc, 2016.

Sen, Amartya K. *Development as Freedom*. New York: Knopf, 1990.
Sen, Amartya K. *L'idea di giustizia*. Translated by Luca Vanni. Milano: Mondadori, 2011.
Sexton, Renard. "Unpacking the Local Resource Curse: How Externalities and Governance Shape Social Conflict." *Journal of Conflict Resolution* 64, no. 64 (2020): 640–673.
Susskind, Lawrence E. "Confessions of a Public Dispute Mediator." *Negotiation Journal* (2000): 129–132.
Susskind, Lawrence E. "Environmental Mediation and the Accountability Problem." *Vermont Law Review*, no. 6 (1981).
Tilly, Charles and Sidney Tarrow. *Contentious Politics*. New York: Oxford University Press, 2006.
Twining, William. "Alternative to What? Theories of Litigation, Procedure and Dispute Settlement in Anglo-American Jurisprudence: Some Neglected Classics." *The Modern Law Review* 56, no. 3 (1993): 380–392.
Yarn, Douglas H. "Environmental Mediation: Great Promise, Some Problems." *Water Environment & Technology*, no. 7 (1995): 80–81.

9

COMPARATIVE ANALYSIS OF THE SINGAPORE CONVENTION IN LIGHT OF THE NEW YORK AND HAGUE CHOICE OF COURT CONVENTIONS

Xiantao Wen (with an introduction by Susan Finder)

Introduction

This chapter provides a focused analysis of the Singapore Convention's core provisions, including the scope of application, general principles, grounds for refusing to grant relief, and reservations as well as a comprehensive interpretation of key concepts like "settlement" and "mediation." It also compares the relevant provisions of the Singapore Convention with those of the Convention on the Recognition and Enforcement of Foreign Arbitral Awards (New York Convention) and the Hague Choice of Court Convention in light of Chinese laws and regulations. Finally, this chapter concludes that China should actively seek to ratify the Singapore Convention and, to that end, improve relevant domestic laws and regulations.

The author negotiated the Singapore Convention on behalf of the Chinese government. It is clear from the article on the drafting of the Singapore Convention by Timothy Schnabel, who was the chief United States negotiator, that the author had an important and positive impact on the process.[1] This has several implications. As seen from the perspective of the Chinese government, the author fully fulfilled his duty to "increase China's voice in international legal affairs," or as seen from another perspective, it showed that China is increasingly involved in shaping international legal norms.[2]

1 Timothy Schnabel, "The Singapore Convention on Mediation: A Framework for the Cross-Border Recognition and Enforcement of Mediated Settlements," *Pepperdine Dispute Resolution Law Journal* 19, no. 1 (2019), https://digitalcommons.pepperdine.edu/drlj/vol19/iss1/1.

2 Robert D. Williams, International Law with Chinese Characteristics: Beijing and the "Rules-Based" Global Order, October, 2020, *Brookings Report*, www.brookings.edu/research/international-law-with-chinese-characteristics-beijing-and-the-rules-based-global-order/; Donald Greenlees, "The Future of the Asia Pacific Rules-based Order: Retaining the US, Integrating China, and Invigorating ASEAN," https://asialink.unimelb.edu.au/asialink-dialogues-and-applied-research/commentary-and-

DOI: 10.4324/9780429354625-13

This chapter may be viewed in the context of an issue that has attracted academic discourse for 20 or more years – legal globalisation and the adopting international norms in China.[3] The impact of the Chinese negotiator on the Singapore Convention shows that this issue has a contemporary twist. Academic discussions have for the most part assumed that the international norms to be adopted in China were those in which China had little or no role in forming. That was accurate when many of these commentators wrote. This chapter relates to a newer phenomenon in how international public law and the Chinese legal system interact – the impact in China of international legal norms to which China, through vigorous negotiators, both official and non-official, contributed. The author of this chapter and other colleagues involved in negotiating the Singapore Convention are now involved in multi-institutional efforts to make the legal and institutional reforms possible for ratification. The Singapore Convention may involve new legislation or substantial amendments to old legislation to establish a legal framework for commercial mediation as well as the courts establishing related new procedures before ratification. The Singapore Convention and the Hague Judgments Convention are two of a new class of international conventions which a representative of the Chinese government played an active part in drafting and which will be linked by efforts by that representative and colleagues to do what is necessary for China to harmonise its legislation and structures with international legal principles in a way appropriate for the Chinese society, economy, and system. It is significant that the author concludes by stressing the importance of legal globalisation and harmonisation in cross-border commercial dispute resolution enforcement matters.

In July 2014, as proposed by the United States, the 47th meeting of the United Nations Commission on International Trade Law (UNCITRAL) decided to draft an international convention that aimed at encouraging dispute resolution through mediation. After four years of work by the UNCITRAL Working Group II, incorporating seven member-state sessions and four commission sessions, the drafting concluded in June 2018. Just like the Convention on Recognition and Enforcement of Foreign Arbitral Awards (the New York Convention), drafted in 1958, this international convention, formally named the United Nations Convention on International Settlement Agreement Resulting from Mediation (hereinafter the Singapore Convention), ushers in a new era for commercial dispute resolution.[4]

---

analysis/the-future-of-the-asia-pacific-rules-based-order; Council on Foreign Relations, "China's Approach to Global Governance," www.cfr.org/china-global-governance/.

3 See, i.e., Pittman Potter, *Law, Policy, and Practice on China's Periphery: Selective Adaptation and Institutional Capacity* (London: Routledge, 2010); Ljiljana Biukovic, "Selective Adaptation of WTO Transparency Norms and Local Practices in China and Japan," *Journal of International Economic Law* 11, no. 4 (December 2008): 803–825, https://doi.org/10.1093/jiel/jgn028; Pittman Potter, *Introduction: Selective Adaptation, Institutional Capacity, and the Reception of International Law under Conditions of Globalization* (Vancouver: UBC Press: Globalization and Local Adaptation in International Trade Law, 2010), 3–20.

4 Schnabel, "The Singapore Convention on Mediation," 1–60; see also Sussman, "The New York Convention. "

The New York Convention greatly facilitates the development of international arbitration, and each provision exerts great influence globally. Currently, the New York Convention has almost 170 signatories.[5] Another similar international convention is the Convention on Choice of Court Agreements (also referred to as the Hague Choice of Court Convention), passed by the 20th Diplomatic Session of Hague Conference on Private International Law in 2005. Entering into force in 2015 and now having almost 40 signatories,[6] the Hague Choice of Court Convention aims to protect parties' exclusive choice of court agreements in international civil and commercial cases by requiring the judgment delivered by the designated court to be recognised and enforced by all signatories. As a member state of the Hague Conference on Private International Law, China participated in the negotiation of the Hague Choice of Court Convention and signed it in September 2017. Furthermore, the Convention on the Recognition and Enforcement of Foreign Judgements on Civil and Commercial Matters (also referred to as the Judgements Convention) was adopted at the 22nd Diplomatic Session of the Hague Conference on Private International Law in July 2019. The Chinese delegates signed the negotiation text (the final document of the conference).[7] The Singapore Convention, the New York Convention, the Hague Choice of Court Convention, and the Judgements Convention are four cornerstone legal instruments for the international recognition and enforcement of civil and commercial dispute resolution. There are great similarities between the structures of the four documents. Because of the different characteristics of mediation, arbitration, and litigation, the four conventions use slightly different rules and terms for settlement agreements, awards, and judgments respectively.[8]

Dispute resolution through mediation reflects greater party autonomy and allows greater consideration of party interests when compared with arbitration and litigation. Whether the parties agree on litigation or arbitration for dispute resolution, they cannot control the result. Mediation means the parties want to resolve their disputes voluntarily. As recognised by the UN General Assembly, dispute resolution through mediation has notable advantages, such as facilitating the administration of international transactions, reducing risks, and maintaining long-term cooperation between the parties to avoid a complete breakdown of business relations.[9] Judicial resources supported by taxpayers should concentrate

5 "Contracting States," New York Convention.

6 "Contracting Parties," Hague Conference on Private International Law.

7 Zhang, "A Review."

8 The Hague Choice of Court Convention and the Convention on the Recognition and Enforcement of Foreign Judgements on Civil and Commercial Matters were formulated by the Hague Conference on Private International Law. The former deals with the jurisdiction by agreement of the parties, and the latter focuses on the legal jurisdiction of the country of origin. Because of the great similarities between the two conventions, this chapter only takes the Hague Choice of Court Convention as the object of comparison and analysis.

9 Resolution 57/18 adopted by the General Assembly during its fifty-seventh session on November 19, 2002. https://digitallibrary.un.org/record/479115?ln=en.

more on maintaining social equality and justice, on criminal cases to protect citizens' personal and property security, and on administrative cases that supervise the operation of the administration of government. Commercial disputes should be encouraged to be resolved by commercial arbitration or, even better, mediation. The Singapore Convention was born out of the need to promote enforcement of settlement agreements more quickly and conveniently.[10]

In its introduction, the Singapore Convention recognises the value of mediation and its advantage over litigation as an alternative form of dispute resolution and envisions that settlement agreements resulting from mediation will contribute to the development of harmonious international economic relations. The main text of the Singapore Convention then defines the "internationality" of a settlement agreement and sets forth its exclusive application to international commercial settlement agreements, establishing the general principle that international commercial settlement agreements are enforceable. The Singapore Convention also recognises a signatory's competent authorities' right to review a settlement agreement. Similar to the New York Convention and the Hague Choice of Court Convention, it provides grounds for refusing to grant relief and limitations on making reservations.

The Meaning of "和解" (he jie, mediation)

The Singapore Convention's use of "settlement agreements resulting from mediation" in its title is a very accurate English expression. Settlement agreement is translated into Chinese as "和解协议" (he jie xie yi). However, the English word "conciliation" matches the Chinese phrase "和解," and the English phrase "settlement agreement" literally means "解决协议" (jie jue xie yi),[11] which does not conform to usual Chinese expressions and tends to confuse listeners. During the discussions of Working Group II, there were also opinions from other countries that the translations from the English words were odd. "Settlement" has a wide

10 See Sun, "Legislative Background"; Wang, "Mediation Skills"; Huang, "Principles and Realization Paths"; Zhu, "Principles and Practices"; Song, "Independent Mediation," 王钢(Wang Gang), *国际商事调解技巧研究* [Research on International Commercial Mediation Skills], 中国民主法制出版社(China Democracy and Legal System Press), 2014 edition; 黄忠顺（Huang Zhongshun）, "商事调解与民事调解的区分原理及其实现路径 – 基于 2012~2013 年中国商事调解研究文献的分析" [the Distinguishing Principles and Realization Paths of Commercial Mediation and Civil Mediation – Based on the Analysis of Chinese Commercial Mediation Research Literature from 2012 To 2013], *北京仲裁* [Beijing Arbitration], no. 3, 2014; 朱楠(Zhu Nan), *商事调解原理与实务* [Principles and Practice of Commercial Mediation], 上海交通大学出版社[Shanghai Jiaotong University Press], 2014 edition; 尹力(Yin Li), 国际商事调解法律问题研究 [Research on Legal Issues of International Commercial Mediation], 武汉大学出版社 (Wuhan University Press), 2007 edition; 宋连斌 (Song Lianbin), "从仲裁与调解相结合到单独调解," [From the Combination Of Arbitration and Mediation to Independent Mediation], *昆明理工大学学报（社会科学版）* [*Journal of Kunming University of Science and Technology (Social Science Edition)*], no. 11, 2009.

11 The explanation of "settlement" from *Black's Law Dictionary* is "an agreement ending a dispute or lawsuit."

range of definitions and can include all sorts of methods that can promote peace. Judging from the Singapore Convention's true intention, the Chinese phrase "和解协议" is the most appropriate translation for it.

New issues keep popping up. According to the *Contemporary Chinese Dictionary*, the word "和解" as a verb means "to stop bickering or hostility, and to reconcile."[12] However, under China's Civil Procedure Law, the phrase has the specific meaning that the disputing parties voluntarily reach a settlement without the participation of a court, an arbitral tribunal, or a People's Mediation Commission. This settlement may be achieved with the help of a neutral mediator, instead of a judge or arbitrator, or achieved through the parties' negotiations without help from a third party. The word "settlement" under the Singapore Convention refers only to settlement reached by involving a third party. China's current law has not distinguished between the aforementioned two methods for achieving settlement, only providing that settlement agreements without judicial confirmation will not be enforceable. In terms of language, Chinese law also distinguishes between settlement agreement ("和解协议"), consent judgment ("调解书"), and mediation agreement ("调解协议").[13]

In many countries, whether or not a third-party mediator participates, a settlement agreement can always be converted into an enforceable ruling or consent judgment as long as an arbitral tribunal or a court confirms the settlement agreement. Does the fact that such conversion can happen in many countries render the Singapore Convention, which aims at promoting cross-border relief for settlement agreements, unnecessary? According to UNCITRAL, the Singapore Convention is necessary because ensuring the enforceability of settlement agreements makes mediation a more effective dispute resolution mechanism.[14] The establishment of such a mechanism will not only save arbitration or litigation costs but also make enforcing settlement agreements more convenient than enforcing or converting a settlement agreement and other forms of dispute resolution mechanisms.

The settlement agreement under the Singapore Convention is reached through mutual agreement and is a kind of commercial arrangement, although different from normal commercial contracts. First, achieving a settlement agreement entails an existing ongoing dispute. Article 1 ("Scope of Application") of the Singapore Convention provides that "this Convention applies to an agreement resulting from mediation and concluded in writing by parties to resolve a commercial dispute ('settlement agreement')." Without a dispute, there is no settlement. In reality, in China, there indeed are practices of "fraudulent settlement" or "advance settlement," in which the parties try to get their "settlement,"

12 3rd edition, 1996, p. 510.

13 Articles 53, 56, 57, 62, and 237 of the Civil Procedure Law of the People's Republic of China, 2017; Article 148 of Interpretation of the Supreme People's Court on the Application of the Civil Procedure Law of the People's Republic of China, 2022.

14 A/CN.9/WG.II/WP.187 – Settlement of Commercial Disputes: Enforceability of Settlement Agreements Resulting from International Commercial Conciliation/Mediation.

"award," or "judgment" recognised by court for tax evasion, money laundering, fraudulent conveyance, or damaging other third parties, when the "disputing parties" are not in dispute. In these cases, fraudulent dispute resolution is not difficult to detect through detailed questioning during judicial review. On June 5, 2018, China's Supreme People's Court issued an official reply regarding "advance arbitral" awards, stating that "the arbitration institution may arbitrate the contract disputes and other property rights and interest disputes that have occurred between the parties" and that

> where a party to a . . . contract applies for enforcing an arbitral award or consent award rendered by an arbitration institution before a dispute occurs, the people's court shall rule that the application should not be accepted; and where an application has been accepted, the people's court shall reject the application for enforcement.[15]

Just like fraudulent litigation, so-called advance arbitration or settlement without dispute is a pseudo-proposition, violating legal procedural requirements, departing from the basic principles and institutional purpose of arbitration and mediation, countering the principles of good faith, and violating public policy as well other fundamental social values.

Second, a third-party mediator is required. The introduction part of the Singapore Convention refers to mediation as "the parties in dispute requesting a third person or persons to assist them in their attempt to settle the dispute amicably" and defines "mediation" in Article 2(3) as a process

> irrespective of the expression used or the basis upon which the process is carried out, whereby parties attempt to reach an amicable settlement of their dispute with the assistance of a third person or persons . . . lacking the authority to impose a solution upon the parties to the dispute.

Therefore, the non-mediated settlement agreement that disputing parties voluntarily reach without third-party assistance is merely a commercial contract, not a settlement agreement under the Singapore Convention. As a result, the role of a mediator is crucial.

"Mediators were charged with harmonising thousands of people's conflicts" (调人掌司万民之难而谐和之, tiaoren zhangsi wanmin zhinan er hexie zhi) in ancient China 3,000 years ago, as recorded in the sub-chapter "Mediator" (调人, tiao ren) of the Han Dynasty Chinese classic *Rites of Zhou Dynasty*.[16]

15 "Advance arbitration" refers to the cases where an arbitration institution delivers an award or mediation before a dispute actually occurs to the "disputing parties." See Official Reply.

16 The Chinese name of the relevant part. There is an annotation given by Zheng Xuan from the Han Dynasty that explains the original characters, saying that "难" equals "相与为仇雠," which means "bear animosity toward each other" in English, and that "谐" refers to "调," which means "mediation."

Sun Yirang, a Qing Dynasty master of Confucian classics, wrote in his book *Corrections and Annotations for Rites of Zhou Dynasty* that "in the ancient times, revenge was not prohibited, but there were mediating officials who were in charge of detecting and soothing animosity." Mediators in ancient China were referred to as "tiao ren," which was at first an official position in the government and then was popularised as a non-official name for intermediaries. The non-official use of "tiao ren" was kept until the Republic of China[17] and was replaced (in the People's Republic of China) by "people's mediator" (人民调解员, ren min tiao jie yuan), which, to some extent, has swung back to official designations.[18]

The Singapore Convention does not require mediators to meet certain standards. The author thinks that mediators should know more "psychological strategies" than arbitrators and judges. An outstanding mediator should be adept in not only law but also psychology and should be equipped with great communication and negotiation skills. A good mediator should truly conciliate and resolve the dispute. A mediator cannot mediate differences by sacrificing principles and pushing for mere compromises with true issues untended, let alone imposing solutions on the disputing parties, which will convert the mediation process into arbitration.[19]

From a linguistic perspective, we can see that many similar designations are used for this phenomenon if it is closely related to people's everyday life. In Chinese, synonyms for "和解" are "调解" (tiao jie), "调停" (tiao ting), "调和" (tiao he), "斡旋" (wo xuan), and so on. Similarly, the word for "mediation" in English has many synonyms. The expressions in the two language systems rarely match each other perfectly.[20] The Singapore Convention uses "mediation"

17 "调人" appeared in the first act of the play *Teahouse* by Lao She – "after the mediators' casual talk, the tens of musclemen started to drink tea and eat bowls of stewed pork noodles as symbols of reconciliation."

18 See People's Mediation Law.

19 Article 1.3, UNCITRAL Model Law.

20 In 2010, the Department of Justice of the Hong Kong Special Administrative Region Government also mentioned in the report from the mediation working group: The general definition of mediation can vary depending upon the context in which it is used in Hong Kong and the roles adopted by the mediator." Department of Justice, The Government of the Hong Kong Special Administrative Region, REPORT OF THE WORKING GROUP ON MEDIATION, 2010, at 9, https://www.doj.gov.hk/en/legal_dispute/pdf/med20100208e.pdf.

'Mediation' (调解 tiaojie/调停 tiaoting) and 'conciliation' (调解 tiaojie/和解 hejie) is often used interchangeably. Both generally refer to a neutral third party assisting the parties in the dispute to communicate and negotiate, and to reach a settlement of conflicts and disputes. However, this is usually the cause of confusion, and the usage of these two terms in the mediation documents and statutory provisions of Hong Kong is also very variable. In Hong Kong, the English terms 'mediation' and 'conciliation' do not have exact Chinese equivalents. In law, mediation is mentioned in multiple legal provisions and is not regulated by a single provision or legal framework; the corresponding Chinese vocabulary used for 'mediation' and 'conciliation' are also different. The disunified usages, especially the interchanging use of words meaning 'mediation' will inevitably cause confusion and misunderstandings among the public and important stakeholders who are conducting mediation procedures in Hong Kong.

instead of "conciliation" because "mediation" is more widely used in practice. The author also thinks that "mediation" more precisely accentuates the neutrality of a mediator.

Review by the Competent Authority

If a commercial settlement is concluded with the assistance of an impartial mediator, signed by competent disputing parties, and not violating the laws and public policies of the place of enforcement, it has met the basic substantive requirements for extraterritorial enforcement of arbitral awards and judgments of the New York Convention and the Hague Choice of Court Convention. Its enforceability is not subject to review by the competent authority of the place of enforcement (which is the people's court in China) for fairness, as its fairness has been recognised by the disputing parties and the mediator(s) at the time of signing. If a party objects to the content of the settlement agreement, it means that either that party is going back on its own word or the disputing parties differ over the interpretation of the agreed terms and conditions. If so, can the competent authority in the place of enforcement directly enforce the agreement according to its own understanding? According to the Singapore Convention,[21] the competent authority can do so in principle. As the final resolution to the dispute, the core principle of "recognition and enforcement" has been recognised by the New York Convention Article III[22] and the Hague Choice of Court Convention Article 8.[23] One difference among the Singapore Convention, the New York Convention, and the Hague Choice of Court Convention is that the object of enforcement of the former two conventions is an award or judgment while that of the Singapore Convention is an "agreement." More stringent requirements for the latter are unnecessary.

Should the competent authority enforce the settlement agreement like a vending machine? Obviously not. A direct enforcement mechanism does not

21 Singapore Convention, Article 3(1): "Each Party to the Convention shall enforce a settlement agreement in accordance with its rules of procedure and under the conditions laid down in this Convention."

22 New York Convention, Article III:

> Each Contracting State shall recognize arbitral awards as binding and enforce them in accordance with the rules of procedure of the territory where the award is relied upon, under the conditions laid down in the following articles. There shall not be imposed substantially more onerous conditions or higher fees or charges on the recognition or enforcement of arbitral awards to which this Convention applies than are imposed on the recognition or enforcement of domestic arbitral awards.

23 Hague Choice of Court Convention, Article 8(1):

> A judgment given by a court of a Contracting State designated in an exclusive choice of court agreement shall be recognised and enforced in other Contracting States in accordance with this Chapter. Recognition or enforcement may be refused only on the grounds specified in this Convention.

mean indiscriminately enforcing every settlement agreement without review. The Hague Choice of Court Convention Article 8 ("Recognition and Enforcement") Section 2 clearly states:

> Without prejudice to such review as is necessary for the application of the provisions of this Chapter, there shall be no review of the merits of the judgment given by the court of origin. The court addressed shall be bound by the findings of fact on which the court of origin based its jurisdiction unless the judgment was given by default.

Although the New York Convention does not have an explicit review mechanism, according to Article V of the New York Convention, when a party questions a signing party's capacity to sign an arbitration agreement, the validity of the arbitration agreement, the scope of arbitration, or the arbitral procedure or binding force of the arbitral award, the competent authority has the power to examine the authenticity and legitimacy of the matter in dispute and may, ex officio, positively examine whether the dispute is arbitrable and whether the arbitral award violates any public policy. Applying the Singapore Convention involves issues such as the authenticity and enforceability of the settlement agreement, parties' capacity, the impact of public policy, and the challenge to mediator conduct. According to the Singapore Convention Article 5 ("Grounds for refusing to grant relief"), all of those matters need to be clarified through review. Different from the New York Convention and the Hague Choice of Court Convention, under the Singapore Convention, whether the settlement agreement has truly resolved the parties' dispute cannot be determined. The Singapore Convention Article 3 ("General Principles") Section 2 makes a special arrangement to resolve this.[24] If a dispute arises concerning a matter that a party claims was already resolved by a settlement agreement, the competent authority of the place of enforcement shall allow the party to prove that the matter has already been "conclusively" resolved.[25] However, what if the parties cannot agree on this issue? The Singapore Convention is silent. The author believes that this issue exceeds the scope of the settlement agreement and the Singapore Convention.

Another particularity of the Singapore Convention is that it does not emphasise the application of "recognition and enforcement" by the parties as the New

24 Singapore Convention, Article 3(2):

> If a dispute arises concerning a matter that a party claims was already resolved by a settlement agreement, a Party to the Convention shall allow the party to invoke the settlement agreement in accordance with its rules of procedure and under the conditions laid down in this Convention, in order to prove that the matter has already been resolved.

25 "In order to conclusively prove that the matter has been already resolved" is the expression of the original draft of the Singapore Convention. During the Working Group discussion at the session, both the United States and China supported this clearer expression of the confirming validity of the settlement agreement. However, as adding the word "conclusively" did not change the meaning of the sentence, it was deleted in the final draft. See supra note 1.

York and the Hague Choice of Court Convention. Instead, it establishes that the parties "seek relief" from the competent authority and that the competent authority "grants relief." The Singapore Convention does not use the term "recognition." As revealed in the Singapore Convention negotiations, "recognition" has different meanings in different jurisdictions and therefore is not a rigorous legal term. Although the New York Convention Article III states that "each contracting State shall recognize arbitral awards as binding and enforce them in accordance with the rules and procedures of the territory where the award is relied upon, under the conditions laid down in the following articles," in practice, "recognition" and "enforcement" are different.[26] Especially in international investment arbitration where the foreign investors sue the host country and even if the competent authority recognises the validity of the arbitral award by the arbitral tribunal, it often invokes the Vienna Convention on Diplomatic Relations and the Convention on the Settlement of Investment Disputes Between States and Nationals of Other States and refuses to enforce the arbitral award on the grounds of its domestic sovereign immunity law.[27] Clearly, "recognition" is only the subjective confirmation of authorisation or particular state,[28] and only "enforcement" can truly protect rights and interests.

Reservations and Limitations on the Applicable Scope of the Singapore Convention

The Issue of "Internationality"

To refer to the object of the Singapore Convention as an "international settlement agreement" easily creates confusion because the settlement agreement in this convention does not mean an agreement governed by public international law between the states or other entities; rather, it is an agreement between commercial entities and subject to private law. Article 1 ("Scope of Application") Section 1 of the Singapore Convention states that "this Convention applies to an agreement resulting from mediation and concluded in writing by parties to resolve a commercial dispute ('settlement agreement') which, at the time of its conclusion, is international." The Singapore Convention explains the term "international" as meaning that "at least two parties to the settlement agreement have their places of business in different States" or "the State in which the parties to the settlement agreement have their places of business" is different from "the State in which a substantial part of the obligations under the settlement

26 "Commentators are in broad agreement that 'recognition' refers to the process of considering an arbitral award as binding but not necessarily enforceable, while 'enforcement' refers to the process of giving effect to an award." Paragraph 7 of point a under Section A of Article I (1), UNCITRAL Secretariat Guide, 9.

27 See Benvenuti & Bonfant, Eastern Timber Corporation, SOADBI, AIG.

28 *Black's Law Dictionary*.

agreement is performed."[29] In other words, the settlement agreement is international when the parties to the settlement agreement have places of business in different countries or when, regardless of whether the parties' business places are in the same country, the place where the settlement agreement is performed is not the same as the parties' place of business. The place where the settlement agreement is performed is often the place where the parties seek relief.

The description of internationality in the New York Convention is relatively simple. According to the New York Convention Article I.1, it applies to "arbitral awards made in the territory of a State other than the State where the recognition and enforcement of such awards are sought" or "not considered as domestic awards in the State where their recognition and enforcement are sought." In short, the New York Convention applies if the competent authority decides the arbitral award was made in a foreign territory. The New York Convention does not state whether the seat of arbitration shall be in a state other than the state where enforcement is sought and whether the parties to the arbitration should be a citizen of the signatory to the convention. Shall the competent authority recognise an arbitral award made by a foreign arbitral institution while all the parties to the disputes are its citizens? The New York Convention does not prohibit the competent authority from doing so.[30]

In China, "internationality" is often referred to as "foreign elements." When Beijing Zhaolai Xinsheng Sports and Leisure Co., Ltd. applied for the recognition and enforcement of a foreign arbitral award, a case ranked as one of the "Top Ten Influential Arbitration Cases in China of 2014," the court relied on the Civil Procedure Law and the Arbitration Law of China to hold that for disputes arising from foreign economic, trade, transportation, or maritime matters, the parties may submit them to Chinese arbitral institutions or other arbitral institutions by including an arbitration clause in the contract or entering into a written after-the-event arbitration agreement, and since the law did not explicitly allow domestic parties to submit to a foreign arbitral institution disputes without foreign elements, the arbitration clause under which the parties agreed to submit their non-foreign dispute to a foreign arbitral institution was invalid.[31] The reasoning of this judgment has been widely questioned in academia. In the field of private law, the absence of legal prohibition means freedom. If the legislation

29 Singapore Convention, Article 3(2):

> If a dispute arises concerning a matter that a party claims was already resolved by a settlement agreement, a Party to the Convention shall allow the party to invoke the settlement agreement in accordance with its rules of procedure and under the conditions laid down in this Convention, in order to prove that the matter has already been resolved.

30 See UNCITRAL Secretariat Guide, 7–8.

31 See Beijing Court, accessed October 4, 2018. See also CNARB, 媒体评出十大有影响力仲裁案例 [The Top Ten Most Influential Arbitration Cases as Rated by the Media], http://victory.itslaw.cn/victory/api/v1/articles/article/aabbbf27-bde1-4d60-9e0a-4545863883c2, archived at: https://web.archive.org/web/20221003132435/; http://victory.itslaw.cn/victory/api/v1/articles/article/aabbbf27-bde1-4d60-9e0a-4545863883c2.

does not explicitly prohibit domestic parties from submitting a dispute that does not involve foreign elements to a foreign arbitral institution, holding such arbitration agreements invalid by expanding the meaning of the legal provision is questionable.[32]

Unlike an international arbitration clause, "internationality" is a compulsory part of a choice of court agreement and a settlement agreement. The Hague Choice of Court Convention Article 1 ("Scope") Section 2 has a detailed description of "internationality" from the reverse perspective of "no foreign factors." If "the parties are resident in the same Contracting State and the relationship of the parties and all other elements relevant to the dispute are connected only with that State," "regardless of the location of the chosen court," there is no internationality. The author believes that this expression is consistent with the meaning of Singapore Convention Article 1(1). Hague Choice of Court Convention Article 1(3) states that "recognition or enforcement of a foreign judgment can be sought when a case is international." Article 20 ("Declarations Limiting Recognition and Enforcement") states that "a State may declare that its courts may refuse to recognize or enforce a judgment given by a court of another Contracting State if the parties were resident in the requested State." This is also consistent with the spirit of the Singapore Convention.

The application of the three conventions only focuses on the internationality of the parties' agreement, award, or judgment, rather than the nationality of the parties, lacking a requirement for the parties to be citizens of the signatories. The Singapore Convention and the New York Convention share the principle that the place of entering into the settlement agreement and the place where the arbitral award is made need not be in a signatory state; the New York Convention allows the signatories to make reciprocal reservations.[33] The Hague Choice of Court Convention Article 3 ("Exclusive Choice of Court Agreements") Section 1 requires the parties to choose courts in a contracting state.[34]

32 李鹏 (Li Peng), 试论无涉外因素争议的外国仲裁裁决 [Foreign Arbitral Awards on Disputes without Foreign Factors], 《行政与法》 [Administration and Law], issue 2013.10, at 120–121 (2013); 牟笛(Mou Di), 《无涉外因素的争议能否在国外仲裁（上）》 [Can Disputes without Foreign Factors be Arbitrated by Foreign an Arbitral Institution], 《商法》 [Commercial Law], issue 2014.03 (2014Li, Analysis on Foreign Arbitral Awards, 120–121; Mou, Disputes without a Foreign Element.

33 New York Convention, Article I(3):

> When signing, ratifying or acceding to this Convention, or notifying extension under article X hereof, any State may on the basis of reciprocity declare that it will apply the Convention to the recognition and enforcement of awards made only in the territory of another Contracting State.

34 Hague Choice of Court Convention, Article 3(1):

> For the purposes of this Convention – a) "exclusive choice of court agreement" means an agreement concluded by two or more parties that meets the requirements of paragraph c) and designates, for the purpose of deciding disputes which have arisen or may arise in connection with a particular legal relationship, the courts of one Contracting State or one or more specific courts of one Contracting State to the exclusion of the jurisdiction of any other courts.

Limitation on the Scope of Application

The Singapore Convention and the Hague Choice of Court Convention share similar limitations on the scope of application. They do not apply to consumer protection, employment and labour, marriage, adoption and succession disputes, and so on. The Hague Choice of Court Convention has a more detailed negative list. Besides the previously listed areas, cases of bankruptcy, transportation, maritime affairs, anti-competition, nuclear damage, personal injury, property damage, real estate rights, intellectual property rights, etc. are also excluded. The commonality of these areas is that they relate to the parties' significant interests as well as to their personal rights. Additionally, the parties to such disputes have disparate bargaining power. Therefore, most countries have relevant special legislation.

Another type of exception relates to comity to an adjacent dispute resolution mechanism. Singapore Convention Article 1(3) states that the convention does not apply to a settlement agreement that was concluded in the course of proceedings before a court or arbitral tribunal or in the course of enforcement of a decision.[35] The Hague Choice of Court Convention Article 2(4) also clarifies that the Convention does not implicate arbitration proceedings.[36] On the other hand, the Singapore Convention Article 1(3) emphasises the enforceability of court judgments and arbitral awards. Some settlement agreements record that the judge or arbitrator participated in the mediation during the settlement process but that they were not enforced by the competent authority as a judgment or arbitral award. Similar situations occurred in China.[37] In order to avoid such a situation where the parties to the settlement agreement cannot seek relief, the Working Group of the Singapore Convention reached a consensus that a settlement agreement cannot be excluded from the scope of the Singapore Convention simply because the settlement agreement is unenforceable because it records that a judge or arbitrator was involved in the mediation. According to the Singapore Convention Article 1(3), only those settlement agreements that are approved by courts or are enforceable as court judgments or arbitral awards by the competent authority are beyond the scope of this convention. This clarifies the different

35 Singapore Convention, Article 1(3):

> This Convention does not apply to: (a) Settlement agreements: (i) That have been approved by a court or concluded in the course of proceedings before a court; and (ii) That are enforceable as a judgment in the State of that court; (b) Settlement agreements that have been recorded and are enforceable as an arbitral award.

36 Hague Choice of Court Convention, Article 2(4): "This Convention shall not apply to arbitration and related proceedings."

37 Interpretation of the Civil Procedure Law, Article 148:I[Interpretation of the Supreme People's Court of the Application of Civil Procedure Law of the People's Republic of China] (promulgated by the Sup. People's Ct., January 30, 2015, effective February 04, 2015) art. 148, (stating that if "the parties enter into an agreement upon settlement or mediation on their own, and request the people's court to make a written judgment in accordance with the settlement or mediation agreement, the people's court shall not allow it."

enforcement mechanisms for settlement agreements reached through mediation, arbitration, and litigation. Each can produce settlement agreements with distinct enforcement procedures, and together they provide a complete framework for enforcing settlement agreements.

Reservation for Whom

Reservations are formal declarations made by a contracting state to exclude or change the legal effect of certain principles or provisions of a convention on itself. The Hague Choice of Court Convention has no "reservations" clause. It gives contracting states the right to make declarations of restrictive application, which essentially allows contracting states to implement the convention with reservations. Similarly, although the term "reservation" does not appear throughout the text of the New York Convention, Article I.3 grants contracting states the right to make reciprocal and commercial reservations.[38]

China declared the two reservations in its accession to the New York Convention in 1986, meaning that China "on the basis of reciprocity applies the Convention to the recognition and enforcement of awards made only in the territory of another contracting state" and "applies the Convention only to differences arising out of legal relationships, whether contractual or not, which are considered commercial under the national law of China."

According to the aforementioned two reservations, China does not apply the New York Convention to "arbitral awards made in the territory of non-contracting states" and "does not include disputes between foreign investors and host governments."[39] However, the practical benefits in making these two reservations are questionable.

The biggest beneficiary of the New York Convention is the winning party who seeks to enforce a foreign arbitral award. If a contracting state makes the reciprocal reservation, it means that it will not recognise an arbitral award made in a non-contracting state, and the result encourages the parties to choose contracting states for place of arbitration. If the property against which the enforcement is sought is in a contracting state with a reciprocal reservation, such reservation can

38 New York Convention, Article I.3:

> When signing, ratifying or acceding to this Convention, or notifying extension under article X hereof, any State may on the basis of reciprocity declare that it will apply the Convention to the recognition and enforcement of awards made only in the territory of another Contracting State. It may also declare that it will apply the Convention only to differences arising out of legal relationships, whether contractual or not, which are considered as commercial under the national law of the State making such declaration.

39 Notice of the Supreme People's Court. Zuigao Renmin Fayuan Guanyu Zhixing Woguo Jiaru De Chengren Ji Zhixing Waiguocaijue Gongyue De Tongzhi (最高人民法院关于执行我国加入的<承认及执行外国裁决公约>的通知) [Notice of the Supreme People's Court on Implementing the Convention on the Recognition and Enforcement of Foreign Arbitral Awards Acceded to by China] (promulgated by the Supreme People's Court, April 10, 1987).

only limit the party's choice of the place of arbitration without bringing practical benefits to the enforcing state.

Further, as the number of contracting states increases, the impact of reciprocal reservations on the scope of application of the convention shrinks. The Singapore Convention does not contain a reciprocal reservation clause, not only because it is not as easy to identify the place where the settlement agreement is reached as the place of arbitration and the adjudicating court but also because determining the country of origin of the settlement agreement is unnecessary. Similarly, the New York Convention does not ask the place of arbitration, and the Hague Choice of Court Convention does not look at the place where the choice of court agreement is reached.

Both the Singapore Convention and the New York Convention recognise the declaration of commercial reservations made by contracting states, but the specifics differ. Article 8 ("Reservation") (1)(a) of the Singapore Convention provides that

> a Party to the Convention may declare that it shall not apply this Convention to settlement agreements to which it is a party, or to which any governmental agencies or any person acting on behalf of a governmental agency is a party, to the extent specified in the declaration.

Accordingly, settlement agreements reached by the government agency of the contracting state as a commercial entity may not be governed by Singapore Convention if the relevant declaration of reservation is made by the contracting state.

Article I.3 of the New York Convention states that "[any contracting state] may also declare that it will apply the Convention only to differences arising out of legal relationships, whether contractual or not, which are considered as commercial under the national law of the State making such declaration." Therefore, it is clear that the reservation provision of the New York Convention focuses on the commercial nature of the dispute while the Singapore Convention focuses on the commercial nature of disputing parties.

The author believes that commercial reservations are not very significant to the enforcing state. The purpose of refusing application of enforcement against property concerning foreign governments can be achieved by invoking the doctrine of sovereign immunity of the enforcing state. Making a reservation while acceding to a convention on enforcement of international commercial dispute resolution is unnecessary. In addition, in all three conventions, the main obligation of the contracting states is enforcement, and the declaration of commercial reservations only means that the competent authorities of the state where enforcement is sought can refuse the application for enforcement involving foreign government property. It cannot protect the government property of the state of enforcement against enforcement in other contracting states lacking the commercial reservation.

The Hague Choice of Court Convention treats this issue more appropriately. Article 2 ("Exclusions from Scope") Section 5 stipulates that "proceedings are not excluded from the scope of this Convention by the mere fact that a State, including a government, a governmental agency or any person acting for a State, is a party thereto," affirming first that the agency and government of contracting states are bound by the convention. Then, in Article 2(6), it clarifies that "nothing in this Convention shall affect privileges and immunities of States or of international organizations, in respect of themselves and of their property."

Further reflection is necessary to answer the question for whom the reservations of the New York Convention are made, although 75 contracting states of the New York Convention have made reciprocal reservations and 47 have made commercial reservations.[40]

In contrast with the other two conventions, Article 8(1)(b) of the Singapore Convention implements a new type of reservation clause, which allows contracting states to declare that the applicability of the convention is contingent upon the explicit agreement of the parties to the settlement agreement.[41] The Working Group discussed "opt out" and "opt in" extensively. The former refers to "the Convention will apply only if the parties agree to apply it in the settlement agreement" and the latter refers to "the Convention will automatically apply unless the parties agree to exclude its application in the settlement agreement." Ultimately, "opt in" is established as the principle of the Singapore Convention while "opt out" is made available as reservation for contracting states. Counting the commercial reservations, the contracting states are not allowed to make other reservations besides the two.

Grounds for Refusing to Grant Relief

First, the conditions for granting relief should be made clear. The basis for granting relief is the validity and enforceability of the settlement agreement under the applicable law and public policy of the state where enforcement is sought. Both the New York Convention and the Hague Choice of Court Convention have similar requirements with analogous language. Article V of the New York Convention requires the parties to have capacity, the arbitration agreement to be valid, the scope of arbitration to be in accordance with party agreement, the arbitration to be properly conducted, the arbitral award to be binding, the subject matter to be arbitrable by the law of the state where enforcement is sought, and the enforcement not be in violation of the public policy of the enforcing state. Similarly, Article 9 ("Refusal of Recognition or Enforcement") of the Hague Choice of Court Convention also requires the parties to be able to reach an

40 "Contracting States," New York Convention.

41 Singapore Convention, Article 8(1)(b): "A Party to the Convention may declare that: (b) It shall apply this Convention only to the extent that the parties to the settlement agreement have agreed to the application of the Convention."

agreement on choice of court, the agreement to be valid, the agreement to be duly reached, no conflict with parallel litigation proceedings, and no apparent violation of the public policy of the requested state. Accordingly, it could be found that most of the wording of Article 9 of the Hague Choice of Court Convention reproduces Article V of the New York Convention.

Unlike arbitration and litigation, reaching a settlement agreement does not require strict procedural rules on court formation, service, defence, etc. But Article 5 ("Grounds for Refusing to Grant Relief") of the Singapore Convention puts forward more detailed requirements on the enforceability of the settlement agreement: the settlement agreement must be final, binding, and cannot be subsequently modified, and the obligations of the agreement must not have been performed and must be clear and comprehensible, etc. The author believes that the requirements on the enforceability of arbitral awards or arbitral mediation agreements in the Provisions of the Supreme People's Court on Several Issues Concerning the Enforcement of Arbitral Awards by the People's Courts may also apply to reviewing settlement agreements. According to Article 3 of this provisions, a settlement agreement should specify the parties with rights and obligations, the amount of money to be paid or a method of calculating the specific amount, a specific piece of property against which enforcement is invoked, and the standard, object, and scope of specific performance. If an arbitral award or a conciliation statement does not meet these requirements, the competent authority of the place where enforcement is sought may refuse granting relief.

Violating public policy of the place of enforcement is an expressly allowed ground for refusing to enforce settlement agreements, arbitral awards, or judgments in all three conventions. The violation of public policy as an exception to the contracting state's obligation to enforce has been extensively discussed in academia. It is difficult to contribute something new to the discussion because public policy (or public interest of the society) is not a pure legal concept. From the perspective of jurisprudence, policy and law are two different social phenomena, and they differ in the nature of will, forms of formulation, enforcement mechanisms, manifestations, and degrees of stability, though they are closely connected. The institution of public policy of the New York Convention refers to the contracting state's right to refuse to enforce arbitral awards on the grounds of public policy when enforcement conflicts with the vital interests, basic policies, fundamental moral concepts, or core principles of law of the state where enforcement is sought. It can be regarded as a protective clause, which grants the competent authorities (courts) of the state where enforcement is sought discretion under specific circumstances.

Public order or good morals maintained by public policy is a temporal and spatial concept. Due to differences in political systems and cultural traditions, different countries may have different interpretations on the connotation of public policy. Moreover, even in the same country, the connotation of public policy will change with the development of the society. In a modern society where pluralism and openness prevail, there is great uncertainty in the definition of public order or good morals, and it is difficult to have only one dominating opinion. Accordingly, public policy ultimately depends on judges' discretion during the judicial examination.[42]

The application of public policy as grounds for enforcement refusal should focus on safeguarding basic societal values; upholding fairness, justice, honesty, and trust; and prohibiting abuse of rights, expropriation without compensation, racial discrimination, pornography harming children's rights and interests, slave trade, and piracy. Most states tend to interpret the public policy clause restrictively. If public policy is interpreted as a basket clause and everything can be packed in it, it will be abused. An abuse of exceptions and public policy clause will be also detrimental to a nation in the international community.

China also adopts the approach of strictly interpreting public policy. In his article "The Application of Public Policy in the Judicial Review of Arbitration," former judge and now procurator Song Jianli summarised the scenarios where China expressly excludes the application of public policy: 1) the violation of the general compulsory provisions of Chinese law, 2) the incorrectness of the application of Chinese law in arbitration, 3) the injustice of the arbitral award, and 4) the misinterpretation or improper comments made on Chinese law in the arbitral award.

In his view, "Public policy is a safety valve for the fundamental interests of a country. Up to now, Chinese courts have annulled or refused to enforce foreign arbitral awards on the ground of violating public policy in judicial practice only on three or four occasions."[43] It shows that China has been an exemplary model in implementing the New York Convention over the past three decades. According to the author's opinion, China's enforcement standards for foreign arbitral awards can be transplanted into the implementation of settlement agreements.

Gaps between Chinese and International Practices to be Filled

Substantive Requirements for Granting Relief Pursuant to Settlement Agreements

At present, China only allows recognition and enforcement of a foreign settlement agreement that is reached by the parties during a court or arbitral proceeding and is converted into a judgment or an arbitral award. In accordance with Articles 281 and 283 of the 2017 Chinese Civil Procedure Law, the party can apply directly to the intermediate people's court for recognition and enforcement of the judgment or award, either in the place of domicile of the party against whom enforcement is sought or the place where his or her property is located.

42 Yang, Research on the New York Convention, 341–371.
43 Song, "The Application of Public Policy," 63–64.

However, for settlement agreements reached abroad by the parties on their own, no applicable law exist for parties seeking enforcement or relief in China.

In 2011, the Supreme People's Court issued Several Provisions of the Supreme People's Court on the Procedure of Judicial Recognition for the People's Mediation Agreements. According to Article 7 of the provisions, a people's court will not recognise the legal force of a mediation agreement under one of these six circumstances: violating the mandatory provisions of law or administrative regulations, harming national interests or public interests, infringing upon the legitimate rights and interests of those who are not parties to the case, impairing public order and good morals, the agreement content being too unclear to recognise, or other circumstances under which the agreement should not be recognised. Although these six circumstances seem more stringent than the practice in enforcing foreign arbitral awards discussed previously, basically, they overlap with the grounds for refusing to grant relief under Article 5 of the Singapore Convention.

The "Mediation Agreement" in the People's Meditation Law Is Inconsistent with the Scope of the Singapore Convention

Article 1(3)(1) ("Scope of Application") of the Singapore Convention clearly stipulates that "this Convention does not apply to: (a) Settlement agreements: . . . (i) That have been approved by a court or concluded in the course of proceedings before a court . . ." This article distinguishes commercial settlement agreements concluded with "the assistance of a third person or persons ('the mediator') and those approved by a court." The latter falls outside the scope of application of the Singapore Convention, but those have "compulsory enforceability" under China's People's Mediation Law. According to Article 33:

> After a mediation agreement is reached through mediation by the People's Mediation Committee, if both parties consider it necessary, they may jointly apply to the people's court for judicial confirmation within 30 days from the effective date of the mediation agreement. The people's court shall timely review the mediation agreement and confirm the effectiveness of the mediation agreement according to law. After the people's court confirms the effectiveness of the mediation agreement according to law, if one party refuses to perform or fails to fully perform, the other party may apply to the people's court for compulsory enforcement.

"Judicial confirmation" mentioned in this article corresponds to the so-called "approved by a court" in the Singapore Convention. Only when the mediation agreement is confirmed to be effective by the people's court can it be enforced. The criteria for the court to review the mediation agreement are embodied in Article 7 of the 2011 Several Provisions of the Supreme People's Court on the Judicial Confirmation Procedure for the People's Mediation Agreements.

The six scenarios of non-confirmation listed in that article are highly similar to Article 5 ("Grounds for Refusing to Grant Relief") of the Singapore Convention. What the author does not understand is the procedural requirements prescribed in Article 33 of the People's Mediation Law, which stipulates that to make the mediation agreement enforceable, both parties must "jointly apply to the people's court for judicial confirmation within 30 days from the effective date of the mediation agreement." What is the legal basis for 30 days? What is the possibility of two parties' joint application? Is there a validity period for a judicial-confirmed mediation agreement? How can we find a recorded judicial-confirmed mediation agreement? Parties seeking enforcement of cross-border mediation agreements are unable to meet so many requirements.

The Singapore Convention and the People's Mediation Law agree that the enforceability of a mediation agreement relies on the judicial review by the competent authority of the place of enforcement. They differ on procedural requirements on granting a mediation agreement compulsory enforceability. The former one is more practical and workable, with no preconditions of reservation, confirmation, and recording. The interference of the competent authority of the place of enforcement happens when a party applies to it for relief after the mediation agreement is not enforced by the other party; then, the competent authority shall review the mediation agreement, confirm its legal effect, and grant it the compulsory enforceability. China needs to promulgate a commercial mediation law that is consistent with the Singapore Convention or take a step further, making a uniform mediation law that can encompass the People's Mediation Law and integrate it with China's Civil Procedure Law and Arbitration Law.

Restrictions on the Mediator

According to China's Civil Procedure Law, Arbitration Law, and the People's Mediation Law, Chinese judicial organs (people's courts) recognise mediation agreements made in the name of the people's court, the arbitration institution, a people's mediation committee, or a duly organised mediation organisation. Mediation agreements reached through a people's mediation committee or mediation organisation cannot be compulsorily unless judicially recognised.[44] Only the legal force of mediation agreements reached through permanent institutions, rather than by individuals or ad hoc mechanisms, are recognisable and enforceable in China. Article I.2 of the New York Convention defines the term "arbitral awards" in the convention as both awards made by arbitrators appointed for each case (ad hoc arbitration) and those made by permanent arbitral bodies, and it allows no room for contracting states to make reservations. Thus, when China acceded to the convention in 1986, it accepted the condition and thus formed a two-track system – foreign awards are recognisable when they are from either permanent or ad hoc arbitral tribunals while in accordance with Arbitration Law,

44 Articles 31 and 33, People's Mediation Law.

while domestic awards are recognisable only when they are made by permanent arbitral bodies. Similarly, the Chinese commercial mediation system cannot integrate with the UNCITRAL Model Law on International Commercial Mediation and International Settlement Agreements Resulting from Mediation (the Model Law). According to Article 1(2) and (3) of the Model Law, "mediator" means a sole mediator or two or more mediators, as the case may be. "Mediation" means a process, whether referred to by "mediation," "conciliation," or other terms of similar meanings, whereby parties request a third person or persons ("the mediator") to assist them in their attempt to reach an amicable settlement of their dispute arising out of or relating to a contractual or other legal relationship. Under the People's Mediation Law, the mediation agreement is legally binding only when it is concluded through mediation by the body designated by law – the people's mediation committee. This clearly restricts societal participation.

In recent years, Chinese judicial authorities are attempting to harmonise with international practices. On October 16, 2017, the Supreme People's Court and the Ministry of Justice issued the Opinions on Implementing the Pilot Program of Lawyer Mediation. According to the opinions, one or more lawyers can preside over mediation as an independent third party and assist parties to resolve disputes through negotiation and reach a mediation agreement. Furthermore, the establishment of an ad hoc arbitration system in China's Free Trade Zones is also under discussion.

The mediator's duties to conform to applicable standards and disclose necessary information are stipulated in Article 5(1)(e) and (f) of the Singapore Convention.[45] However, as an international convention, it cannot establish qualification standards for mediators. At present, China has qualification requirements for people's mediators and lawyer mediators but not commercial mediators in general. Competent authorities where recognition and enforcement are sought obviously cannot further require foreign arbitrators, judges, or mediators to pass relevant qualification tests. The New York Convention, Choice of Court Convention, and Singapore Conventions lack such a requirements.

Establishing an Incentive Mechanism to Resolve Commercial Disputes by Mediation

Compared with commercial mediation, arbitration and litigation are more time consuming, use more judicial resources, and end in uncertain results for parties.

45 Singapore Convention, Article 5(1):

> The competent authority of the Party to the Convention where relief is sought under article 4 may refuse to grant relief at the request of the party against whom the relief is sought only if that party furnishes to the competent authority proof that: (e) There was a serious breach by the mediator of standards applicable to the mediator or the mediation without which breach that party would not have entered into the settlement agreement; or (f) There was a failure by the mediator to disclose to the parties circumstances that raise justifiable doubts as to the mediator's impartiality or independence and such failure to disclose had a material impact or undue influence on a party without which failure that party would not have entered into the settlement agreement.

Mediation can help the parties re-establish communication that is interrupted by disputes, foster mutual understandings of expectations and difficulties, face and solve problems through cooperation, and finally achieve reconciliation and re-establish cooperative business relationships. Therefore, compared with arbitration and litigation, reconciliation – based on mediation consisting of the trilogy of consolation, evaluation, and facilitation – is more conducive to thoroughly resolving disputes and contributing to constructing a harmonious society.

The Chinese nation has a long-lasting tradition of upholding harmony as the overarching principle of conducting oneself in society. However, people tend to misunderstand the meaning of "harmony." Either they understand it narrowly, as in the traditional sayings – "tolerance and generosity," "loss is a blessing," and "giving up the little and saving the great" – which shows the lack of a long-term perspective. Or they would go to the other extreme, stubbornly holding on to petty claims that are not economically reasonable, such as "striving with your life" and "fighting for dignity if not for bread." These are all acts far from the true meaning of reconciliation. Commonly, for a commercial dispute with a substantial amount of money at stake, rational parties tend to think more carefully, view facts more objectively, and apply laws more accurately. In addition, well-qualified mediators analyse and evaluate the case from both sides' perspectives in a comprehensive way. Given these characteristics, solving disputes by mediation is more beneficial to the parties' interests than arbitration and litigation.

States should encourage resolution of commercial disputes through mediation by enacting legislation, letting the parties understand the advantages and benefits of mediation. Second., states should facilitate the enforcement of settlement agreements. For example, the Hong Kong judiciary issued practice direction PD31 in 2010, which stipulates that "legal representatives shall advise their clients of the possibility of the Court making an adverse costs order where a party unreasonably fails to engage in mediation."[46] Such practice is a good reference for mainland China. Finally, the most crucial thing is to promote commercial mediation with commercial thinking. According to Article 4 of the current People's Mediation Law, "A people's mediation committee shall not charge any fees for mediating civil disputes," which obviously blocks the development of commercial mediation and is inconsistent with the spirit of the UNCITRAL Conciliation Rules issued in 1980 and proposals for amendments. Mediation is an idiosyncratic way of dispute resolution; it is different from litigation and arbitration and is an independent developing legal industry. Excellent mediators not only should have a sense of professionalism but also should accumulate excellent skill sets in settling disputes through systematic training and experience. The sustainable development of commercial mediation cannot be promoted by only emphasising "voluntary labour."

46 https://legalref.judiciary.hk/lrs/common/pd/pdcontent.jsp?pdn=PD31.htm&lang=EN.

Applicability of the Convention in Hong Kong and Macau

The three conventions are unified in their treatment of "non-unified legal systems." According to Article 13(1) of the Singapore Convention,

> If a Party to the Convention has two or more territorial units in which different systems of law are applicable in relation to the matters dealt with in this Convention, it may, at the time of signature, ratification, acceptance, approval or accession, declare that this Convention is to extend to all its territorial units or only to one or more of them, and may amend its declaration by submitting another declaration at any time.

Article X.1 of the New York Convention,[47] which was made 60 years ago, and Article 28 ("Declarations with Respect to Non-unified Legal Systems") Section 1 of the Hague Choice of Court Convention,[48] which China signed in 2017, have similar provisions. When China accedes to these conventions, it should clarify how the convention will be applied in Hong Kong and Macau, where a "one country, two systems" policy is implemented. Even though these two regions had not yet returned when China acceded to the New York Convention in 1986, China needed to make a supplementary clarification after their return.

If no such declaration is made, according to Article 13(4) of the Singapore Convention[49] and Article 28(3)[50] of the Hague Choice of Court Convention, the conventions extend to all territorial units of China. This provision is based on Article 29 ("Territorial Scope of Treaties") of the 1969 Vienna Convention on the Law of Treaties, which provides that "unless a different intention appears from the treaty or is otherwise established, a treaty is binding upon each party in respect of its entire territory."[51] Similarly, many of the bilateral investment agreements signed by China in the early years also did not mention their applicability in Hong Kong and Macau, prior to their return to China. After their

47 New York Convention, Article X1:

> Any State may, at the time of signature, ratification or accession, declare that this Convention shall extend to all or any of the territories for the international relations of which it is responsible. Such a declaration shall take effect when the Convention enters into force for the State concerned.

48 Hague Choice of Court Convention, Article 28:

> Declarations with respect to non-unified legal systems (1) If a State has two or more territorial units in which different systems of law apply in relation to matters dealt with in this Convention, it may at the time of signature, ratification, acceptance, approval or accession declare that the Convention shall extend to all its territorial units or only to one or more of them and may modify this declaration by submitting another declaration at any time.

49 Singapore Convention, Article 13(4): "If a Party to the Convention makes no declaration under paragraph 1 of this article, the Convention is to extend to all territorial units of that State."

50 Hague Choice of Court Convention, Article 28 (3): "If a State makes no declaration under this Article, the Convention shall extend to all territorial units of that State."

51 Tza Yap Shum; Sanum Investments Limited.

return, the application of those previous international investment agreements to Hong Kong and Macau has caused much controversy among both practitioners and academics.

Conclusion

Even 20 years ago, "legal globalisation"[52] was viewed as an absurd term and aroused controversy among academics in China.[53] With "economic globalisation" now coming true, the civil and commercial laws of many countries, from procedural rules to substantive, are increasingly similar. With the field of human economic interaction expanding beyond the national borders, "legal globalisation" has also gained momentum and has become the fundamental trend of legal development of the world as well.

In March 2018, China's National People's Congress passed the constitutional amendment which revised "developing diplomatic relations and economic and cultural exchanges with other countries" in the preamble to "developing diplomatic relations and economic and cultural exchanges with other countries and promoting the building of a community with a shared future for mankind." Such amendment suggests that besides the worldview of harmonising and the outlook of sustainable development that China proposed previously, it has gradually developed a new view of international power, common interests, and global governance that features interdependency.[54] These new ideas not only provide basic values and foundations for building a community with a shared future for mankind but also offer a theoretical basis for legal globalisation.

Litigation, arbitration, and mediation are the three major pathways to commercial dispute resolution. The enforcement of relevant judgments, awards, and settlement agreements is dispute resolution's ultimate end. Enforcing foreign judgments, arbitral awards, and settlement agreements suggests recognising foreign judicial principles as well as civil and commercial rules. Such recognition is an important indicator of legal globalisation and is also an important manifestation of the interdependence and mutual cooperation of the community with a shared future for mankind. After the policy of isolation was abolished in the last century, China commenced reform and opening up. It then acceded to the first two conventions discussed, which were viewed as two important steps to integrate with global judicial trends. China should draw lessons and research the Singapore Convention seriously as soon as possible. Early accession to the

52 From the perspective of legal history, the idea of legal globalisation can be traced back to ancient Rome. At that time, the famous political thinker Cicero inherited the natural law ideas of the late Stoics in ancient Greece and the viewpoint of "universal human rationality" and proposed that there are universal natural laws in the "world government of heaven." He believed that for the reason that man and God share rationality, the natural laws of heaven are embodied in human society as the common laws of the nations of the world.

53 Liu, "Legal Globalization."

54 China's Peaceful Development, State Council.

Singapore Convention will be an important step in China's diversifying commercial dispute resolution.

Acknowledgement

Wen, Xiantao thoroughly participated in UNCITRAL's Working Group II Session 62 to Session 68, discussing the Convention's draft and proofreading its Chinese version.

Susan Finder thanks STL graduates Guo Qianru, Li Haiyan, Hu Yue, Peng Sheng, Ni Xiang, Jin Xiaojia, and Sun Dongyu for their work on the translation.

Bibliography

AIG Capital Partners, Inc. and CJSC Tema Real Estate Company v. Republic of Kazakhstan (Award, 2003) ICSID Case No. ARB/01/6 (AIG).

Beijing Court 北京法院. "Beijing fayuan canyue anli di shisi hao)" 北京法院参阅案例第14号：北京朝来新生体育休闲有限公司申请承认和执行外国仲裁裁决案"No.14 Reference Case of Beijing Court: Beijing Chaolai Xinsheng Sports and Leisure LLC Applying for Recognizing and Enforcing the Foreign Arbitration Award. www.bjcourt.gov.cn/article/newsDetail.htm?NId=50000024&channel=100015002&m=zdal%EF%BC%8C

China's Peaceful Development, State Council. http://english.www.gov.cn/archive/white_paper/2014/09/09/content_281474986284646.htm.

The Civil Procedure Law of the People's Republic of China (2017 Amendment), lawinfochina. www.lawinfochina.com/display.aspx?id=23601&lib=law.

"Contracting Parties." Hague Conference on Private International Law. www.hcch.net/en/instruments/conventions/status-table/?cid=98.

"Contracting States." New York Convention. www.newyorkconvention.org/countries.

Di, Mou. "Can Disputes without a Foreign Element Be Arbitrated outside China?" *China Business Law Journal*. https://law.asia/can-disputes-without-a-foreign-element-be-arbitrated-outside-china/.

Gang, Wang 王钢. "Guoji Shangshi tiaojie jiqiao yanjiu" 国际商事调解技巧研究 [Research on International Commercial Mediation Skills]. Bejing: Zhonguo minzhu fazhi chubanshe, 2014.

Hague Conference on Private International Law, Convention of 30 June 2005 on Choice of Court Agreements. www.hcch.net/en/instruments/conventions/full-text/?cid=98

Honglei, Yang 杨弘磊. *Zhongguo Neidi Sifa Shijian Shijiao Xia De Niuyue Gongyue Wenti Yanjiu* 中国内地司法实践视角下的《纽约公约》问题研究 *[Research on New York Convention in the View of Legal Practice in Mainland China]*. Beijing: Falv chuban she, 2006.

Huang, Zhongshun黄忠顺. "Shangshi tiaojie yu minshi tiaojie de qufen yuanli ji qi shixian lujing – jiyu 2012–2013 nian Zhongguo shangshi tiaojie yanjiu wenxian de fenxi" 商事调解与民事调解的区分原理及其实现路径 – 基于 2012~2013 年中国商事调解研究文献的分析 [The Distinguishing Principles and Realization Paths of Commercial Mediation and Civil Mediation – Based on the Analysis of Chinese Commercial Mediation Research Literature from 2012 to 2013]. *Beijing Zhongcai* 北京仲裁 3 (2014): 50–68.

The Interpretation of the Supreme People's Court on the Application of the Civil Procedure Law of the People's Republic of China, lawinfochina, www.lawinfochina.com/display.aspx?id=19211&lib=law&SearchKeyword=CIVIL%20PROCEDURE&SearchCKeyword=.

Jiangli, Song 宋建立. "Gonggong zhengce zai zhongcai sifa zhong de shiyong" 公共政策在仲裁司法审查中的适用 [The Application of Public Policy in the Judicial Review of Arbitration]. *Renmin sifa* 人民司法 1 (2018): 61–64.

Li, Yin 尹力. *Guoji shangshi tiaojie falv wenti yanjiu*国际商事调解法律问题研究 *[Research on Legal Issues of International Commercial Mediation]*. Wuhan: Wuhan daxue chubanshe, 2007.

Lianbin, Song 宋连斌. "Cong Zhongcai yu tiaojie xiang jiehe dao dandu tiaojie" 从仲裁与调解相结合到单独调解 [From the Combination of Arbitration and Mediation to Independent Mediation]. *Kunming ligong daxue xuebaon* (社会科学版) 昆明理工大学学报（社会科学版） *[Journal of Kunming University of Science and Technology]* 11 (2019): 94–99.

Liberian Eastern Timber Corporation v. Republic of Liberia (Award, 1986) ICSID Case No. ARB/83/2 (Eastern Timber Corporation).

Nan, Zhu 朱楠. *Shangshi tiaojie yuanli yu shiwu* 商事调解原理与实务 *[Principles and Practice of Commercial Mediation]*. Shanghai: Shanghai jiaotong daxue chubanshe, 2014.

New York Arbitration Convention. *United Nations Convention on the Recognition and Enforcement of Foreign Arbitral Awards (New York, 10 June 1958)*. www.newyorkconvention.org/english.

Official Reply of the Supreme People's Court on the Application of Law on Placing the "Advance Arbitral" Awards or Mediations of Arbitration Institutions on File for Enforcement, lawinfochina. www.lawinfochina.com/display.aspx?id=28478&lib=law.

Peng, Li 李鹏. "Shilun wu shewai yinsu Zhengyi de waiguo zhongcai caijue" 试论无涉外因素争议的外国仲裁裁决 [Analysis on Foreign Arbitral Awards on Disputes without Foreign Factors]. *Xingzheng yu fa* 行政与法 10 (2013): 120–123.

Peng, Zhang 张鹏. "Yiwen zonglan guoji minshangshi zhengyi jiejue xin jinzhang – Chengren yu zhixing waiguo minshangshi panjue gongyu" 一文纵览国际民商事争议解决新进展 – 《承认与执行外国民商事判决公约》签署确认 [A Review of the New Progress in the Settlement of International Civil and Commercial Disputes – the Execution and Confirmation of the Convention on the Recognition and Enforcement of Foreign Judgments on Civil and Commercial Matters]. www.zhonglun.com/content/2019/07-10/1345030601.html.

People's Mediation Law of the People's Republic of China, lawinfochina. www.lawinfochina.com/display.aspx?id=8266&lib=law.

Sanum Investments Limited v. Lao People's Democratic Republic (Judgment of the Court of Appeals of Singapore, 2016), UNCITRAL, PCA Case No. 2013–13.

S.A.R.L. Benvenuti & Bonfant v. People's Republic of the Congo (Award, 1980) ICSID Case No. ARB/77/2 (Benvenuti & Bonfant).

Schnabel, Timothy. "The Singapore Convention on Mediation: A Framework for the Cross-Border Recognition and Enforcement of Mediated Settlements." *Pepperdine Dispute Resolution Law Journal* 19, no. 1 (2019): 1–60. https://digitalcommons.pepperdine.edu/drlj/vol19/iss1/1.

Société Ouest Africaine des Bétons Industriels v. Republic of Senegal (Award, 1988) ICSID Case No. ARB/82/1 (SOADBI).

Sussman, Edna. "The New York Convention Through a Mediation Prism." *Transnational Dispute Management* 12, no. 1 (2010). www.transnational-dispute-management.com/article.asp?key=1593.

Tza Yap Shum v. Republic of Peru (Decision on annulment, 2015) ICSID Case No. ARB/07/6 (Tza Yap Shum).

UNCITRAL. *UNCITRAL Model Law on International Commercial Mediation and International Settlement Agreements Resulting from Mediation, 2018 (Amending the UNCITRAL Model Law on International Commercial Conciliation, 2002)*. https://uncitral.un.org/sites/uncitral.un.org/files/media-documents/uncitral/en/annex_ii.pdf.

UNCITRAL. *UNCITRAL Secretariat Guide on the Convention on the Recognition and Enforcement of Foreign Arbitral Awards (New York, 1958)*. 2016 ed. www.uncitral.org/pdf/english/texts/arbitration/NY-conv/2016_Guide_on_the_Convention.pdf.

UNCITRAL. *United Nations Convention on International Settlement Agreements Resulting from Mediation*. https://uncitral.un.org/sites/uncitral.un.org/files/singapore_convention_eng.pdf.

UNGA. *Settlement of Commercial Disputes: Enforceability of Settlement Agreements Resulting from International Commercial Conciliation/Mediation: Note by the Secretariat*, UNCITRAL Working Group II, 62ed session, UN 9/11/22 Doc A/CN.9/WG.II/WP.187. Nov. 27, 2014. undocs.org/en/A/CN.9/WG.II/WP.187.

Wei, Sun 孙巍. "Lianheguo guanyu tiaojie suo chansheng de guoji hejie xieyi gongyue lifa beijing ji tiaowen shiyi" <联合国关于调解所产生的国际和解协议公约>立法背景及条文释义 [Legislative Background and Interpretation of the Provisions of the United Nations Convention on International Settlement Agreements Resulting from Mediation]. Bejing: Falv chubanshe, 2018.

Zhiyun, Liu 刘志云. "Falv quanqiuhua yiyu hu, jianyushenling xiansheng shangque" 法律全球化,呓语呼 – 兼与沈宗灵等先生商榷 [Legal Globalization, Crazy Talk: A Discussion with Mr. Shen Zongling, etc]. *Fujian Zhengfa ganbu guanli xueyuan xuebao* 福建政法干部管理学院学报 3 (2002): 19–23.

"Zuigao Renmin Fayuan Guanyu Zhixing Woguo Jiaru De Chengren Ji Zhixing Waiguocaijue Gongyue De Tongzhi" (最高人民法院关于执行我国加入的<承认及执行外国裁决公约>的通知) [Notice of the Supreme People's Court on Implementing the Convention on the Recognition and Enforcement of Foreign Arbitral Awards Acceded to by China]. www.lawinfochina.com/display.aspx?id=11873&lib=law&SearchKeyword=Recognition%20and%20Enforcement&SearchCKeyword=.

SECTION IV

ADR Developments and Reform in Mainland China

10

FLEXIBILITY AND AUTHORITY

Keys for Informal Justice to Succeed

Xin He and Yang Su

Introduction

Over the last decade, China has witnessed a resurgence of mediation in dispute resolution. Institutionally, many agencies, such as government bureaus, community organizations, and courts, have been called upon to proactively mediate disputes, resulting in "the Grand Mediation." Although adjudication and arbitration continue to be utilized, mediation has been aggressively pursued and has become the preferred method of the Chinese regime. According to official statistics, 63 percent of the 1,332,000 labour disputes in 2012 were settled by mediation (Labournet.com 2012).

Is mediation an effective means of dispute resolution? Answers vary, based on different perspectives and data. Fieldwork from rural China – for example Xiong (2014) – has shown that judicial mediation remains effective and important. Focusing on medical disputes, Ding (2015) contends that mediation is "a dose to cure 'medical chaos.'" Huang (2015) suggests that securities dispute mediation has the potential to become a successful forum. On the other hand, the literature is critical of this revived mediation. Minzner (2011) dubs this resurgence a "turn against law," which in the long run undermines the legal spirit. A recent study (He 2007) demonstrates that in divorce cases, judicial mediation in the shadow of stability concerns has undermined legal principles. Some (Ng and He 2014) argue that there are internal contradictions in judicial mediation. When judges conduct mediation, role conflicts are widely registered (Chen 2015; Xian 2015). Judges, especially those who receive formal legal education, seem resistant to the renewed mediation (Fu and Cullen 2011). As a result, many call for a "rethinking" of the mediation campaign (Zhang 2015; Zhao 2015).

However, few studies have systematically assessed the effectiveness of mediation. We all know that from the pre-reform era to the mid-1980s, mediation was

DOI: 10.4324/9780429354625-15

the most important form of dispute resolution for the so-called "internal conflicts among the people" in China (Lubman 1999). It then declined in the 1990s. The political ideology, personnel, organizational capacity, and supporting systems that made mediation effective in the pre-reform period have either vanished or eroded (Di and Wu 2009; Halegua 2005). Will the revived mediation be different?

Drawing on archival records from a commonly used forum known as the Labour Inspection Brigade in Western China, supplemented with interviews of relevant officials and complainants and secondary literature, this chapter examines the case flow; assesses its effectiveness, or lack thereof; and explores institutional conditions. Given the vast size of China and its immense regional variation, data from a single county over only two years do not provide a comprehensive and accurate picture for the country as a whole. It will, however, allow us to track the trajectories of a group of labour disputes in China from beginning to end, including both those that reach a formal legal forum and those that do not. We try to determine how many of these are resolved and by which channels, the extent to which they are resolved, and how their nature affects their final resolutions. We also assess the level of their effectiveness. Comparing our findings with other dispute resolution forums, we examine how the effectiveness of a particular forum is related to its social and political setting. We argue that the combination of flexibility and authority is crucial in order for informal justice to be effective.

Labour Mediation and the LIB

The Labour Inspection Brigade, or LIB, is one subsidiary of the labour bureau – the government branch that regulates labour relations. The responsibilities of the LIB are mainly to, through inspections, oversee companies, contractors, and small business owners on issues regarding safety, the environment, and employment contracts. Dealing with labour-related complaints had primarily fallen within the domain of another subsidiary – the arbitration committee. Since the revival of the mediation policy, however, the LIB has become one of the leading offices in handling labour disputes; it promotes its role in resolving labour disputes through various channels. Posters proclaiming that the LIB provides free and efficient means to collect unpaid wages and to regulate harmful working environments have been hung not only in the offices of the LIB but also at construction sites and in the streets. These posters provide a hotline for potential disputants to report their grievances. With its changed role, the LIB hopes to eliminate any possibility that minor disputes are transformed into social protest, suicides, or petitions, all of which are categorized as social instability incidents.

Procedurally, the LIB is informal and flexible. While visitors must state their identity, they do not have to submit written complaints. Indeed, many complaints are not filed in person, but rather by telephone or email. LIB officials usually accept every complaint submitted. They do not have to match them to different categories; collective cases or cases with significant influence are filed in a special folder. Nor is there any need for the complainant to provide any evidence. Although the officials ask what happened, they take the complainant at his or her word. According to our interview with an LIB official, "most workers there are trustworthy. They have no incentive to come here and say something baseless." Once a complaint is filed, the officials respond to the complainant, usually after contacting the party towards whom the complaint was targeted. Of course, there is no guarantee that every complaint will be addressed.

The LIB has thus become an informal channel, in addition (and parallel) to the formal channel. Officially, the formal resolution process in labour disputes consists of three methods: mediation conducted by a state enterprise's labour dispute mediation committee; arbitration conducted by the arbitration centre in the labour bureau; and litigation (i.e. filing suits in court). Legally, only when one party is unsatisfied with the decision of the arbitration centre can a suit be filed in court.

In achieving the goal of social stability or social control, the LIB stands with the existing formal legal channel. Despite apparent differences in the duties and responsibilities of the two branches, they often overlap. The LIB thus often intervenes in ongoing conflicts or acts as the mediator. There is also much crossover from one body to the other, and a case may be referred back to the LIB when a plaintiff in the arbitration committee refuses to carry on after realizing the process is too protracted and expensive. For example, the LIB, where we conducted our fieldwork, has taken on far more cases than the formal channel. In 2005, it registered more than 400 cases, while the county courts took less than 50 labour cases. Of course, the cases the LIB registered might have been smaller and more casual, whereas the cases with which the court dealt could have been more serious. Nonetheless, the changed role of the LIB is a response to the perceived failure of the formal legal system.

Methods

Studying dispute resolution in the Chinese government presents tremendous methodological challenges. For the LIB, labour issues, especially those related to social protest, collective action, and petitioning, remain sensitive. Any mishandling may lead to incidents which could threaten social stability. Both the LIB and its officials are thus wary of any inquiry from researchers outside of mainland China. This is also why the existing literature relies primarily on sporadic interviews, anecdotes, survey data, and news reports.

To overcome these challenges, we have adopted unconventional methods. Having gained the trust of several LIB officials from our previous projects, we were welcomed to conduct fieldwork investigations in County Z during 2011 and 2012. During our empirical work, we stressed that our research was anonymous and that any details that could leak the identity of the informants would be removed so as to ensure the authenticity of our data. We were allowed to sit beside the hosting officials and silently observe how they handled disputes. We also had casual talks with the complainants at their convenience, both before and after they arrived at the office. A total of 21 petitioners agreed to provide information for this study. In addition, we managed to interview the hosting officials after their sessions had ended, so as to understand their approaches towards the disputes. Five officials agreed to such interviews, and the interviews lasted between 30 minutes and one hour. Last, we also interviewed seven employers – the targets of the complaints. They explained to us the reasons why they had either not paid or had decided to pay and when this had been requested by the LIB officials.

County Z is located in Sichuan Province in China's western heartland, far from the booming coastal cities leading China's economic development. Over 75 percent of its 780,000-plus population is rural, suggesting that agriculture has remained the pillar of the local economy. According to official statistics, County Z's GDP per capita was only 9,975 yuan (1,200 USD) in 2005, about one-third of the more developed coastal areas. The region's underdevelopment has led the central government to mount the "Grand Western Development" campaign to attract high-profile investment projects. At the time of our fieldwork, the county seat was experiencing a construction boom. The construction workers were farmers who had come from villages both within the county and from surrounding areas.

During our fieldwork in County Z, the formerly intimidating government compound was open to labourers. They passed the guards without being stopped and proceeded straight to the fourth floor where the LIB was located. Some of their quests for justice eventually might reach the Arbitration Committee and even the courthouse, but the engagement with an LIB official was the starting point. The first encounter typically lasted between 15 minutes and half an hour. Based on our observations, if the amount in dispute was tiny and straightforward, officials would take action directly, without recording anything. Only when the officials felt a written record was necessary would they then require the complainants to provide written documentation – they usually asked them to fill out a standardized form. The form included the identity and contact information of the complainants and the other parties, as well as a brief outline of the disputed issue. If the complainants were illiterate or had poor writing skills, the officials would fill out the forms for them while simultaneously raising questions. One incident, instead of one complainant, constituted a form. As a result, one form might include a batch of complainants against a single employer. According to some LIB officials, the recorded disputes were only 60 percent of the total disputes reported to the LIB. At year's end, these forms, collected in the Daily Log of Complaints (台账) of the LIB, were bound and archived. Since the LIB is an informal dispute resolution agency, it is understandable that some information was missing from the Daily Log. Labourers would occasionally not fill in all the blanks, or the dispute would be swiftly resolved, rendering the recording of information unnecessary. Some disputes might have reached beyond the capabilities of the LIB and were thus unrecorded.

Towards the end of our fieldwork investigations, the local officials kindly agreed to make available to us the Daily Log of Complaints in 2004 and 2005.

There were 810 disputes in total. In the chapter, we refer to these 810 disputes registered in the LIB as the "Daily Log Sample" (see Tables 10.1 and 10.2). With all pages running continuously and consistent with the content at the beginning, it was clear that no cases had been removed due to their sensitivity or other concerns. Six years had passed since the disputes had been filed, which may have desensitized the records, and this could have been why the officials felt comfortable granting access. If we were to have chosen the dates, we could have chosen more recent years to conduct our research. Nonetheless, the six-year gap between the recorded disputes and our fieldwork investigation should not have affected our overall analysis because the national policy on dispute resolution has been oriented towards mediation since the early 2000s. If anything, the tendency towards outcome-based settlements was only more pronounced in 2011. The outcome would have been more effective had the disputes been handled in 2011.

More valuable for the sake of this project was that most of the records had kept the contact information of the complainants. This allowed us to conduct follow-up interviews for each dispute. Of course, some contact information was outdated since migrant workers may have migrated to other locales. Nonetheless, we were successful in reconstructing the entire life cycle of 225 disputes. We will refer to these 225 disputes as the "Interview Sample" (see Tables 10.3 to 10.5). While the data are incomplete, they offer a rare peek into the systematic evolution of labour disputes and how (in)effective the LIB was in handling them.

Tracing how these disputes are handled offers a systematic picture of how they evolve. Aided by two research assistants, we used the complainants' phone numbers registered in the Daily Log to conduct interviews to find out how these cases had fared and how they had ended by the year 2012. This interval of several years between the occurrence of the disputes and the interview ensured that most disputes had been settled by the time of the interview. After briefly introducing ourselves and the goal of the research, we asked the complainants to relate their stories. In 225 cases, the respondents kindly accepted our interviews. There were also cases in which the complainants forgot the details. Regardless, we retrospectively recorded the trajectories of these disputes' life courses by asking the following questions:[1] Was a second government agency involved? Did the complainant use street protest? Did the case ultimately end up in arbitration or in court? What was the outcome? Was the grievance addressed, and in what way? We then ran statistical analyses on the data collected.

In our multivariate analysis, we ran regression models on two dependent variables. One is a dichotomous variable in the life cycle of the dispute, whether a case has ever entered the legal channel – defined as either appearing in court and a government-run arbitration committee. Of the 225 petitions in the interview

1 There are two reasons for this low success rate. First, there had been long intervals between many of the disputes and the ensuing round of interviews. Many workers had already migrated to other parts of the country and thus changed their phone numbers, and some of the numbers were no longer in service. Second, some workers simply did not want to answer our questions.

sample, 25 (11 court cases and 14 arbitration cases), or 11.11 percent, are such petitions (see Table 10.3). In the other dependent variable, we measured the outcome of the dispute – whether the petitioner ended up obtaining monetary compensations, recorded as 1 if yes and 0 if no. For both dependent variables, logistic regression models were appropriate.

Among the key independent variables, we included one dichotomous measure to indicate whether the dispute had been processed by the LIB. This measure is important in predicting both of the aforementioned dependent variables: whether the LIB's process reduced the likelihood of a dispute moving upward towards the formal legal channels and whether such processing by the LIB helped the petitioners satisfy their demands. In the models predicting the dispute outcome, another key independent variable is whether it entered the legal system. We were curious if entering the legal system had a positive or negative effect on achieving the petitioner's goal.

We investigated these relationships in the context of controlling for other factors that may obscure them. We used the following measures as the control variables in our models:

- Petitioner's gender, coding male as 1, female as 0
- Type of petition, coding those that involved wages and employment deposit as 1, the others as 0
- Whether the petitioner was a local resident (i.e. from within the county); coding yes as 1, no as 0
- Whether the petitioner was an urban resident or a peasant, coding urban as 1, peasant as 0
- Size of the company being targeted by the petition, coding large company as 1, the others as 0
- Number of petitioners involved
- Whether the dispute involved any collective actions, coding yes as 1, no as 0
- The amount of the money claimed by the petitioner

Typically, quantitative research bases its argument on its regression models. However, our research is different. While we present statistical tables and multivariate regression models, it is important to emphasize the mixed-methods nature of our research: it provides both quantitative and qualitative angles to investigate the process of a set of Chinese labour disputes. Not only do we examine the dispute process from "outside in" by interviewing disputants on their personal experience and the process as they perceive, but we also investigate the same process from "inside out" via our in-depth ethnographic fieldwork inside the government agency. Thus, our thesis about flexibility and authority rests on both quantitative data and ethnographic narratives.

The former, with descriptive statistics and regression models, presents a collective profile of the disputes that were initiated in and processed by the LIB and assesses the results of these disputes. The message in this part of the analysis suggests a certain level of effectiveness. Unlike the situation depicted in the classic dispute pyramid, the majority of the disputes entering the LIB in County Z were processed, and many of them ended with an outcome favourable to the petitioner. The latter, with interview data with the government officials and the participatory observations of the government action, explains why the disputes turned out as they did. In sum, while we use regression models as an important step to build our thesis, our thesis does not rest solely on the quantitative findings; it also incorporates the findings of our ethnography of the LIB.

Trajectories and Outcomes

Using the Daily Log Sample, Table 10.1 presents the profiles of the disputes in terms of their characteristics such as the issues of complaints, the numbers of individuals involved, the monetary value involved, and the types of employers.

Small but Significant Disputes

Other than those lacking details, all were labour related: 784 of 810 records showed that they were either related to wages, job deposits,[2] retirement, welfare, work injury, or lay-off severance. More than three-quarters (77 percent) of the disputes concerned wage or job deposit issues. As shown in the following, issues surrounding wage arrears and the unfair withholding of job deposits were more straightforward than the others.

These disputes involved small amounts of money; 22 percent of the 810 disputes involved sums equal to 1,000 RMB (approximately 120 USD as of 2005 rates) or less, while 23 percent were between 1,000 and 10,000 RMB. Only 8 percent had a stake greater than 100,001 RMB (or 12,048 USD), which usually involved multiple individuals. Of the 810 cases in the daily log sample, 61 percent involved one individual complainant. The rest were registered on behalf of a collective: 18 percent had been filed by two individuals, 17 percent involved between 10 and 100 individuals, and 26 cases (3 percent) had been filed on behalf of 100 or more workers. Those with higher amounts in dispute usually involved multiple complainants. Since the Daily Log only recorded those relatively complicated disputes, leaving many straightforward disputes unrecorded, the LIB handled primarily small disputes.

All disputes had been filed by employees. Approximately three-quarters of the complainants were migrant workers, the rest being local residents of the city. Among the targets of the complaints, 9 percent were *ge-ti-hu* (individual households). Legally speaking, the LIB had no power against this group because they were natural persons rather than employers: the LIB can only inspect employers.

2 It is common practice for employers to require their employees to put down a deposit when they are hired, and many do so. Whether or not the deposit is returned to an outgoing worker often becomes a source of dispute.

TABLE 10.1 Profile of Disputes Registered by Labour Inspection Brigade of County Z

		Number of cases	*Percent*
Issue of complaints	Wage or job deposit	625	77.16
	Retirement and welfare	61	7.33
	Work injury compensation	39	4.81
	Lay-off severance	59	7.28
	Other issues related	23	2.84
	No information	3	0.70
	Total	810	100.00
Number of individuals involved	1	497	61.36
	2 to 10	148	18.27
	11 to 100	139	17.16
	More than 100	26	3.21
	Total	810	100.00
Monetary account at stake (RMB)	0	32	3.95
	1–1,000	146	18.02
	1,001–10,000	183	22.59
	10,001–100,000	133	16.42
	100,001 or above	65	8.02
	No information	251	30.99
	Total	810	100.00
Type of employers	State/collective owned	48	5.93
	Mid-size private company	320	39.91
	ge-ti-hu (individual households)	72	8.89
	Private small business	253	31.23
	Other	87	10.74
	No information	30	3.7
	Total	810	100.00

Data Source: Daily Log Sample.

Another 40 percent were mid-size private businesses. State-owned businesses only accounted for 6 percent of the sample.

The Role of the LIB

Again based on the Daily Log Sample, Table 10.2 reports the actions taken by the LIB once a disputant came to the office for petition. In the table, we only report the initial actions; for the further actions in the later stages of the dispute, see our follow-up interview reports.

Upon reaching the LIB, disputes were processed immediately by the official on duty, often on the same day. The forms for 80 percent of the 810 cases

TABLE 10.2 Initial Processing of Labour Disputes by Labour Inspection Brigade

		Frequency	*Percent*
Initial processing	Phone the petition target party	469	57.90
	Visit the company	49	6.05
	Ask the target party to explain	85	10.49
	Transfer case to other agency	39	4.81
	Legal channels suggested	10	1.23
	Did not get processed	19	2.35
	No information	139	17.16
	Total	810	100.00
Result of initial processing	Complete at LIB	379	46.79
	Transferred to other agency	39	4.81
	Next step suggested	207	25.56
	Not processed or pending	158	19.50
	Total	810	100.00

Data Source: Daily Log Sample.

in our Daily Log Sample had been marked with at least one specific means of processing, including making phone calls, paying visits, interviewing the target, transferring the case, or suggesting other channels. In total, 58 percent of the targeted employers had received a phone call inquiry, and 10 percent had been asked to come to the LIB to explain the situation. In 49 cases, an official had visited the company to investigate. After the initial processing, only 19.50 percent of disputes are still marked as pending or unprocessed; 46.79 percent are marked complete, and 25.56 percent of them are suggested for a second step.

From the standpoint of the disputants, 46.79 percent indicates a high level of responsiveness of the government to their claims. If we refer back to the dispute pyramid, we know that due to the lack of recourse, the majority of disputes end up being lumped or otherwise set aside. A tiny proportion of them are processed by the public authorities, including the court. The percentage varies, of course, but 46.79 percent is by no means insignificant because most legal systems tend to ignore these small claims.

The Dispute Pyramid

To follow the entire life cycle of the disputes, we successfully interviewed 225 petitioners five years after the initial petition. Table 10.3 used this Interview Sample to report actions taken after the initial stage.

Our findings confirm the established pattern of the dispute pyramid – only a tiny proportion of disputes reached the "apex" of the formal legal process

TABLE 10.3 Subsequent Trajectories and Outcomes of Labour Disputes

		Frequency	*Percent*
Processed by second agency	None	147	65.33
	Other branch of Labour Bureau	9	4.00
	Arrears Clearance Office	4	1.78
	Letter and Petition Office	3	1.33
	Media	1	0.44
	Arbitration committee	14	6.22
	Court	11	4.89
	Other	31	13.78
	No information	5	2.22
	Total	225	100
Was protest involved?	Yes	8	3.60
	No	217	96.40
	Total	225	100.00
Was lawyer involved?	Yes	15	6.67
	No	210	93.33
	Total	225	100.00
Winning reward	Yes	105	46.67
	No	120	53.33
	Total	225	100.00

Data Source: Interview Sample.

(Michelson 2007; Felstiner et al. 1980–1981). Contrary to traditional wisdom, however, our data suggest that many other disputants did not simply dump their cases, nor were their grievances silenced without resolution. Instead, the government agency intervened with various third-party efforts. Ultimately, many of the outcomes favoured the initial disputants.

The data from 225 follow-up interviews help reveal what happened after the initial processing by the LIB: 147 disputes, or 65 percent, ended without a second agency. This result is fairly consistent with the data from the Daily Log Sample, which reports that 46.79 percent of the disputes were deemed "complete" by the LIB after the initial processing. The higher percentage here may indicate some of these cases reached the conclusion because the petitioner stopped perusing the recourse midway. Apart from the five cases lacking details, the rest all went to a second government agency: the Arrears Clearance Office (4), the Letter and Petition Office (3), media organizations (1), the Arbitration Committee (14), the court (11), another branch of the Labour Bureau (9), or an unspecified agency (31). Since the formal legal channel includes the Arbitration Committee and the court, of the 225 disputes, 25, or 12 percent, reached them. The complainants in 15 of the 225 disputes reported that they retained a lawyer, and 8 of the 215 disputes reported protesting.

Only a minority of the disputes resorted to the formal legal channel (12 percent), yet most of "the other cases" obtained third-party interventions in one way or another. These interventions came from the LIB or other government agencies. As reported in the last panel of Table 10.2, such interventions produced positive relief for about half of the disputes (46 percent).

A clear pattern emerges: while most disputes did not achieve the status of a legal case, they did not just disappear during the dispute resolution process. They were processed with the assistance of government agencies, whose simple interventions tipped the balance in favour of the employee, thus enabling the employee to obtain a certain amount of compensation from the employer.

Which Types of Disputes Were Transformed into Litigation?

To ascertain the effect of the initial processing, we control for the other characteristics of the disputes, including the dispute type, the claim size, the petitioner's socio-economic status, the type of targeted party, and the number of petitioners involved. These characteristics potentially have their own effects on whether a dispute will reach the legal channels. We ran two regression models in Table 10.4 to investigate. Model 1 is a fuller model in terms of sample size with 225 cases; we also introduced a control variable indicating the size of the petition claim, which results in some missing cases. In Model 2, the sample becomes 153. In both models, however, the message is the same: if the case had been processed by the LIB first, it may have ended there with a resolution: it would have been less likely to have escalated into a court case.

Other factors being equal, there are two significant effects, shown in the statistical results. The first is the dispute type – specifically, whether the dispute involves issues of wages or job deposits. Take Model 2 as an example. This factor

TABLE 10.4 Coefficients of Logistic Regression Predicting Likelihood of Dispute Entering Legal Channels

	B	*Odds ratio*	*B*	*Odds ratio*
Intercept	0.057	1.059	1.487	4.422
Petitioner being male	−0.251	0.778	−0.844	0.430
Wage or deposit related	−1.606[2]	0.201	−1.767[1]	0.171
Petitioner from within county	−0.155	0.856	−0.740	0.477
Petitioner being urban resident	−0.708	0.493	−0.694	0.500
Target being large company	−0.113	0.893	−0.325	0.723
Number of people represented	0.007	1.007	0.038	1.039
Dispute involving protest	0.313	1.367	1.838	6.281
Dispute processed by LIB	−1.144[1]	0.319	−1.913[2]	0.148
Amount of the claim			−0.013	0.987
N	225		153	
2 x log likelihood (df)	137.08 (8)		75.71 (9)	

[1] = $p < .05$; [2] = $p < .01$

Data Source: Interview Sample.

has a strong negative effect. That is, wage- or deposit-related disputes were less likely to develop into litigation, with a negative coefficient, −1.767. The corresponding odds ratio, as shown in the table, is 0.171 (i.e. exp[−1.767]), indicating that the likelihood of this type of dispute is a fraction of that of the other types. The likelihood for a wage- or deposit-related dispute to go to channels, measured in terms of odds, decreased by 82.9 percent, in comparison with the other types of disputes.

The second was the effect of the initial processing of the LIB. Once they were processed by the agency, the likelihood of disputes later being litigated decreased by a negative coefficient of −1.913, with the odds ratio being 0.148. That means processing by the LIB decreased the odds of entering the legal channels by 85.2 percent.

Which Elements Facilitated Positive Outcomes?

As shown in Table 10.3, most disputes received by the LIB were processed, and about half of the 225 disputes in our interview sample obtained a positive outcome. Why can "winning reward" be an indicator of effectiveness of the dispute resolution? The reason lies in the lopsided power relationship between migrant labourers and the business. The migrant workers were routinely mistreated, with the wage arrears being the most severe problem. Previous research has amply documented the plight of the disadvantaged (Lee 2012). In particular, He et al. (2013) and Zhuang and Chen (2015) detail the length of time for the workers to get their wages back.

Our further multivariate regression analysis was to ascertain which elements were crucial to achieving the aforementioned outcomes.

In the logistic regression models in Table 10.5, we employed a set of independent variables to estimate the likelihood of the disputes achieving monetary compensation, as a positive outcome for the initial petitioner. With other factors controlled, three findings stand out. The first is the effect of government assistance. The LIB's processing increased the likelihood of redress by a factor of between 4.368 (see the odds ratio in Model 3) and 5.241 (see the odds ratio in Model 2). This finding is consistent with the previous discussion.

Second, "target being large company" is a negative significant factor in predicting the likelihood of monetary awards by an odds ratio of between 0.385 (in Model 2) and 0.420 (in Model 3). This suggests that large companies might be more capable of thwarting workers' claims. The claims against them might therefore have fewer positive outcomes.

Third, entering the legal channels in fact would decrease the likelihood of being compensated. As shown in Table 10.5, in the first two models (Models 1 and 2), the effect is negative and significant, with the odd ratios between 0.305 and 0.229. This indicates that if a dispute could not be resolved by the LIB and become a legal case, its prospects of a favourable resolution were worse than the other cases. This is perhaps because disputes that failed to be resolved by the LIB

TABLE 10.5 Coefficients of Logistic Regression Predicting Monetary Reward in Dispute Resolution

	Model 1		*Model 2*		*Model 3*	
	B	*Odds ratio*	*B*	*Odds ratio*	*B*	*Odds ratio*
Intercept	0.986[3]	2.679	−0.455	0.634	−1.520[2]	0.219
Petitioner being male	−0.159	0.853	−0.179	0.836	−0.180	0.836
Petitioner from within county	−0.536[1]	0.585	−0.520	0.595	−0.423	0.655
Petitioner being urban resident	−0.230	0.794	−0.029	0.972	0.145	1.156
Target being large company	−0.907[3]	0.404	−0.954[3]	0.385	−0.868[2]	0.420
Number of people represented	0.000	1.000	0.000	1.000	−0.003	0.997
Dispute entering legal channel	−1.189[2]	0.305	−1.475[2]	0.229	−0.487	0.614
Dispute involving protest	0.171	1.186	0.325	1.385	0.067	1.070
LIB processed the case			1.656[3]	5.241	1.474[2]	4.368
Lawyer involved			1.664	5.280		
Wage or deposit related					1.428[2]	4.170
N	225		225		225	
2 x log likelihood (df)	290.25 (7)		270.34 (9)		258.56 (9)	

[1] = $p < 0.1$; [2] = $p < .05$; [3] $< = p < .01$

Data Source: Interview Sample.

were the more difficult ones to begin with. Indeed, after controlling for the dispute type, the negative effect of going through legal channels is less pronounced (odds ratio being 0.614 in Model 3).

Finally, the data also show that while the involvement of a lawyer had a positive effect, it was not significant. This contradicts previous studies which have found that lawyers are important for case outcomes (He and Su 2013). A plausible explanation is that since the LIB intervention was effective, it restricted lawyers' room. Of course, one should not read too much into this, since less than 7 percent of the petitioners in the interview sample had legal representation (see Table 10.3).

These patterns challenge the conventional wisdom of dispute resolution in two ways. First, those disputes that did not reach the "apex" of the pyramid – the formal legal channel – do not fail per se; they do obtain a form of redress.

Second, the government agency plays a crucial role in achieving this. This factor is so prominent that the effectiveness of the formal means – lawyers and courts – is overshadowed: it seems that they do not advance the chances of gaining relief.

Flexibility and Authority

The prior analysis finds that the government agency plays a crucial role in resolving disputes. Our fieldwork investigations, including interviews with officials and participation observation, suggest that the effectiveness of government involvement lies in the nature of the LIB as an informal dispute resolution institution: flexibility and authority. As an informal dispute resolution institution, it does not enjoy the kind of power that can directly determine the outcome of a dispute; it is informal in nature. However, this frees it from the rigidity of the formal institution and thus enables it to address disputes effectively, especially for certain types of disputes. It also allows the LIB to transmit its power as a regulator to authority in dispute resolution.

First, the flexible nature of the LIB attracts specific genres of dispute. As shown in the Daily Log, most registered disputes concern small amounts; they are straightforward and predominantly involve migrant workers. In many instances, the employers did not disagree with workers' requests, they just did not pay as promised when a claim was initially made. Many cases could be simply resolved through a phone call. In the LIB Daily Logs, few cases involved complex legal disputes.

Second, in part due to their limited power, LIB officials employ flexible means and techniques. According to our observations, the officials were usually friendly towards complainants. Patiently listening to the labourers ensured that they understood the causes of complaints; subsequently, they would suggest a solution. In cases they believed to be credible, they immediately offered to call the employer. In their interaction with the employers, the most commonly used technique was to elaborate upon the employees' predicament and ask the employers to place themselves in the employees' shoes. "Persuading with emotion and reason" (以情动人，以理服人) was crucial in communicating with the employers, according to an official interviewed. For many disputes, this technique was effective. With a nudge from the LIB officials, most minor labour disputes, such as this, were resolved.

Third, the LIB's flexibility also means that their dispute resolution is pragmatic. For many labour complainants, this is the most attractive aspect of the LIB. While the court may offer a full set of compensation to the plaintiff, the court decision may not be enforced, and the legal process itself takes much longer. Many migrant workers, eager to get paid, did not have the time, expertise, or money to go through the formal process. The ultimate goal of the LIB officials was to get the wage arrears back for the migrant workers. The LIB officials try to find a balance between the requests of the migrant workers and their employers. For government officials, as long as it was acceptable to the other parties, it was a good deal. In their own words, "to get both parties to accept is a triumph" (抹平就是水平). In essence, what the LIB offers is raw justice, but timely raw justice is better than late justice, let alone an unenforceable court judgment obtained after a lengthy and expensive legal battle.

Finally and most important, the LIB is not bound by rigid procedural rules. Unlike the judges, the LIB officials were not bound by the rigidity of evidence rules, so they could act efficiently and effectively to resolve disputes. Furthermore, the LIB has taken up many disputes outside of its jurisdiction. Labour law has a clear definition of what constitutes the employment relationship. For many migrants who did not even have a labour contract with their employer, which is common in the construction business (Pun et al. 2010), their claims, legally speaking, should not have been regarded as labour cases. According to both our observations and the data, in many situations the LIB officials did not even bother to ask the nature of the complained business before they made the call. Sometimes, regardless of the absence of a legal relationship, they would request the developer, the contractor, the project managers, the group leaders, and the representatives of the migrant workers to convene at the LIB office and work out a solution.

In addition to flexibility, the other characteristic critical to the success of the LIB is power. In the court and the Arbitration Committee, the judges and the arbitrators have the formal power to determine the outcome of cases, but they are not the regulators of the employers. The LIB, however, has become both regulator and adjudicator in handling disputes. Although the LIB's formal power to issue administrative penalties is limited, it has the power to regulate employers' behaviour. For example, the LIB is empowered to inspect the safety of the working environment. It can also inspect whether or not labour contracts comply with legal requirements. For instance, in 2002, a migrant worker from a construction company committed suicide by jumping off a rooftop. Lacking the administrative power to impose a penalty for this incident, the LIB imposed a fine of 3,000 RMB on the company for non-compliant behaviour in labour contracts (Wang 2009: 94).

Formally the LIB is a regulator, and informally it is a dispute resolver. Even though it does not have legal teeth, it does have administrative teeth, and those teeth are arguably more powerful – or at least more petty and available.

Beyond the LIB

This section looks to instances of effective mediation or informal justice beyond the LIB in China. The aim here is to highlight a common dynamic: to identify analogies that can make sense of details that otherwise would seem accidental. While remaining attentive to variation stemming from a host of factors, we can begin to assess the generality of the findings from China's LIB and avoid wrapping a conclusion around a single case.

The first example, the fate of China's People's Mediation Committee (the PMC) before and after the reforms, illustrates the crucial role of authority in the effectiveness of informal justice forums. In Mao's China, the PMC was forceful. This was because the mediation system, including the PMC, was politicized (Lubman 1967). The mediators were both activists and cadres, collaborating with the police. Following state policy and political standards, they helped repress the enemies of the people and "educate" or "persuade" bad elements to reform (Lubman 1967: 1348). They combined the power to persuade with the power to sanction. They might have lacked explicit coercive power, but they could trigger more authoritative actions leading to criticisms and greater sanctions than could the judges. In sum, "mediators are integral parts of the mechanism of Party rule" (Lubman 1967: 1349). In a word, the authority of the PMC before the reforms was formidable. In the reform period, however, the PMC's authority declined. While 7.4 million cases were handled by the PMC in 1990, this dropped to 5 million by 2000 and fell to just 3.1 million cases in 2002 – roughly 40 percent of the 1990 figure. One reason for the decline, according to Halegua (2005), is the lack of authority for the institution of the PMC and the mediators (see also Di and Wu 2009: 242; Wu 2014: 121–122). The state has put more emphasis on rule of law and court professionalism and has thus sidelined the PMC.

If the shrunken effectiveness of the PMC reveals the importance of authority in an informal justice forum, the fate of judicial mediation in China suggests that its inflexibility eclipses its effectiveness. Since the Grand Mediation policy was put into place in the mid-2000s, judicial mediation has been required for most court cases. The revived judicial mediation, however, has not been as effective as intended. Although the mediation rate has become a crucial criterion for assessing the performance of the judges and the courts, many judges, especially those with formal legal training, resist this requirement. While official statistics claimed that the percentage of civil cases resolved by mediation has increased (*China Law Yearbooks* various years), Li et al. (2016: 3) found that "mediation rate increases at first were largely the result of low-level court involvement in mediation practices outside of the courtroom" and that "the mediation rate was produced strategically by seeking the highest increase possible under the discretion of the definition of mediation in the incentive structure with the lowest cost and risk to the court." A recent study (Ng and He 2014) documented that of 25 cases they observed during their two weeks of fieldwork, only one was successfully mediated, and that was accidental. According to Ng and He (2014), one reason for this ineffective policy is that "when the rather rigid format of adjudication is carried over to in-trial mediation, it curtails the flexible, non-legalistic approach that mediation is meant to promote."

This contrasts with the effectiveness of judicial mediation in Mao's China. In that era, the judges had not been bound by the format of procedural rules, and they investigated neighbourhoods to understand the causes of disputes. As illustrated by Huang (2010), the hearings were held in the neighbourhood or government buildings, with the participation of government officials. The judge would also provide government-funded remedies, in addition to the legal remedies provided by the litigation parties themselves.

The crucial role of flexibility and authority has also been shown in the mediation of various businesses in contemporary China. While scant systematic research is available, preliminary studies suggest the importance of flexibility and authority also here. For example, Huang (2015: 187) suggests that securities dispute mediation in China has been welcomed by the market as a useful mechanism for resolving disputes. On the contrary, in explaining the failure of the mediation of environmental disputes, Zhao (2015: 242) argues that a lack of legal force is the primary culprit.

Flexibility and authority are also the key to the effectiveness of informal justice forums in societies with advanced legal systems. For example, in the US, consumer protection bureaus are associated with the state attorney general's office; New York initiated this trend in 1957, and 44 states had established such bureaus by 1973 (Johnson et al. 1977). The law enforcement activities of the bureaus are related only tenuously to the dispute-settling process (Steele 1975: 1119). They handle complaints through a combination of persuasion, education, mediation, and litigation. Of these, studies have found mediation to be the most effective (cf. Johnson et al. 1977, note 87).

What is the secret to this effectiveness, when other informal forums had produced mixed results, and many had run into frustrating obstacles? The existing literature on ADR, particularly that written as advocacy for non-state solutions and informality, emphasizes the magic of mediation – its non-adversarial features aiming at pragmatic solutions with flexible procedures. Indeed, in dealing with consumer complaints, the bureaus' priority is obtaining compensation for consumers, not reinforcing general rules. The aim "is to get money back as promptly as possible for the citizen who has been cheated or defrauded" (Johnson et al. 1977: 67). In his study, Steele (1975) also resorts to flexibility in explaining mediation's success.

Do most ADRs not share these same features – non-adversarial character, modest goals, and flexible procedures? Why are the US consumer protection bureaus and Chinese LIBs more effective than most others? The explanation lies in the agencies' authority over the disputing parties – in this case, over the companies and retailers. As Johnson and his colleagues put it, consumer bureaus are able to back up their "suggestions" for resolutions with potent sanctions such as injunctions and other orders (1977: 67). This point echoes the "informal power" possessed by the Chinese LIB over businesses under its jurisdiction: as described, sanctions range from holding up clearance for sanitary inspections to confiscating operating licenses. The difference between the two agencies is that the Chinese LIB does not have the power to adjudicate cases directly. This power is vested in its sister branch – the arbitration committee.

A moment of reflection on other ADR practices may reinforce this point. One of the most ingenious ADR experiments in the US was the Neighborhood Justice Center, which reached its height in the late 1970s and early 1980s

(Cook et al. 1980; Tomasic and Freeley 1982; Hofrichter 1987; Harrington 1982, 1985). Its advocates insisted on its community character as a solution outside the state. In reality, most of the centres were the product of state legislature and were funded by the government. Initial assessments were mostly positive, but the "success" of the Neighborhood Justice Center, mainly promoted by the scholars who themselves were its advocates, is disputed by critics for lacking a rigorous empirical base (Harrington 1985). More important, by the end of the 1980s, most Neighborhood Justice Centers had run out of funds and had closed, joining the legion of failures in the history of "informal" or "popular" justice.

The termination of funding may have been the logical extension of failure, rather than the cause. The heart of the problem is a lack of authority (Abel 1982). Unlike traditional townships and villages, the "neighbourhood" in contemporary American cities does not comprise an organic unit. It thus lacks the cultural infrastructure necessary to generate community authority on behalf of the "neighbourhood."

Conclusions and Implications

This chapter presented a systematic study in which an executive branch of the local government functions as an informal dispute resolution forum by way of its flexibility and authority over the potential disputants. As our findings suggest, the LIB, a state-backed channel, effectively resolves a large portion of disputes which would have otherwise been denied access to justice. We argue that flexibility and authority are the essence of this kind of administrative mediation. It is flexible because it is outside the formal court system, and the executive powers are used "tactically" as a force to compel disputants to comply with its decisions. Its authority stems from its regulatory position in the government.

Flexibility allows government-sponsored administrative agencies to attract specific types of cases, which are usually screened out by the procedural rigidity of the formal channel. It also allows the handling of disputes in less confrontational ways and with more room for compromise. The authority of the administrative agencies also demands respect for their suggestions, and disputants are thus less resistant to the final resolutions.

The combination of these two factors provides a unique perspective on the formal legal channel and its relationship with informal justice. The formal legal system in the US, characterized as adversarial legalism by Kagan (2003), enjoys authority but lacks flexibility. Its formality and rigidity have prevented many disputes from reaching its dockets. That is why informal justice, and especially the ADR movements, has arisen.

Viewed from this perspective, the formal and informal justice channels do not replace each other but are complementary, like different business models catering to the needs of different clients. Reducing the rigidity of formal justice would certainly increase its accessibility to the general public, but resolving disputes through informal channels may not necessarily be a bad idea. Our study thus suggests an alternative agenda to traditional scholarship on access to justice (Sandefur 2008): while it is important to reduce the rigidity and the cost of the formal channel, it is equally important to set up informal mechanisms with the authority to deliver justice. Indeed, as more cases vanish from the formal channel and are diverted into alternative forums (Galanter 2004), this task becomes more pressing.

However, the effectiveness of informal justice should not be overstated. Without formalities established to ensure procedural neutrality, the informal channels of justice are more susceptible to corruption and arbitrariness (Fiss 1984). The success of the LIB illustrates, in a roundabout way, the weakness of the law in China. The Chinese government's goal in establishing such channels is to better control society, and thus labourers' rights are not the top priority; no institutional arrangement is put in place to prevent similar violations from recurring in the future. The coerciveness of mediation in Communist China is a telling example of how cases can turn wild in informal justice. When an adjudicator is also the regulator, there can be many undesirable consequences, which is why administrative laws are established to prevent the abuse of power. Allowing the further combination of judicial power and administrative power is the opposite of specialization and professionalism in the development of the rule of law; it will impede legal development in the long run. In a way this weakness of the legal development continues into the Xi era: the regime now emphasizes rule of law and legal professionalism, but informal justice and control of society are not less stressed (Ng and He 2017). The role of administrative power remains prominent, and the sacrifice of labour rights persists. Moreover, since the informal channels of justice tend to be more suitable for small claims disputes, the efforts made to establish informal forums are not intended to replace the formal channels that are more suitable for complicated and difficult cases.

Acknowledgement

An earlier version of this chapter was published with the title "Authority and Flexibility: Resolving Labor Disputes in a County Government in Western China," in *Law & Society Review* 53(4): 1341–1376, 2019.

References

Abel, Richard L. "The Contradictions of Informal Justice." In *The Politics of Informal Justice (Volume I)*, edited by Able Richard, 267–320. New York: Academic Press, 1982.

Chen, Yongzhu. "The Judge as Mediator in China and Its Alternatives: A Problem in Chinese Civil Justice." *American Journal of Comparative Law* X, no. 2 (2015): 106–125.

China Law Yearbooks (中国法律年鉴). Beijing: China Law Yearbooks Press, Various Years.

Cook, Royer F., Janice A. Roehl and David I. Sheppard. *Neighborhood Justice Centers: Field Test.* U.S. Department of Justice National Institute of Justice Office of Program Evaluation, 1980.

Di, Xiaohua and Yuning Wu. "The Developing Trend of the People's Mediation in China." *Sociological Focus* 42 (2009): 228–245.

Ding, Chunyan. "A Dose to Cure 'Medical Chaos': Medical Mediation in China." *American Journal of Comparative Law* X, no. 2 (2015): 158–176.

Felstiner, William, Richard Abel and Austin Sarat. "The Emergence and Transformation of Disputes: Naming, Blaming, Claiming . . ." *Law & Society Review* 15 (1980–1981): 631–654.

Fiss, Owen M. "Against Settlement." *Yale Law Journal* 93 (1984): 1073–1090.

Fu, Hualing and Richard Cullen. "From Mediatory to Adjudicatory Justice: The Limits of Civil Justice Reform in China." In *Chinese Justice: Civil Dispute Resolution in Contemporary China*, edited by Margaret Y. K. Woo and Mary E. Gallagher, 25–57. Cambridge: Cambridge University Press, 2011.

Galanter, Marc. "The Vanishing Trial: An Examination of Trials and Related Matters in Federal and State Courts." *Journal of Empirical Legal Studies* 1, no. 3 (2004): 459–570.

Halegua, Aaron. "Reforming the People's Mediation System in Urban China." *Hong Kong Law Journal* 35 (2005): 715–747.

Harrington, Christine. "Delegalization Reform Movements: A Historical Analysis." In *The Politics of Informal Justice*, edited by Able Richard, 35–71. New York: Academic Press, 1982.

Harrington, Christine. *Shadow Justice: The Ideology and Institutionalization of Alternatives to Court*. New York: Greenwood Press, 1985.

He, Xin. "'No Malicious Incidents': The Concern for Stability in China's Divorce Law Practice." *Social & Legal Studies* 26 (2007): 467–489.

He, Xin and Yang Su. "Do the 'Haves' Come Out Ahead in Shanghai Courts?" *Journal of Empirical Legal Studies* 10 (2013): 121–146.

He, Xin, Lungang Wang and Yang Su. "Above the Roof, Beneath the Law: Perceived Justice among Migrant Wage Claimants in China." *Law & Society Review* 47 (2013): 703–737.

Hofrichter, Richard. *Neighborhood Justice in Capitalist Society: The Expansion of the Informal State*. New York: Greenwood Press, 1987.

Huang, Philip C. C. *Chinese Civil Justice, Past and Present*. New York: Rowman & Littlefield Publishers Inc, 2010.

Huang, Robin Hui. "Securities Dispute Resolution in China." *Journal of Comparative Law* X, no. 2 (2015): 177–188.

Johnson, Earl, Valerie Kantor and Elizabeth Schwartz. *Outside the Courts: A Survey of Diversion Alternatives in Civil Cases*. Denver: National Center for State Courts, 1977.

Kagan, Robert. *Adversarial Legalism: The American Way of Law*. Cambridge, MA: Harvard University Press, 2003.

Labournet.com.cn. "Statistics for Labor Disputes Settlement (劳动争议处理统计数据)." (2012). www.labournet.com.cn/ldzy/ckzl/ckzl.asp (accessed 23 April 2017).

Lee, Ching Kwan. "Durable Subordination: Chinese Labour Regime through a South Korean Lens." In *East Asian Capitalism: Diversity Continuity and Change*, edited by Andrew Walter and Xiaoke Zhang, 110–131. Oxford: Oxford University Press, 2012.

Li, Yedan, Joris Kochen and Benjamin van Rooij. "Understanding China's Court Mediation Surge: Insights from a Local Court." *Law & Social Inquiry* 43, no. 1 (2016): 58–81.

Lubman, Stanley. "Dispute Resolution in Communist China." *California Law Review* 55 (1967): 1284–1358.

Lubman, Stanley. *Bird in a Cage: Legal Reform in China after Mao*. Stanford: Stanford University Press, 1999.

Michelson, Ethan. "Climbing the Dispute Pagoda: Grievances and Appeals to the Official Justice System in Rural China." *American Sociological Review* 72 (2007): 459–485.

Minzner, Carl. "China's Turn Against Law." *American Journal of Comparative Law* 59 (2011): 935–984.

Ng, Kwai Hang and Xin He. "Internal Contradictions in China's Judicial Mediation." *Law & Social Inquiry* 39 (2014): 282–312.

Ng, Kwai Hang and Xin He. *Embedded Courts: Judicial Decision Making in China*. New York: Cambridge University Press, 2017.

Pun, Ngai, Huilin Lu and Huipeng Zhang. *On the Grand Construction Site* 大工地上. Hong Kong: Commercial Press (商务印书馆), 2010.

Sandefur, Rebecca. "Access to Civil Justice and Race, Class, and Gender Inequality." *Annual Review of Sociology* 34 (2008): 339–358.

Steele, Eric. "Fraud, Dispute, and the Consumer: Responding to Consumer Complaints." *University of Pennsylvania Law Review* 123 (1975): 1107–1186.

Tomasic, Roman and Malcolm M. Feeley. *Neighbourhood Justice: Assessment of an Emerging Idea*. New York: Longman, 1982.

Wang, Lungang. *The Struggle for Rights and Interests by Migrant Workers in the China's Legal Development (法治进程中当代中国农民工非正式的利益抗争)*, Doctoral Dissertation, Southwestern University of Finance and Economics, China, 2009.

Wu, Yuning. "People's Mediation in China." In *The Routledge Handbook of Chinese Criminology*, edited by Liqun Cao, Ivan Y. Sun and Bill Hebenton, 116–129. Oxford: Routledge, 2014.

Xian, Yifan. "Grassroots Judges of China in the Resurgence from Adjudicatory to Mediatory Justice." *Journal of Comparative Law* X, no. 2 (2015): 126–141.

Xiong, Hao. "The Feasibility of Court Mediation in the Grassroots Society of Southwest China: A Case Study from Yunnan." *Hong Kong Law Journal* 44 (2014): 277–302.

Zhang, Xianchu. "Rethinking the Mediation Campaign." *Journal of Comparative Law* X, no. 2 (2015): 44–64.

Zhao, Yuhong. "Mediation of Environmental Disputes." *Journal of Comparative Law* X, no. 2 (2015): 237–253.

Zhao, Yun. "Mediation in Contemporary China: Thinking about Reform." *Journal of Comparative Law* X, no. 2 (2015): 65–83.

Zhuang, Wenjia and Feng Chen. "'Mediation First': The Revival of Mediation in Labor Dispute Resolution in China." *China Quarterly* 222 (2015): 380–402.

11

WEARING TWO HATS

Problems of "In-Trial" Mediation in China

Kwai Hang Ng

Introduction

Within the familiar Anglo-American context, the word "alternative" in the common acronym ADR suggests the alternative and thereby different character of mediation to adjudication. For some, mediation is meant to enable the pursuit of quality alternative solutions outside of litigation.[1] That remains the goal even when mediation is facilitated under the auspices of the court. Judicial mediation in the United States, for example, commonly means court-annexed mediation hosted either by a trained mediator or a judge specially assigned to facilitate settlement meetings. The judge or legal professional who mediates a case is not the same individual who is assigned to try the case. Some courts have rules stipulating that the trial judge should not be informed of any positions that parties take during an ADR proceeding. The only information that the settlement judge reports to the trial judge is the outcome of whether or not settlement is reached.[2]

In China, to say that mediation is an "alternative" to adjudication is, both in theory and in practice, an understatement. For many who study the courts there, it also sounds a bit off-key. The Chinese model may be characterised as reformist;[3] the system is designed to blur the line that separates adjudication and mediation.[4] Mediation is everywhere in the country. Outside of the courts,

1 Carrie Menkel-Meadow, "Pursuing Settlement in an Adversary Culture: A Tale of Innovation Co-Opted or 'the Law of Adr'," *Florida State University Law Review* 19 (1991); "Dispute Resolution," in *The Oxford Handbook of Empirical Legal Research*, ed. Peter Cane and Herbert M. Kritzer (Oxford: Oxford University Press, 2012).

2 Wayne Brazil, "Judicial Mediation of Cases Assigned to the Judge for Trial," *Dispute Resolution Magazine* (2011).

3 Sally E. Merry, "Sorting out Popular Justice," *Social and Legal Studies* 1 (1992).

4 This point is certainly not new. Scholars such as Jerome Cohen, Stanley Lubman, and Philip Huang have pointed out the term "mediation" in the Chinese context is complex. See Jerome A. Cohen,

DOI: 10.4324/9780429354625-16

there are various overlapping systems of mediation. Take labour dispute as an example. An employee may try to mediate a dispute internally at the mediation committee in her work unit or company or take the dispute outside to the local peoples' mediation committee. The ubiquitous peoples' mediation committee is an expansive network that still handles civil disputes of different kinds while boasting very high rates of settlement countrywide.[5] These many local and enterprise-based mediation networks are considered extrajudicial, as they exist outside of the judicial system proper. For labour, family, and other civil disputes, it is reasonable to assume that many have been mediated at some point, in some cases multiple times, before they make their way to the basic-level courts of China. Article 18 of the People's Mediation Law (2011) states: "Where a dispute is suitable to be resolved through people's mediation mode, the basic-level people's court or public security organ may, prior to accepting and hearing it, notify the parties to apply to the people's mediation committee for mediation."

The use of local mediation committees to resolve civil disputes can at least be dated back to the Republican era in the 1930s.[6] But its cultural root is often traced further back to the Confucian tradition that favours harmonious social relations over conflicts. The institution survived the regime change in 1949 and was incorporated into the socialist model of justice that dominated the 1950s.[7] The Maoist mass line approach added new flavours to the Chinese model, including the involvement of the community (the term used then was "people-initiated") and the emphasis on persuasion and education.[8] As recent as in 1989, the party state still promoted the ratio of 80 percent (mediation) versus 20 percent (adjudication).[9] The prevalence of mediation reached its high watermark during the early 2000s, when mediation, which in Chinese is expressed as *tiaojie* 调解, literally meaning harmonising and resolving, was touted as the way to promote the ideal of "harmonious society."

For obvious reasons, the Chinese model of incorporating mediation into the adversarial process has attracted much scholarly attention. Some hail it as an extension of the country's non-confrontational cultural tradition. Some argue that judicial mediation maintains pre-existing social relationships and reduces judicial cost. Other believe that the practice contributes to social harmony and

---

"Chinese Mediation on the Eve of Modernization," *Journal of Asian and African Studies* 2, no. 1–2 (1967); Stanley B. Lubman, "Mao and Mediation: Politics and Dispute Resolution in Communist China," *California Law Review* 55 (1967); Philip C. C. Huang, *Chinese Civil Justice, Past and Present*, Asia, Pacific, Perspectives (Lanham, MD: Rowman & Littlefield, 2010).

5 Knut B. Pissler, "Mediation in China: Threat to the Rule of Law?" in *Mediation: Principles and Regulation in Comparative Perspective*, ed. Klaus J. Hopt and Felix Steffek (Oxford: Oxford University Press, 2013), 992.

6 The Republican government promulgated a Civil Mediation Law (Minshi tiaojie fa) in 1930. See Huang, *Chinese Civil Justice, Past and Present*, 198.

7 William Partlett and Eric C. Ip, "Is Socialist Law Really Dead?" *New York University Journal of International Law and Politics* 48, no. 2 (2016).

8 Lubman, "Mao and Mediation: Politics and Dispute Resolution in Communist China."

9 Huang, *Chinese Civil Justice, Past and Present*, 89.

stability, a paramount goal now pursued by the ruling communist party.[10] But the mediation-heavy system of China has also attracted critics. Some worry that the use of mediation would stray the courts away from the rule of law. Carl Minzner,[11] in a well-known article, characterises the obsession with mediation shown by the Chinese judiciary as a "turn against the law." Minzner is worried that the overt reliance of mediation continuously undermines the court as a rules-based legal institution. Famed Chinese legal scholar Zhu Suli expresses the scepticism of a realist. He doubts the efficacy of judicial mediation in dealing with growing volumes of disputes, as the different regions of China have grown further apart socially and economically.[12]

In practice, how does mediation affect adjudication in China? This article addresses the question by drawing from field work at various grassroots courts, supplemented by some systematic court statistics I recently collected about the Beijing grassroots courts. I focus on divorce cases. There are obvious reasons why divorce disputes as a group provide a clear view of the relation between adjudication and mediation. In the United States, ADR in civil cases was created in the 1970s to first resolve disputes in family law.[13] In China, it is also the one area of law in which mediation is most institutionalised. In fact, mediation is mandatory in contested divorce disputes.[14] In practice, when dealing with contested divorces, courts much prefer settlement over judgment. In the next section, I take a closer look at the characteristics that differentiate the Chinese model from the Anglo-American ADR model. I characterise the Chinese model as an extreme case of integration. In practice, they interlace each other. Analytically, the integration of mediation and adjudication can be separated into three key aspects – procedural integration, judicial role integration, and valuation integration. I move on to present some problems created by this extreme form of integration. The final part of the chapter argues that mediation in China in practice does not work as "an alternative" to adjudication. Quite the contrary, mediation is the dominant process as adjudication is the subordinate process in the Chinese courts. It is more accurate to view adjudication as the fallback option for mediation. The subordination of adjudication to mediation is reflected by how judges are strongly inclined to turn down petitions in their first trials. Rejecting first-time petitions is also a way to push parties to agree to judge-led settlements.

10 Xin Xu, *Jiufen Jiejue Yu Shehui Hexie [Dispute Resolution and Social Harmony]* (Beijing: Law Press, 2006); Liming Wang, "Characteristics of China's Judicial Mediation System," *Asia Pacific Law Review* 17 (2009).

11 "China's Turn against Law," *American Journal of Comparative Law* 59, no. 4 (2011): 940.

12 "Guanyu Nengdong Sifa Yu Datiaojie [on Judicial Activism and Grand Mediation]," *Zhongguo faxue [China Legal Science]* 1 (2010).

13 Robert A. Baruch Bush, "Staying in Orbit, or Breaking Free: The Relationship of Mediation to the Courts over Four Decades," *North Dakota Law Review* 84 (2008).

14 Article 32 of the Marriage Law of the People's Republic of China. It states: "In dealing with a divorce case, the people's court should carry out mediation between the parties. Divorce shall be granted if mediation fails because mutual affection no long exists."

The Chinese Integrative Model

Procedural Integration

In the United States, judicial or court-annexed mediation is an out-of-court affair. It is not part of the trial process. It is presided over mostly by a mediator who is not the judge presiding over the case. The mediator may not even be a professional judge. Parties mediate before or after the adversarial court proceedings commence. In fact, it is common for parties to settle in the middle of a trial, as they come to form a more realistic and informed view about their chances of winning the case. Whether mediation takes place before or during the trial, mediating proceedings are separate proceedings that take place outside of the courtroom. For that reason, when parties settle, they are said to settle "out of court." In contrast, the Chinese model embeds mediation in the adversarial trial procedure. From the Anglo-American perspective, this may look conceptually confusing. But the Chinese model does not view adjudication and mediation as two distinct processes. The merged model is evident when one looks at how the Chinese trial is organised. The trial is made up of four stages: court investigation, court discussion, court mediation, and announcement of the decision. Each stage is an integral component of the civil trial. Mediation, if agreed upon by the litigating parties, literally takes place in the middle of the trial. No separate session is held for mediation.[15]

By law, in-trial mediation is voluntary in China. The Civil Procedural Law of the People's Republic of China stipulates that the court may or may not conduct mediation after court discussion. That is to say, if a party does not want to mediate, the trial, in theory, moves on to the next stage. Spearheaded by the Supreme People's Court (SPC) president Xiao Yang, the courts in the late 1990s and early 2000s adopted an adjudication-centred approach to civil justice that de-emphasised mediation. But it was a short-lived campaign as the party state was alarmed by the growing number of petitions. The judiciary quickly reverted back to its reliance on mediation.[16] The SPC believed this would allow for more access to justice and more effective dispute resolution. In the decade of the 2000s when the policy of building of a "socialist harmonious society" was promoted by the leadership of the Chinese Communist Party, the SPC made a strong push for mediation. The SPC Provisions on Court's Civil Mediation Work in 2004 state that "all cases that can be mediated should be mediated." In this period, mediation rates of all levels of courts experienced noticeable spikes. The national average percentage of mediated cases reported by the SPC reached the zenith of the high 60s in the early 2010s (e.g., the national average was 68.2

15 See Article 142 of the Civil Procedure Law of the People's Republic of China (2017). Unlike in Japan, mediation and conciliation mean basically the same process in China. See Kwai Hang Ng and Xin He, "Internal Contradictions of Judicial Mediation in China," *Law and Social Inquiry* 39, no. 2 (2014).

16 Margaret Y. K. Woo and Mary Elizabeth Gallagher, *Chinese Justice: Civil Dispute Resolution in Contemporary China* (Cambridge and New York: Cambridge University Press, 2011).

percent in 2012).[17] Many courts offered extra incentives, in the form of year-end bonuses, to encourage judges to mediate more and adjudicate less. Grassroots courts also used mediation rate as an important indicator for evaluating judges' performances. Some local courts reported a mediation percentage in the 80s or even 90s.[18] Courts in economically less developed regions of China particularly leaned on mediation to resolve cases.[19] It is no secret that these courts prefer mediation over adjudication for stability maintenance.[20] Some courts even claimed that their goal was to achieve zero adjudication, meaning that all the cases processed by a court were to be resolved by means of mediation.[21]

The model is even more integrative in practice than on paper. In trials that I observed, the first three stages of a trial as stipulated by the Civil Procedure Law – that is, investigation, discussion, and mediation – often blended as one continuous process. There were no clear breaks separating one stage from another in trials.[22] In a sense, the Chinese model presages the routinisation of mediation in the United States. Critics of court-annexed mediation in the United States lament that as mediation becomes more popular, it deviates from its original goal of promoting *alternative* form of dispute resolution, as success is now measured exclusively by the volume of settlements produced.[23] In the case of China, mediation has never been viewed as an alternative vision of justice. The judicial system has been settlement oriented from its early days. Judicial mediation often turns into explicit bargaining in the shadow of an impending judgment. This is compounded by the fact that court hearings are supposedly open to the public.[24] In mediation, the exchange between parties bargaining with each other is heard by everyone present in the courtroom. Mediation, in the Anglo-American context, is confidential and private. What one says in mediation should not be used to the detriment of the person in trial later.

Role Integration

To my knowledge, China is one of the very few jurisdictions in the world that ask the sitting judge to also serve as the mediator of the same case. By far the

17 Jian Ma, "Shixian Shenpan Fuwu Jingjishehuifazhan De Xinchangtai," *People's Court Daily*, May 14, 2015.

18 Yedan Li, Joris Kocken, and Benjamin van Rooij, "Understanding China's Court Mediation Surge: Insights from a Local Court," *Law & Social Inquiry* 43, no. 1 (2018).

19 Hao Xiong, "Two Sides of Court Mediation in Today's Southwest Grassroots China: An Empirical Study in T Court, Yunnan Province," *Asian Journal of Law and Society* 1, no. 2 (2014).

20 Kwai Hang Ng and Xin He, *Embedded Courts: Judicial Decision-Making in China* (New York: Cambridge University Press, 2017).

21 Shizhong Peng, "Nengdong Sifa Shiyexia Minshi Tiaojie Gaige De Jingxiang Xuanze [Paths of the Civil Mediation Reform from Judicial Activism Perspective]," *Jinan xuebao (zhexue shehui kexue ban) [Journal of Jinan University (Philosophy and Social Sciences)]* 1 (2011).

22 Ng and He, "Internal Contradictions of Judicial Mediation in China."

23 Nancy A. Welsh, "Making Deals in Court-Connected Mediation: What's Justice Got to Do with It?," *Washington University Law Quarterly* 79 (2001).

24 In civil trials, litigants are usually accompanied by family members and friends and sometimes their lawyers.

more common practice is for another person, whether a judge, a member of the judicial personnel, or a certified or court-appointed mediator, to host settlement negotiations.

The Chinese judge plays the dual role of mediating and adjudicating. During the stage of court investigation, the Chinese equivalent of Western-style adversarial proceeding, the parties are asked to present competing evidence to challenge and contradict each other. A judge is supposed to play the part of an investigator guiding the process. She often gets herself involved during this stage. She probes into the details of the case by asking questions to the plaintiff and defendant.[25] During the process, confidential information may be disclosed that the judge would not otherwise have known. And it could be difficult, even for a judge, to separate the information that comes out during mediation from the evidence presented during court investigation. At the same time, the same judge is heavily involved in mediating parties to reach a settlement. What the trial judge says during mediation may lead parties to think that she has already taken a stance on certain crucial issues that have yet to be decided. Parties may already feel pressured to agree to settle at trial when they have doubts about the impartiality of the judge. The conflicting expectations of the roles are difficult for many judges to navigate.

Besides the lack of separation between mediation and adjudication at trial, there is a lack of closure after the hearing is finished. In theory, as soon as parties disagree to mediate or fail to reach an agreement after trying mediation, a trial moves on to its final stage of decision. In practice, judges almost without exception reserve judgments. In between the trial and the day judgment is handed down, the judge would step up her effort to urge parties to settle. The constant effort to push for mediation is at loggerheads with the distinct "day in court" style of justice that the Chinese system now promotes.

Valuation Integration

Many civil disputes are about economic loss. Even for cases that are not ostensibly about economic loss, non-economic loss such as loss of companionship is awarded in the form of monetary compensation. In mediation, a plaintiff is likely to learn about the defendant's view about how much, if any, the person is willing to pay. They are also likely to learn about the mediator's view of the "fair value" of the claim during the process. But when the mediator is the judge, it is virtually difficult to tell at what point adjudication ends and mediation begins. Some Chinese judges are openly evaluative in their approach; they let parties know what they think of as "fair values." In systems in which the judge and the mediator are different individuals, the mediator's opinion on value at least has no direct bearing on the adjudication process, even when parties decide not to settle. A mediator is by definition a third party who has no power to render a decision or enforce

25 Xin He and Kwai Hang Ng, "Inquisitorial Adjudication and Institutional Constraints in Chinese Civil Justice," *Law & Policy* 35, no. 4 (2013).

an agreement.[26] But in this case, the person who invests much of her time and effort to facilitate a settlement is the same person who decides on the outcome if parties do not settle. At mediation, the parties may also discuss other issues that could affect the judge's overall assessment of values – for example, things such as how one feels about the other party and matters such as hurt feelings and emotion.

A Case in Point

The example here is a case of "successful mediation" reported in a co-authored article (with Xin He) on judicial mediation in China.[27] I reproduce the part that addresses directly the themes I identified prior. The example illustrates how easily adjudication and mediation bleed into each other in a trial. The case is typical in many ways. A husband (the plaintiff) fought over various accusations with his estranged wife (the defendant) at the trial. It was a hotly contested case. The defendant especially was overwhelmed with emotion during the early part of the trial. The sitting judge, a woman judge in her thirties, decided to move quickly to the stage of mediation. As is often the case with trials in grassroots courts, there was no clear break between the stages of investigation and mediation. The judge did not formally announce that the investigation and discussion stages were over. In the second half of the trial, the judge talked with the parties about the value of the conjugal home. The discussion remained difficult. Neither side was in the mood of conciliation. The judge then moved on to the thorny question of child support. The following excerpts reproduce the part of the discussion when the parties negotiated about child support.

Excerpt 1

[JUDGE] Yes, can you increase your offer on child support?
[DEFENDANT'S LAWYER] 800 yuan is not that much –
[PLAINTIFF] That's not possible.
[JUDGE] You said 500 yuan. Is that all you can give?
[PLAINTIFF] Yes.
[JUDGE] Defendant, what do you think?
[DEFENDANT'S LAWYER] We think 500 yuan is not enough.
[JUDGE] How about 600 yuan, is that possible?
[PLAINTIFF] This –
(A relative in the audience is saying things to the plaintiff out loud)
[JUDGE] Please don't . . .

26 Susan S. Silbey and Sally E. Merry, "Mediator Settlement Strategies," *ibid.* 8, no. 1 (1986).
27 Ng and He, "Internal Contradictions of Judicial Mediation in China."

In Excerpt 1, the judge's hands-on and interventionist style is in display. She is no mere facilitator. She bargains openly to try to find a figure that is agreeable to both parties.

Excerpt 2

[JUDGE] What's your decision, plaintiff?

[PLAINTIFF] OK. I still insist that the most I can give is 500 yuan.

[JUDGE] Right.

[DEFENDANT'S LAWYER] Let the court rule then.

[JUDGE] Still only 500 yuan?

[A RELATIVE IN THE AUDIENCE] What's going on here? I'll pay that 100 yuan for you!

[JUDGE] Who is this person? Who are you?

[DEFENDANT] He's his second elder brother.

[PLAINTIFF'S LAWYER] That's a different matter. But according to the legal rule, child support only amounts to 20 to 30 percent of a person's income. (*Note: according to the plaintiff, his monthly income is 2,000 yuan.*)

[JUDGE] So, how much is the child support if it is 30 percent of his income?

[PLAINTIFF'S LAWYER] But according to the rule, you don't have to use the upper limit of the range for your calculation.

[JUDGE] (*louder*) But am I not allowed to use the upper limit for my ruling?

[PLAINTIFF'S LAWYER] The calculation should consider the circumstances faced by the plaintiff.

[JUDGE] That isn't necessarily true. If you want to talk about the law, I'll discuss the law with you. It's 20 to 30 percent.

[JUDGE] (*turning to the plaintiff*) Your brother already said he could pay the remaining 100 yuan for you. But is this really necessary? This money is for your own son, not for a stranger.

[PLAINTIFF] Now I don't care. Where would my salary go? I don't care now.

[JUDGE] Don't be difficult.

[PLAINTIFF] . . . just 2,000 yuan.

[JUDGE] Whether your salary is really 2,000 yuan, you know it better than I do.

[PLAINTIFF] Is that right? You can ask my wife . . .

The plaintiff rebukes the judge's suggestion to raise the offer to 600 yuan. His lawyer challenges the judge for suggesting the figure. The counsel's comment points to the tension the judge inherits by playing the two roles at once. The lawyer talks as if the judge already ruled that the plaintiff would pay a monthly child support of 600 yuan. This is the problem of valuation integration identified previously. The lawyer challenges if the judge is applying the law properly. But 600 yuan is supposedly just a number proposed during mediation. Yet this is not how the lawyer views the number. To him, mediation is clearly a bargaining that takes place in the shadow of an impending ruling, a ruling that requires the lawyer's client to pay 600 yuan per month. The merging of mediation and adjudication makes what the judge suggested at mediation potentially coercive. It also makes mediation difficult. What could well have been probing for grounds for a settlement is now viewed by the parties in a different light.

As the transcript shows, the elder brother of the plaintiff offers to pay 100 yuan a month to his nephew. The judge takes up the offer as part of the "settlement package" and goes on to lecture the husband about his duty as a father. She invokes the Confucian filial ideal of fatherhood – a responsible father should take care of his son. The judge reminds the plaintiff that the money is for supporting his own son. The blended nature of mediation and adjudication deviates even from the principles that the SPC set out for the grassroots courts.[28] In "Some Provisions of the SPC on Evidence in Civil Procedures" (最高人民法院关于民事诉讼证据的若干规定) that was announced in 2001, it stated explicitly that anything unfavourable disclosed in mediation cannot be used to the detriment of the party disclosing the information.[29] But in the example, the judge uses the "offer" given by the plaintiff's brother to further push the plaintiff into agreeing to 600 yuan. Given the way mediation and adjudication are conducted hand in hand, it is simply impossible for the judge to separate the information obtained from the two procedures.[30] And in her all-out attempt to get the settlement done, there is no point for her to keep the information separate. In the end, the plaintiff agrees, albeit reluctantly, to pay 600 yuan each month for child support.

Evidence from Court Statistics

In this section, I zoom out from individual case examples to look more broadly at the relation between mediation and adjudication. I present some statistics collected from the grassroots courts of Beijing to show the effects of mediation on adjudication in contested divorce petitions. Scholars have acknowledged the difficulties of gathering quality empirical data on ADR mechanisms and court-annexed mediation in particular.[31] As a preliminary study, I analyse the outcomes of divorce cases during a period of two and a half years in Beijing to see how adjudication and mediation affect each other. I present some preliminary

28 If we use the terms derived by Huang, this would be a case of "adjudicative mediation." See Huang, *Chinese Civil Justice, Past and Present*, 158.

29 See Supreme People's Court, "Some Provisions of the Supreme People's Court on Evidence in Civil Procedures" (2001). At the time when I observed the case (early 2010s), the 2001 provision was still in place. Perhaps noticing how impractical the provision was, the SPC, in a new set of provisions on civil procedure announced in 2019, deleted the specific article (Article 67). See "Some Provisions of the Supreme People's Court on Evidence in Civil Procedures" (2019).

30 Article 67 of the old 2001 provisions was taken out in the new 2019 version. Compare two "Some Provisions of the Supreme People's Court on Evidence in Civil Procedures."

31 Shahla F. Ali, *Court Mediation Reform: Efficiency, Confidence and Perceptions of Justice* (Northampton, MA: Edward Elgar Pub., 2018).

findings of an analysis of about 10,000 decisions handed down by the grassroots courts in the Beijing municipality from 2014 to 2016.

The dataset is constructed by scraping online judgments released by the courts on their websites. Since January 2014, the SPC ordered every level of Chinese courts to make their judgments available online for public perusal.[32] In practice, courts have not made all judgments available. Hence, the dataset is not exhaustive. Yet the overall level of access has markedly increased since the SPC announced the policy in 2014. This is especially the case with the courts in major metropolitan areas.[33] By the SPC's own calculation, up to September 2017, there have been around 35 million court cases available online, and this number continues to increase. My collaborator and I used Beijing as the site for the study.[34] Beijing is the capital city of China. Administratively, it is also a big, directly governed municipality with a mix of urban and rural districts. Within Beijing the municipality, there are a total of 16 basic-level courts, each corresponding to the 16 districts that make up the municipality, from which their judgments on contested divorce petitions made up our dataset. Districts such as Dongcheng and Xicheng are the most urbanised and densely populated spots in all of China. But outlying districts such as Mentougou and Fangshan remain quite rural. The dataset includes all the available decisions on divorce petitions from the 16 courts handed down between January 2014 and June 2016.

Online Judgments

The data are made up of the decisions scrapped from the website of Beijing's High People's Court (HPC).[35] My search yields a return of 10,738 first-instance

32 Supreme People's Court, "Provisions on People's Courts Release of Judgments on the Internet," (2013).

33 Chao Ma, Xiaohong Yu, and Haibo He, "Big Data Analysis: Report on Public Access to Legal Documents Online," *Zhongguo Falü Pinglun* 2016, no. 4 (2016).

34 Yu Wang and I collaborate on this ongoing project. For fuller details, please see Yu Wang and Kwai Hang Ng, "By the Law? – How Chinese Judges Rule on Contested Divorces," *Journal of Comparative Law* XV, no. 2 (2020). Some of the data presented in this chapter are taken from the article.

35 Several websites with different affiliations make judgments from basic-level courts available to the public or paid subscribers. They vary in both quantity and content. We searched three major websites of court judgments using the keyword "contested divorce" (离婚纠纷[lihun jiufen]) and a filter to only retrieve the "judgments" (判决书 [panjueshu]) from all-level courts in Beijing and compared their returned results. The three websites are namely China Judgment Documents Website (中国裁判文书网[zhongguo caipanwenshu wang]) (SPC's own website), Beijing Court Judgment Information Website (北京法院审判信息网[beijingfayuan shenpan xinxiwang]) (Beijing's HPC website), and Beida Fabao (北大法宝), a subscription-required commercial legal reference database licensed and managed by Peking University. We also use the dossier serial number of each case to compare how the contents of the same case vary across the three websites. We found Beijing Court Judgment Information preserved the most complete information among the three. Our comparison of the three sources led us to choose Beijing Court Judgment Information Website as the source for compiling the dataset.

TABLE 11.1 Descriptive Statistics

	Total (N = 10,639)		*Contested (N = 7,035)*					
			Total contested		*Returning (N = 2,068)*		*First time (N = 4,967)*	
Variable	*Mean*	*SD*	*Mean*	*SD*	*Mean*	*SD*	*Mean*	*SD*
Defendant disagree (1 = disagree)	0.66	0.47	/	/	/	/	/	/
Returning petition	0.32	0.47	0.29	0.46	/	/	/	/
Petition rejected	0.59	0.49	0.83	0.37	0.58	0.49	0.94	0.24
Male plaintiff	0.46	0.50	0.50	0.50	0.52	0.50	0.49	0.50
Age of plaintiff	39.83	11.60	40.40	11.86	42.89	12.45	39.37	11.46
Age difference (plaintiff-defendant)	−0.62	5.33	−0.50	5.21	−0.39	5.36	−0.55	5.15

judgments.[36] After removing empty entries, there are a total of 10,639 judgments for the dataset. As mentioned, the cases made available by the courts online do not represent the entire corpus of contested divorce cases. The online judgments available, however, are the most comprehensive data source for studying contested divorces. I believe that divorce cases as a category are relatively non-political. Grassroots courts are less inclined to filter out divorce judgments and withhold releasing them. It is reasonable to assume that a substantial proportion of the contested divorces in Beijing during the period are captured by the dataset. Analysing these cases offers a preliminary survey of the landscape of contested divorces in China.

Table 11.1 presents the descriptive statistics of the surveyed judgments. It reports the means and standard deviations of the outcomes in the full and restricted sample (contested cases only). It also includes the means and standard deviations of three basic demographic variables – namely, gender of plaintiff (male coded as 1), age of plaintiff, and age difference between plaintiff and defendant. A few observations follow here. Only 66 percent of the cases handled by the courts involved contestation of a divorce petition. Of the other 34 percent of cases in the full sample, plaintiffs and couples agreed to divorce but contested over issues such as child custody and the ownership of marital property. Almost up to 60 percent of the petitions were rejected by the courts. The figure is consistent with the numbers reported elsewhere.[37] This percentage applies to all of the divorce cases handled by the courts. If we focus on the *contested* petitions proper,

36 Judgments were identified and collected by searching the Chinese keywords 离婚纠纷 ("contested divorce").

37 The SPC's "Special Report on Judicial Big Data: Divorce Disputes" (2016) officially reports a similar percentage of 63 percent for its nationwide statistics.

the rejection rate was as high as 83 percent. In China, getting a divorce when both sides agree is now easy. But getting a divorce when the other party disagrees is not as straightforward. In fact, it remains difficult.

Among the contested divorce cases proper, there were a total of 4,967 first-time petitions made to the courts during the surveyed period. In comparison, there were 2,068 returning petitions in the same period. Assuming there was no substantial fluctuation of the total number of couples who sought to divorce from the first year to the second year, this suggests that the total of the returning petitions that were adjudicated is about 41.6 percent of the total of the ruled first-time petitions. In other words, in between the end of the first hearing and the end of the second hearing, close to 60 percent of these petitions were either settled or withdrawn. That was a high diversion rate, especially when one takes into account the fact that most of the petitions had been repeatedly mediated by the courts and other bureaucracies by the time they were adjudicated (see prior). And among returning petitions, 58 percent of them were disapproved. This means that the odds of getting an approval for a returning petition were still less than half. Yet this was a marked improvement from the odds of getting an approval for first-time petitions. The disapproval rate of this group of petitions was an overwhelming 94 percent. The figure suggests that the courts reject first-time petitions by default. It seems that courts are trying to create more intervention points for mediation by denying the bulk of the petitions repeatedly. Though I have no systematic data to support it, I suspect this tendency to fall back on disapproval is even higher in the economically less developed parts of the country. The primary role of adjudication remains to create more opportunities for mediation.

Discussion

The evidence suggests there is a role reversal between adjudication and mediation in the Chinese courts. As said, in the Anglo-American context, the mainstream model is to see mediation as the alternative (hence the "A" in ADR) and adjudication as the default. Mediation is conceptualised as an alternative, not so much in terms of outcomes (far more cases are settled than adjudicated in the United States, for example, for costs and time consideration) but in the conceptual sense that the most difficult cases should be adjudicated after attempts to mediate fail. The belief is that cases in which parties cannot come to a common ground should be decided by going through the most elaborate and rules-specific procedures. The Chinese civil justice model is different in the sense that it is left to mediation to deal with the most difficult cases. In the area of divorce disputes, the courts deal with the most acrimonious type of divorce disputes, *contested* divorces. What the data suggest is that judges tend to reject a first-time petition to give parties more time to go through more rounds of mediation. And if the parties still fail to reach a settlement, they will return to courts again.

As mediation has assumed an increasingly prominent role in the United States, some have suggested that aspects of the Chinese model may be adopted to promote the further integration of adjudication and mediation. Others argue that the Chinese model brings about a more restorative "third-way" justice not available in the divided adjudication and mediation systems of the West.[38] Some scholars propose deeper integration between adjudication and mediation.[39]

No matter how prevalent mediation has become, there remains a procedural separation between it and adjudication in the case of the United States. Once a trial commences, a judge seldom assumes an active role in mediation.[40] All the judge can do is urge parties to settle out of court. In contrast, judge-led mediation in China is both a stage of the adversarial trial and an ongoing effort after the trial has supposedly ended. The Chinese model opts for full integration of mediation and adjudication. This integrative approach is clearly underscored in the "Several Opinions of the SPC on Further Displaying the Positive Roles of Litigation Mediation in Building of a Socialist Harmonious Society" (最高人民法院关于进一步发挥诉讼调解在构建社会主义和谐社会中积极作用的若干意见) that was published in 2007.[41] At every step of the way, judges are to give priority to mediation. Judges must consider the suitability of mediation at all stages of the litigation life cycle, starting from filing to trial, appeal to retrial, and eventually execution.[42]

Is the Chinese model better? In a paper co-authored with Xin He, we argue that, based on courtroom observations of contested divorce trials, there exists elements of coercion in this seemingly very effective system of Chinese-style judicial mediation.[43] As they turn more professionalised, the Chinese courts have become more aware of the tension created by the integrated model. Some of the big city courts, including those in Beijing, Guangzhou, Shanghai, and Shenzhen, have set up elaborate and more formalised programs of *pre-trial* mediation, as distinct from the *in-trial* mediation that judges are asked to carry out. The purpose of these pre-trial pilot programs is certainly not to fully replace in-trial mediation but to at least shift the focus of mediation from in trial to before trial and to offload part of the burden of mediation from trial judges. In a recent research paper written by Tengda Lu of Shanghai No. 2 Immediate People's Court, the researcher reports some statistics from his court's pilot pre-trial program that deserved closer study. The success rates of the pre-trial program for

38 Michael T. Colatrella, "'Court-Performed' Mediation in the People's Republic of China: A Proposed Model to Improve the United States Federal District Courts' Mediation Programs," *Ohio State Journal on Dispute Resolution* 15 (2000).

39 Michael Hogan, "Judicial Settlement Conferences: Empowering the Parties to Decide through Negotiation," *Williamette Law Review* 27 (1991); Carrie Menkel-Meadow, "For and against Settlement: Uses and Abuses of the Mandatory Settlement Conference," *UCLA Law Review* 33 (1985).

40 Though in some state courts, a judge may first try mediation, and if mediation fails, the same judge may preside over the subsequent trial. Brazil, "Judicial Mediation of Cases Assigned to the Judge for Trial."

41 Supreme People's Court, "Several Opinions of the Supreme People's Court on Further Displaying the Positive Roles of Litigation Mediation in Building of a Socialist Harmonious Society" (2007).

42 In its 2007 opinion, the SPC directed lower courts to actively consider the use of mediation in cases in which mediation is appropriate. The underlying policy is to give priority to mediation in different stages of the litigation process and to combine mediation with adjudication. Ibid.

43 "Internal Contradictions of Judicial Mediation in China."

civil and commercial cases in 2015 and 2016 (the most recent years in his survey) were both around 19 percent (see Table 11.2).[44] Even among those years when mediation was most heavily promoted by then SPC president Wang Shengjun (2011–2013), the pre-trial mediation rate of Shanghai grassroots courts hovered around 30 percent. The total mediation/withdrawal rates were consistently at around 67 percent in the years of the Wang era.[45]

What do the numbers tell us? To some, they might confirm the superior effectiveness of in-trial mediation, as the 36.5 percent success rate of the in-trial mediation system still exceeds the 19 percent of the pre-trial system by a wide margin, if we pick 2016 as an example. I would, however, argue that the high rates of judicial mediation in China are an artefact created by a highly conservative approach to adjudication that pushes litigants to settle. In fact, the possibility that parties may agree to settle is the most oft-used reason by frontline judges for seeking a deadline extension to close a case.[46] The numbers show that, absent of the de facto mandatory and possibly coercive quality of in-trial mediation, pre-trial mediation in China yields a substantially lower, but conceivably more natural, percentage of settlements among civil and commercial cases.

Mediation does not happen in a social vacuum. As the Chinese society becomes more urbanised, it appears inevitable that rates of judicial mediation are going to fall across the country. Insisting on near-perfect mediation rates has produced unnecessary strains for many grassroots courts. It seems that the next step for developing a more rules-based civil justice system of China is to shift from the current ostensibly voluntary but potentially coercive system of in-trial mediation to a formally mandatory system of pre-trial mediation. Given the emphasis on mediation there, pre-trial mediation can be mandated for certain types of cases – for example, family, inheritance, personal injury, labour disputes.

TABLE 11.2 Pre-Trial and In-Trial Mediation Rates among Basic-Level Courts in Shanghai 2011–2016[47]

Year	*Cases mediated before trial*	*Total commercial/ civil cases filed*	*Cases successfully mediated before trial (%)*	*Cases withdrawn or successfully mediated in trial (%)*
2011	78,841	262,828	30.0	36.5
2012	86,376	272,985	31.6	35.8
2013	88,600	302,218	29.3	38.0
2014	82,174	350,926	23.4	39.5
2015	80,020	412,678	19.4	39.4
2016	88,032	463,141	19.0	36.5

44 Tengda Lu, "Research on Legal Regulation of Pre-Mediation Procedure of Civil Disputes [in Chinese]," *Present-Day Law Science* 16, no. 2 (2017).

45 Ibid.

46 Kwai Hang Ng and Peter C. H. Chan, "'What Gets Measured Gets Done' Metric Fixation and China's Experiment of Quantified Judging," *Asian Journal of Law and Society* 8, no. 2 (2021).

47 Ibid.

The SPC already recommends six types of cases to be mediated first before going through adjudication.[48] Surprisingly, despite its prevalence, mediation is only legally mandatory in divorce cases in China.[49]

Doing so is not going to address all criticisms of the current practice. For example, for proponents of mediation as a genuine form of ADR that enables the pursuit of quality solutions, the proposed court-annexed mediation might be still too close to the adjudicative process. Yet the potential payoff of this separation is to make adjudication more independent and rules based. As mentioned, the context in which judicial mediation is put in place is quite unique. The biggest payoff of limiting court-sponsored mediation to the pre-trial stage is not so much to offer, as Menkel-Meadow puts it, some form of "process pluralism."[50] Mediation is already everywhere in China. The payoff is instead to rein in the ubiquitous presence of mediation. By keeping mediation at arm's length, adjudication can turn more rules based and single minded. At the time of writing, the SPC just launched a nationwide pilot program to separate civil cases into simple and complicated ones.[51] The idea is to further expand pre-trial mediation to deal with easier cases and then leave more complex cases to adjudication. Meanwhile, the SPC has also proposed a "diversified dispute settlement" scheme.[52] The scheme attempts to bolster the strengths of various out-of-court mediation channels (people's mediation, administrative mediation, industry mediation, commercial mediation) to help lighten the load of judicial mediation. These new measures can be perceived as the Chinese state's continued promotion of mediation. But hopefully this also signals a development to further separate the process of mediation from adjudication in the future.

Conclusion

This chapter analyses the problems produced by the Chinese integrated model of combining adjudication and mediation. The more integration is not necessarily

48 In a directive published in 2003, the SPC also states that mediation *shall* be conducted in six types of cases, including marriage and domestic disputes and succession disputes; disputes over labour contracts; disputes over damages that result from traffic or work injury accidents and in which the rights and obligations are relatively clear; disputes over home sites and neighbor relationship; disputes over partnership agreements; and disputes in which the subject matters of action are of relatively small amount. See Supreme People's Court, "Several Provisions of the Supreme People's Court on the Application of Summary Procedures in the Trial of Civil Cases," (2003).

49 As stated, this is mentioned in Article 32 of the Marriage Law. The Labour Law of China also specifies that the labour dispute arbitration committee should first mediate a labour dispute. Article 42 of the Labour Dispute Mediation and Arbitration Law states: "The arbitral tribunal shall mediate before making an award. Where an agreement is reached after mediation, a statement of mediation shall be prepared by the arbitral tribunal."

50 Menkel-Meadow, "Dispute Resolution."

51 Supreme People's Court, "Notice by the Supreme People's Court to Carry out the Pilot Program of the Reform of Separation of Cases into Complicated Cases and Simple Ones in Civil Procedure" (2020).

52 "Opinions of the Supreme People's Court on People's Courts Further Deepening the Reform of Diversified Dispute Resolution Mechanism" (2016).

the merrier. Mediation shades into adjudication to the extent that the latter becomes subservient to the former. Erasing the institutional boundary between adjudication and mediation creates some persistent structural problems for the Chinese model.

Judicial mediation in China is an interesting case of how adjudication serves to facilitate mediation as the end goal, rather than treating the latter as a diversifying mechanism to provide more choices. Whether it was justified by the Confucian ideal of reconciliation and forbearance or the Maoist idea of "non-antagonistic contradictions among the people," mediation was, and still is, the preferred mode of resolution.[53] This may have to change. The current arrangement was developed at a time when the Chinese courts were less professionalised. More important, the integrative model took shape at a time when the courts were tasked mainly with handling interpersonal and family disputes. The judicial system was not set up to serve a massive state-directed market economy and to deal with the growing volume of disputes that come with it. Commercial cases are more transactional in nature. They have been the fastest growing sector of cases in recent years. Between 2013 and 2017, the top two fastest growing categories of civil cases were credit card disputes and product liability cases.[54] Indeed, they now make up a substantial part of the total caseloads of the courts. Contractual cases make up 64 percent of all civil disputes.[55]

With the new enhanced focus on trial procedures, it is time for Chinese courts to remove mediation from the courtroom. I argue that judicial mediation should be reorganised as a standalone alternative – before trial rather than in trial, court annexed but not judge directed. This will offer more separations between adjudication and mediation. This will also give adjudication a stronger status in a rules-based system.

References

Ali, Shahla F. *Court Mediation Reform: Efficiency, Confidence and Perceptions of Justice.* Northampton, MA: Edward Elgar Pub., 2018.

Brazil, Wayne. "Judicial Mediation of Cases Assigned to the Judge for Trial." *Dispute Resolution Magazine* (2011): 24–27.

Bush, Robert A. Baruch. "Staying in Orbit, or Breaking Free: The Relationship of Mediation to the Courts Over Four Decades." *North Dakota Law Review* 84 (2008): 705–768.

Cohen, Jerome A. "Chinese Mediation on the Eve of Modernization." [In English]. *Journal of Asian and African Studies* 2, no. 1–2 (1967): 54–76.

Colatrella, Michael T. "'Court-Performed' Mediation in the People's Republic of China: A Proposed Model to Improve the United States Federal District Courts' Mediation Programs." *Ohio State Journal on Dispute Resolution* 15 (2000).

53 See Huang, *Chinese Civil Justice, Past and Present*, 145–185.

54 Supreme People's Court, "Report on the Work of the Supreme People's Court," (Beijing: Law Press China, 2018).

55 "Report on the Work of the Supreme People's Court," (Beijing: Law Press China, 2019).

He, Xin and Kwai Hang Ng. "Inquisitorial Adjudication and Institutional Constraints in Chinese Civil Justice." [In English]. *Law & Policy* 35, no. 4 (October 2013): 290–318.

Hogan, Michael. "Judicial Settlement Conferences: Empowering the Parties to Decide through Negotiation." *Williamette Law Review* 27 (1991).

Huang, Philip C. C. *Chinese Civil Justice, Past and Present*. Lanham, MD: Rowman & Littlefield, 2010.

Li, Yedan, Joris Kocken and Benjamin van Rooij. "Understanding China's Court Mediation Surge: Insights from a Local Court." *Law & Social Inquiry* 43, no. 1 (2018): 58–81.

Lu, Tengda. "Research on Legal Regulation of Pre-Mediation Procedure of Civil Disputes." [in Chinese]. *Present-Day Law Science* 16, no. 2 (2017): 75–85.

Lubman, Stanley B. "Mao and Mediation: Politics and Dispute Resolution in Communist China." *California Law Review* 55 (1967): 1284–1359.

Ma, Chao, Xiaohong Yu and Haibo He. "Big Data Analysis: Report on Public Access to Legal Documents Online." [In Chinese]. 大数据分析：中国司法裁判文书上网公开报告*]. Zhongguo Falǜ Pinglun* 2016, no. 4 (2016): 195–246.

Ma, Jian. "Shixian Shenpan Fuwu Jingjishehuifazhan De Xinchangtai." *People's Court Daily*. May 14, 2015.

Menkel-Meadow, Carrie. "Dispute Resolution." In *The Oxford Handbook of Empirical Legal Research*, edited by Peter Cane and Herbert M. Kritzer, 597–625: Oxford: Oxford University Press, 2012.

Menkel-Meadow, Carrie. "For and Against Settlement: Uses and Abuses of the Mandatory Settlement Conference." *UCLA Law Review* 33 (1985): 485–514.

Menkel-Meadow, Carrie. "Pursuing Settlement in an Adversary Culture: A Tale of Innovation Co-Opted or 'the Law of Adr'." *Florida State University Law Review* 19 (1991).

Merry, Sally E. "Sorting Out Popular Justice." *Social and Legal Studies* 1 (1992): 161–176.

Minzner, Carl. "China's Turn Against Law." American Journal of Comparative Law 59, no. 4 (Fall 2011): 935–984.

Ng, Kwai Hang and Peter C. H. Chan. "'What Gets Measured Gets Done' Metric Fixation and China's Experiment of Quantified Judging." *Asian Journal of Law and Society* 8, no. 2 (2021): 255–281.

Ng, Kwai Hang and Xin He. *Embedded Courts: Judicial Decision-Making in China*. New York: Cambridge University Press, 2017.

Ng, Kwai Hang and Xin He. "Internal Contradictions of Judicial Mediation in China." [In English]. *Law and Social Inquiry* 39, no. 2 (Spring 2014): 285–312.

Partlett, William and Eric C. Ip. "Is Socialist Law Really Dead?" *New York University Journal of International Law and Politics* 48, no. 2 (2016): 463–511.

Peng, Shizhong. "Nengdong Sifa Shiyexia Minshi Tiaojie Gaige De Jingxiang Xuanze [Paths of the Civil Mediation Reform from Judicial Activism Perspective]." *Jinan xuebao (zhexue shehui kexue ban) [Journal of Jinan University (Philosophy and Social Sciences)]* 1 (2011): 52–58.

Pissler, Knut B. "Mediation in China: Threat to the Rule of Law?" In *Mediation: Principles and Regulation in Comparative Perspective*, edited by Klaus J. Hopt and Felix Steffek, 959–1009. Oxford: Oxford University Press, 2013.

Silbey, Susan S. and Sally E. Merry. "Mediator Settlement Strategies." *Law & Policy* 8, no. 1 (1986): 7–32.

Supreme People's Court. "Notice by the Supreme People's Court to Carry out the Pilot Program of the Reform of Separation of Cases into Complicated Cases and Simple Ones in Civil Procedure." 2020. http://www.lawinfochina.com/display.aspx?id=32123&lib=law.

Supreme People's Court. "Opinions of the Supreme People's Court on People's Courts Further Deepening the Reform of Diversified Dispute Resolution Mechanism." 2016. http://lawinfochina.com/Display.aspx?lib=law&Cgid=273230.

Supreme People's Court. "Provisions on People's Courts Release of Judgments on the Internet." 2013. https://www.chinalawtranslate.com/en/spc-regulation-on-releasing-opinions-online/.

Supreme People's Court. "Provisions on Several Issues Concerning the Civil Mediation Work of the People's Court." 2004. http://www.lawinfochina.com/display.aspx?lib=law&id=3735&CGid.

Supreme People's Court. "Report on the Work of the Supreme People's Court." Beijing: Law Press China, 2018.

Supreme People's Court. "Report on the Work of the Supreme People's Court." Beijing: Law Press China, 2019.

Supreme People's Court. "Several Opinions of the Supreme People's Court on Further Displaying the Positive Roles of Litigation Mediation in Building of a Socialist Harmonious Society." 2007. http://www.lawinfochina.com/display.aspx?id=5930&lib=law.

Supreme People's Court. "Several Provisions of the Supreme People's Court on the Application of Summary Procedures in the Trial of Civil Cases." 2003. http://www.lawinfochina.com/display.aspx?lib=law&id=3141&CGid=.

Supreme People's Court. "Some Provisions of the Supreme People's Court on Evidence in Civil Procedures." 2001. http://www.lawinfochina.com/display.aspx?lib=law&id=2197&CGid=&EncodingName=big5.

Supreme People's Court. "Some Provisions of the Supreme People's Court on Evidence in Civil Procedures." 2019. http://www.lawinfochina.com/display.aspx?id=31964&lib=law.

Supreme People's Court. "Special Report on Judicial Big Data: Divorce Disputes." 2016. https://www.court.gov.cn/upload/file/2016/12/22/16/58/20161222165843_23070.pdf.

Wang, Liming. "Characteristics of China's Judicial Mediation System." *Asia Pacific Law Review* 17 (2009).

Wang, Yu and Kwai Hang Ng. "By the Law? – How Chinese Judges Rule on Contested Divorces." *Journal of Comparative Law* XV, no. 2 (2020): 223–249.

Welsh, Nancy A. "Making Deals in Court-Connected Mediation: What's Justice Got to Do with It?" *Washington University Law Quarterly* 79 (2001): 787–861.

Woo, Margaret Y. K. and Mary Elizabeth Gallagher. *Chinese Justice: Civil Dispute Resolution in Contemporary China*. Cambridge and New York: Cambridge University Press, 2011.

Xiong, Hao. "Two Sides of Court Mediation in Today's Southwest Grassroots China: An Empirical Study in T Court, Yunnan Province." *Asian Journal of Law and Society* 1, no. 2 (2014): 367–394.

Xu, Xin. *Jiufen Jiejue Yu Shehui Hexie [Dispute Resolution and Social Harmony]*. Beijing: Law Press, 2006.

Zhu, Suli. "Guanyu Nengdong Sifa Yu Datiaojie [On Judicial Activism and Grand Mediation]." *Zhongguo faxue [China Legal Science]* 1 (2010): 5–16.

12

THINKING ABOUT CONSUMER MEDIATION IN CHINA

Some Examples from Shenzhen

Ling Zhou

Introduction

As the People's Republic of China (PRC) over the past four decades has moved from a planned to a (socialist) market economy, there has been a much greater need to consider the rights and interests of the consumer. The social and economic changes have turned 'comrades' into 'customers' in many aspects of life. From a comparative perspective, in many jurisdictions around the world, it is not easy for consumers to find redress in a cost-effective and proportionate manner. Disagreements between consumers and businesses over consumer transactions often have one or more distinctive features which directly or indirectly impact on dispute resolution. These features may make securing remedies difficult for an aggrieved consumer. First, there may well be significant power imbalances between the parties; particularly, there may also be significant differences in the levels of technical knowledge about the product or service in question, with any disparity in expertise likely disadvantaging the consumer. Second, the value of the dispute is often relatively small, but the number of consumers affected may be relatively large. Going to court may thus be financially difficult, and representation of consumers of diffused interests at the court is challenging. Third, consumer disputes may take on a wider significance when adopted by civil society actors as reflections of the need for greater reform in society and as a result may become politically sensitive.[1] As a result, there is something of a global trend of greater use of ADR processes to handle consumer disputes.

1 For example, 'Naderism', referring to Ralph Nader's early legal work on the Project for Corporate Responsibility from the 1960s, sought to represent small parties handicapped by power imbalances in their struggle against large corporation producers of (defective) consumer goods. See Jo Littler, *Radical Consumption: Shopping for Change in Contemporary Culture* (Maidenhead, UK, & New York, NY: Open University Press & McGraw-Hill Education, 2009).

DOI: 10.4324/9780429354625-17

The Law for Protecting the Rights and Interests of Consumers (1993, revised 2013) and other relevant legislation contain provisions that encourage aggrieved consumers in the PRC to take their cases to court by means of robust provisions on punitive damages,[2] class action–type mechanisms,[3] and the development of small claims courts.[4] However, these cost-spreading court-based mechanisms do not seem popular in consumer dispute resolution practice in China, and the system seems weak at providing adjudicative justice for consumers. Instead, cost-avoiding processes – extra-judicial mediation and government administrative intervention – continue to dominate in the resolution of disputes in China's now flourishing consumer culture, as we see in the following.

To a significant extent, this reflects well-known and intensifying ideological and policy pressures to rely on mediation as the 'first line of defence' in civil disputes in the interests of political stability and social harmony.[5] At the same time, consumer mediation has distinctive features that set it apart from other from more common types of mediation in China, such as people's mediation.[6] The administrative nature of the bodies that predominantly handle consumer disputes indicates that consumer protection is primarily seen as a governmental responsibility and that consumer mediation is in effect a type of 'administrative mediation' in China.[7] Also, administrative power has an important role to play in, for example, the negotiation processes between the disputing parties. Such an administrative ethos in consumer dispute resolution is very much due to both Chinese traditions of paternalistic governance and the specific economic structure of contemporary China. In this structure, state-owned enterprises continue to enjoy a dominant economic status in the market, and there has been only an imperfect transition to a market economy, with legacies from the state planning era. While much has been written about the various forms of civil dispute resolution in China, and significant attention has been given to administrative

2 Article 55 of the Consumer Protection Law (revised 2013); Article 148, Food Safety Law (last revised 2019).

3 Article 47 of the Consumer Protection Law (revised 2013) empowers consumer associations at the provincial level to represent consumers in court.

4 Article 162 of the Civil Procedure Law (last revised 2017) for the first time set a lower barrier for simpler cases, which indeed created the small claims procedures and applied 'the first instance as the final instance' (*yishen zhongshen zhi*) principle.

5 See, for example, Ling Zhou Review, "Wang, Zhiqiong June and Chen, Jianfu *Dispute Resolution in the People's Republic of China: The Evolving Institutions and Mechanisms*," *Journal of Comparative Law* 16, no. 2: 779–782.

6 People's mediation focuses on handling civil disputes and minor criminal disputes between two equal parties, while in consumer mediation, one party is the business with stronger power. Since 2010, the People's Mediation Law has allowed parties to seek recognition by the court for enforcement power of the settlement agreement resulting from people's mediation.

7 See, for example, Yuhong Zhao, (2015) "Mediation of Environmental Disputes," *Journal of Comparative Law*, 10, no. 2: 237–253. Professor Zhao's work provides another example of 'administrative mediation' – in her case, in the handling of environmental disputes in China.

litigation, administrative review, and letters and visits,[8] very little attention has been given to mediation by administrative and quasi-administrative bodies.[9]

Through analysis of consumer disputes and observations based on my fieldwork studies in this area, this chapter looks at the system that has developed to offer consumers access to justice at the local level and how that system actually works.[10] This helps us understand better the place of mediation in consumer dispute resolution more generally in China. More specifically, this chapter addresses the following questions: what are the distinctive features of consumer mediation in Shenzhen, China, and how does the mediation process facilitate consumers' access to justice in Shenzhen, China? The study is based on intensive fieldwork recently carried out over one year in the local consumer dispute resolution bodies and their handling of consumer grievances in Shenzhen, giving particular attention to the manner in which consumer disputes are handled by these bodies.

The Consumer Council and Its Dispute Resolution

In Shenzhen, the main consumer dispute resolution bodies are the Shenzhen Consumer Council (SZCC) and the Market Supervision Administration (MSA) bureau.[11] The SZCC is an agency that provides consumer advice, conducts product comparison tests, publishes consumer guidance, and, most importantly, handles consumer disputes.[12] The SZCC is a municipal-level organization, and there are also district consumer associations. Together they are part of the national consumer association network headed at the national level by the China Consumers' Association (CCA). The SZCC, however, has considerable powers of its own. It has the authority, discretion, and capacity to innovate in consumer dispute handling for Shenzhen city. The dispute resolution processes in the SZCC are mainly negotiation and mediation, leading to a settlement outcome, but how best to distinguish between the two modes of resolution is a question that raises interesting issues. Faced with an increasing number of disputes, the SZCC has in recent years moved its working platform to online in a search for greater efficiency. There is continuing extensive use of an old office automation system shared with the MSA, but the SZCC in 2014 also established a mobile application that allows consumers to make complaints and follow up their grievances.

8 Letters and visits is the petitioning system for seeking justice from levels of the government superior to those whose alleged misconduct gave rise to grievances, and it is one of the primary tools for dispute resolution in China.

9 See, for example, Margaret YK Woo, & Gallagher, Mary E (eds) *Chinese Justice: Civil Dispute Resolution in Contemporary China*, (New York, NY: Cambridge University Press, 2013), and my review in *China Quarterly*, 218 (2014): 561–564.

10 The 'law in action' approach is important in understanding negotiation and mediation practices, as doctrinal analysis often can only provide a small part of the story.

11 The English language name has recently changed to Shenzhen Administration for Market Regulation.

12 The official webpage is at: www.sz315.org.

Complaints received from this portal are distributed between the SZCC and the district Consumer Councils for handling.

Settlement Process

If the complaint is made against a business that has joined the 'fast-settlement' channel (*kuaisu hejie tongdao*) established by the SZCC, the complaint will be forwarded to the business (by one click of the mouse) to attempt a business-led settlement. Such a 'fast-settlement' process is in effect a negotiation-based process, and the business will key in the outcome of the negotiation in the SZCC's working platform. In such a process, SZCC staff set up a venue for negotiation, and they will not intervene in the negotiation process.

In such cases, it is likely that the consumer may well have attempted negotiation with the business using the in-house complaint process of that business. However, feedback from the field is that the staff in the business who handle disputes received from the in-house complaint channel seem, to aggrieved consumers, to be significantly less polite and less professional than those who handle complaints delivered by the SZCC. Moreover, the business's personnel who handle complaints made through the SZCC often enjoy higher status and possess greater authority to make compromises for the benefit of aggrieved consumers. For example, in their hands, they may agree to a maximum of 200 RMB compensation (or offer a fixed amount coupon for redemption by the consumer) without seeking a superior's approval. Thus, negotiations are conducted in effect under the supervision of the SZCC, and if negotiation between disputing parties fails, the dispute will be sent for SZCC mediation.

Mediation and Mediators

Face-to-face mediation in the SZCC's offices, or on-site mediation conducted by the SZCC, is one of its main dispute resolution processes in SZCC. But it is not used as much as might be expected, largely because of the inconvenience faced by some aggrieved consumers of travelling to the SZCC offices and the difficulties faced by SZCC staff when making on-site visits. Most of the disputes, instead, are resolved through phone-based mediation. These are, in effect, mediator caucusing meetings rather than round-table, face-to-face discussions.

According to official reports, the SZCC and district councils altogether handled 220,496 cases in 2019, about the same as the numbers for 2017 and 2018 combined.[13] These case numbers are impressive in that the SZCC has less than 20 permanent staff for handling consumer disputes and a smaller number of dispute handlers in each district council.[14] As a solution for this shortage of full-time

13 The SZCC's report on consumer complaints in 2019 is available at: www.cqn.com.cn/ms/content/2020-03/27/content_8436890.htm.

14 General information of the SZCC's personnel is available at: www.sz315.org/html/show-43-8926.html. There were 25 permanent staff members in the SZCC in 2020.

dispute handlers, the SZCC has developed a group of volunteer mediators (or the '315 mediators', 315 *tiaojieyuan*) that help handle consumer mediation cases. Because phone calls are the main channel for conducting their caucusing type of mediation, the volunteer mediator can work from home, with her or his mobile number connected to the online working platform of the SZCC.

The standards or criteria for selecting the volunteer mediator, however, are not very robust. There do not seem to be what might be termed 'professional' requirements for becoming a SZCC 'mediator' – the group of volunteers consist of persons who, as the SZCC's own recruitment adverts stress, have a basic command of computing, strong communication and cooperation skills, resilience, patience, and an ability to deal with details.[15] This broad selection criteria, and lack of any accreditation scheme, may reflect the fact that the style of mediation in these situations is generally well known in Chinese society. Such informal third-party intervention was and still is a significant part of Chinese legal culture. In a sense, the skills used are those of everyday social interaction, rather than trained skills or professional knowledge. Accordingly, a brief two hours' online mediators' training is all that is provided. This training explains how to use the online working platform and conveys some basic ideas about mediation and mediators' techniques. It does not come with an assessment, and there is no certificate formally entitling the mediators to practice. Volunteer mediators are gathered into a group by use of a WeChat[16] group function. The WeChat group becomes a forum where mediators' own experiences and knowledge are shared. The group includes a member of the SZCC permanent staff who will advise mediators on such matters as how best to contact the defendant business when a consumer has a grievance against a company.

It is noted that although the mediation service provided by the SZCC is free, volunteer mediators do receive a small payment for their work, and their volunteering hours are accumulated in the 'volunteer system'[17] in Shenzhen. However, there is a slight difference between an 'unsuccessful' case and a 'successful' case – mediators will receive 30 yuan for a successful mediation while they will only be given 20 yuan for a failed mediation. Their volunteering hours are calculated as three hours for a successful mediation but only two hours for a failed case. A successful case may refer to situations where consumers have not obtained their expected outcome but agree to withdraw the case or abandon taking further actions such as filing lawsuits, making complaints to the regulator, letters and

15 The basic recruitment requirements are posted in adverts for a volunteer mediator published in the WeChat public account of the SZCC. These were also the basic skills for a mediator in traditional China. In terms of formal requirements, the standards are low, but in terms of social skills, the performance standards are high.

16 A popular instant messaging mobile application in China.

17 The 315 mediators are registered as volunteers with the Shenzhen Volunteers' Association (SVA, Shenzhen Yigong Lian), a social organization created by the Chinese Communist Youth League's (CCYL) Shenzhen Committee. It is composed of volunteers from all levels of society. Each 315 mediator has an SVA number and may use its online system to join other volunteer activities. SVA's website is available at: www.sva.org.cn.

visits, and so on. Thus, the intention of incentivizing mediators for a successful handling of the consumer's grievance is obvious.

Telephone Mediation Style

In telephone mediation, which has developed in large part because of the perceived inconvenience of local travel as noted prior, as well as the ubiquitous use of the mobile phone in China, the style of meditation used by the lay mediators often draws on a mix of traditional values, communist party values, and common sense. Law provides a backdrop for the mediation, and more importantly, mediators sometimes draw upon consumer law as they understand it in order to persuade and educate the parties, so as to encourage them towards a compromise outcome.

Since the matter is handled over the telephone in caucused calls, the process is in effect one of indirect facilitated negotiation. The telephone mediator seeks to gather information, keep the complainants' anger down, and dissolve the dispute. Aggrieved consumers are listened to and allowed to vent their feelings to some extent. The telephone mediator then seeks to develop rapport with the complainant but also encourages the complainant to see the dispute more logically by understanding the other (usually business) party's point of view. Moral principles and precepts expressed in everyday terms may be stressed. Objective facts are pointed to, and efforts are made to lower the complainants' expectations. The case is then taken up with the seller or supplier, using the same techniques. Both parties are encouraged to see the value of harmony, compromise, and cooperation. The hope is that after several such calls, the parties can find a mutually agreeable solution. Because such an agreement is an oral agreement made through a phone call, it is possible that parties will walk away from the agreement. In most situations, mediators will need to make a follow-up phone call with the aggrieved consumer to confirm enforcement of the agreement and more generally to ensure that the dispute is completely resolved.

The Regulator's Complaint and Report Channel

An important issue in consumer dispute resolution systems is sometimes the nature of the relationship between the dispute resolution agency and the regulatory body for consumer affairs. In China, including in Shenzhen, the MSA – namely, the former State Administration of Industry and Commerce (SACI) – is the regulator for commercial activities, including consumer goods and services standards, in the market. Resolving consumer disputes is not its main concern, but the MSA does provide complaint channels for consumer grievances. These differ from the SZCC mediation processes. The MSA has two routes for consumer complaint – a normal 'complaint' (*tousu*) route and a 'report' (*jubao*) route. In theory, a 'report' is made by a citizen with the aim of disclosing to the regulator the malpractice of business so that the regulator can start an investigation over such malpractice. This may lead to the imposition of a fine on the business party. In practice, these two routes may both lead to a similar outcome in which the consumer secures a settlement with the business party.

'Ordinary' and 'Professional' Consumers

Relevant here is a distinction that may be drawn between the 'ordinary' consumer and the 'professional' consumer.[18] The latter is somebody who frequently buys substandard or fake products knowingly and then uses the consumer redress processes to secure, say, compensation. The distinction between the two types of consumer is important. For example, if a case goes the court, the judge may place considerable stress on the difference and may be alert to the details of claims made by a 'professional', suspecting that the professional is being very strategic in the kind of complaint that is the basis for bringing suit. At the heart of the practice of 'professional' consuming is the possibility of claiming punitive damages. In the search for such damages, employing the punitive damages articles from the Consumer Protection Law (last revised 2013) and the Food Safety Law (last revised 2019),[19] a professional may be able to make money from such activity, especially when, in claiming punitive damages, the professional consumer has managed to purchase a large quantity of the same defective good from different chain stores.

'Reporting' as a Dispute Resolution Process

The 'report' system of the MSA is favoured by many professional consumers. These social actors are 'repeat players' in the system. They use the system in order to claim punitive damages that are often much higher than normal compensatory damages.[20] A professional consumer buys a problematic product, files a report with the MSA, and then negotiates with the business to get a settlement deal which is much lower than the fine that may be put on the business by the MSA if the MSA proceeds with an investigation for the report. These professional consumers employ techniques in enhancing their bargaining power with

18 They are called anti-counterfeit professionals (*zhiye dajia ren*) in mass media, as a public figure, Wang Hai, was coined as an anti-counterfeit hero in the 1990s, and his followers showed up after that.

19 Article 55 of the Consumer Protection Law, revised 2013, states:

> Business operators that practice fraud in providing goods or services shall, on the demand of consumers, increase the compensation for their losses by an amount that is three times the payment made by the consumers for the goods purchased or services received, or in the amount of 500RMB if the increased compensation is less than 500RMB.

Article 148 of the Food Safety Law (last revised 2019) provides that aggrieved consumers 'may claim for punitive damages which are ten-times of the price of the [defective] food product purchased or three-times of the loss of the buyer'. However, the latest revision of the law adds a provision excluding cases that concern minor issues such as defects on labels and instructions in an attempt to limit the activities of the professionals.

20 See footnote 19 for provisions on punitive damages.

the business: they may put pressure on the MSA by not only buying loads of defective goods but also by filing an enormous number of reports at the same time. They might also request disclosure of government information, inter alia, so as to create still more administrative work for the MSA. In addition, they may well file administrative lawsuits against the MSA over procedural issues when it handles the report. As a result, MSA officials as well as many judges dislike these professionals and criticize them as abusing the report process, using it to get the business to make compromises that will give the professional consumer a better settlement deal.[21]

Despite the controversy over the conduct of professional consumers, there is no doubt that the 'report' system is the most effective way to pressure a business to pay compensation. The MSA in this process is a third party or go-between in the dispute handling process. In theory, a report cannot be withdrawn – the system (like that of punitive damages in the Consumer Protection Law 1993, revised 2013) is created for the purpose of incentivizing citizens to report malpractices of the business to the regulator so that the business will receive its due punishment. However, professional consumers have brought in many reports critical of business parties, and the regulator (the MSA) is reluctant to investigate the reports one by one. This is because to investigate every report means a heavy workload, and in the eyes of officials, the issues concerned with the defective product or service are minor details. Such small issues include erroneous production information, fake product certification, incorrect packaging labels, and so on. These issues are seen as minor by MSA officials in the sense that they do not seem directly to cause personal injury. In most situations, local MSA officials will seek to help the parties reach a settlement agreement so that an investigation will not occur and time and energy are saved.

So, a distinctive type of consumer mediation has emerged, one which is an innovative process used by Chinese professional 'consumers' to enhance their bargaining power. In theory, mediation is based upon mutual agreement of the two parties, and the mediator, as a neutral third-party facilitator, does not have the power to push the defendant business parties to make compromises. However, the MSA, as an authoritative body, is able to influence businesses' decision-making in agreeing to compensation. This forms something of a contrast with the SZCC's more relaxed style of mediatory intervention. The MSA has local offices in the commercial areas of Shenzhen, and it regulates the local businesses' various forms of market activity. The degree of intervention of the government into economic activities may mean that the regulatory body has some 'authority' as an intermediary. Thus, a mediation meeting called by the regulator will likely create a more compliant attitude on the part of the defendant business, leading to the success of an attempted mediation in that the outcome is an agreed settlement.

21 Details of such practice are provided in my book, Zhou, Ling (2020) *Access to Justice for the Chinese Consumer: Handling Consumer Disputes in Contemporary China*, (Oxford, Hart Publishing, 2020), Chapter 5.

Features of Chinese Consumer Mediation

Consumer cases cover a broad range of issues. They stretch from buying daily necessities to the purchase of automobiles and real estate. Broadly speaking, this means consumers are those who buy products or use services for daily consumption purposes, which is the definition of consumers in the PRC's Consumer Protection Law of China (article 2). Although this chapter has focused on Shenzhen, the nature of the consumer bodies and mediation processes in China suggests that the features examined here are broadly shared by consumer mediation systems and processes in many other parts of China. The Shenzhen practice may involve some innovative technology for enhancing case-handling efficiency, but in terms of mediation style and mediation effectiveness, it has little or no difference from that of other urban areas in mainland China. In some respects, however, there are significant differences from consumer mediation in other parts of the world.

Consumer Mediation Works Well

In Shenzhen, mediation works well in several ways for resolving consumer disputes. Fieldwork shows that the informal forum facilitates resolution of consumer disputes. The mediation services are free of charge, save plaintiffs considerable time, and often result in settlement agreements that can be executed immediately – for example, getting a compensation payment from the business party right after the mediation meeting has been concluded. In consumer disputes involving everyday consumer issues, most cases are very small in value and sometimes may even not involve any monetary claims – some disputes against the telecommunication giants concern values as low as 5 or 10 yuan, while others may involve securing an apology for a shop assistant's bad manners.

To some extent, the nature of consumer mediation in China resembles that of people's mediation – a didactic process which involves evaluation for the parties. As a consumer body, the SZCC sees its role as one of protecting consumers' rights and interests. Therefore, in the mediation process, the consumer dispute handler may have a heavy responsibility for persuading the defendant business to make compromises: such concessions are not only what consumers expect the SZCC to deliver but also are a key factor in getting the parties to reach a settlement agreement. In the mediation meeting, staff regularly advise the business of the negative social impact and possible illegality of its conduct. Since the mediation process is voluntary, at least in theory, whether a settlement agreement can be reached often depends on how much compromise a business is prepared to yield. As the SZCC does not have enforcement powers, the willingness of the defendant business to carry out the terms of the agreement is also important. In early 2020, disputes over purchases of surgical masks and cancellations of prepaid services, including gyms, overseas wedding photography, preschool education, and so on, were major issues arising from the arrival of Covid-19.

Many enterprises found that doing business was much tougher than before and lost much money. At this difficult time, many businesses refused to compensate consumers for the cancellation of services even though aggrieved consumers were eligible for such compensation under the terms of their contract with the business concerned. Most such consumer complaints, in these difficult circumstances, ended up with consumer grievance apathy – in many cases, a 'lumping' of the grievance by the consumer.

Consumer mediation in China is not a neutral third-party facilitative style of intervention. It is evaluative and looks to support and speak for the consumer. As a result, the mediation process often does deliver substantive justice in the sense that the grievant consumer secures all or most of what he or she seeks from the other party. Also, in terms of procedural justice, the process is relatively fair from the perspective of the consumer, with the mediators dealing effectively with both parties, despite the power imbalances between the parties that often exist.

Lack of Professionalism in Practice Style

In terms of style, the consumer mediation service in China is carried out in an ad hoc and loosely structured manner and lacks professionalism and formal enforceability. The lack of professionalism is a common problem for the extra-judicial Chinese style of mediation. Mediators are selected from the general public, do not have any formal training in mediation, and are not bound by any formal code of practice. The techniques mediators use come from their own life experience, and they hone their skills on the job. Thus, we may say that the normative framework within which consumer mediation operates is one that lies in the shadow of the law but is infused with moral values of everyday Chinese society.

As in mediation more generally, while settlement negotiation and mediation take place in the shadow of the legal system, in reality what is important is the negotiation process between the parties. In the Chinese context, evaluation may be as much moral as it is legal, as mediators may try to persuade or educate parties with moral norms during mediation meetings. Business defendants may be taught to maintain a good temper, learn from their own life experience, and treat consumers better in their delivery of goods or services. The consumers themselves, hoping perhaps that the business can give them a tailored settlement compensation plan so as to cover their claimed losses, are as likely to use moral arguments as they are the legal issues arising from their claims.

However, law and legal issues are now becoming more important in negotiation. Mediators have started to get themselves better equipped with legal knowledge, in particular to enhance their success rate in persuading businesses to compromise. Among the 315 volunteer mediators, knowledge and experience are exchanged through a WeChat group, so that mediators learn their skill on their job. In general, consumer mediation is slowly becoming more professionalized and modernized, so it is somewhat less didactic and educational nowadays. This change is taking place slowly, especially as there is no code of practice to restrict mediators from being didactic and evaluative in their approach to mediatory intervention, and so much depends on the individual mediator's character.

The case acceptance threshold is very low in both the SZCC and the MSA mediation services. As noted prior, claims as small as several yuan or claims without a monetary dimension are all within the case acceptance threshold. In Hong Kong, Shenzhen's neighbour, the Hong Kong Consumer Council (HKCC) is equipped with a professional dispute handling team of more than 70 people, with well-researched annual reports published every year.[22] Although the case acceptance threshold of the SZCC is very low, the value of some claims can go up to thousands of RMB. A report shows that the SZCC successfully mediated and secured compensation of more than 80,000 RMB for a consumer in one recent home renovation service case.[23] Such large claims cases may be about issues of interior decoration; purchases of automobiles, laptops, and other high-value electronic devices; cancellation of prepaid services, and so on.

The Mix of the Consumer Council and the Regulator

Although the SZCC is not officially a governmental body, and its staff are not civil servants, the consumer mediation it delivers is in effect a form of administrative mediation. This is because the two main bodies that handle the consumer disputes, the Consumer Council and the regulator (the MSA), liaise very closely, use the same office automation (OA) system to handle consumer complaints, share the same complaint hotline 12315, may even sometimes deal with the same case, and in the eyes of the public are seen as sharing the same 'brand name'. Moreover, it is not easy for local consumers to distinguish between these two bodies, and so they sometimes expect the SZCC to make regulatory-type decisions and are puzzled when it does not do so.

On the other hand, the fact that both the SZCC and the MSA have the authority to resolve disputes can be problematic. Both bodies sometimes use mediation as an excuse to indulge in what is called locally as playing Tai Chi[24] – that is, passing the consumer grievance between themselves in order to avoid management of and responsibility for the case. Faced with a difficult case, the Consumer Council staff may claim that they cannot meet the consumer's expectations because they do not have the authority to regulate the area of business in which the defendant is involved and about which the complaint has been made.

22 It might also be noted that that HKCC had over 155 staff members in year 2020, while there are only some 25 permanent staff in the SZCC. So the HKCC has significantly more mediators and more support staff. Annual reports are available at: www.consumer.org.hk.

23 The case is reported by the MSA on its webpage at: http://amr.sz.gov.cn/szsscjdgljwzgkml/szsscjdgljwzgkml/qt/gzdt/content/post_9027511.html, accessed September 5, 2021.

24 Tai Chi is a kind of traditional Chinese shadow-boxing, in which a person's hands move in circles as they push and pass in the air.

In contrast with a formal judgement or order of the court, a mediation settlement agreement does not have enforcement power. This should not be a major obstacle to achieving informal justice, as in an informal voluntary process such as mediation, compliance with the voluntary agreement is usually very high. However, problems do occur. The parties may agree orally on the spot but fail to record the agreed terms in writing. Sometimes, on reflection, one of the parties, usually the consumer, may feel that the mediated outcome is in fact unfair and does not meet expectations. While it is easy for consumers to lump their grievance, it is also easy for them to change their minds and reject a disadvantageous settlement agreement. As a result, there may be a lack of finality in the outcome, and a consumer may use the free service of either the SZCC or MSA mediation again by making a simple phone call or filling in a mobile app form to send to the consumer bodies. Moreover, their rights to bring suit in the people's court are undiminished by the fact of the mediated settlement agreement.

The Social Welfare Approach to Consumer Mediation

Consumer mediation is in some ways a form of social welfare in China – the party-state leadership seeks to foster an image of paternalistic car, as part of its efforts to contain social unrest at the local level. The consumer organizations are all carried out directly or indirectly by state administrative bodies. In practice, there are no major consumer NGOs in China that work specifically on protecting consumers' rights and interests.

Moreover, consumer complaining has become a cathartic channel where consumers may in effect grumble about their difficult life, using the Consumer Council as a place to vent their anger about various injustices and other social problems they experience in China's rapidly changing economy and society. Sometimes, even in mediations that I have carried out myself for the SZCC as a volunteer, I found that aggrieved consumers sometimes were very emotional, even threatening suicide. The Consumer Council, to some extent, has become a 'letters and visits' venue for petitions about citizens' economic rights and interests. Citizens take advantage of the free service provided by the state to air their voice about social injustice and social problems. The mobile phone–based complaint portal has made it even easier for the consumer to make complaints to the SZCC, and the number of complaints has increased significantly in recent years. As a result, the need for social stability is emphasized, and efforts are made to contain and resolve such problems, where possible, at the local level.

The process of consumer mediation service is perhaps best seen as part of the social welfare gifted by the state to citizens who have not fully shared in the benefits of China's fast-growing economy and whose rights and interests have been sacrificed for ensuring the rapid growth of the market economy. Even with punitive damages articles, the consumer protection standard or administrative sanction imposed on companies is still very low, thereby failing to prevent the company from violating the regulations again.[25] On the other hand, the state is still a significant shareholder in many companies, and state-owned enterprises (SOEs) play an important role in the economy. These SOEs, including China's three telecommunication giants, have enjoyed many policy-orientated benefits in their development. Lack of competition in the telecommunication market may have, to some extent, discouraged incentives for improving telecommunication services.

Consumer mediation in China differs from people's mediation, especially in its administrative dispute resolution tone, but it is nevertheless also – as is people's mediation – something of a 'social clinic' – dispensing 'social prescriptions', as Hazel Genn has elsewhere put it.[26] Surprisingly, the major reason for taking citizens' social problems into hospitals, Genn explains, is that the GP service is absolutely free in the UK. This has encouraged her idea of establishing a pro bono legal advice centre in the same building with the GPs. Her pilot spot seemed to be successful for helping patients resolve their personal social problems, but there is concern about the sustainability of the legal advice centre, as it is all free.[27]

In the shadow of 'administration' power, the Consumer Council is in effect prescribing social medicine to consumers. The emphasis of public consumer bodies is more on resolving social problems than it is on facilitating negotiations between parties and encouraging exchange of information during mediation meeting. This indicates that the systemic concerns with political stability and social harmony have shaped the nature of Consumer Council work in China so that it has become something like a 'social clinic'. Seen in this light, consumers are patients with problems, and the quasi-government body, free of cost, tries to prescribe a settlement compensation plan to resolve the social problem and maintain the good order of the society. Such an approach does not aim at correcting the power imbalances in the bargaining process but may be seen as a tool for management of the society through protecting citizens' interests (wealth).

Chinese consumer mediation has effectively synthesized the provision of accessible, cheap justice with a broad coverage of different types of claims. However, in my view, it needs to develop more to provide professional standards in its mediation. Moreover, much emphasis on informalism may result in two main problems. First, consumers may need to spend even more time on getting what is their right or getting the result that they perceived as reasonable and acceptable. Through fieldwork, I have learned about the attitudes of mediators

25 Since punishment is not very heavy, businesses do not clean up their act, thereby giving professionals chances to keep on spotting the same errors by the business and seeking compensation.

26 Hazel Genn "When Law is Good for Your Health: Mitigating the Social Determinants of Health through Access to Justice," *Current Legal Problems* 72, no. 1, (2019): 159–202. The clinics refer to GPs in the UK who have been turned for help for resolving patients' social problems alongside patients' physical health problems. These social problems, such as personal debt, social benefits, jobs, etc., emotionally affect patients' status and thus may further affect their physical health.

27 As Genn stressed in a seminar at Hong Kong University in 2019, the centre mainly relies on law students helping on a pro bono basis and thereby avoiding costs for patients.

in the Consumer Council and the MSA. They focus too much on resolving the single dispute and making sure that the consumer complainant will not come to the consumer body for further trouble. They do talk about laws, but this is not their main concern. They often make simple judgements on the dispute and use techniques of persuasion and conciliation to try to narrow down differences. At times, they may advise consumers to seek help from other possible channels rather than hanging around their own place (such as to dial the government complaint hotline).

The second problem of too much informalism in Chinese consumer dispute resolution points directly to an important criticism of ADR: Laura Nader's concept of harmony ideology warns of the danger of using informal means to contain social conflicts – for example, that the weaker party (the consumer) may be coerced to accept an unjust result due to power imbalances between the parties. In many situations, consumers are faced with options of either accepting a low compensation outcome or simply lumping their grievance. Consumer disputes in China have become more of a social problem which need to be handled carefully, and mediation, as a soft approach for dispute resolution, carries the danger of suppressing rights assertion of citizens, who feel pressured to accept a mediated outcome with which they are dissatisfied, instead of bringing suit. Moreover, the incorporation of mediation into court processes means that, by going to the court, consumers may get even less than what they can get in mediation outside the court, and punitive damages are unlikely to be applied by the court even though the product in question is obviously fake.

In this sense, the state tries to ensure consumers' pursuit of their individual economic interests – mediation services provided by the Consumer Council and the MSA are best seen as a kind of social welfare that the state is willing to deliver. However, by providing such welfare, the state has largely limited the channels for consumers to assert their rights and to lobby for social change – the civil and political rights of a 'citizen' (or, indeed, a 'consumer') have been confined. The absence of independent consumer civil associations reflects that consumer groups and consumers' collective efforts to secure redress is not favoured by the state.

Despite the difficult situation for consumer protection associations, a bottom-up force – the professional consumers – have nevertheless formed their own community by creating chat rooms on social media and sharing their experience and knowledge about how to spot substandard goods, file administrative lawsuits, and other forms of public means to put pressure on the regulator, such as requesting disclosure of government information. Their fights with the administrative bodies (even with the court, sometimes) are perhaps the strongest example of tolerance by the state for consumer activism. Even so, because there is controversy over their 'motives' for doing their work – especially given that some professionals employ unlawful and threatening methods to secure compensation from defendant businesses – the anti-counterfeiting practices by the professionals have been largely restricted by the court in recent years. Judges are more on the alert and show a more questioning attitude when plaintiffs seek punitive damages. The criteria used by the courts when assessing whether the professionals are 'consumers' as defined by the law and whether their claims will be supported have changed with the increasing numbers of the professionals engaged in the art of seeking and securing punitive damages, or along the way of securing a favourable settlement in the shadow of the punitive damages, and vary greatly from place to place.[28] The Supreme People's Court (SPC) has also published a formal reply to the regulator (at the state level), stressing that except for food and drug issues concerning public health, the profit-making anti-counterfeiting practices of the professionals should be restricted by the court.[29] The SPC clearly has tried to limit activities of the professionals that it sees as 'excessive', but it does not fully close the door for their cases.

The welfare approach to consumer dispute resolution is not a stand-alone phenomenon in China's system of social management. In the Chinese context, various 'social protection laws' have also been introduced in order to safeguard the rights and interests of vulnerable groups such as women, children, elders and the disabled. Consumers are also characterized as in need of such social protection. The paternalistic policies of the government intended to protect the welfare of these marginal and vulnerable members of society are dominant – while much less official support is given to the possibilities of bottom-up change through allowing greater civil and political action. Individual consumers may well secure moderate compensation through settlement, and exit their dispute moderately satisfied, but find it difficult to reform the rules governing consumer rights through court decisions or by joining pro-consumer social movements. This welfare approach to consumer dispute resolution may work well in the short term, as consumers are often reasonably compensated in the sense that they get most of what they ask for. In the longer term, however, consumers with an increasing awareness as citizens of society likely will feel the need to press for changes to rules unjust to them. The market economy must be based on rule of law, and consumers are important potential forces for progressing reforms for a better market environment.

Conclusions

China's dominant approach to handling consumer disputes is social and informal. Mediation is the main form of consumer dispute resolution and is performed in a relatively ad hoc manner with little attention given to developing mediators' professionalism and putting in place procedural standards and ethical

28 See different judgements in Liqun Yang, "Shipin Lingyu Zhiye Dajia Xingwei de Sifa Rending" [Judicial Determination of Professional Anti-Counterfeiting in the Food Field], *Faxue* [*Law Science*] 8 (2020): 257–263.

29 Reply by the General Office of the Supreme People's Court to Recommendation No. 5990 of the Fifth Session of the Twelfth National People's Congress May 19, 2017. The Supreme People's Court believes that at present 'we may consider gradually restricting the profit-making anti-counterfeit behaviour of the professionals, except for the purchases of food and drug.'

norms. The whole consumer dispute resolution system rests within the hands of administrative bodies – both the Consumer Council and the regulator provide consumer mediation service, and there is no major consumer civil society–type association that has dispute resolution functions. The core reasons for mediation's centrality in the consumer dispute resolution arrangement are cultural, political, and economic. The long-existing dispute resolution practice in China is a didactic process with educational purposes and a goal of restoring social relationships, and consumer mediation is no exception. Although the Chinese socialist market economy is thought to require a law-based dispute process and greater professionalism for dispute resolution services, most mediators are lay mediators, and the court does not seem to play an important role in consumer dispute resolution, especially when punitive damages and group litigation processes do not function in practice. The lingering memories of state planning and administration of the economy also make the use of administrative mediation for resolving today's market-related disputes seem more natural.

Bibliography

Genn, Hazel. "When Law is Good for Your Health: Mitigating the Social Determinants of Health through Access to Justice." *Current Legal Problems* 72, no. 1 (2019): 159–202.

Littler, Jo. *Radical Consumption: Shopping for Change in Contemporary Culture.* Maidenhead and New York: Open University Press and McGraw-Hill Education, 2009.

Woo, Margaret Y. K. and Mary E. Gallagher, eds. *Chinese Justice: Civil Dispute Resolution in Contemporary China.* New York: Cambridge University Press, 2013.

Yang, Liqun. "Shipin Lingyu Zhiye Dajia Xingwei de Sifa Rending [Judicial Determination of Professional Anti-Counterfeiting in the Food Field]." *Faxue [Law Science]* 8, no. 2 (2020): 257–263.

Zhou, Ling. *Access to Justice for the Chinese Consumer: Handling Consumer Disputes in Contemporary China.* Oxford: Hart Publishing, 2020.

Zhou, Ling. Review. "Wang, Zhiqiong June and Chen, Jianfu *Dispute Resolution in the People's Republic of China: The Evolving Institutions and Mechanisms.*" *Journal of Comparative Law* 16, no. 2 (2021): 779–782.

Zhou, Ling. Review. "Woo, Margaret YK & Gallagher, Mary E (eds). *Chinese Justice: Civil Dispute Resolution in Contemporary China.* (2013). *China Quarterly* 218 (2014): 561–564.

INDEX

For Product Safety Concerns and Information please contact our EU representative GPSR@taylorandfrancis.com Taylor & Francis Verlag GmbH, Kaufingerstraße 24, 80331 München, Germany